SCHOOL CRIME AND JUVENILE JUSTICE

School Crime and Juvenile Justice

Richard Lawrence

New York   Oxford
Oxford University Press
1998

Oxford University Press

Oxford   New York
Athens   Aukland   Bangkok   Bogotá   Bombay
Buenos Aires   Calcutta   Cape Town   Dar es Salaam   Delhi
Florence   Hong Kong   Istanbul   Karachi
Kuala Lumpur   Madras   Madrid   Melbourne
Mexico City   Nairobi   Paris   Singapore
Taipei   Tokyo   Toronto
and associated companies in
Berlin   Ibadan

Published by Oxford University Press, Inc.,
198 Madison Avenue, New York, New York 10016

Library of Congress Cataloging–in–Publication Data

Lawrence, Richard (Richard A.)
    School crime and juvenile justice/Richard Lawrence.
        p.   cm.
    Includes bibliographical references and index.
    ISBN 0-19-510164-2 (cloth).—ISBN 0-19-510165-0 (paper)
    1. School violence—United States—Prevention.   2. Juvenile
delinquency—United States—Prevention.   3. Juvenile justice,
Administration of—United States.   I. Title
LB3013.3.L38   1997
371.5'8—DC20   96-34162
                                                          CIP

9 8 7 6 5 4 3 2 1

Printed in the United States of America
on acid-free paper

To my mother and to the memory of my father—
two teachers who met during hall duty; who dedicated their lives to
teaching; and who touched many other lives, especially mine.

Contents

Acknowledgements

Schools are an important part of every person's life. We have all been there, done that. For some persons school, teaching, and teachers take on even greater importance. I grew up with two teachers: my parents. They met in a small school in North Dakota, during their first year of teaching. Growing up with teachers sensitized me at an early age to the pressures placed on them. Even students in a small town of 2,000 in North Dakota could make life difficult for teachers. As a child playing in my father's classroom while he completed work on weekends, I recall finding "contraband" items like water guns that he had confiscated from his students. Some students had a way of getting back at teachers. Halloween nights were particularly harrowing, like the year Dad's trailer was found turned upside down in the backyard! Despite the difficulties with some students, my parents loved teaching. Together, they dedicated about fifty years of their lives to teaching.

I respected them for that, but I was determined not to become a teacher. Instead, I ended up working with juvenile delinquents as a probation officer. My career choice took me onto the streets, into the homes, and into the schools of young offenders on probation. I saw how teachers and principals were faced with more resistance, disruption, and delinquent behavior—often from the delinquent students on my caseload. I came to see that probation officers and teachers have much in common. They are expected to work with many youth who are not willing participants. They do not want to be in school. They dislike school, and teachers. They act out their dislike by disrupting the classroom, harassing other students, and creating an environment of frustration and fear. Juvenile delinquents on court-ordered probation are unwilling participants.

They do not like their probation officer and the authority he or she represents. They dislike the court-ordered rules imposed on them, and they violate those rules whenever they think they can get away with it. As a probation officer, I was expected to be sure my delinquent students stayed in school, in spite of their resistance. School attendance was part of their "rehabilitation." The intent of the court process was to get two major social institutions, the schools and the courts, to work together in correcting young offenders. The juvenile court would help reinforce the importance of school attendance and compliance with school rules. I observed as a young probation officer, however, that school rules and court orders are insufficient by themselves to help turn around many troubled young people. First, we needed more communication and more cooperative efforts between educators and juvenile court officials. Second, we needed more support and involvement from parents if we were to help their children to achieve in school and avoid delinquent behavior. Third, we needed more resources and support from the community if we were to accomplish the goals of improving school attendance and academic achievement and to reduce disruptive and delinquent behavior in schools and in the community. Fourth, we needed to recognize that the problems of school failure and delinquency could not simply be blamed on the youth, their peers, their parents, or the school. This was a community-wide problem, with multiple causes that varied with each individual case.

Young people do not start out life choosing to be bad, failing in school, or unwilling or unable to work for a living and a rewarding lifestyle. Parents have high hopes when they bring a new child into the world. Unfortunately, the excitement and anticipation of the new family fades as it faces the awesome responsibilities of parenting. The task is made more difficult for those with limited resources, poor education, few job skills, and few examples for how to be a responsible parent and provider. Those responsibilities then often fall to community social services, the schools, and the courts. This book has been dedicated to two special teachers in my life—my parents. It is also dedicated to those teachers, social service providers, and juvenile probation officers who give so much of their time, energy, and skills to help young people who have "fallen into the cracks." Special thanks go to those teachers who helped me, through their patience and persistence, pushing me when I seemed to have less confidence in my own ability than they did. Thanks also to my colleagues in the juvenile court. We often felt overwhelmed and on the verge of "burnout," but somehow the cameraderie and group experiences helped us find humor in our kids, their families, and our fellow law enforcement and juvenile justice colleagues. A special acknowledgement goes to my friends in juvenile probation and juvenile correctional facilities who are still there after two or three decades, long after I "bailed out" to the comfortable confines of academia.

Finally, special acknowledgement to Susan Perry, who encouraged me to get that first book proposal out there; to Gioia Stevens and Karen Shapiro, excellent editors who saw this project through to completion; to my colleagues at St. Cloud State University, for their support and encouragement; and special thanks to Dorothy, my favorite teacher, my best critic, my companion.

R. L., July 1996

SCHOOL CRIME AND JUVENILE JUSTICE

1

Delinquency and the Schools

- Twenty percent of students in New York City schools were found to carry weapons (*New York Times*, October 11, 1991); more than 3,843 violent incidents were reported in New York City schools (*The Economist*, Nov. 30, 1991).
- Two students were shot to death outside Thomas Jefferson High School in Brooklyn, New York—moments before a visit to the school by Mayor David Dinkins (*New York Times*, Feb. 27, 1992).
- Violent crimes have moved from the streets into school hallways, prompting legislation for school safety measures (Levy, *Minneapolis Star-Tribune*, Sept. 3, 1995).
- Shootings at schools prompt new concerns about violence, and officials wonder how to address the problem (*New York Times*, March 3, 1996).

An Introduction to the Problem

Walter had been suspended several times for disrupting class, talking back to teachers, coming late, just "being a troublemaker," as the principal put it. He missed two weeks of school while he was locked up in Juvenile Detention after committing his third crime this year (a burglary). One of his court-ordered probation rules was to attend school regularly and obey all school rules, but the only way he could be readmitted would be to have his probation officer bring him for a conference with the principal. We went in, and the principal began asking about his crime problems and whether he was willing to get along in school, not miss a day, obey all the rules—the usual questions. I told Walter to expect this, to just answer the questions, keep a cool attitude, and convince Mr. P. that he was going to give his best. But Walter lost his cool after a few minutes of questioning and said something to the principal about always being picked on, singled out for classroom troubles. The principal said he hadn't changed a bit, wasn't ready to come back to this school. Before I could intervene, Walter made some remark about things at this school not changing any, either—he was still being picked on. That's all it took! The principal ordered us out of his office and the school, immediately. I had to run out after Walter, who was fuming as he hurriedly left the school building, convinced he was once again a victim of injustice. —A Juvenile Probation Officer

The newspaper headlines and this example from a juvenile delinquent's school experience illustrate two sides of the problem of schools and delinquency. We are seeing an increasing amount of crime in and around schools—and teachers and administrators find it difficult to cope with disruptive and delinquent students as they carry out their educational task. This book was written to address these two separate but related problems. It seeks to answer a number of questions: How extensive and serious is school crime? Who commits school crime? Who are the victims? What are the characteristics of schools with more crime? What are the characteristics of youth who commit crime in and around schools? To what extent do school experiences contribute to delinquent behavior? What can schools do to help prevent delinquency? How can schools, families, and juvenile justice and social agencies combine their efforts to reduce delinquency?

Schools are blamed for many problems that originate within the family and the community. In addition to their primary educational role, schools are expected to fulfill many of the functions previously filled by parents, families, the church, and the community. We begin by addressing the context of schools and crime and the role of the school with respect to delinquent students.

Crime in Schools

Disorder and delinquency are growing problems in our schools. The public perception of most inner-city high schools is that they are dangerous places for students and teachers, that drugs are rampant, and that growing numbers of students carry weapons, including guns. Media attention to school problems has heightened public fears and concerns about problems in our schools. Newspaper and news magazine headlines rivet our attention on school problems: "Kids and Guns: A Report from America's Classroom Killing Grounds" (Morganthau, 1992: 25); "More kids bringing weapons to school" (Walsh, 1992: 1B); "Reading, Writing, and Murder" (Reed, 1993: 44; "America's Schools Confront Violence" (Boothe et al., 1994: 33); "Today's Lesson: Safety at School—Rise in Violence Spurs Action" (Levy, 1995: 12A). School violence occurs more frequently in inner-city schools, but the problem is not limited to New York and to other cities with reputations for high crime. Suburban and rural schools are now experiencing similar problems. A headline from the *New York Times Educational Supplement* declared that "Discipline problems now affect the 'rural havens' " ("Discipline Problems," 1988: 7). The level of violence and the use of firearms among school children is on the increase in the United States in both rural and urban areas. An honor student at a high school in Grayson, Kentucky, killed his teacher and a custodian, then held his fellow students hostage. The "tragedy in Room 108" forever changed the small Kentucky town (Buckley, 1993). According to a 1993 survey of 16,000 students by the national Centers for Disease Control and Prevention, more than one in ten (11.8 percent) of high school students reported that they had carried a weapon on school property; 24 percent said they were offered, sold, or given drugs on campus; about 7.3 percent said they were threatened or injured with a weapon in school; and 4.4 percent said they had skipped school at least one day in the previous month because they felt unsafe (Levy, 1995: 12A). According to a U.S. Education Department report, violent crime strikes every six seconds on or near public schools (Vidulich, 1993: 5).

Schools are a reflection of the community. As crime has increased in cities and communities, so also has it increased in the school environment. The problems no longer are restricted to inner-city schools or to neighborhoods characterized by lower socioeconomic levels. The types of crimes most often committed in schools involve drugs and alcohol, theft and vandalism, and weapons and violence. Alcohol and drugs have been a problem for some time, but now students are bringing guns and other weapons to school. School equipment and property are vulnerable to theft, and administrators have had to step up security precautions to protect the property from vandalism. Violence is a pervasive problem, as students now carry weapons for self-protection, and teachers and students face the risk of assault.

The public concern about our schools is not greatly exaggerated. Congressional hearings as long as twenty years ago reflected the public concern about school disorder, and the testimony at these hearings confirms an image of deviance and disorder in schools (U.S. Senate, 1975). Public officials have joined parents and students in expressing alarm about problems of school disorder and violence. School crime and violence have been the subject of research for more than two decades. It is not a recent problem. A number of researchers have attempted to identify the sources, the characteristics, and the effects of school crime (Baker and Rubel, 1980; McPartland and McDill, 1977; Polk and Schafer, 1972; Rubel, 1977). The extent and the nature of school disorder and violence have been a major focus of much government-funded research, such as *Violent Schools—Safe Schools: The Safe School Study Report to Congress* (National Institute of Education, 1977), as well as more research funded by the U.S. Department of Education and National Institute of Education (National Institute of Education, 1978; Gottfredson and Gottfredson, 1985).

School Crime: Community Problem or School Problem?

A popular belief is that crime in schools is a recent phenomenon that is the result of such factors as more disrespectful students or increasingly lax discipline policies. This view is not shared uniformly. Some have suggested that school violence is simply one manifestation of the modern violent urban society—and American society has been urbanized since the early eighteenth century (see Berger, 1974; Wilson, 1977). This raises the question of whether school crime is simply a reflection of crime in the community or whether it is a function of problems within the school itself. The question, in short, is whether school crime is an internal or an external problem.

A School Problem

According to the *Safe School Study*, school crime is not merely a reflection of social ills in society. The National Institute of Education (NIE) study concluded that schools can do much to reduce school violence and disruption, through such policies as: (1) increasing efforts in student governance and rule enforcement; (2) treating students fairly and equally; (3) improving the relevance of subject matter to suit students' interests and needs; and (4) having smaller classes, with teachers instructing a smaller number of different students (NIE, 1977: A13–A14).

The study also found that outsiders are *not* responsible for most problems of school crime and violence. Except for cases of trespassing and incidents of breaking and entering, between 74 and 98 percent of all offenses are committed by youngsters enrolled in the school. This finding is contrary to the claim of many that school dropouts and outsiders are responsible for most school crime.

If school crime indeed is primarily an internal problem, then schools are responsible for improving the school climate, student discipline policies, and other changes that may reduce crime and disruption. The *Safe School Study* found that many variables that are not under the school's control (such as unemployment, poverty, and neighborhood conditions) are not so important in school crime. School variables such as class size, pupil-teacher ratio, and the principal's firmness, fairness, and consistency of discipline may be more important in curbing school crime. The finding that nonstudents are not the cause of most school crime has a direct bearing on the types of security programs that school districts and individual schools should develop. If school administrators institute security programs on the belief that their schools are more at risk from outside trespassers, then those programs may be misdirected and ineffective. The overall implication of school crime as an internal problem is that schools may have less to fear from the type of neighborhood in which they are located. According to this view, schools can do much to reduce disruption, crime and violence; but it also means that schools are responsible for dealing with their own crime problems.

A Community Problem

Viewing school crime as an external problem means viewing the school in the context of the community. Bill Larson, assistant superintendent of the St. Paul, Minnesota, schools, believes that "school is a microcosm of society. What happens in the community and on the streets invariably spills into schools" (Levy, 1995: 12A). Nancy Riestenberg, a violence prevention specialist for the Minnesota Department of Education, echoed that belief and stated that "schools reflect what's going on in our culture. Whatever is happening in a town, city, or state will happen in a school" (Levy, 1995: 12A). In a discussion of crime in schools, James Q. Wilson noted that

> we must realize that crime does not occur in the schools in isolation from crime in the rest of society. Indeed, much of what is called "crime in the schools" is really crime committed by young persons who happen to be enrolled in a school or who happen to commit the crime on the way to or from school. (Wilson, 1977: 48)

Gold and Moles (1978) analyzed data from the 1972 National Survey of Youth (a self-report survey of 1,395 boys and girls eleven through eighteen years old) and concluded that delinquent behavior that occurs in school is not an isolated phenomenon but rather is the same kind of behavior committed outside school and tends to be committed by the same individuals. They claim that proportionately less delinquency occurs in school given the amount of time youths spend there, since youths spend about 20 percent of their waking hours in school but report that 13 percent of their offenses are committed in school (Gold and Moles, 1978: 115).

To view school crime as an external rather than an internal problem is to see school crime as inseparable from, and a function of, crime in the community. This view has important implications for explaining and preventing school crime. To view school crime as an internal problem is to place the blame squarely on the schools and to hold schools responsible for solving what may be more of a community problem. McDermott (1983) emphasized that this approach has unfortunate consequences:

> First, the blame is placed solely on the schools, or more precisely, on school officials, administrators, and teachers. Second, solutions are almost always school-related: better teachers, smaller classes, fair and equal treatment of students, relevant subject matter in courses, and tighter discipline. (1983: 278)

Policies such as these may surely help minimize school disruption, and of course they are positive steps toward quality education beyond any effect they may have on school crime. However, if school crime is primarily a reflection of crime in the community, then relying on improved teaching and discipline may not significantly reduce levels of school crime. McDermott argued that crime in schools does not exist apart from crime in the community, and this concept has important implications for school crime prevention efforts. She suggested that concentrating efforts in the school probably will not have a significant impact in the long run for those schools located in high crime communities:

> Law and order approaches such as tighter security, stricter rule enforcement and fortresslike alterations in a school's physical plant may reduce acts of crime and violence in school, only to displace them to the community. Similarly, expelling or suspending troublemakers puts them on the street with nothing to do. Lowering the level of crime in schools may have no real impact on reducing the total amount of crime committed by young people. (McDermott, 1983: 281)

McDermott also questioned the assumption that offenders and victims are different groups, with one preying on the other. She presents evidence that three groups of young people—offenders, victims, and the fearful—are not mutually exclusive (1983: 281). Some youth who become offenders have been victimized and are themselves fearful of crime. The fear experienced by victims of crime often drives them to actions that are unlawful. Many students unlawfully bring weapons to school for self-protection and not primarily to use them offensively.

A view of school crime as a reflection of community crime receives support from other researchers. In a reanalysis of the *Safe School Study* data, Gottfredson and Gottfredson (1985: 188) presented evidence that school crime was as much a reflection of community disorganization and crime as it was the result of internal school problems. Analyses of data from the School Crime Supplement of the National Crime Survey show that fear of being attacked at school is related to reports of street gangs at school and to how students get to and from school. Students who walk to school are more likely to fear being attacked than students on school buses, and those on buses report more fear than students who get to school by car (Pearson and Toby, 1991). A longitudinal analysis using National Crime Survey data examined victimization of juveniles in schools, homes, and streets or parks. More assaults, robberies, and larcenies occurred in homes than in schools or streets and parks. The authors concluded that one of the causes of victimization in schools is in the community surrounding the school, and they suggest that increases or decreases in victimization rates outside schools will be reflected by increases or decreases inside schools (Parker, Smith, Smith, and Toby, 1991). They add a caution, however:

> (O)ur results do not suggest that school administrators should ignore factors inside the school which may have an impact on this problem, since they have a great deal more control over what happens in school than they do over what happens outside or over what students are like when they come into the school. (Parker et al., 1991: 15–16)

The consensus from recent research is that a view of school crime as an internal problem is incomplete and inaccurate. Concentrating crime prevention efforts only on the school is not likely to have a long-term significant impact, especially for schools located in high-crime communities. School policies that focus on tighter security, more strict discipline, and similar crime control approaches may well reduce disruption and crime in the school but simply displace the problems to the community. Likewise, suspending or expelling disruptive students without referral to an alternative program simply puts them out on the street with nothing to do. If concerted efforts aimed at both school and community crime do not occur, then schools will continue to face problems of disruption, crime, and victimization in the hallways and on the school grounds. Crime in schools must be seen as an extension of crime in our communities. That means we must view it as a larger social problem. It is not just the responsibility of the school board, administrators, and teachers. School crime, like crime in the community, must become the responsibility of citizens, parents, and students—as well as police and juvenile court officials.

Schools and Crime

In addition to the problem of crime *in* schools, the second objective of this book is to address the subject of crime *and* schools. That is, how are schools expected to deal with disruptive and delinquent students? To what extent do effective schools help prevent crime, and does school failure contribute to dropout and delinquency? The first step in answering these questions is to understand the school's role as an important *social institution*; its function as an instrument for *social change*; the *expectations and demands* placed upon schools; and the claim that schools are often a *source of juvenile delinquency*.

An Important Social Institution

From a broad perspective, public education of all citizens is viewed as essential in a democratic society. Along with the family, the school is important for the socialization of young people. In addition to providing knowledge and skills for effective living and working, schools are expected to instill in young people the values that contribute to an ordered and productive society. Education has played an important role in developing America. The framers of our Constitution, in forging a democratic form of government, understood early on that this radical experiment in government for the people and by the people would not succeed without an informed, educated citizenry. Thomas Jefferson and Benjamin Franklin, among others, advocated strongly for the development of schools that were publicly supported. America's leaders have placed high expectations on education for its role as an important social institution in forming a democratic society.

John Dewey became well known as an educational reformer when he published *The School and Society* in 1899. Dewey established a Laboratory School at the University of Chicago in 1896 to develop and test his educational ideas (see Rippa, 1980). Like leaders before him, Dewey recognized the importance of public education in a democracy. Because of changes in society, he believed the school must take on some of the functions formerly performed by the home. He called for a more active role of the child in education and supported teaching styles that encouraged thinking and problem solving. Dewey was optimistic that education could improve students' lives and eliminate social problems.

Demands on Education for Social Change

Schools have been expected to serve as the primary institution for social change. A major function of the schools during the influx of immigrants to the United States in the early twentieth century was to ensure that immigrant children were given American values and to socialize them. The school teacher was forced to become a parent substitute for many immigrant children. The living conditions of the early immigrants were deplorable. Jacob Riis, a police reporter and crusading journalist, was appalled by the physical squalor and poverty in the New York City tenement houses and by the parental neglect of children who roamed the streets poorly clothed. Writing in 1892, he stated, "The immediate duty which the community has to perform for its own protection is to school the children first of all into good Americans, and next into useful citizens" (cited in Rippa, 1980: 173). School leaders responded to many similar demands to assist needy children by developing special schools and educational programs in cities across the country where immigrants were working and struggling to survive. Thus, by the turn of this century schools were trying to cope with the demands of business and industry, the needs of immigrants, and the social effects of urbanism.

The idea that schools should be instruments of social change and take on responsibilities beyond basic education has been promoted by the U.S. Congress and has resulted in considerable legislation. One of the earliest congressional initiatives was the Smith-Hughes Act promoting vocational education in high schools (Maeroff, 1982: 9).

America has undergone dramatic changes in the twentieth century, and education has been a central part of those changes. In addition to meeting educational demands, schools have assumed the responsibilities of fostering youths' personal development, tasks that previously belonged to the family and the church. The social and political problems of the 1960s and 1970s presented challenges to education. While schools were being asked to assist students in personal and social adjustment, the challenges of the space age brought criticism that American schools had weak academic standards.

Expectations and Demands on Schools

The 88th and 89th Congresses, with the prodding of President Lyndon B. Johnson, passed legislation that gave unprecedented support for education. Among the goals of the legislation was the use of schools to address social problems such as poverty, unemployment, crime, violence, and racial discrimination. At the White House Conference on Education in 1965, Vice President Hubert Humphrey said that our country would achieve historical acclaim for using its educational system to overcome problems of illiteracy, unemployment, crime and violence, and even war among nations (Goodlad, 1984: 4, 33). Barely more than a decade after those optimistic expectations were raised, legislators and the public were calling for school reform to "get back to basics" and to raise educational standards. American youths were falling behind in school achievement, particularly in math scores but also in reading and writing skills.

At the same time that more has been expected of schools, changes in American society have meant that there is less support for public education. Declining birth rates and growing numbers of older Americans means that there are fewer persons directly involved in our school system. This largely accounts for the defeat at the polls of proposed tax increases for education in many parts of the country. The success of public education depends on the public. It is difficult to convince a majority of citizens that the relationship exists and that schools require their support. It is more difficult when many people believe that schools are failing to fulfill their role and that raising school taxes is not the answer.

Although schools have been given responsibilities other than teaching reading, writing, and arithmetic, the criterion on which schools are evaluated is still academics. Books critical of schools bear titles such as *Why Johnny Can't Read*, *Crisis in Education, Educational Wastelands*, and *Crisis in the Classroom*; Goodlad notes that public criticism of schools accompanied a general loss of faith in government, the judicial system, the professions, and even ourselves (see Goodlad, 1984: 2–3). This represents a dramatic change from the optimistic expectations Americans had for schools which were supposed to bring about economic and social change. Our past expectations for education have actually been quite unrealistic.

Some are critical of the numerous responsibilities placed upon schools in addition to their primary function of education. Maeroff (1982) questioned the unrealistic expectations placed on schools. He noted that turning to schools has become a common response in attempting to deal with a social dilemma. Schools are expected to take on responsibilities that traditionally have been taken care of in the home, churches, hospitals, and other institutions. In the apparent belief that nearly every task that involves children and youth is best handled by schools, they have been given such responsibilities as addressing the nutritional needs of children and providing alcohol and drug abuse education, driver education, and even inoculations (see Maeroff, 1982: 10–11). The extra demands on schools makes it all the more difficult for them to accomplish their primary responsibility of educating youth.

The Public Schools as a Source of Delinquency

The schools have not only failed to meet the expectations of social change, vocational preparation and academics; they have been cited as a source of delinquency. In the Task Force Report on Juvenile Delinquency and Youth Crime, Schafer and Polk (1967) noted several practices and deficiencies within the school system that tend to promote delinquency. They cited evidence suggesting that "delinquent commitments result in part from adverse or negative school experiences of some youth, and . . . there are fundamental defects within the educational system . . . that actively contribute to these negative experiences," thereby increasing the probability of delinquent behavior (1967: 223). Schafer and Polk asserted that because of its important role in the lives of youth, the school has the potential to partly offset or neutralize the pressures toward delinquency that may originate in the family and community. They proposed a number of recommendations for educational changes that they believed would alleviate the school-delinquency problem. McPartland and McDill (1977) echoed the charge that schools are partially responsible for crime and violence and asserted that schools can aggravate the problem or reduce it depending on teaching and disciplinary practices. They also believed that student violence could be reduced through reforms in school structure (1977: 21–22).

Schools appear to be facing insurmountable difficulties. Teachers and administrators find it increasingly difficult to carry out their educational function because of the growing problem of crime in schools. At the same time, they are charged with being a source of crime, because of their ineffectiveness in teaching and disciplining students. Our country has placed high demands and expectations on schools, some of which may be unrealistic. Furthermore, we might question whether it is fair to hold schools responsible for delinquent behavior, which more often has its source in family and community problems. Yet, as a major social institution, schools do play an important role in youth development. For those youth who for a number of reasons do not succeed in school, the result is too often unemployment, poverty, and crime.

It is essential that we attempt to understand the school-delinquency relationship by examining the factors that lead to school failure, frustration, dropout, and delinquency. In subsequent chapters we address the more specific questions of how schools may cause or prevent delinquency. In Chapter 3 we examine some explanations of delinquency, which include the school as a variable in delinquency causation or prevention. Chapters 4 and 5 deal respectively with the role of families, peers, and gangs in school and the problem of dropout and delinquency. Chapters 6 and 7 discuss the relationship between delinquency and school size, structure, teaching and administrative policies and school rule enforcement and disciplinary procedures. Chapters 8 and 9 provide an overview of juvenile law, the justice process, and correctional programs. We conclude in chapter 10 with a discussion of school-based delinquency prevention programs and evaluations of their effectiveness. Before we address the school's role in delinquency causation, we examine in Chapter 2, how much crime there is in schools, according to a number of measures.

Summary

We are seeing an unprecedented increase in school crime and violence. The problem has attracted the attention of the public and the media and is the subject of growing concern. The purpose of this book is to address school crime as a two-dimensional issue: the problem of crime in schools and the role of schools in preventing delinquency and dealing with delinquent students. In this chapter we examined the question whether school crime is primarily a school problem or a community problem. Evidence seems to indicate that crime does not occur in the schools in isolation from crime in the rest of society and that school crime must be viewed as a broader community problem. As a major social institution, education has tried to meet the high demands and expectations that have been placed on it. Schools are expected to play a major role in educating and socializing young people and are believed to contribute to delinquency when poor quality teaching or lack of proper discipline results in dropout and delinquency.

References

Baker, Keith, and Robert J. Rubel, eds. 1980. *Violence and Crime in the Schools.* Lexington, Mass.: Lexington Books.

Berger, Michael. 1974. *Violence in the Schools: Causes and Remedies.* Bloomington, Ind.: Phi Delta Kappa Educational Foundation.

Boothe, James E., Leo H. Bradley, T. Michael Flick, Katherine E. Keough, and Susanne P. Kirk. 1994. "America's Schools Confront Violence." *USA Today Magazine* 122(2584):33.

Buckley, Jerry. 1993. "The Tragedy in Room 108: An Angry Teen Killed His Teacher." *U.S. News & World Report* 115(18):41f.

"Discipline Problems Now Affect the 'Rural Havens'." 1988. *New York Times Educational Supplement,* June 3, 7.

Gold, Martin, and Oliver C. Moles. 1978. "Delinquency and Violence in Schools and the Community." In J. A. Inciardi and A. E. Pottieger, eds., *Violent Crime: Historical and Contemporary Issues.* Beverly Hills, Calif.: Sage.

Goodlad, John I. 1984. *A Place Called School.* New York: McGraw-Hill.

Gottfredson, Gary D., and Denise C. Gottfredson. 1985. *Victimization in Schools.* New York: Plenum Press.

Levy, Paul. 1995. "Today's Lesson: Safety at School." *Minneapolis Star-Tribune,* September 3, 12A.

Maeroff, Gene I. 1982. *Don't Blame the Kids: The Trouble with America's Public Schools.* New York: McGraw-Hill.

McDermott, Joan. 1983. "Crime in the School and in the Community: Offenders, Victims, and Fearful Youths." *Crime & Delinquency* 29:270–282.

McPartland, James M., and Edward L. McDill, eds. 1977. *Violence in Schools: Perspectives, Programs and Positions.* Lexington, Mass.: Lexington Books.

Morganthau, Tom. 1992. "Kids and Guns: A Report from America's Classroom Killing Grounds." *Newsweek* 119 (March 9): 25.

National Institute of Education. 1977. *Violent Schools—Safe Schools: The Safe School Study Report to the Congress—Executive Summary.* Washington, D.C.: U.S. Department of Health, Education, and Welfare.

National Institute of Education. 1978. *Violent Schools—Safe Schools: The Safe School Study Report to the Congress,* vol. I. Washington, D.C.: U.S. Department of Health, Education, and Welfare.

Parker, Robert N., William R. Smith, D. Randall Smith, and Jackson Toby. 1991. "Trends in Victimization in Schools and Elsewhere, 1974–1981." *Journal of Quantitative Criminology* 7:3–17.

Pearson, Frank S., and Jackson Toby. 1991. "Fear of School-Related Predatory Crime." *Sociology and Social Research* 75:117–125.

Polk, Kenneth, and Walter E. Schafer, eds. 1972. *Schools and Delinquency.* Englewood Cliffs, N.J.: Prentice-Hall.

Reed, Susan. 1993, "Reading, Writing and Murder: A Survey of Death in America's Public Schools." *People Weekly* 39(23):44f.

Rippa, S. Alexander. 1980. *Education in a Free Society: An American History,* 4th ed. New York: Longman.

Rubel, Robert. 1977. *The Unruly School: Disorder, Disruptions, and Crimes.* Lexington, Mass.: Lexington Books.

Schafer, Walter E., and Kenneth Polk. 1967. "Delinquency and the Schools." In *Task Force Report: Juvenile Delinquency and Youth Crime.* Washington, D.C.: U.S. Government Printing Office.

U.S. Senate, Committee on the Judiciary. 1975. *Our Nation's Schools—A Report Card: "A" in School Violence and Vandalism.* Preliminary Report of the Subcommittee to Investigate Juvenile Delinquency. Washington, D.C.: U.S. Government Printing Office.

Vidulich, Dorothy. 1993. "Students Return to More Than School This Fall." *National Catholic Reporter* 29(40):5.

Walsh, James. 1992. "More Kids Bring Weapons to School." *Minneapolis Star-Tribune*, April 7, 1B.

Wilson, James Q. 1977. "Crime in Society and Schools." In J. M. McPartland and E. L. McDill, eds. *Violence in Schools.* Lexington, Mass.: D.C. Heath.

2

School Crime and Violence

School violence casualties in the first weeks of a new school year:

- August 27: A fifteen-year-old girl at a suburban Orlando, Florida, high school gashed a classmate repeatedly.
- August 31: A ninth-grader was killed and a tenth-grader wounded when another student opened fire in the crowded cafeteria of an Atlanta high school (the incident followed a fistfight the previous day).
- September 7: A fifteen-year-old was shot at a Los Angeles high school while waiting in line for a permit to transfer into the school.
- September 8: A fourteen-year-old student at a rural North Carolina high school was arrested for shooting a classmate as school was dismissed.
- September 9: Two students at a Washington, D.C., junior high school were charged with spraying the school grounds with semiautomatic weapon fire, sending students diving for cover.
- September 16: A seventeen-year-old at a New Jersey high school was charged with attempted murder after allegedly shooting another student.
- September 17: A seventeen-year-old was gunned down as he sat in his car in a high school parking lot near Chicago. Another student walked over, put a gun to his head, and pulled the trigger. Friction between the two had begun days earlier, when the suspected assailant reportedly blew smoke in the face of the victim's twelve-year-old brother (Toch, 1993: 32).

The reports of violent crime in and around schools in the first weeks of a new school year are alarming. News magazines and newspapers draw public attention to the crime problem in a dramatic manner. The cover photo of an issue of *U.S. News & World Report* that featured a high school student drawing a handgun from inside his jacket was subtitled "Even suburban parents now fear the rising tide of violence." Other news magazine cover stories in past years have focused on the "youth crime plague" and on teenage gangs. Such stories dramatically portray an image of the juvenile delinquent today as a hardened, ruthless criminal—and the youth crime problem as pervading all cities and most suburbs.

The cases used as illustrations are correct. They are not fabrications. And yet, such media portrayals of youth crime tend to overgeneralize and exaggerate the problem in at least two ways: by not reporting the variations in crime in different cities and regions and by not reporting the *rates* of crime (number of crimes per 100,000 population). To say that media stories are exaggerations is not to deny that youth crime is a serious problem about which we should be concerned. But inaccurate reports of the true extent and nature of youth crime often lead to targeting certain youth and attacking the perceived problem with extreme policies. Accurate measures provide the basis for a more reasoned, rational approach to the problem.

Measuring the Extent of School Crime

Crime statistics in general are not a precise measure of the true extent of crime. Crime is underreported by most police and court statistics. A major reason that more crimes occur than are reported is that many persons do not report the crime. Results of the National Crime Survey indicate that the public reports only about one-third of the crimes that affect members of households. Other crimes are not recorded because there may be no victim or witness present. So-called "victimless crimes," such as alcohol and drug violations, are unlikely to be reported to police as long as the incidents go undetected by anyone else. The problem of unreported crime led criminologists to devise other methods of measuring crime. Self-report measures and victimization studies are the two most common. In self-report measures, samples of youth are asked to report on their own involvement in delinquent activities, whether or not they were ever caught. Self-reports provide a more complete picture of juvenile delinquency but are not completely error-free, since they depend on subjects' honesty and reliability of memory. Victimization surveys, which are administered to a sample of the population, ask people whether and how often they have been victims of crime. These surveys may also ask about the perpetrators and circumstances of the crime, and they have the advantage of asking if the crime was reported—and if not, why it was not reported. These "unofficial" measures of crime are not perfect, error-free measures, nor are they intended to replace official police statistics. They do, however, serve as a valuable supplement to official statistics and provide information about crime that is not available from police and court statistics.

Research on school crime has suffered because of imprecise and incomplete methods of measuring the extent of the problem. There have been no widely accepted criteria for identifying and recording the kinds and incidents of school crime (Garrett, Bass, and Casserly, 1978). In recording incidents of vandalism, for example, some school systems include certain categories of apparently accidental damage, while others do not; some include all destruction, while others include only acts for which a perpetrator is identified; some exclude damage covered by insurance, while others do not. Until uniform reporting practices are adopted, we will not have a complete measure of the extent of school crime and cannot draw meaningful comparisons among different school systems.

Police and Court Statistics

Official statistics of juvenile offenders include those gathered by police and reported nationally by the FBI Uniform Crime Reports and juvenile court statistics, reported by the Office of Juvenile Justice and Delinquency Prevention (OJJDP) and by the National Center for Juvenile Justice. Neither of these sources specifies the extent of crime in schools, but only crime in general. Additional analyses would be required to identify the location or the victim of these crimes, such as property damage against schools or victims in and around schools. In order to have a basis for comparing reports of school crime with other reported crime, it is helpful to summarize police and court statistics of all reported juvenile crimes. Table 2–1 reports the number of arrests of juvenile age youth, by gender, for Part I and other selected offenses in 1994.

Table 2–1
Juvenile Arrests in 1994
(Persons under 18 years of age)

Part I Offenses	*Males*	*Females*
Murder & nonnegligent manslaughter	2,838	178
Forcible rape	4,555	93
Robbery	42,010	4,258
Aggravated assault	54,875	12,523
Burglary	100,110	10,568
Larceny-theft	268,385	126,949
Motor vehicle theft	61,299	9,919
Arson	7,769	1,088
Other Offenses		
Other assaults	121,580	43,612
Stolen property: buying, receiving, possessing	30,703	3,913
Vandalism	104,738	12,033
Weapons (carry/possess)	46,363	4,062
Drug abuse violations	112,327	14,898
Driving under the influence	8,583	1,407
Liquor laws	63,124	25,421
Drunkenness	11,746	2,290
Curfew and loitering violations	72,382	29,434
Runaways	65,193	86,706

Source: Federal Bureau of Investigation. 1995. *Uniform Crime Reports for the United States 1994.* Washington, D.C.: U.S. Department of Justice, p. 226

It is important to note that the FBI arrest statistics report the number of arrests for crime, not the number of different juveniles arrested. Studies have shown that a relatively small number of youth is responsible for most serious crimes. One study found that 22 percent of male delinquents born in Philadelphia in 1958 accounted for 61 percent of all offenses involving males by the time they were eighteen years and for an even larger share of serious juvenile offenses (Tracy, Wolfgang, and Figlio, 1985). The findings of other studies that have examined the delinquent behavior of youth cohorts confirm that a relatively small number of youth account for most serious juvenile crime (see, e.g., Dinitz and Conrad, 1980; Hamparian et al., 1985).

Juvenile court statistics provide another measure of juvenile delinquency. *Juvenile Court Statistics 1993* reports the number of cases disposed of by juvenile courts in the United States. Table 2–2 reports the number of delinquency cases

Table 2–2
Juvenile Court Cases by Offense, 1993

	Number of Cases[a]	*Percent Change* 1989–1993	*Percent Change* 1992–1993
Person Offenses	318,800	52	6
Homicide	2,800	45	13
Rape	6,100	48	12
Robbery	35,600	56	5
Aggravated assault	77,500	59	1
Simple assault	166,400	51	10
Property Offenses	808,900	15	−3
Burglary	149,700	14	−4
Larceny-theft	353,700	11	−2
Motor vehicle theft	61,100	−10	−14
Arson	8,200	21	0
Vandalism	117,100	41	0
Trespassing	60,500	22	5
Stolen property	27,400	16	−7
Drug Law Violation	89,100	14	24
Public Order Offense	272,800	24	8
Disorderly conduct	71,200	49	4
Weapons offenses	47,200	87	16
Liquor law violations	13,200	−16	3
Violent Crime Index	122,000	57	3
Property Crime Index	572,600	9	−4
Total[b]	**1,489,700**	**23%**	**2%**

[a] Numbers have been rounded.   [b] Some categories are not reported here; those reported may not equal the total.
Source: J. Butts, H. Snyder, T. Finnegan, A. Aughenbaugh, & R. Poole. 1996. *Juvenile Court Statistics 1993.* Washington, D.C.: Office of Juvenile Justice and Delinquency Prevention, p. 5

by offense in 1993, and Table 2–3 reports the number of juvenile court cases by sex and race for 1989 and 1993, with the percent of change in the four years.[1]

In 1993 juvenile courts processed an estimated 1,489,700 delinquency cases, a 2 percent increase from 1992 and 23 percent more than in 1989 (see Butts et al., 1996, and Table 2–2). Between 1989 and 1993 the number of cases for person offenses increased 52 percent; property offense cases increased 15 percent; drug cases increased 14 percent; and public order offense cases went up 24 percent. The number of person offense cases handled by juvenile courts has increased significantly more than motor vehicle theft and liquor law violations, which decreased from 1989 to 1993. The increases in juvenile court cases parallels the increases in arrests of persons under the age of eighteen as reported by the FBI (Butts et al., 1996: 5).

Table 2–3
Juvenile Court Cases by Sex and Race, 1989–1993

| | Number of Cases[a] | | Percent |
Offenses	1989	1993	Change
Male	984,200	1,192,300	21%
Person	167,200	248,300	49
Property	576,200	647,900	12
Drugs	67,100	78,100	16
Public Order	173,800	217,900	25
Female	227,600	297,400	31%
Person	41,900	70,400	68
Property	128,900	161,000	25
Drugs	10,900	11,000	1
Public Order	46,000	54,900	19
White	816,300	962,100	18%
Person	116,400	181,400	56
Property	501,600	555,900	11
Drugs	44,900	50,400	12
Public Order	153,400	174,400	14
Black	354,000	472,700	34%
Person	86,100	127,700	48
Property	177,300	218,700	23
Drugs	31,500	36,600	16
Public Order	57,000	89,700	52
Other Races	41,600	54,800	32%
Person	6,500	9,600	48
Property	26,200	34,300	31
Drugs	1,500	2,100	36
Public Order	7,400	8,800	18

[a] Numbers have been rounded.

Source: J. Butts, H. Snyder, T. Finnegan, A. Aughenbaugh, & R. Poole. 1996. *Juvenile Court Statistics 1993*. Washington, D.C.: Office of Juvenile Justice & Delinquency Prevention, p. 21, 26

Police and court statistics report only those youth who have been arrested and brought before a juvenile court for offenses. To that extent, they are not complete measures of the full extent of delinquent behavior, since many youth who commit crimes are never apprehended and referred to juvenile court. There is evidence that juvenile arrests vary by race and social class, so lower-class and minority youth may be more likely to be arrested and referred to court (Regoli and Hewitt, 1994: 65–68). Jensen and Rojek estimated the prevalence rates of youth who are arrested and processed by juvenile courts, using 1982 data from the National Center for Juvenile Justice. They estimated that

> out of over three million youths age 12 or younger in 1980, about one-half million will have been referred to the juvenile court by their 18th birthdays, which represents about 18 percent of them. About 25 percent of boys and 12 percent of girls will come to the attention of the juvenile justice system for some form of delinquency before they are eighteen. . . . In sum, it appears safe to conclude that about one-fourth of males in the United States get into trouble with the law before they are 18 years of age and that girls are less than one-half as likely as boys to do so. (Jensen and Rojek, 1992: 83)

The number of young males who get into trouble with the law—one-fourth— is an astounding figure. Most of the delinquent activities are neither violent nor serious property crimes, however. Only a small percentage of all delinquent activities are violent, and most youth who get into some trouble with the law before their eighteenth birthday do not engage in further crime as adults.

School Crime According to Survey Data: *The Safe School Study*

The National Institute of Education (NIE) released the *Safe School Study Report to Congress* in January 1978. Congress passed legislation and funded this three-year, $2.4 million study in 1974 to assess the nature and extent of crime, violence, and disruption in the nation's schools. The nationwide survey gathered data on school crime from principals, teachers, and students in thousands of schools.[2] The results of this study are still relevant for examining the extent and nature of school crime, even though the data are now nearly twenty years old. This study is the only available national study of school violence. No other more recent surveys have been conducted in schools on such a large sample of principals, teachers, and students (see Toby, 1994).

Crimes Against Students

According to reports of students, theft was the most common type of school crime, with 11 percent (2.4 million) of the nation's secondary school students reporting that something worth more than $1 was stolen from them in a month (items such as money, sweaters, books, notebooks, and similar property found in lockers). Only one-fifth of the reported thefts involved money or property worth $10 or more (National Institute of Education-NIE, 1977: 2). An estimated 1.3 percent (282,000) of secondary school students reported that they were attacked at school in a typical one-month period. Twice as many (2.1 percent) junior high students reported attacks. About two-fifths of the reported attacks resulted in some injury, but only 4 percent involved injuries serious enough to require medical treatment. Only one-half of 1 percent (about 112,000) of students reported being robbed (money or property taken by force, weapons, or threats) (NIE, 1977: 2). When the amount of time spent at school is taken into account, the risk of violence to teenagers is greater in school than elsewhere. While youth spend up to 25 percent of their waking hours in school, 40 percent of the robberies and 36 percent of the assaults on urban teenagers occurred in schools (NIE, 1977: 2).

Crimes Against Teachers

Survey data from the *Safe School Study* estimated that 12 percent of the teachers in secondary schools have something worth more than $1 stolen from them, about the same proportion as students (11 percent) (NIE, 1977: 3). One out of 200 secondary school teachers (about 5,200) are physically attacked at school each month. About twenty percent or 1,000 of the attacks on teachers each month required medical treatment (compared to only 4 percent of assaults on students) (NIE, 1978: 75). Attacks on teachers were predominantly in urban schools, and junior high schools showed higher percentages than senior highs.

In summary, teachers are more likely to be victimized if they teach in junior high schools; have large classes with more low-ability students, underachievers, and behavior-problem students; or work in schools with higher proportions of minority students and with classes that exceed thirty pupils. Most school violence is not committed by outsiders intruding into the school. In most attacks and robberies, the offender is recognized by the victim and known by him or her by sight or by name. Most attacks and robberies in school involved only one offender. The offender and victim are usually of the same sex (generally males victimizing other males), and they are similar in age, contrary to the belief that older students are preying on younger students (NIE, 1978: 113).

Junior high school students show more overt hostility toward teachers than do older students (NIE, 1978: 70–71). Two-thirds of secondary school teachers in large urban settings report that students swore or made obscene gestures at them in one month. This compares with 41 percent of rural and 48 percent of suburban secondary school teachers. The study found that 90 percent of all assaulted teachers also reported having been sworn at in the previous month. These hostile encounters affect teachers' responses to student misbehavior. The teachers were asked whether they hesitated to confront misbehaving students out of fear for their own safety; 12 percent indicated that had happened at least once or twice in the past month. A higher percentage of teachers in urban areas experienced fear and hesitated to confront students. There was no difference between junior high and senior high teachers, in spite of the greater verbal abuse in junior highs. It is likely that the greater age and size of senior high youth increases the fear and hesitation of teachers.

Insults and threats against teachers are in general associated with increased risks of victimization, particularly in urban junior high schools. The report noted:

> In seriously affected schools, they (hostility and conflict) are likely to be part of a general turbulance in which violent acts are common. . . . Moreover it seems that extensive personal violence in a school is likely to be just one part of a negatively charged social environment in which many things go wrong. (NIE, 1978: 71)

Crimes Against School Property

The principals' reports covered offenses against schools, rather than persons. Most widespread were property offenses—trespassing, breaking and entering, theft of school property, and deliberate property destruction or vandalism, which was the most common. Data indicated that in the late 1970s one in four schools was vandalized, at an average cost of $81 per incident. One in ten schools was broken into, at an average cost of $183 per incident. Schools were about five times as likely to be burglarized as were commercial establishments. Estimates of the annual cost of school crime nearly twenty years ago ran from about $50 million to $600 million, with most estimates in the $100 to $200 million range (NIE, 1977: 3).

Unfortunately, there are no current national statistics available on the costs of school crime. Robert Rubel, an authority on school crime and former director of the National Alliance for Safe Schools, noted that the *Safe School Study* was the last national research effort to collect data on the costs of school crime. National estimates of the costs are very difficult to obtain because of the many variables involved and the different measures used by school districts across the country in counting damages, glass breakage, and vandalism (Rubel, 1996). Peter Blauvelt, an expert on school security and currently executive director of the National Alliance for Safe Schools, has noted that individual school districts have estimates of the cost of school crime and vandalism but that no state or national figures are available. The National Center for Educational Statistics stopped collecting damage and cost measures in the early 1980s, and there is no state or federal legislation that requires the reporting of costs of damage and theft of school property (Blauvelt, 1996).

Arson raises special concerns for school administrators and for police and fire officials, because it is a crime against property and a crime of violence. School fires often involve present or former students who have had problems with teachers or have experienced school failure ("On the Fire Line: Fighting Arson at School," 1995). The St. Paul, Minnesota, Department of Fire and Safety Services tracked 108 children who had played with fire at least once, and they found that 13 percent had set fire to schools or on school buses ("Officials Note Flareup in Arson-Related School Fires," 1994: B7). As with other school crimes, it is difficult to measure the cost of arson, since several factors must be considered. The monetary cost ranges from a few thousand to millions of dollars. The average cost of property damage for all types of structures for the 102,009 arson offenses reported in the 1992 Uniform Crime Reports was $28,343. The cost to repair and rebuild Burnsville High School in Minnesota after an arson-suspected fire in April 1995 is an estimated $7 million.

The costs of school vandalism and arson, however, cannot be measured only in financial terms. Crimes against school property also have a profound effect on students, teachers, and school staff, including:

•negative publicity related to school safety

•increased insurance rates (29 cents of every insurance dollar now goes to pay the cost of intentionally set fires)

•loss of study and work time due to injuries or canceled classes

•loss of irreplaceable items such as personal keepsakes, lecture notes, and student files, projects, and writing

•lowered morale or reduced productivity due to a persisting sense of fear and/or violation (Ramsey, 1994: 8; see also "On the Fire Line: Fighting Arson at School," 1995: 2).

A number of school districts have developed programs to reduce vandalism and arson. The most effective programs are those that have been jointly developed with local police and fire departments and that involve students, teachers, and school staff members. Vandalism and arson must be treated as serious crimes, with penalties ranging from school expulsion to police arrest and judicial action. Improved security practices can reduce the incidents of vandalism and arson. School efforts that help students develop a sense of pride and ownership in their school will help reduce property damage and theft. The tremendous cost of school property damage is an additional drain on tight school budgets. School districts should develop a school safety task force to carefully analyze the problem and to develop possible solutions in collaboration with police, the fire department, parents, and community organizations (see the March 1995 issue of *School Safety Update* of the National School Safety Center, 1995).

Location and Perpetrators of School Crime

According to the *Safe School Study,* offenses tended to be higher in the Northeast and the West than in the North Central and the Southern states. Violent offenses were more common in urban, inner-city schools, and in junior highs rather than senior highs. For property offenses there was little difference between urban and suburban metropolitan areas. The per capita cost of school crime was actually higher in the suburbs than in the cities. According to secondary school students, beer, wine, and marijuana were widely available in schools throughout metropolitan areas, especially senior high schools (NIE, 1977: 4; NIE, 1978: 71–73).

Except for trespassing and breaking and entering, most reported school crimes were committed by current students enrolled at the school, and the offender was usually recognized by the victim. The majority of the attacks involved victims and offenders of the same age, sex, and race, although 42 percent of the attacks and 46 percent of the robberies were interracial, and the risks of violence were greater in schools with less than 40 percent white students (NIE, 1977: 5).

Factors Associated with School Crime

The *Safe School Study* identified some factors that were associated with school crime (NIE, 1977: 5; NIE, 1978: 111–113). First, the amount of crime in the neighborhood around the school is a factor. The presence of fighting gangs in the school's attendance area tends to increase the level of violence. The more crime and violence to which students are exposed outside the school, the greater the problems in the school. A school's proximity to students' homes can make it a convenient target for vandalism. The presence of nonstudent youths around the school also increases the risk of property loss. Schools in which discipline is firm and those with higher proportions of students from two-parent families suffer less vandalism. There is more violence in schools with lower secondary grades and where there are higher proportions of male students.

School size and structure are factors in crime and disruption. The probability of victimization is greater if the teacher has large classes (more than thirty students); large numbers of low-ability students, underachievers, and behavior-problem students; and a high percentage of minority students (NIE, 1978: 111). Larger schools, and schools with larger classes, tend to have more violence and vandalism. The impersonality of large schools often creates feelings of alienation and frustration in students, which in turn may erupt in disruption and violence. When teachers and administrators can establish personal relationships with students, the risks of violence decrease. Thus, school governance is a related factor. A firm, fair, and consistent system for running a school seems to be a key factor in reducing violence. Where the rules are known and where they are firmly and fairly enforced, less violence occurs. Good coordination between the faculty and administration also promotes a better school atmosphere. On the other hand, if students perceive a hostile or authoritarian attitude on the part of the teachers, vandalism may result.

The degree of student commitment to education and the school is a factor. Students need to feel that their courses are relevant and that they have some control over what happens to them at school. Findings indicate that academic competition may decrease the risk of disruption and violence in schools. Violent students are more likely to be those who have given up on school, do not care about grades, find courses irrelevant, and feel that nothing they do makes any difference. Such students might take out their frustration through disruption in the classroom or violence against teachers or other students. Caring about grades and seeing relevance in education can be an important step toward commitment to the school and one's own future. Overall, the results of the *Safe School Study* seemed to stress the importance of a rational structure of incentives, both positive and negative, that serve to increase student commitment and to structure perceptions, expectations, and behavior (NIE, 1977: 5).

Evaluation of Safe School Study Findings

The *Safe School Study* was the first comprehensive assessment of the extent and nature of school crime in the United States. While the report provided a wealth of descriptive data and a sound basis for further research, some of the methods and statistical analyses of the report have come under criticism (see Emrich, 1978, and Gottfredson and Gottfredson, 1985). Gottfredson and Gottfredson reexamined the *Safe School Study* data to control statistically for community and demographic characteristics while examining the relative contribution of school governance, school climate, and other school characteristics. The *Safe School Study* focuses on in-school variables such as student characteristics, school governance, and rule enforcement. A major theme running through the report is the role of administrators and teachers in reducing school disruption. The message of the report is that school administration and policies make a difference. While the NIE study acknowledged that schools with more disruption and crime were located in communities with more crime, the report virtually ignored community factors and focused on the school variables. In their reanalysis of the data, Gottfredson and Gottfredson combined a number of variables into an index of social disorganization and found that schools with high rates of teacher victimization are located in communities characterized by poverty and disorganization and are in central cities.

> The results . . . have documented powerful links between the community context within which a school exists and disruption within the school. . . . (T)hese associations . . . accord with theory and earlier ecological research in implying that delinquency is related to community social organization. (Gottfredson and Gottfredson, 1985: 73–74)

The reexamination of the *Safe School Study* data revealed several influences on student and teacher victimization that were beyond the control of school administration and staff. Characteristics of the community and school social composition that are associated with more victimization but are beyond the school's control include:

1. Schools located in areas characterized by poverty, unemployment, and a high proportion of female-headed families
2. Urban schools (teacher victimization)
3. Schools located in high crime communities
4. Schools where large proportions of the students are black, rated as low in ability, and come from families on welfare (teacher victimization)
5. Schools located in areas where the general population has little education and is not affluent (senior high schools only)
6. Schools in which most students are at the lower grade levels (senior high schools only)
7. Schools where a large proportion of students are male (senior high schools only)
8. Schools where desegregation programs exist (e.g., busing or court-ordered desegregation programs; junior high schools only) (Gottfredson and Gottfredson, 1985: 133–4)

Contrary to recent reports that school disorder is an acute crisis, the evidence from the Gottfredsons' reanalyses is that there are some chronic disciplinary problems in many schools and that victimization in schools resembles the kind of victimization outside the schools. Although crime in the schools is not more serious than crime in the community, they emphasize that any victimization experiences in schools are serious problems because they disrupt education, increase teacher job dissatisfaction, and create negative impressions of some schools as places where no one would want to work or study.

In sum, the *Safe School Study* was the first comprehensive national assessment of the extent and nature of school crime. In spite of some methodological weaknesses, the report has contributed to our understanding of the problem and has generated more research and analyses of school crime.[3] The *Safe School Study* statistics are rather dated now, however, so we turn next to the most current national measure of crime victimization in schools.

National Crime Victimization Survey

A special School Crime Supplement of the National Crime Victimization Survey (NCVS) was conducted from January through June of 1989 (Bastian and Taylor, 1991). The 10,449 respondents included students between the ages of twelve and nineteen who had attended a public or private school at any time during the six months preceding the interview and were enrolled in junior and senior high schools. Data from the survey represent an estimated 21.6 million students between ages 12 and 19. The students were questioned their perceptions of various school crime problems: How difficult were drugs or alcohol to obtain at school? How prevalent were street gangs in school? How fearful were students of being attacked at school? The major findings of the survey are summarized in Table 2–4.

The NCVS findings indicate that an estimated 9 percent of students ages 12 to 19 were victims of crime in or around their school during the first six months of 1989 (Bastian and Taylor, 1991: 1). Thus, nearly two million of the 21.6 million twelve- to nineteen-year-old youth enrolled in the nation's public and private schools are estimated to be victims of at least one crime. Six percent of students have avoided some place in or around their school because they thought someone might attack or harm them; school hallways and restrooms were most often mentioned as places students avoided (Bastian and Taylor, 1991: 9). Even greater fear was expressed by students who had been robbed or assaulted the previous six months (25%) and who had experienced a theft or attempted theft (10%). Public school students (22%) were more likely than private school students (13%) to report some fear of attack at school; students from families with low incomes were most likely to be afraid of attacks and avoid places in school; and inner-city students expressed more fear than suburban or nonmetropolitan area students (Bastian and Taylor, 1991: 10–11).

The National Crime Survey is a rich source of data for secondary analysis. Garofalo, Siegel, and Laub (1987) noted that while more than half of the personal crimes of violence committed against adults are reported to the police,

Table 2–4
The Extent and Nature of School Crime
[National Crime Victimization Survey Data]

• Seven percent of all students were victims of property crime, and 2 percent were victims of violent crime.

• Public school students were more likely to be crime victims than were private school students—9 percent versus 7 percent.

• Students in central cities were more likely than suburban students to fear attack at school and to avoid certain places.

• About 24 percent of the black students in central cities and 18 percent of the white students feared being attacked going to and from school.

• Among suburban youth, 15 percent of black students and 12 percent of white students feared attack going to and from school.

• Generally, students from families with low incomes were the most likely to fear being attacked at school, but violent crime victimization rates showed no consistent relationship to family income levels.

• Students whose families had moved twice or more during the previous five years were more likely to report being afraid of attack at school than were students who had moved less frequently.

• Public school students were substantially more likely than students in private schools to indicate some level of fear of attack at school.

• Six percent of students said they avoided some place in or around their school because they thought someone might attack or harm them there. School restrooms were most often mentioned as places to avoid.

• Overall, 14 percent of white students, 20 percent of black students, and 32 percent of Hispanic students said there were gangs in their schools.

• Among students who said gangs were or might be in their schools:

• 37 percent said gang members never fought at school.

• 19 percent said gang fights occurred once or twice a year.

• 12 percent said gang fights happened at least once a week.

• Students who said their schools had gangs were about twice as likely as students from schools without gangs to be afraid of attack, both at school and on the way to or from school.

• Sixteen percent (representing more than 3 million students) said they knew of attacks on or threats to a teacher at their school in the six months before the interview.

Source: Adapted from Lisa D. Bastian and Bruce M. Taylor. 1991. *School Crime: A National Crime Victimization Survey Report*. Washington, D.C.: U.S. Department of Justice, pp. 1–11

the figure is only one-third for victims ages 12 to 19, and only 15 percent of school-related juvenile robberies and assaults were reported (1987: 335). Their examination of interviewers' narrative reports revealed more about the causes and nature of school crime. A large proportion of school-related victimizations stem from peer interactions that occur in the course of routine daily activities and escalate into victimizations. Many incidents result from frictions among peers that arise from normal school-day activities. Stealing items often originates not in criminal intent but in teasing and youthful horseplay (Garofalo, Siegel, and Laub, 1987: 332–3).

Recent School Crime Surveys

Teacher Survey on Safe, Disciplined, and Drug-Free Schools

A survey of teachers was conducted by Westat, Inc., for the National Center for Education Statistics during the 1990–91 school year. A national sample of 1,350 public school teachers responded to questions concerning the extent of school crime, disruption, and discipline problems and the extent and effectiveness of current policies and drug education programs (Mansfield, Alexander, and Farris, 1991). Among the highlights of the survey report were these findings:

- Student alcohol use was considered a serious or moderate problem by 23 percent of teachers.
- Student drug use was considered a serious or moderate problem by 17 percent of teachers.
- Prevention programs and policies for school alcohol and drug use were considered not very effective in reducing student alcohol and drug use.
- Nineteen percent of teachers reported verbal abuse by a student during the past four weeks; 8 percent had been threatened with injury within the past twelve months; and 2 percent had been physically attacked within the past twelve months.
- Almost 50 percent of teachers indicated that a lack of alternative placements/programs for disruptive students limited their ability to maintain order and discipline in their school.
- Nearly all teachers indicated that they felt safe in the school building during school hours; 90 percent felt safe after school hours, on school grounds, or in the neighborhood of the school (Mansfield et al., 1991: iii).

The 1991 Youth Gun Survey

A survey was conducted to determine the extent of weapon possession and victimization in inner-city high schools (Sheley, McGee, and Wright, 1995; see also Sheley and Wright, 1995). The sample included 1,591 students (758 males, 833 females) in ten inner-city high schools in California, Louisiana, New Jersey, and Illinois. (The overall study also included surveys of adjudicated juveniles in correctional facilities in those states.) Enrollments in the selected high schools ranged from 900 to 2,100. Selection of research sites focused on areas in which gun-related activities were considered extensive. The findings of this survey therefore are not generalizable to many other cities or states. Major findings of the survey were these:

- A total of 39 percent of the students reported that male relatives carried guns outside their homes.

•A total of 35 percent had friends who carried guns outside the home.

•Twenty-three percent considered guns easy to get in their neighborhoods.

•Eighty percent reported that other students carried weapons to school; 66 percent personally knew someone who had done so.

•Two-thirds personally knew someone who had been shot at, stabbed, or assaulted while in school.

•More than one-third (38 percent) of the students stated that there is "a lot of violence in this school" (Sheley, McGee, and Wright, 1995: 7).

The findings of this survey are clearly not representative of most high schools throughout the nation. The survey does indicate, however, that weapon-related victimization is not uncommon among students in troubled inner-city schools. Joseph Sheley and his associates noted some implications of the survey findings: many students in the sample reported engaging in behaviors that increased the risk of violent victimization (criminal and gang activities, carrying weapons); a strikingly high level of danger characterized many students' social environments; schools do not generate weapon-related violence as much as they represent the location where violence in the neighborhood around the school occurs; schools can do much to prevent violence on their grounds, using metal detectors and increased security, but reducing weapon possession and violence among students requires a comprehensive community-level effort (Sheley et al., 1995: 10–11).

National Household Education Survey

The National Household Education Survey was conducted by Westat, Inc., for the National Center for Education Statistics (National Center for Education Statistics, 1995). Data were collected from January through April 1993 from a sample of 6,504 students in grades 6 through 12. Weights were applied to make the survey estimates applicable to the entire population of students in grades 6 through 12. This survey expanded the definition of victimization to include knowledge or witness of crime incidents or bullying at school (the NCVS findings reported earlier included only direct personal experience, threats, or harm). The rationale for including students' knowledge or witnessing of school crime and bullying is that awareness of and fearing school crime have a pervasive effect on students besides those who are direct victims. The incidents reported were bullying (repeated threat of harm), physical attacks, and robbery (taking something directly by force or threat of force). Students were asked to report on these crime incidents at their schools or on their way to or from school from the beginning of the 1992–93 school year. Students were asked whether they knew of each type of incident; whether they had seen any incidents; whether they worried that such an assult might happen to them; and whether they had personally been a victim of an incident. Results of the summary are reported in Figure 2–1.

The survey method, including awareness of, witnessing, or worrying about being a crime victim at school and going to or from school, was expected to

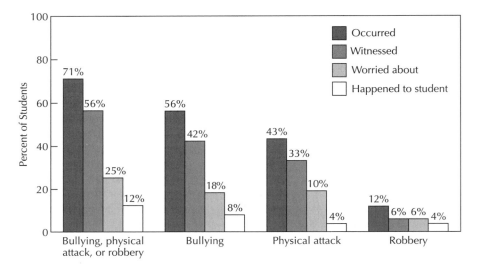

Figure 2–1. Sixth- through twelfth-graders' reports of the occurrence of, witnessing, worry about, or victimization by crime, by selected incidents, 1992–93

*Students who reported more than one type of incident are included in the overall victimization percentages only one time. Source: U.S. Department of Education, National Center for Education Statistics, National Household Education Survey, 1993

result in a significant proportion of students responding affirmatively. The results bear this out. A majority of students (71 percent) reported knowing about bullying, physical attack, or robbery at their schools during that year. The largest percentage of students reported knowing about bullying incidents (56 percent), followed by physical attack (43 percent) and robbery (12 percent). Even though many students had knowledge of or had witnessed such incidents, fear of crime at school is rather low: 18 percent worried about being bullied, 10 percent worried about being attacked, and only 6 percent worried about being robbed. The percentage who reported having been personally victimized was even lower, as reported in Figure 2–1.

Bullying in Schools

As the data just presented indicate, one of the most common victimization experiences reported by students is bullying. Most persons have witnessed or been a victim of bullying at some time during their school experience. Bullying has not been recognized as a serious problem in the United States until fairly recently. It has often been downplayed as simply teasing or minor harassment that is a "normal" but unpleasant part of going to school. More attention and research has been devoted to bullying in Scandinavian countries (Olweus, 1978). Research on bullying among schoolchildren has attracted attention in other countries, including Great Britain, Canada, and the United

States only since the 1980s and early 1990s (Farrington, 1993). Surveys of more than 150,000 Norwegian students indicated that 15 percent of students in grades 1 through 9 have been involved in bullying incidents, either as bullies (about 7 percent) or as victims (about 9 percent) (Olweus, 1994). Data from other countries indicate that the bullying problem is at least comparable to or greater than that in Norwegian schools. More boys than girls bully other students. A large percentage of girls report that they are mainly bullied by boys, but a somewhat larger percentage of boys are victims of bullying. Bullying is a greater problem among boys, although girls are also involved in bullying. Bullying among boys tends to be more physical; girls typically use more subtle forms of harrassment, such as slandering, spreading rumors, exclusion from a group, and manipulating friendship relations (Olweus, 1994). Contrary to what many believe, bullying is not a consequence of large schools or class sizes; nor is it explained as a reaction to school failure or frustration. Research suggests that bullying is more closely related to personality characteristics of bullies and victims. Bullies have a greater acceptance of violence than do other students, are often characterized by impulsivity and a need to dominate others, and express little empathy for victims (Olweus, 1994: 2).

School Crime in Perspective

School crime receives widespread publicity. We are led to believe that crime and disruption in schools are pervasive, affecting the majority of all schools. To the contrary, survey measures of crime show that few serious incidents occur in most schools during any one-month period. It is difficult to conclude that schools are violent places, when data indicate that on the average 99 percent of students are free from attack in a month's time. There is no strong evidence that serious crime in schools is an extensive problem or that the problem has increased significantly; serious physical injuries or financial loss are rare in schools, although minor victimizations and verbal threats do occur regularly (see Gold and Moles, 1978; Gottfredson and Gottfredson, 1985; and Garofalo, Siegel, and Laub, 1987). According to the *Safe School Study* and National Crime Victimization Survey data, most crimes that occur in school are petty theft, damage to school property, or minor assaults. Some urban schools in high-crime communities do have more serious crime, but violent schools are not the norm. Students and teachers are safer in most schools than they are in other parts of the community.

Then why has there been so much publicity about school crime and violence? Scarcely a week goes by without some report on television, radio, newspapers and magazines about crime, drugs, and guns in schools. A number of factors seem to explain the attention and publicity given to school crime. Many crime incidents, including those in schools, are more likely to be reported today than previously. More public attention is focused on urban problems, and the problems of inner-city schools tend to form the public's image of all schools. While minor thefts and school property damage do occur in suburban and rural schools, serious victimization of students and teachers is much more likely to occur in inner-city schools—schools located in neighborhoods that are also marked by more crime. Victimization trends in the homes located near the schools and in the streets surrounding the schools have a direct effect on victimization rates inside the school (Parker, Smith, Smith, and Toby, 1991). Incidents such as serious assaults, students carrying guns, and gang activities tend to be dramatized by the media. The publicity, more reporting, and frequent minor incidents when coupled with verbal harassment and bullying of a few students, create a fearful environment in many schools. Thus, despite the fact that students and teachers in most schools actually have a low probability of being victims of crime in school, their fears and feelings of vulnerability affect the school environment.

Fear of School Crime

Whether theft, property damage, or violent crime is high or low in schools, the interruption of the learning process and the fear of crime are serious problems. Thirty-three percent of junior high school students in large cities state that they avoid places in school, such as restrooms, out of fear. The *Safe School Study* found that 7 percent of metropolitan junior high students reported that they were afraid most of the time; 8 percent said they stayed home at least one day each month out of fear. Overall, at schools surveyed, 56 percent of attack victims and 18 percent of nonvictims said they were sometimes afraid that someone would hurt or bother them at school; and 29 percent of victims and 9 percent of nonvictims reported that they often brought something to school to protect themselves (NIE, 1978: 116–17). According to the National Crime Survey, about 24 percent of black students and 18 percent of white students in central cities and 15 percent of black students and 12 percent of white students in suburban areas feared being attacked going to and from school (Bastian and Taylor, 1991: 11). The fear of school crime poses a serious problem when it disrupts the learning process and contributes to absenteeism. In addition to the personal and educational impact, there is an economic impact, as absenteeism affects schools' average daily-attendance computations, which are tied in turn to per-pupil cost reimbursements (Rubel, 1978: 264).

The public and political reaction to fear of school crime is often to demand the use of more security personnel. Police and security officers patrolling the hallways may help diminish fear and incidents of crime. They may also bring a prisonlike atmosphere to the school and may be unnecessarily intrusive. Studies suggest that the presence of school personnel alone may be sufficient to reduce school victimizations. Hallways, stairs, toilets, cafeterias, and locker rooms—places where teachers' and principals' supervision is least likely—are the locations of most school victimizations (Toby, 1983: 23). Getting to and from school is another source of fear. Students who walk to and from school report the most fear. Students who ride a school bus are less likely to fear attack, and (except for students in central cities) students who use public transportation express still less fear. Pearson and Toby suggest that school bus and public bus drivers act as potential guardians against attack (1991: 119). Likewise, greater presence of school personnel in those areas that are least supervised and where students fear being victimized may reduce student conflicts and threatening behaviors (Garofalo, Siegel, and Laub, 1987: 333–334). More adult supervision throughout schools will not prevent all school crime, but it will certainly reduce the incidence of student conflicts and threatening behavior.

The picture of school crime drawn by the survey data is not one of widespread random violence such as the media suggest. This is not to deny that some schools experience serious violence. Serious incidents in any schools deserve our attention. A reasoned assessment of the extent and nature of most school crime reveals that most victimizations result from frequent interactions among students in a confined setting. Teasing, threats, and conflicts often escalate into more serious victimization. Fortunately, much of this behavior can be deterred through the presence of school personnel. There are limitations on how much control school personnel can exert on student interactions that may become disruptive and threatening, however.

> [I]t is unlikely that many of these victimizations can be prevented by trying to decrease the exposure of adolescents to each other or by trying to increase the presence of capable guardians. Kids still have to go to school, and their interactions cannot be kept under constant surveillance. (Garofalo, Siegel, and Laub, 1987: 337)

Garofalo, Siegel, and Laub (1987) suggest that we can prevent much school victimization by helping students change their attitudes and the behaviors that lead to assaults and thefts. Providing juveniles with the skills to settle their disputes will reduce many of the conflicts that escalate into victimization. Some schools, beginning with the elementary grades, have introduced programs to help students deal with hostile interactions and to develop mediation skills to resolve disputes before they escalate into serious threats and assaults.

Summary

Newspapers and news magazines regularly feature dramatic accounts of youth crime and portray it as a widespread and growing problem. We have yet to develop accurate and reliable measures of the true extent of crime in general, and police and court statistics do not provide specific measures of school crime. The extent and nature of school crime is assessed through survey measures, such as the *Safe School Study* and the National Crime Survey. Contrary to media accounts of school crime, survey measures indicate that there is no strong evidence that serious crime in schools is an extensive problem or that the problem has increased significantly. Minor victimizations do occur frequently in some schools, but serious physical injuries or financial loss are rare in most schools. Most crimes that occur in school are damage to school property and minor thefts and assaults that escalate from student conflicts and disputes. The verbal harassment, threats, and bullying of a few students do create fear among students about getting to and from schools and foster a fearful environment inside many schools. Many of the problems can be reduced through greater adult supervision and by providing students with skills to prevent conflicts and disputes from escalating into violence.

Notes

1. The report includes youth who are juveniles under the statutes of each state. In most states the upper age of juvenile jurisdiction is seventeen, but the top age ranges from fifteen to eighteen. Juvenile court statistics are compiled from the National Juvenile Court Data Archive, which is maintained by the National Center for Juvenile Justice for the Office of Juvenile Justice and Delinquency Prevention.

2. The study was completed in three phases. Phase I was a mail survey of 5,578 schools selected through a probability sample, representing a profile of all the nation's schools. School principals responded to a questionnaire on illegal or disruptive activities and prepared reports on incidents during a one-month period. Phase II included on-site surveys of 642 junior and senior high schools. Phase III consisted of detailed, qualitative case studies of ten schools in which problems of violence had dramatically and rapidly decreased. Survey return rates were very high. In Phase I, 97 percent (3,910) of the principals returned their questionnaires. In Phase II, 91 percent (582) of the schools returned incident reports; 23,895 teachers (76 percent) returned their questionnaires; 31,373 students (81 percent) responded to questionnaires; and 6,283 students (83 percent) responded to in-depth interviews. (See also Robert J. Rubel [1978], "Analysis and Critique of HEW's *Safe School Study Report to the Congress*," *Crime & Delinquency* 24: 257–265; and Jackson Toby, 1994, "Everyday School Violence: How Disorder Fuels It," American Educator [Winter]: 4–9, 44–48.)

3. Criticisms include poor conceptualization of "seriousness" of crimes; survey methods that have questionable validity and reliability; and reliance on cross-tabulation statistical analyses, which can analyze data only categorically and provide a weak basis for sound policy recommendations.

References

Bastian, Lisa D., and Bruce M. Taylor. 1991. *School Crime: A National Crime Victimization Survey Report*. Washington, D.C.: U.S. Department of Justice.

Blauvelt, Peter. Personal telephone interview conducted on May 17, 1996.

Butts, J., H. Snyder, T. Finnegan, A. Aughenbaugh, & R. Poole. 1996. *Juvenile Court Statistics 1993*. Washington, D.C.: Office of Juvenile Justice and Delinquency Prevention.

Dinitz, Simon and John Conrad. 1980. "The Dangerous Two Percent." In D. Shichor and D. Kelly, eds., *Critical Issues in Juvenile Delinquency*. Lexington, Mass.: Lexington Books.

Emrich, Robert L. 1978. "The Safe School Study Report to the Congress: Evaluation and Recommendations." *Crime & Delinquency* 24:266–275.

Farrington, David P., 1993. "Understanding and Preventing Bullying." In M. Tonry, ed., *Crime and Justice: A Review of Research*, vol. 17. Chicago: University Chicago Press.

Federal Bureau of Investigation. 1995. *Uniform Crime Reports for the United States 1994.* Washington, D.C.: U.S. Department of Justice.

Garofalo, James, Leslie Siegel, and John Laub. 1987. "School-Related Victimizations among Adolescents: An Analysis of National Crime Survey (NCS) Narratives." *Journal of Quantitative Criminology* 3:321–338.

Garrett, John R., Scott A. Bass, and Michael D. Casserly. 1978. "Studying School Crime: A Prescription for Research-Based Prevention." In E. Wenk and N. Harlow, eds., *School Crime and Disruption.* Davis, Calif.: Responsible Action.

Gold, Martin, and Oliver C. Moles. 1978. "Delinquency and Violence in Schools and the Community." In J. A. Inciardi and A. Pottieger, eds., *Violent Crime: Historical and Contemporary Issues.* Beverly Hills, Calif.: Sage.

Gottfredson, Gary D., and Denise C. Gottfredson. 1985. *Victimization in Schools.* New York: Plenum Press.

Hamparian, D., J. Davis, J. Jacobson, and R. McGraw. 1985. *The Young Criminal Years of the Violent Few.* Washington, D.C.: U.S. Department of Justice.

Jensen, Gary F., and Dean G. Rojek. 1992. *Delinquency and Youth Crime*, 2nd ed. Prospect Heights, Ill.: Waveland Press.

Mansfield, Wendy, Debbie Alexander, and Elizabeth Farris. 1991. *Teacher Survey on Safe, Disciplined, and Drug-Free Schools.* Washington, D.C.: National Center for Education Statistics.

National Center for Education Statistics. 1995. *Statistics in Brief: Student Victimization at School.* Washington, D.C.: U.S. Department of Education.

National Institute of Education. 1977. *Violent Schools—Safe Schools: The Safe School Study Report to the Congress—Executive Summary.* Washington, D.C.: U.S. Department of Health, Education, and Welfare.

National Institute of Education. 1978. *Violent Schools—Safe Schools: The Safe School Study Report to the Congress*, vol. I. Washington, D.C.: U.S. Department of Health, Education, and Welfare.

National School Safety Center. 1995. *School Safety Update* (newsletter). March.

"On the Fire Line: Fighting Arson at School." 1995. *School Safety Update* (March): 1–4.

Olweus, Dan. 1978. *Aggression in the Schools.* London: Hemisphere Publishing Corporation.

Olweus, Dan. 1994. "Bullying: Too Little Love, Too Much Freedom." *School Safety Update* (May): 1–4.

Parker, Robert N., William R. Smith, D. Randall Smith, and Jackson Toby. 1991. "Trends in Victimization in Schools and Elsewhere, 1974–1981." *Journal of Quantitative Criminology* 7:3–17.

Pearson, Frank S., and Jackson Toby. 1991. "Fear of School-Related Predatory Crime." *Sociology and Social Research* 75:117–125.

Ramsey, Robert D. 1994. "Arson: Hot Workplace Issue for the 90s." *National Research Bureau*, no. 9 (September): 8.

Regoli, Robert M., and John D. Hewitt. 1994. *Delinquency and Society*, 2nd ed. New York: McGraw-Hill.

Rubel, Robert J. 1978. "Analysis and Critique of HEW's Safe School Study Report to the Congress." *Crime & Delinquency* 24:257–265.

Rubel, Robert, 1996. Personal telephone interview conducted May 17, 1996.

Sheley, Joseph F., and James D. Wright. 1995. *In the Line of Fire.* New York: Aldine De Gruyter.

Sheley, Joseph F., Zina T. McGee, and James D. Wright. 1995. *Weapon-Related Victimization in Selected Inner-City High School Samples.* Washington, D.C.: U.S. Department of Justice.

Toby, Jackson. 1983. "Violence in Schools." In M. Tonry and N. Morris, eds., *Crime and Justice: An Annual Review of Research*, vol. 4. Chicago: University of Chicago Press.

Toby, Jackson. 1994. "Everyday School Violence: How Disorder Fuels It." *American Educator* (Winter): 4–9, 44–48.

Toch, Thomas (with Ted Gest and Monika Guttman). 1993. "Violence in Schools: When Killers Come to Class." *U.S. News & World Report* 115 (November 8): 32.

Tracy, P. E., M. E. Wolfgang, and R. M. Figlio. 1985. *Delinquency in Two Birth Cohorts: Executive Summary*. Washington, D.C.: U.S. Department of Justice.

3

Explaining Delinquency and School Crime

I started getting in trouble the summer after seventh grade. . . . I guess my friends would say I'm wild, crazy. . . . I'm a clown. I'll say stupid things and everybody will laugh. I like attention; I'll admit it. Some of my friends are good students, but some are not.—Nicole (Strother, 1991: 14–15)

Most persons have some opinions about what causes crime and delinquency. Popular opinions blame poverty, unemployment, family problems and a loss of traditional family values, rational choices of "bad" persons, or laws and punishments that are not tough enough. Social scientists have sought for years to better understand and explain the complex origins and etiology of crime and delinquency. Explanations have ranged from those that focus on the individual to those that locate the origins of crime in society. In the process of attempting to explain crime, social scientists have come up with a number of theories—ideas and observations that help to explain facts. Theories are constantly being developed, tested, and revised on the basis of research studies that may either support or question their accuracy. The best theories are ones that are (1) clear and simple, (2) testable, (3) based on observations and research data, and (4) logically consistent.

The number and complexity of theories that explain crime and delinquency can be overwhelming, as criminologists seem to be competing with each other for the most correct and comprehensive theoretical perspective. In reality, however, the diversity of theories that attempt to explain crime and delinquency attests to the complexity of the problem and its variation among subcultures and social classes and across gender, ethnic, and racial lines. No single theory can adequately explain all the reasons behind deviant behavior and delinquency of youth, but the predominant theories, when considered together, are able to explain most delinquent behavior. Several criminologists have developed integrated theories of crime, which combine the best features of several theories.

Why Study Theories of Crime and Delinquency?

A problem such as crime that so pervades society, instilling fear among people and costing billions of dollars, demands our utmost attempts to understand its origins and causes. Social scientists have spent years studying the varieties of criminal behavior and the factors that seem to underlie the problem. The study of crime theories is not simply an academic or intellectual exercise, however. Understanding the causes of crime is essential in order to make rational, informed responses to the problem of crime. All policies, laws, and crime prevention programs are based on some beliefs about what causes the problem. Thus, persons who argue in favor of passing tougher laws to combat crime assume that offenders are acting rationally and may be deterred by tougher laws and harsh punishment. On the other hand, those who argue for more rehabilitation and treatment programs assume that some underlying psychological problems or alcohol or other drug abuse have impaired offenders' judgment or caused them to commit crime. Both of these approaches are correct—in some circumstances, for some offenders, some of the time. To assume that one crime prevention strategy will work effectively for all offenders under all circumstances, however, is naive and doomed to failure. Thus, as with any problem facing society, it is incumbent upon us to attempt to understand the origins and causes of crime in order to make policy decisions that are realistically in line with the true nature of the problem. Of course, no single explanation can account for the variety of delinquent behaviors of youth; in fact, most of the major explanations of delinquency do offer accurate descriptions of the reasons youths become involved in delinquency under different circumstances. Just as there are a variety of causes, therefore, policymakers must also take a variety of approaches to deal with the problem.

Explanations of Criminal Behavior

Explanations of crime and delinquency fall into one of two broad categories: rational theories and positivist theories.[1]

Rational Choice Theory

According to *rational theories of crime*, persons commit crime simply because they have made a voluntary, rational decision to do so. Positivists, on the other hand, believe that external conditions beyond the individual's control affect the decision to engage in criminal behavior. The theory originated as the "classical school of criminology" in eighteenth-century Europe and England with Cesare Beccaria and Jeremy Bentham. Their primary concern was not so much to explain criminal behavior as to develop a legal system by which the punishment would fit the crime. It was assumed that since crime was a rational choice, criminal offenders could be deterred by punishment. Punishment was justified because of its practical usefulness in preventing crime. Classical theory has thus been referred to as a utilitarian approach to crime. Rational explanations of crime currently receive wide support among those who believe that crime occurs when an offender decides that the probable gain from illegal behavior outweighs the possible costs of getting caught, convicted, and punished. (See, e.g., Bartollas, 1993: 105–106; Regoli and Hewitt, 1994: 78–82, for a more complete discussion and explanation.)

Rational choice theory has become one of the most popular theoretical approaches in criminology, economics of crime, political science, and law (see, e.g., Cornish and Clarke, 1986; Akers, 1990). This explanation assumes that crime results from a rational process in which offenders make decisions and choices, often planning their criminal activity so as to maximize the benefits and avoid the risks (see Cornish and Clarke, 1986: 1–2). Lawrence Cohen and Marcus Felson (1979) developed a version of rational theory called "routine activity theory" to explain trends and cycles in the crime rate since the 1960s. They concluded that crime is closely related to the interaction of three variables associated with the "routine activities" of everyday life: the availability of suitable targets of crime; the absence of capable guardians; and the presence of motivated offenders. Thus, as more homes are unoccupied during the day as their occupants go to work (and as there are fewer neighbors, family members or relatives to look after them), they are more likely to be targeted by unemployed teens or young adults. The routine activity approach links delinquency to social changes that increase the opportunities for crime and emphasizes the role the victim's lifestyle and behavior play in the crime process. Felson (1994) described how social changes in large and small cities and the increasing number of large schools have increased the likelihood that crime will occur. (Crime as a "routine activity" in large schools is discussed in chapter 6.)

Critics of rational choice theory question the degree to which criminal behavior is always a rational, free-will process. Ronald Akers (1990) questions whether offenders really make rational decisions to commit crime based on knowledge of the law and possible punishments and whether those decisions are made in the absence of any situational factors that tend to influence crime. Rational choice proponents do not always hold to a strict definition of rationality but acknowledge that situational factors do affect individuals' choices, and there are efforts to integrate rational choice theory with other explanations (see, e.g., Felson, 1986; Hirschi, 1986). Certainly many crimes reflect rational choices of persons, and this holds true especially for so-called white-collar crimes, which are often committed in workplace situations that pose relatively little risk of detection, conviction, or punishment. Much juvenile crime reflects rational choice, especially when youths perceive that their chances of being caught are low; even if caught, many are well aware that the punishment for juvenile crime is often much less than for comparable crimes committed by adults.

At the beginning of this chapter, we noted that all responses to crime by legal and social institutions are based on some assumptions about the causes. The logical response to crime as rational behavior is tougher punishment as a deterrent. Deterrence theory holds that punishment has a *general* effect, discouraging the general public from engaging in criminal activity by creating fear of punishment. *Specific deterrence* discourages offenders from repeating their crimes by threatening to punish them more harshly the next time. Punishment and the threat of punishment *are* effective as deterrents against crime: most persons (including offenders), after all, do obey most of the laws most of the time. The effectiveness of punishment as a deterrent to crime, however, depends on three factors: certainty, speed, and severity. Offenders will be deterred from crime only if they believe they are likely to be caught, convicted, and punished. Furthermore, punishment is more effective if it is administered soon after the violation and if it is sufficiently severe. The last requirement, severity, is the one that lawmakers rely on most and that is easiest to achieve. It is more difficult to increase the certainty of police arrest and court conviction, however. That requires additional funding for hiring more police to increase the certainty of arrest and more judges and attorneys to process more cases through the courts. Tougher laws are effective only when they are accompanied by a higher probability of quick and certain enforcement. This is a difficult task, and one that generates heated debate throughout the political process at all levels of government and among citizens. Many persons attribute students' disrespect and disruption in schools to the limitations placed on teachers' and principals' ability to punish students. Lack of support from superintendents, school boards, and parents often limits the ability of teachers to maintain discipline in their classrooms. (This issue is addressed in more detail in Chapter 7.)

Positivist Theories

The second category of explanations for delinquency is referred to as *positivist theories.* Proponents hold that behavior is determined, or caused, by factors over which individuals have no control. Positivist explanations originated with the nineteenth-century criminologist Cesare Lombroso, who is credited with being the first person to use the scientific method to study crime. Lombroso was an Italian physician who noted what he believed to be distinguishing physical characteristics of criminals in prison. Lombroso documented his findings in *The Criminal Man* in 1876, in which he described certain characteristics—or "stigmata"—such as an irregularly shaped head and face, a large jaw, protruding ears, and receding chin. He linked such stigmata to "atavism," a lower stage of biological development, and believed these to be related to criminal tendencies. Lombroso's original findings have since been largely discounted, but the influence of his early work provided the incentive for subsequent criminologists to apply the scientific method to studying criminals.

Positivist theorists have developed explanations of delinquency based on individual factors such as heredity, intelligence, and psychological characteristics; on social structures within society and on social processes within groups of persons; and on political and economic structures of society. Proponents of positivist theories argue that much criminal behavior is not the result of rational choice but stems from a variety of individual and social factors that influence delinquent behavior. Since crime, according to these theorists, is not a rational choice but rather results from conditions over which individuals have little or no control, the theorists are critical of overreliance on punishment to deter crime. Focusing laws and policies primarily on legal sanctions and punishment as the single best answer to crime reduction assumes that most illegal activity is a rational choice. Positivists question that assumption and the tendency of lawmakers to focus on legal sanctions and harsher punishment as the primary response to crime. They believe that individual and social factors that cause crime must be addressed, and many of them have been instrumental in pushing for educational and social programs as alternative means of crime prevention. (We review some of the prominent school-based delinquency prevention and intervention programs in Chapter Ten.)

Individual explanations. Following the initial work of Lombroso, others have posited biological causes of crime. In the 1930s, Earnest Hooton, an American anthropologist, compared physical measurements of 10,000 male prisoners with those of noncriminals and discovered some distinctive differences. The physical differences, such as ear shapes, eye colors, or hair distributions, had no clear connection to crime other than a statistical correlation, however. In the 1940s, William Sheldon (1949), a physician, developed a system for classifying human physique types (endomorphy, mesomorphy, and ectomorphy) and found that these have some correlation with personality and temperament. Mesomorphs tend to be characterized by high activity levels, restlessness, and aggressiveness and tend to seek adventure and danger. Sheldon reported that male and female offenders tended to be mesomorphs.

Genetic influences on delinquency have been examined through studies of twins and adopted children. Glenn Walters (1992) analyzed thirty-eight family, twin, and adoption studies on the gene-crime relationship and found that only the older, poorly designed studies claim to show a relationship. The newer (1975–1989), better designed studies provide less support for the gene-crime hypothesis. Rather than viewing criminal behavior as a product of nature *or* nurture, it seems preferable to examine the relative contributions of genetic and environmental concerns (Walters, 1992: 608). David Rowe and D. Wayne Osgood (1984) view genetic factors as contributing to certain individual differences that in turn interact with specific sociological and environmental conditions that influence delinquent behavior.

Individual explanations of delinquency and school crime have focused primarily on the subjects of intelligence, learning problems, psychological characteristics, and biochemical factors.

Intelligence. The relationship between IQ and delinquency received much attention in the early part of this century. Henry Goddard (1920) found that some juveniles in training schools were what he called "feebleminded," and he created much debate when he concluded that half of all juvenile delinquents were mentally defective. Relatively few studies were published on the topic again until the 1960s and 1970s. D. J. West and D. P. Farrington (1973) conducted a longitudinal study of 411 English boys and found that those who later became criminals had lower IQ scores than those who did not become criminals, leading them to conclude that intelligence is a predictive factor of future delinquency. Lis Kirkegaard-Sorensen and Sarnoff Mednick (1977) conducted a similar longitudinal study of 311 Danish children. Results on intelligence tests supported the West and Farrington study: adolescents who later committed criminal acts had significantly lower intelligence-test scores than their more law-abiding peers (1977: 271). Travis Hirschi and Michael Hindelang (1977) examined several research studies, including Hirschi's data from his California study; Wolfgang and associates' data from the Philadelphia studies; and Weis's data from studies in the state of Washington. They concluded that IQ is more important than race or social class for predicting delinquency. The findings of these studies were supported by analyses of data on Danish students, which demonstrated that low IQ is related to delinquent involvement independent of the effects of socioeconomic status (Moffitt et al., 1981: 155). The authors suggest that the IQ-delinquency relationship is likely explained in part by the lower verbal ability of children with low verbal IQ scores, who experience frustration and failure in school. The frustrating school experiences may contribute to delinquency by creating a negative attitude toward authority, by leading the failing student to seek rewards in less socially desirable settings, or by making the student more vulnerable to delinquent peer pressure when peers provide a source of self esteem (Moffitt et al., 1981: 155). Wilson and Herrnstein believe there is clear evidence for an association between intelligence and crime.

> A child who chronically loses standing in the competition of the classroom may feel justified in settling the score outside, by violence, theft, and other forms of defiant illegality. School failure enhances the rewards for crime by engendering feelings of unfairness. In addition, failure in school predicts, to a substantial degree, failure in the marketplace. For someone who stands to gain little from legitimate work, the rewards of noncrime are relatively weak. Failure in school therefore not only enhances the rewards for crime, but it predicts weak rewards for noncrime. (1985: 171)

Others have questioned the IQ-delinquency relationship. Rosenbaum (1976) argued that the practice of curriculum tracking may depress the IQ scores of students placed in the lower tracks, and Simon (1978) suggests that IQ can change in response to environmental factors and is therefore unstable over time. Scott Menard and Barbara Morse (1984) believe that the practice of tracking, which tends to generate failure, may affect IQ itself and confound the relationship between IQ and academic performance. They concluded from an analysis of longitudinal data of San Diego high school students that the correlation of IQ with delinquency occurs not because IQ has a causal effect on delinquent behavior. Rather, it is one of many individual characteristics that schools tend to select for differential treatment among students.

Proponents of the IQ-delinquency hypothesis nevertheless insist that there is ample evidence to support a statistically significant relationship. Robert Gordon (1987) compared delinquency prevalence rates and concluded that the higher arrest rates and court appearance rates of minority males are best explained by differences in IQ, and not by geographical location, city size, or socioeconomic status. Gordon concludes that because there are differences in IQ between black and white students before they enter school, and because the differences remain throughout schooling, we should seriously consider race differences in IQ when confronting the crime problem (Gordon, 1987: 91–92). Wilson and Herrnstein (1985) suggest that intelligence makes a difference in the types of crimes committed by offenders, that more intelligent offenders tend to commit crimes that have a lower risk of arrest and prosecution and that involve preparation and planning. Less intelligent offenders, on the other hand, are more likely to commit crimes with an immediate payoff or gratification—generally crimes of violence that are acted on impulsively (1985: 166–167). Empirical evidence from research studies does indicate that there is a relationship between intelligence and types of crimes committed by delinquents. Anthony Walsh (1987) analyzed IQ and offense data from the files of male delinquents and concluded that those with lower IQs commit impulsive and spontaneous crimes that offer instant gratification, while more intelligent offenders are more "future-oriented" and tend to commit crimes that require planning and offer deferred gratification but that also lead to more valuable payoffs (1987: 288–289). Longitudinal research provides additional evidence of a relationship between early intelligence scores and later involvement in delinquent behavior. Paul Lipsitt, Stephen Buka, and Lewis Lipsitt (1990) analyzed data of 3,164 children involved in the Brown University cohort of the National Collaborative Perinatal Project. Children who scored lower on IQ tests at ages 4 and 7 had a significantly higher risk of later delinquent involvement. Their findings suggest that children with lower IQs who are identified as disruptive and as behavior problems at an early age may be helped to avoid further delinquent behavior in adolescence if they receive early intervention from school counselors and family therapists (see Gordon, 1990: 207).

Learning disabilities were identified in the 1960s and were believed to affect children's ability to perform effectively in the classroom. The term refers not to lower intelligence but to difficulties in the use of spoken or written language and in the ability to focus and attend to verbal tasks. The most accepted definition of learning disabilities is the one adopted by the National Advisory Committee on Handicapped Children and reported by Hobbs in 1975:

> Children with special learning disabilities exhibit a disorder in one or more of the basic psychological processes involved in understanding or using spoken written languages. These may be manifested in disorders of listening, thinking, talking, reading, writing, spelling or arithmetic. They include conditions which have been referred to as perceptual handicaps, brain injury, minimal brain dysfunction, dyslexia, developmental aphasia, etc. They do not include learning problems which are due to visual, hearing, or motor handicaps, to mental retardation, emotional disturbance, or to environmental disadvantages. (cited in Podboy and Mallory, 1978: 26)

There clearly appears to be a relationship among learning disabilities, learning problems in school, and juvenile delinquency. John Podboy and William Mallory analyzed intelligence test and aptitude test scores of 250 juveniles in a detention facility in California and found that 12.9 percent were developmentally disabled and 48.9 percent were learning disabled (1978: 31). The juveniles with learning disabilities tended to come from larger families, had poorer school performance and poorer English grades, and were likely to have been in a remedial reading class. The researchers' findings led them to conclude that approximately 13 percent of those who enter the juvenile justice system may be below average in IQ, and close to 50 percent of the juvenile delinquent population may be learning disabled (1978: 33). One type of learning disability is attention deficit and hyperactivity disorder (referred to as "ADD" or "ADHD"). David Offord and his associates (1979) compared thirty-one delinquent children who were also hyperactive with thirty-five delinquents who were not hyperactive. The hyperactive delinquents had more antisocial symptoms and an earlier onset of symptoms, and they were characterized as being more reckless and irresponsible and more involved in fighting and drug abuse than the nonhyperactive delinquents. The two groups did not differ in socioeconomic status, IQ, or school performance prior to the onset of antisocial behavior.

There are two theories for the link between learning disabilities and juvenile delinquency (see Post, 1981: 60–61). Proponents of the first theory, the *susceptibility rationale*, argue that the impulsiveness and poor learning ability of LD children makes it difficult for them to learn from experience and to be receptive to social cues. Their learning disability leads to uncontrollable antisocial behavior, and they develop negative self-images because they are then grouped with children who perceive delinquent behavior as part of their expected roles. The second theory, the *school failure rationale*, is based on the labeling process. The LD child is labeled as a problem, which results in a negative self-image and is reinforced by the adults and peers around him. In spite of how hard they may try, LD children are faced with failure each day in the school setting. The daily experience of failure and frustration leads such children to withdraw and not participate in classwork; they may attempt to gain recognition by acting out in the classroom or in the community, many through truancy and other status offenses, some through more serious and aggressive actions (Post, 1981).

Terrie Moffitt (1990) analyzed longitudinal data of a birth cohort of 435 boys, comparing self-reported delinquency scores and assessments for attention deficit disorder (ADD). She found that delinquents with ADD began life with significant motor skills deficits and more family adversity; they had difficulty meeting the demands of school, experienced reading failure soon after entering school, and fell further behind their peers in reading as they approached high school. The antisocial behavior of the ADD boys was more persistent than that of non-ADD boys and became significantly worse over the years. The link between attention deficit disorder and delinquency appears to be highlighted by her finding that the greatest increase in antisocial behavior of the ADD boys coincided with their entry into school and identified reading failure (1990: 906). Britt Klinteberg, David Magnusson, and Daisy Schalling (1989) analyzed longitudinal data including scores on personality and impulsiveness scales for subjects in their teens and again at age 26–27 years and found that early indications of hyperactive behavior was an important predictor of adult impulsivity. They suggested that boys who were hyperactive at an early age are a high risk for delinquency at a young adult age (1989: 48).

Studies showing that a higher proportion of LD children are arrested and incarcerated provide additional support for the relationship between learning disabilities and delinquency. It is estimated that about 10 percent of children in the general population have learning disorders; estimates of LD among adjudicated delinquents range from 26 percent to 73 percent (Zimmerman et al., 1981). Studies that show a link between delinquency and learning disabilities have been criticized for methodological weaknesses, however. Robert Pasternack and Reid Lyon (1982) found no support for the contention that the majority of juvenile delinquents exhibit learning disabilities. They found no significant difference between prevalence of learning disabled youth from a juvenile delinquent sample and that for the public school population, when age was held constant. They suggested that the contradiction between their results and those of previous studies supporting a JD-LD link stems from differences in definitions of learning disabilities and in the diagnostic procedures used to identify them (1982: 11). It may be that LD youths are not involved in more delinquent behavior than non-LD youths, but they may be more likely to be arrested, adjudicated, and incarcerated than other youth.

In summary, while there are some questions about the exact association between juvenile delinquency and learning disabilities, it is clear that many children with learning disabilities do fail in school; many of them do act out in response to their experience of failure and frustration; and many of them do find their way into the justice system. The delinquent behavior of many of these youth justifiably brings them to the attention of juvenile authorities, but it is also apparent that decisions of juvenile justice officials to process them through the system may be influenced by the learning problems and school failure as well as by the antisocial behavior of these youth.

Psychological explanations of delinquency focus on personality characteristics and individual differences in learning. August Aichhorn (1936) drew upon the psychoanalytic theories of Sigmund Freud and suggested that juvenile delinquents had difficulty conforming to parental and societal expectations because they had not developed a healthy superego. Fritz Redl and David Wineman (1951) also argued that juvenile delinquents had an inadequate superego so that they tended to follow the impulses and drives of the id. These psychoanalytic theories have been criticized because it is impossible to establish a causal relationship between a person's mental state and delinquent behavior.

Sheldon and Eleanor Glueck (1950) compared 500 juvenile offenders and 500 nonoffenders and found that the delinquents were more extroverted, resentful, hostile, suspicious, defensive and defiant toward authority than the nondelinquents. Conger and Miller (1966) found that delinquents were more emotionally unstable, impulsive, suspicious, hostile, irritable, and egocentric than nondelinquents. Other researchers have found no conclusive evidence of personality differences between delinquents and nondelinquents (see Schuessler and Cressey, 1955; Waldo and Dinitz, 1967; and Tennenbaum, 1977).

Psychological learning theories include behaviorism, social learning, and moral development. According to B. F. Skinner (1953), behavior is conditioned by the reinforcements and punishments that it produces. Reinforcements increase the likelihood that the behavior will be repeated and punishments decrease the probability of the behavior being repeated. Skinner is regarded as the most influential psychologist of the twentieth century. Behaviorism has contributed a great deal to understanding human behavior, but critics contend that it falls short of explaining the role of cognitive mental processes involved in behavior. Social learning theory attempts to explain why some adolescents engage in delinquent behavior while others, in similar environments, do not. According to this theory, behavior is a reflection of people observing and imitating other people (see Bandura, 1977). Evidence suggests that some delinquent behavior is a result of observing the actions of others; and many believe that television and movie viewing may affect aggressive and violent behavior (Josephson, 1987). Social learning theory is a popular explanation for delinquent behavior, but it has been criticized because it does not account for the role of free will and it does not completely examine the relationship between a persons' thought processes and their behavior. Moral development theories (see Piaget, 1932; Kohlberg, 1964) focus on how children learn social rules and make judgments on the basis of those rules. In terms of Kohlberg's theory, delinquents are at a lower level of moral development than nondelinquents. They are more likely to define right and wrong in absolute terms, they focus more on external consequences, act to avoid punishment, and show little concern for the feelings of others. Nondelinquents, in contrast, have internalized societal rules and expectations. Research comparing the moral judgments of delinquents and nondelinquents showed mixed results. Critics note that Kohlberg's work focused on reasoning, not behavior; he found that moral and immoral behavior is inconsistent and situation-specific. Psychologists have discovered that children at different stages of moral development can behave similarly and children at the same stages of moral development can behave differently. In summary, psychological theories of delinquency are difficult to test and verify and the relationship between personality factors and delinquent behavior has not been proven conclusive by research (see Regoli and Hewitt, 1994).

Biochemical factors focus on chemical imbalances in the body that may influence delinquent behavior. Researchers have found evidence that chemical imbalances in the body bring about changes in perception and hyperactivity (Hoffer, 1975). The connection between nutrition and delinquent behavior has received considerable attention in the juvenile justice system (Schauss, 1981). Stephen Schoenthaler and Walter Doraz (1983) observed that a reduction in the sugar intake of institutionalized youths brought about a corresponding reduction in the number of assaults, fights, thefts, and defiant acts.

In another study they found that improving the diets of public school students was correlated with improved school performance (Schoenthaler, Doraz, and Wakefield, 1986).

Researchers have discovered that exposure to toxic substances such as lead interferes with brain functions and affects behavior. Herbert Needleman and his colleagues (1979) found that children with higher dentine lead levels had lower IQ test scores and exhibited more attention difficulties that resulted in poor classroom performance. Research on the long-term effects (on many of the same lead-contaminated children) indicated that they were more likely to have a reading disability, increased absenteeism, lower class standing in high school, and/or to have dropped out of high school (Needleman, Schell, Bellinger, Leviton, and Allred, 1990). In a recent study Needleman and his associates found a relationship between lead poisoning and delinquency (Needleman, Riess, Tobin, Biesecker, and Greenhouse, 1996). The most common cause of lead poisoning is lead-based paint. Though it is no longer produced, lead-based paint is still on the walls, woodwork, and windows of many older homes and apartment buildings. The children of lower-income families are more vulnerable to the effects of lead toxicity. Fortunately, lead poisoning as a cause of school failure and delinquency is preventable. Knowledge of the dangers of lead poisoning and proper building maintenance can minimize this source of learning and behavior problems among children.

The relationship between drugs and behavior is another biochemical factor in explaining delinquency. Pharmacology experts know that drugs affect human emotions, but drugs have not been proven to cause aggressive behavior. Persons react differently to the influence of drugs, with certain personality types being more affected (McCardle and Fishbein, 1989). Whether a person engages in aggressive or antisocial behavior while under the influence of drugs depends on individual and environmental conditions (Fishbein, 1990). Alcohol and drugs are clearly associated with aggressive behavior and violent crimes, but criminologists do not agree on the exact causal relationship. Studies have not clearly demonstrated that alcohol and drug use are a cause of crime and delinquent behavior (Huizinga, Loeber, and Thornberry, 1994). Relatively few juvenile offenders have reported committing a crime while using drugs, and most youths appear to commit crime for reasons other than drug use (Altschuler and Brounstein, 1991). Elliott, Huizinga, and Ageton (1985) concluded that delinquent peer associations increase the likelihood of delinquency and drug use. That is, youths who associate with friends who use drugs and engage in delinquency are more likely themselves to use drugs and commit crime. In summary, psychological and biochemical factors are associated with delinquency, but whether they cause individuals to commit crime depends on environmental circumstances and social influences.

Structural-strain theories. Social structure and strain explanations of delinquency focus on the social and cultural environment in which adolescents grow up or on the subcultural groups in which they become involved. Social structure theorists, relying on official statistics as the primary measure of crime, claim that such forces as cultural deviance, social disorganization, and status frustration lead lower-class youths to become involved in delinquent behavior. This theory is often referred to as the "Chicago School" after Clifford Shaw and Henry McKay (1942), of the Chicago School of urban criminology, and Walter Miller (1958), a social anthropologist from the University of Chicago.

Delinquency is assumed to be caused primarily by disruption and instability in the structure and institutions of society. Uncertainty and confusion result from social disorganization, often producing a state of "anomie" or "normlessness" and leaving individuals vulnerable or susceptible to delinquent behavior (Merton, 1957). The weakened social structure and institutions are presumably most pronounced among the lower or working classes. These theories were developed to explain lower-class delinquency and were based on official measures such as police statistics.

Albert Cohen (1955) developed a theory of delinquency that specifically emphasized the role of the school. Cohen focused on lower-class youths and the strain that resulted from the middle-class measuring rod. Four assumptions of Cohen's theory were:

1. Many lower-class youths (especially males) do poorly in school.
2. School performance is related to delinquency.
3. Poor school performance is a result of a conflict between the dominant middle-class values of the school system and the youths' lower-class values.
4. Lower-class male delinquency is largely gang delinquency and a means of gaining positive self-concept and maintaining antisocial values.

Cohen's first assumption is generally true: more lower-class youth *do* perform poorly in school than middle-class youth. Cohen's second thesis has also been supported by research. School performance *is* related to delinquency, but scholars disagree as to the causal ordering of school problems, dropout, and delinquency. Elliott and Voss (1974) studied the school performance and delinquency records of 2,000 California youths and found that, while those who dropped out did have higher rates of delinquency, the rates of delinquency were higher before dropping out and declined after leaving school. Thus, dropping out may reduce rather than cause delinquency. Thornberry and his associates (1985) failed to replicate the Elliott and Voss study, however, finding that arrest rates of school dropouts increased soon after the youths dropped out. Thornberry et al. concluded that their results did not support Cohen's theory but did support control theory (discussed later in this chapter). The relationship between dropout and delinquency is discussed more completely in Chapter 5.

Cohen's claim that school problems were class-related has not been well documented by research. Middle-class values and norms that are purportedly related to school performance include punctuality, neatness, cleanliness, drive and ambition for achievement and success, individual responsibility, willingness to postpone immediate gratification of desires, courtesy and self-control, and control of violence and aggression. Polk, Frease, and Richmond (1974) examined the relationship among social class, school experience, and delinquency and found that school failure, but not social class, is directly related to delinquency. "Boys who do poorly in school, regardless of their class background, are more likely to be delinquent than those who are performing adequately at school. *Both* white-and blue-collar adolescents who have low grade point averages show relatively high rates of delinquency" (1974: 92).

Cohen's contention that lower-class delinquency is a gang phenomenon by which youths reduce their frustration and gain a more positive self-concept has received mixed research support. There is little question that delinquency tends to be group behavior, but the extent to which delinquency (lower- or middle-class) is associated with structured, deviant gangs or whether gang membership increases youths' self-esteem is questionable (Jensen and Rojek, 1992: 234).

In summary, social structure and strain explanations claim that delinquent acts are often an expression of frustration resulting from limited educational and employment opportunities, particularly for lower-income and disadvantaged youth. Opportunity-structure theorists note that most young people accept middle-class goals and aspire toward the middle-class lifestyle, but those from disadvantaged backgrounds often find illegitimate means for achieving those goals that have been blocked to them by barriers, including unequal educational and vocational opportunities. Whether or not there is outright discrimination, the verbal and social skills, family reputation, and social contacts necessary to compete educationally and vocationally often exclude children from poor families. Delinquent acts are viewed as reactions to the frustration caused by blocked opportunity. Disruption in school classrooms often results from such frustration. Because schools present barriers and are sources of frustration to many youth, they are easy targets for youthful aggression. Vandalism, theft, and assaults at schools are thus seen as resulting from the frustration of restricted opportunities. Criminological theories that emphasize this theme are referred to as "strain" or "structural" theories.

Subcultural explanations. Researchers who endorse subcultural explanations of delinquency point to observations that values and attitudes of lower-class youth differ from mainstream middle-class values. Youth from neighborhoods and communities characterized by poverty, social problems, and crime develop different values and attitudes. Where crime and violence are more common, persons' attitudes toward the law and its enforcement are different, and violent behavior may be viewed as a common and acceptable part of life. Law violations such as theft, dealing drugs, and prostitution are viewed by some as one way to overcome unemployment and poverty. Threats and physical attacks, rather than verbal negotiation, are the preferred means of resolving conflicts in some subcultures.

Social process explanations. Social process explanations of delinquency focus not on societal structures but on social interactions between individuals and environmental influences that may lead to delinquent behavior. *Differential association theory* holds that delinquency is a learned behavior acquired as youth interact closely with other deviant youth. Differential oppression is a new theoretical development that explains delinquency as resulting from emotional, verbal, and physical abuse from parents, elders, and authority figures. Social process explanations that have specifically included school experiences as a variable in delinquency are *control theory* and *labeling theory*. They differ on the major emphasis in delinquency explanation, but are grouped together here because the focus is on the social process. Control theories explain delinquency as evolving from the nature of juveniles' social interactions; labeling theory explains delinquency as a result of societal reactions to deviant behavior of some youth.

Differential association theory was developed by Edwin Sutherland, who believed that delinquency is learned behavior as youths interact with each other. The theory is founded on a number of propositions (Sutherland and Cressey, 1974):

- Criminal behavior, like other behavior, is learned.
- Criminal behavior is learned as youths are involved and communicate with each other, primarily through intimate groups.
- The learning process includes methods of committing crimes and the motives, drives, rationalizations, and attitudes to support criminal behavior.
- A youth becomes delinquent because of an excess of definitions favorable to violation of law over definitions unfavorable to violation of the law.
- The differential association process varies in frequency, duration, priority, and intensity.

Sutherland's differential association theory remains an important explanation for juvenile delinquency. It is difficult to argue against a theory that maintains that criminal behavior is learned like other behaviors. This explanation also has a positive appeal, since it holds that youth are changeable and can be taught prosocial behavior. Delinquency prevention efforts may be effective when they are directed at reducing the criminal influence among groups of antisocial youths. Sutherland's differential association theory has stimulated considerable research on explaining delinquent behavior. Burgess and Akers (1966) reformulated the differential association theory according to operant conditioning principles, and Akers (1985) further developed an explanation of deviant behavior according to a social learning approach.

Control theories, which are based on concepts that go back to the nineteenth century, have a long history. The basic idea of control theories is that human beings must be held in check, or controlled, if delinquent behavior is to be prevented. The means of control vary from internal sources, such as the self-concept, to external sources, such as the family and the school. An assumption of control theories is that deviance and delinquency are to be expected. The focal question therefore is not "Why did he do it?" but rather "Why did he not do it?" Walter Reckless (1961) posited that internal factors such as self-control and external factors such as parental supervision, discipline, and social institutions help to "insulate" or "contain" persons from crime. Reckless and his associates' primary contribution was the emphasis on inner containment, or self-concept, which they believed was a major variable in steering youth away from delinquency (Reckless, Dinitz, and Kay, 1956: 744–746). While there are problems in operationalizing and measuring self-concept, studies have confirmed that the greater the self-esteem, the less likely a youth is to become involved in delinquent behavior (Jensen, 1973).

Travis Hirschi (1969) holds that four elements of the social bond explain delinquency: attachment, commitment, involvement, and belief. *Attachment* refers to the ties of affection and respect that youth have to parents, teachers, and friends; these ties help youth avoid the temptation to commit delinquent acts. *Commitment* to socially acceptable activities and values, such as educational and employment goals, likewise helps youth avoid delinquency by increasing the cost and risks involved. *Involvement* in conventional activities keeps youth occupied and reduces their opportunities to commit deviant acts. *Belief* refers to respect for the law and societal norms and derives from close relations with other positive role models, especially parents. Hirschi tested and supported his control theory by giving a self-report survey to more than 4,000 junior and senior high school youth in California. The theory has generated a considerable amount of research.

Control theory has several strengths. It has clear concepts that lend themselves to empirical research and testing. Others have used the social control model to develop integrated theories patterned on the social bond (Elliott, Ageton, and Canter, 1979). Hirschi's control theory has made valuable contributions to our understanding of the relationship between delinquency and the major social institutions of family and the school. He examined the role of attachment to parents and the relative importance of peer relationships as youth mature. He addressed educational aspirations and goals, student-teacher relationships, and the role of school performance and behavior in delinquency.

Control theory does have some weaknesses. First, the measure of the social bond is limited, and the delinquency measure lists only a few relatively minor behavior problems. Second, the chain of events that weaken the social bond is not clearly defined, and the division of youth into socialized or unsocialized tends to ignore the wide range of delinquent activities. Last, there are many causal factors of delinquency that are not explained by social control variables. Nevertheless, social control theory has more empirical support than any other explanation of delinquency.

In support of school attachment, Hirschi found that students who perform poorly in school reduce their interest in school and related activities and increase the likelihood of committing delinquent acts. Students' perceived academic ability and actual performance affect their bond to school, and his data show that these are associated with delinquent involvement (1969: 120). Those with weak attachments to parents tend to show less respect for teachers and to dislike school (Hirschi, 1969: 131–132).

The nature of peer relationships has an intervening effect on parental attachment, school experiences, and delinquency. Attachment to peers does not necessarily mean less attachment to parents. It appears to depend on *to whom* one is attached and the nature of one's peer attachments. Linden and Hackler (1973) found that self-reported delinquency was inversely related to ties to parents and conventional peers but positively related to ties to deviant peers. Others suggest that parental attachment affects delinquency, which affects school performance, which in turn affects parental attachment (Liska and Reed, 1985: 556–557). Parents, not schools, are the major institutional sources of delinquency control—for lower-class more than for middle-class youth (Liska and Reed, 1985: 557–558). According to Hirschi's control theory, delinquents are less dependent on peers than are nondelinquents—a finding that has been supported by other research. In a study comparing the personality factors of nondelinquent high school students and adjudicated delinquents, the delinquents scored higher on the "self-sufficiency" personality factor, while nondelinquents scored higher on "group dependence" (Lawrence, 1985: 77).

The role of parents, peers and school as factors in promoting or preventing delinquent behavior deserves careful examination, particularly for practical and policy implications. One study of school performance, peers, and delinquency analyzed self-report data from the National Youth Survey, comparing youths' school attachment and how many of their friends had committed delinquent acts (Lawrence, 1991). Results indicated that peer relationships have a greater influence on delinquent behavior than does attachment to school. (Measures of school attachment included items such as "How important has school work been?," "How important is it to have teachers think of you as a good student?," "How do teachers think you are doing?," "How important is a high grade point average?") Youth who had fewer friends who had committed delinquent acts reported less delinquent involvement themselves, regardless of high or low school attachment. Youth with more friends who had engaged in delinquent behavior reported a higher number of delinquent acts, even among those with higher school attachment. Those with more delinquent friends and lower school attachment reported the highest self-reported delinquency rate. The findings indicate that the nature of peer relationships is more important than school attachment in explaining delinquent behavior (Lawrence, 1991: 64–65).

School involvement tends to reduce involvement in delinquency. Boys in Hirschi's sample who felt they had nothing to do were more likely to become involved in delinquent acts. He theorized that lack of involvement and commitment to school releases youth from a major source of time structuring (1969: 187–196). Hirschi's claim for the positive benefit of involvement has been supported by other studies. The results of a self-report survey of 1,400 high school students in San Antonio, Texas, showed that, compared to delinquents, nondelinquents tend to participate in or attend more extracurricular school activities (Lawrence, 1985: 76).

Labeling theory. Labeling theory begins with the understanding that most youth engage in some deviant acts, and labeling theorists use findings from self-report studies to support that contention. Initial deviant and delinquent activities of youth have many varied causes. The primary assumption of the labeling perspective is that repeated delinquent behavior is caused by society's reaction to minor deviant behavior. Frank Tannenbaum (1938) first suggested that the very process of identifying and segregating deviant persons as criminals increased the liklihood that the behavior would continue. Lemert (1951) and Becker (1963) are the other major proponents of labeling theory. Lemert differentiated between "primary deviance," referring to behavior of the individual, and "secondary deviance," resulting from society's response to that behavior, which resulted in a status, role, or individual identity. Becker proposed that those in society who make and enforce the rules "create" deviants by labeling persons, who in turn tend to act out the deviant behaviors consistent with their new identity.

There has been only limited research support for labeling theory. Jensen (1973) found that having a delinquent record was related to having a delinquent self-concept for young white males (but not for black youth). Jensen concluded that an official label of delinquency may not affect black youth because such labels are more common and because the label is given by outsiders. Ageton and Elliott (1974) studied youths over a six-year period and concluded that police contact was followed by a greater delinquency orientation among both lower- and upper-class boys. Other studies show mixed or negative support for labeling theory. Foster, Dinitz, and Reckless (1972) found no changes in personal relationships or parental attitudes toward boys following a juvenile court appearance. Most (90 percent) of the boys showed no evidence of being negatively labeled; they believed their official delinquency record would not pose difficulties for their finishing school. Hepburn (1977) compared the self-concepts and attitudes of nondelinquent and delinquent males. He found that the delinquents did have greater definitions of themselves as delinquents, more commitment to future delinquency and to other delinquents, poorer self-concepts, and less respect for the police. However, he found that, when other variables such as socioeconomic status and self-reported delinquency were considered, an arrest record had no direct effect on self-concept or delinquent identification.

Labeling theory does have a number of strengths. It provides an explanation for why many youths who become involved in minor deviance continue delinquent acts following initial contact with police and juvenile authorities. The theory emphasizes the important role of rule making, power, and reactions of society and justice system authorities. As part of the symbolic interactionist perspective, labeling theory points out that some persons *do* tend to take on the roles and self-concepts expected of them.

Labeling theory has many weaknesses. It lacks clear-cut definitions and testable hypotheses (Gibbs, 1966) . It does not explain why youth intially commit deviant or delinquent acts and tends to minimize the importance of delinquency. The theory appears to excuse the behavior of the delinquent and make society the culprit. The reasons or motives behind delinquency are not explained. Overall, labeling theory has been widely criticized and has little empirical support.

Labeling theory does have some important applications to school practices, however. It is common practice in schools to classify students according to their learning ability, and place them into groups, or "tracks," with other students who supposedly perform at a similar level. Such tracking ideally makes it possible for teachers to direct their efforts at the appropriate ability level for slower and faster learners. Tracking has been criticized, however, for a number of reasons: more minority and lower income students are in the basic or low-ability tracks; placement in the tracks tends to be permanent, with little movement up or down in spite of students' learning and progress; and tracking has a labeling and stigmatizing effect, so teachers expect less of the lower-track students, and frequently their expectations are correct. Schafer, Olexa, and Polk (1972) found that even when IQ and previous ability factors were controlled, blacks and low-income students were still more likely to be found in the basic or low-ability tracks. They also found that track assignment was virtually irreversible, operating much like a rigid caste system. Kelly and Grove (1981) claim that race, social class, and other nonacademic factors (such as the father's occupation or student misconduct) are criteria for tracking. They cite evidence that students are routinely assigned to a low-ability track on the basis not of IQ or current ability and performance but often of their past academic record. School tracking affects a student's (1) personal identity (i.e., how the individual views self), (2) *public identity* (i.e., how others view the individual), and (3) *self-image* (i.e., how the individual evaluates self) (Kelly and Pink, 1982: 55). Teachers, peers, parents, and others come to expect less from students in low-ability tracks, while more is expected of students in high-ability tracks. The expectations are often fulfilled. Misconduct and behavior problems are also often expected of students in lower tracks: "When such a student engages in school crime, he or she is probably not only living up to teacher, peer, parental, and self expectations, but . . . may also be striving to obtain some measure of success and well-being. . . . [T]he misbehavior serves to confirm the initial diagnosis and labeling as a potential troublemaker (Kelly and Pink, 1982: 55).

Critics of school tracking claim that schools produce failure by the very organization and educational processes they adopt and that they are responsible for various forms of school misconduct and crime. A study tested whether placement in a noncollege curriculum track causes losses in self-esteem and increased delinquency and presented results that did not support the hypothesis (Wiatrowski et al., 1982). Polk questioned the methodology and data interpretation of that study. He argued that the data indicated that grades, school attachment, self-esteem, and tracking were interrelated and that school experiences were significantly correlated with delinquency (Polk, 1982: 284). The relationship of school tracking, performance and delinquency is unclear, but the issue surely directs our attention to school structure and the educational process and the effects that these have on school experiences and delinquency.

In summary, social process explanations of delinquency focus on individual youths' interactions with others and on societal reactions to deviant behavior. Control theories differ from structural-strain explanations in the emphasis on sociopsychological differences, including individual differences in personality and self-image. The emphasis is on how behavior is learned through influences in an individual's environment, especially the home and family. Parental abuse, rejection, neglect, and lack of affection toward the child are contributing factors that lead to deviant and delinquent behavior. Nurturing parents, consistent discipline practices, and positive parent-child relationships help to steer a child from delinquent behavior. Thus, family and peer values exert an influence on youths' values and life goals. Commitment to educational and vocational goals are important in a young person's avoidance of delinquent behavior, regardless of social class. The theme of this explanation is that delinquent behavior is due not to social class or subculture but to social influences on the individual. A strength of the theories is their contribution to explaining delinquent behavior among middle- and upper-class, as well as lower-class, youth.

Societal reaction or labeling refers to a process of stereotyping youth and fostering a self-image of delinquency. According to this view, most youth commit some minor deviant acts. The problem lies with societal reactions (of parents, teachers, authorities), which tend to label a young person as a serious troublemaker. Youth who are unfairly labeled come to see themselves as bad and accept a delinquent self-image. This is often referred to as a self-fulfilling prophecy.

Differential oppression theory. *Differential oppression theory* is a recent explanation of delinquency developed by Robert Regoli and John Hewitt (1994). It suggests that juvenile delinquency often results as children react to oppressive relationships with parents and other authority figures. Oppressive adult-child relationships are said to take place when adults' perceptions of children establish them as inferior, subordinate, and troublemakers and when disciplinary efforts to establish order in the home and in school become extreme to the point of oppression. Regoli and Hewitt believe that children who are raised in an atmosphere of lovelessness and emotional and verbal abuse often retaliate through rebellion against the people and the social institutions that they blame for causing their oppression (1994: 211). School vandalism often occurs because a student was angry at a teacher or principal, and some youth retaliate against oppressive parents by assaulting them (Regoli and Hewitt, 1994: 211).

Differential oppression theory is based primarily on the established relationship between child abuse and delinquency. Research indicates that serious crimes are committed much more often by youth who have been rejected, abused, and neglected (McCord, 1983). Delinquency that is a result of oppressive, abusive relationships may be prevented when adults respect children and treat them as valued persons (Regoli and Hewitt, 1994).

Summary

Explanations of delinquency fall into one of two broad categories: classical, or rational, theories and positivist, or determinist, theories. We have summarized and briefly discussed those explanations that include some reference to school problems. Individual explanations focus on the biological, genetic, and psychological causes of delinquency. The major sociological theories include social structure or strain; subcultural; and social process and social control theories. While all of the major theoretical explanations make some contribution to our understanding of delinquent behavior, control theory has received the most extensive research support. A measure of a good theory is not only how well it explains the causes of delinquency but also whether it provides clear, workable strategies for delinquency prevention.

Note

1. The explanations of delinquency presented here are not intended to be a complete and comprehensive discussion of all major criminological theories. I have provided only an overview and general explanation of crime theories and focused on those that more specifically explain delinquent behavior in the context of school experiences. For a more complete discussion of explanations of delinquency, readers are encouraged to review Bartollas, 1993; Jensen and Rojek, 1992; Regoli and Hewitt, 1997; Shoemaker, 1996; and Siegel and Senna, 1997.

References

Ageton, Suzanne and Delbert S. Elliott. 1974. "The Effects of Legal Processing on Delinquent Orientations." *Social Problems* 22:87–100.
Aichhorn, August. 1936. *Wayward Youth.* New York: Viking Press.
Akers, Ronald L. 1985. *Deviant Behavior: A Social Learning Approach*, 3rd ed. Belmont, Calif.: Wadsworth Publishing Co.
Akers, Ronald. 1990. "Rational Choice, Deterrence, and Social Learning theory in Criminology." *Journal of Criminal Law and Criminology* 81: 653–676.
Altschuler, David M. and Paul J. Brounstein. 1991. "Patterns of Drug Use, Drug Trafficking, and Other Delinquency Among Inner-City Adolescent Males in Washington, D.C." *Criminology* 19:589–622.
Bandura, Albert. 1977. *Social Learning Theory.* Englewood Cliffs, N.J.: Prentice-Hall.
Bartollas, Clemens. 1993. *Juvenile Delinquency*, 3rd ed. New York: Macmillan Publishing Co.
Becker, Howard S. 1963. *The Outsiders.* New York: Free Press.
Burgess, Robert J., Jr., and Ronald L. Akers. 1966. "A Differential Association-Reinforcement Theory of Criminal Behavior." *Social Problems* 14:128–147.
Cohen, Albert. 1955. *Delinquent Boys.* New York: Free Press.
Cohen, Lawrence, and Marcus Felson. 1979. "Social Change and Crime Rate Trends: A Routine Activities Approach." *American Sociological Review* 44:588–608.
Conger, J. J. and W. C. Miller. 1966. *Personality, Social Class, and Delinquency.* New York: Wiley.
Cornish, Derek B., and Ronald V. Clarke, eds. 1986. *The Reasoning Criminal: Rational Choice Perspectives on Offending.* New York: Springer-Verlag.
Elliott, Delbert, David Huizinga, and Suzanne Ageton. 1985. *Explaining Delinquency and Drug Use.* Beverly Hills: Sage Publications.
Elliott, Delbert S., Suzanne S. Ageton, and Rachell J. Canter. 1979. "An Integrated Theoretical Perspective on Delinquent Behavior." *Journal of Research in Crime and Delinquency* 16:3–27.
Elliott, Delbert S., and Harwin L. Voss. 1974. *Delinquency and Dropout.* Lexington, Mass.: D.C. Heath.

Felson, Marcus. 1994. *Crime and Everyday Life*. Thousand Oaks, Calif.: Pine Forge Press.

Felson, Marcus. 1986. "Linking Criminal choices, Routine Activities, Informal Control, and Criminal Outcomes." In D. B. Cornish and R. V. Clarke, eds., *The Reasoning Criminal*. New York: Springer-Verlag.

Fishbein, Diana. 1990. "Biological Perspectives in Criminology." *Criminology* 28:27–72.

Foster, J. D., Simon Dinitz, and Walter C. Reckless. 1972. "Perceptions of Stigma Following Public Intervention for Delinquent Behavior." *Social Problems* 20:202–209.

Gibbs, Jack P. 1966. "Conceptions of Deviant Behavior: The Old and the New." *Pacific Sociological Review* 9:9–14.

Glueck, Sheldon and Eleanor Glueck. 1950. *Unraveling Juvenile Delinquency*. Cambridge, Mass.: Harvard University Press.

Goddard, Henry. 1920. *Efficiency and Levels of Intelligence*. Princeton: Princeton University Press.

Gordon, Robert A. 1987. "SES versus IQ in the Race-IQ-Delinquency Model." *International Journal of Sociology and Social Policy* 7:30–96.

Hawkins, J. David, Paul A. Pastro, Jr., Michelle Bell, and Sheila Morrison. 1980. *Reports of the National Juvenile Justice Assessment Centers: A Typology of Cause-Focused Strategies of Delinquency Prevention*. Washington, D.C.: U.S. Department of Justice.

Hepburn, John R. 1977. "The Impact of Police Intervention Upon Juvenile Delinquents." *Criminology* 15:235–262.

Hirschi, Travis. 1969. *Causes of Delinquency*. Berkeley: University of California Press.

Hirschi, Travis. 1986. "On the Compatibility of Rational Choice and Social Control Theories of Crime." In D. B. Cornish and R. V. Clarke, eds., *The Reasoning Criminal*. New York: Springer-Verlag.

Hirschi, Travis, and Michael Hindelang. 1977. "Intelligence and Delinquency: A Revisionist Review." *American Sociological Review* 42:471–486.

Hoffer, Abraham. 1975. "The Relation of Crime to Nutrition." *Humanist in Canada* 8:3–9.

Huizinga, David, Rolf Loeber, and Terence Thornberry. 1994. *Urban Delinquency and Substance Abuse: Initial Findings*. Washington, D.C.: Office of Juvenile Justice and Delinquency Prevention.

Jensen, Gary F. 1973. "Inner Containment and Delinquency." *Criminology* 64:464–470.

Jensen, Gary F., and Dean G. Rojek. 1992. *Juvenile Delinquency*, 2nd ed. Lexington, Mass.: D.C. Heath.

Johnson, Richard E. 1979. *Juvenile Delinquency and Its Origins*. Cambridge: Cambridge University Press.

Josephson, W. L. 1987. "Television Violence and Children's Aggression." *Journal of Personality and Social Psychology* 53:882–890.

Kelly, Delos H., and Winthrop D. Grove. 1981. "Teachers' Nominations and the Production of Academic 'Misfits'." *Education* 101:246–263.

Kelly, Delos H., and William T. Pink. 1982. "School Crime and Individual Responsibility: The Perpetuation of a Myth?" *Urban Review* 14(1):47–63.

Kirkegaard-Sorensen, Lis, and Sarnoff A. Mednick. 1977. "A Prospective Study of Predictors of Criminality: Intelligence. In S. A. Mednick and K. O. Christiansen, eds. *Biosocial Basis of Criminal Behavior*. New York: Gardner.

Klinteberg, Britt A. F., David Magnusson, and Daisy Schalling. 1989. "Hyperactive Behavior in Childhood and Adult Impulsivity: A Longitudinal Study of Male Subjects." *Personality and Individual Differences* 10(1):43–49.

Kohlberg, Lawrence. 1964. "Development of Moral Character and Moral Ideology." In Martin Hoffman and Lois Hoffman, Eds., *Review of Child Development Research*, vol. 1. New York: Russell Sage Foundation.

Lawrence, Richard. 1985. "School Performance, Containment Theory, and Delinquent Behavior." *Youth and Society* 17:69–95.

Lawrence, Richard. 1991. "School Performance, Peers, and Delinquency: Implications for Juvenile Justice." *Juvenile and Family Court Journal* 42(3):59–69.

Lemert, Edwin M. 1951. *Social Pathology*. New York: McGraw-Hill.

Linden, Eric, and James C. Hackler. 1973. "Affective Ties and Delinquency." *Pacific Sociological Review* 16:27–46.

Lipsitt, Paul D., Stephen L. Buka, and Lewis P. Lipsitt. 1990. "Early Intelligence Scores and Subsequent Delinquency: A Prospective Study." *American Journal of Family Therapy* 18:197–208.

Liska, Allen E., and Mark D. Reed. 1985. "Ties to Conventional Institutions and Delinquency: Estimating Reciprocal Effects." *American Sociological Review* 50:547–560.

Matza, David. 1964. *Delinquency and Drift*. New York: John Wiley.

McCardle, Lynn and Diana Fishbein. 1989. "The Self-Reported Effects of PCP on Human Aggression." *Addictive Behaviors* 4:465–472.

McCord, Joan. 1983. "A Forty-Year Perspective on Effects of Child Abuse and Neglect." *Child Abuse and Neglect* 7:265–270.

McPartland, James M., and Edward L. McDill, eds., 1977. *Violence in Schools: Perspectives, Programs and Positions*. Lexington, Mass.: Lexington Books.

Menard, Scott, and Barbara J. Morse. 1984. "A Structuralist Critique of the IQ-Delinquency Hypothesis: Theory and Evidence." *American Journal of Sociology* 89:1347–1378.

Merton, Robert K. 1957. *Social Theory and Social Structure*. New York: Free Press.

Miller, Walter. 1958. "Lower Class Culture as a Generating Milieu of Gang Delinquency." *Journal of Social Issues* 14:5–19.

Moffitt, Terrie E. 1990. "Juvenile delinquency and Attention Deficit Disorder: Boys' Developmental Trajectories from Age 3 to Age 15." *Child Development* 61:893–910.

Moffitt, Terrie E., William F. Gabrielli, Sarnoff A. Mednick, and Fini Schulsinger. 1981. "Socioeconomic Status, IQ, and Delinquency." *Journal of Abnormal Psychology* 90(2):152–156.

Needleman, Herbert, Charles Gunnoe, Alan Leviton, Robert Reed, Henry Peresie, Cornelius Maher, and Peter Barrett. 1979. "Deficits in Psychologic and Classroom Performance of Children with Elevated Dentine Lead Levels." *The New England Journal of Medicine* 300:689–695.

Needleman, Herbert, Julie Riess, Michael Tobin, Gretchen Biescecker, and Joel Greenhouse. 1996. "Bone Lead Levels and Delinquent Behavior." *Journal of the American Medical Association* 275:363–369.

Needleman, Herbert, Alan Schell, David Bellenger, Alan Leviton, and Elizabeth Allred. 1990. "The Long-Term Effects of Exposure to Low Doses of Lead in Children." *New England Journal of Medicine* 322:83–88.

Nettler, Gwynn. 1984. *Explaining Crime*, 3rd ed. New York: McGraw-Hill.

Offord, D. R., K. Sullivan, N. Allen, and N. Abrams. 1979. "Delinquency and Hyperactivity." *Journal of Nervous and Mental Disease* 167(12):734–741.

Pasternack, Robert, and Reid Lyon. 1982. "Clinical and Empirical Identification of Learning Disabled Juvenile Delinquents." *Journal of Correctional Education* 33(2):7–13.

Piaget, Jean. 1932. *The Moral Judgment of the Child*. London: Kegan Paul.

Podboy, John W., and William A. Mallory. 1978. "The Diagnosis of Specific Learning Disabilities in a Juvenile Delinquent Population." *Federal Probation* 42:26–33.

Polk, Kenneth. 1982. "Curriculum Tracking and Delinquency: Some Observations." *American Sociological Review* 48:282–284.

Polk, Kenneth, Dean Frease, and F. Lynn Richmond. 1974. "Social Class, School Experience, and Delinquency." *Criminology* 12(1):84–96.

Post, Charles H. 1981. "The Link Between Learning Disabilities and Juvenile Delinquency: Cause, Effect and 'Present Solutions'." *Juvenile and Family Court Journal* 31:58–68.

Reckless, Walter C. 1961. "A New Theory of Delinquency and Crime." *Federal Probation* 25:42–46.

Reckless, Walter C., Simon Dinitz, and Barbara Kay. 1956. "Self-Concept as an Insulator Against Delinquency." *American Sociological Review* 21:744–746.

Redl, Fritz and David Wineman. 1951. *Children Who Hate.* New York: Free Press.

Regoli, Robert M., and John D. Hewitt. 1994. *Delinquency in Society,* 2nd ed. New York: McGraw-Hill.

Rosenbaum, J. E. 1976. *Making Inequality: The Hidden Curriculum of the High School.* New York: John Wiley.

Rowe, David C., and D. Wayne Osgood. 1984. "Heredity and Sociological Theories of Delinquency: A Reconsideration." *American Sociological Review* 49:526–540.

Schafer, Walter, Carol Olexa, and Kenneth Polk. 1972. "Programmed for Social Class: Tracking in High School." In K. Polk and W. E. Schafer, eds., *Schools and Delinquency.* Englewood Cliffs, N.J.: Prentice-Hall.

Schauss, Alexander. 1981. *Diet, Crime, and Delinquency.* Berkeley: Parker House.

Schoenthaler, Stephen and Walter Doraz. 1983. "Types of Offenses Which Can Be Reduced in an Institutional Setting Using Nutritional Intervention." *International Journal of Biosocial Research* 4:74–84.

Schoenthaler, Stephen, Walter Doraz, and James Wakefield. 1986. "The Impact of a Low Food Additive and Sucrose Diet on Academic Performance in 803 New York City Public Schools." *International Journal of Biosocial Research* 8:185–195.

Schuesler, Karl and Donald Cressey. 1955. "Personality Characteristics of Criminals." *American Journal of Sociology* 55:476–484.

Shaw, Clifford R., and Henry D. McKay. 1942. *Juvenile Delinquency and Urban Areas.* Chicago: University of Chicago Press.

Sheldon, William. 1949. *Varieties of Delinquent Youth.* New York: Harper & Row.

Shoemaker, Donald J. 1996. *Theories of Delinquency,* 3rd ed. New York: Oxford University Press.

Siegel, Larry J., and Joseph J. Senna. 1991. *Juvenile Delinquency,* 4th ed. St. Paul, Minn.: West Publishing Co.

Simon, R. L. 1978. "The Meaning of the IQ-Delinquency Relationship." *American Sociological Review* 43:268–70.

Skinner, B. F. 1953. *Science and Human Behavior.* New York: Macmillan Publishing Co.

Strother, Deborah Burnett, ed. 1991. *Learning to Fail: Case Studies of Students at Risk.* Bloomington, Ind.: Phi Delta Kappa.

Sutherland, Edwin H., and Donald R. Cressey. 1970. *Principles of Criminology.* New York: J.B. Lippincott.

Tannenbaum, Frank. 1938. *Crime and the Community.* New York: Columbia University Press.

Tennenbaum, D. J. 1977. "Personality and Criminality: A Summary and Implications of the Literature." *Journal of Criminal Justice* 5:225–235.

Thornberry, Terence P., Melanie Moore, and R. L. Christenson. 1985. "The Effect of Dropping Out of High School on Subsequent Criminal Behavior." *Criminology* 23:3–18.

Waldo, Gordon and Simon Dinitz. 1967. "Personality Attributes of the Criminal: An Analysis of Research Studies 1950–1965." *Journal of Research in Crime and Delinquency* 4:185–201.

Walsh, Anthony. 1987. "Cognitive Functioning and Delinquency: Property Versus Violent Offenses." *International Journal of Offender Therapy and Comparative Criminology* 31:285–289.

Walters, Glenn D. 1992. "A Meta-Analysis of the Gene-Crime Relationship." *Criminology* 30:595–613.

West, D. J., and David P. Farrington. 1973. *Who Becomes Delinquent?* London: Heinemann.

Wiatrowski, Michael D., Stephen Hansell, Charles R. Massey, and David L. Wilson. 1982. "Curriculum Tracking and Delinquency." *American Sociological Review* 47:151–160.
Wilson, James Q., and Richard J. Herrnstein. 1985. *Crime and Human Nature.* New York: Simon & Schuster.
Zimmerman, Joel, William Rich, Ingo Keilitz, and Paul Broder. 1981. "Some Observations on the Link Between Learning Disabilities and Juvenile Delinquency." *Journal of Criminal Justice* 9:9–17.

4

Families, Peers, Schools, and Delinquency

We must first strengthen families in their role as children's first and primary teachers in providing guidance, discipline and sound values.—John Wilson, Office of Juvenile Justice and Delinquency Prevention

The family is the most important source of nurturance and socialization in a child's life. Parents are role models for children, providing examples for interacting with others, for ethical and legal behavior, for instilling work habits, and for fulfilling responsibilities. Nurturing parents who are positive role models and who maintain a positive home environment provide support to help children resist negative peer influence in schools and on the streets. Good parents and family settings provide the kind of home environment that helps youth succeed in school and resist antisocial behaviors even when growing up in high-crime neighborhoods.

On the other hand, children who grow up in families marked by parental conflict and tension or with parents who are absent or neglectful or who frequently engage in verbal abuse are predisposed to factors that promote antisocial and delinquent behavior. There is little question that family problems contribute to school problems, absenteeism, and failure and to deviant and delinquent behavior. The nature of parent-child relations also affects youths' relations with their peers and their selection of friends. At some point in every youth's life, friends begin to have an influence equal to or greater than the influence of the parents. Youth who feel rejected by their parents often turn to peers for support. The emergence of juvenile gangs is a manifestation of youths' need for acceptance and a sense of belonging. The kind of friends with whom a young person associates therefore has great importance. Parental and peer relationships differ for boys and girls, and there are gender differences in how parental neglect leads to school problems and delinquent behavior. There is little question, however, that family problems and peer influence are major contributing factors to juvenile delinquency. Exactly how and under what conditions the process occurs is not agreed upon by researchers. This chapter examines the role of the family and peers in school problems and juvenile delinquency and looks at some of the unique problems of female delinquency.

Changes in Family and Parental Roles

The American family has undergone many changes in the past few decades and is faced with serious problems, including divorce, single-parent families, teenage mothers bearing children outside of marriage, unemployment, poverty, alcohol and drug abuse, verbal abuse, family conflict, and violence.

The divorce rate in the United States has had a major impact on family life. One in four of the nation's youth now live with only one parent, typically the mother; among black families, more than half of young people do not have a father in the home (Dryfoos, 1990: 17) . This increase in female-headed households presents a dramatic change in what Americans have viewed as the "ideal family"—father at work, mother at home, with considerable "quality time" together after dad returns from work and the kids return home from school. In countless homes today, the father lives elsewhere, mother is at work, and the kids return home from school (one hopes they have attended!) to an empty home.

Female-headed households face special difficulties, centered primarily around low income levels resulting from unemployment or underemployment. U.S. Census Bureau figures for 1993 indicate that 22 percent of young people under 18 years of age are in families with incomes below the poverty level (Statistical Abstract of the U.S., 1995: 480). Female-headed families have a much higher percentage of poverty than do other families. The percentage of all families in poverty is 11 percent, but 46 percent of female-headed households that include children are in poverty (Dryfoos, 1990: 18). The median income for all U.S. families in 1993 was about $37,000, but female-headed families had a median annual income of just slightly more than $17,000 (Statistical Abstract of the U.S., 1995: 477). Being raised in a single-parent family or in poverty does not necessarily cause a child to become delinquent, but those factors certainly place stress on the family environment that may increase the tendencies and temptations to become involved in deviant and delinquent behaviors. There is substantial evidence that children raised in poverty and under adverse conditions have a higher probability of becoming delinquent.

The Family and Delinquency

The role of parents and families is important in explaining delinquent behavior. The problem seems clear to juvenile justice officials, policymakers, and concerned citizens. Juvenile probation officers often remark that they work with "as many delinquent parents as we do delinquent children!" John Wilson, acting administrator of the U.S. Department of Justice Office of Juvenile Justice and Delinquency Prevention, emphasizes that family cohesiveness is needed to reduce youth crime. Speaking at a hearing of the House Criminal Justice Subcommittee on ways to strengthen the juvenile justice system, Wilson said we must first "strengthen families in their role as their children's first and primary teachers in providing guidance, discipline and sound values" ("Family Cohesiveness," 1994). Criminologists have been less clear on the role of the family in delinquency. After some extensive research in the 1950s and 1960s, less attention has been given to studying the family as part of the effort to understand delinquency. There seem to be at least two reasons for this. First, attention turned more to social structure and social problems that seemed to lend themselves to change, such as gangs and drugs. Second, researchers emphasized those factors that seemed amenable to change in reducing delinquency, and it was unclear whether family intervention or training could be done and whether it would have any effect on delinquency.

Different explanations have been offered to explain the association between family problems and delinquency. The structure of the family—whether one or two parents are present and the size of the family—is believed by some to explain delinquency. Others argue that "functional" factors or "quality of life" in families, such as family relationships, parent-child interactions, and the quality of supervision and discipline explain whether children become delinquent (Wilkinson, 1974; Rosen, 1985). Researchers have developed a sizable body of literature in their attempts to explain family structure, processes, and the relationship with juvenile delinquency (see Gove and Crutchfield, 1982; Lincoln and Straus, 1985; Loeber and Stouthamer-Loeber, 1986; Pope, 1988).

The Broken Home

The "broken home" refers to a family structure that has been disrupted (or "broken") by separation, divorce, or death of a parent. Research by Sheldon and Eleanor Glueck (1950) showed that 60 percent of delinquents but only 34 percent of nondelinquent youth came from broken homes. There is evidence that a broken home increases the probability that some types of youth will participate in delinquency (Datesman and Scarpitti, 1975; Rankin, 1980). In a longitudinal study of men who had been involved in a delinquency prevention program, McCord (1982) found that more than half of the fathers of boys reared in broken homes were known to be alcoholics or criminals; and close to half of the sons of alcoholic or criminal men had been convicted for serious crimes (1982: 123). The lack of supervision in these broken homes accounted for much of the criminal behavior of these children raised by only one parent. Absence of the father was not found to be important in explaining the boys' criminal behavior, however. The quality of home life, rather than the number of parents, is most important in explaining youths' criminal behavior (McCord, 1982: 124). Gove and Crutchfield (1982) noted gender differences in family variables relating to delinquency. Boys in single-parent homes are more likely to be delinquent, but marital variables have little impact on girls' delinquency. For boys in intact families, delinquency was strongly related to marital interaction, and physical punishment was strongly related to delinquency. Marital status has little effect on girls, but the quality of the parent-child interaction and parental control (including knowledge of friends) is more strongly related to misbehavior among girls. The parents' feeling toward their children was found to be most strongly related to delinquency (Gove and Crutchfield, 1982: 316). Other research indicates that the broken home is associated only with running away and truancy (Rankin, 1977, 1980); there is a moderate relationship with status offenses (Van Voorhis et al., 1988) but a weaker relationship for serious delinquent behavior (Wells and Rankin, 1991). Several studies have challenged the notion of the broken home as a cause of delinquency. Cernkovich and Giordano (1987) believe there are no broken home effects on delinquency but rather that family interaction variables such as caring, trust, control, and supervision are more important than family structure.

Researchers have concluded that there is a relation between official measures, but not self-report measures of delinquency, and broken homes (Johnson, 1986; Laub and Sampson, 1988; Wilkinson, 1980). Laub and Sampson (1988) reanalyzed the Gluecks' data and concluded that their original conclusion in favor of a relationship between delinquency and broken homes is not supportable. The Gluecks' data were based on official delinquency measures, not on self-report data. Self-report measures of delinquency show few if any differences between youth from intact homes and those from broken homes. Decisions by school and juvenile justice officials, however, are often influenced by family status. Youth from single-parent homes are believed to be in greater need of intervention and supervision than youth with two parents, so officials often process cases that might be dropped for youth with two parents, who are perceived as being less in need of court intervention. Thus, youth from broken homes are disproportionately represented in referrals to the justice system (Johnson, 1986; Laub and Sampson, 1988).

In summary, the reemergence of research on the broken home has contributed to our understanding of one- and two-parent families and delinquent behavior. The exact connection between broken homes and delinquency remains unclear, however, and involves more than simply the dichotomous description of broken versus intact home (Wells and Rankin, 1986, 1991). Nevertheless, the percentage of the population that is divorced and the percentage of households headed by women are among the most important predictors of crime rates. Most studies indicate that children from intact homes have lower crime rates than children from broken homes. It would be an oversimplification to claim that broken homes are a cause of delinquency, however. Most youth from broken homes, after all, are not delinquent, and intact families are not a guarantee against delinquent involvement of youth. Rather, it is the quality of the parent-child relationship, whether it involves one or two parents, that is important in explaining youth involvement in delinquent behavior. When all else is equal, one parent is sufficient for child-rearing. However, "all else" is rarely equal (Hirschi, 1983: 62). Single-parent families do face more difficulties in discipline, supervision, and economic viability. The single parent (usually a woman) faces considerable responsibilities to maintain both employment and a household and to devote time to numerous child-rearing tasks, often without the psychological, social, and financial support of a former spouse. Given the high rate of divorce in this country, it is appropriate that family courts and legislative bodies have placed a high priority on the well-being of the child in custody and support decisions. More attention has been given lately to enforcing child-support responsibilities of the noncustodial parent. This is an important step in minimizing the difficulties faced by children of broken homes.

Family Size

The number of children in a family is also related to delinquency and, as with the broken home, this variable also needs explanation. A sizable number of youth who come in contact with police are from larger families. Loeber and Stouthamer-Loeber (1986) suggest three reasons for this apparent relationship: (1) it is harder for a parent to discipline and supervise a larger number of children; (2) parents often delegate the authority to supervise younger children to their older siblings; and (3) larger familes are often associated with other social problems, such as illegitimacy, poverty, and crowding in the home (1986: 100–101). Families of any size with adequate financial means, quality parent-child relations, and good discipline and supervision are less likely to have children who are involved in delinquent behavior. Studies indicate that a broken home is less important than the quality of the parent-child relationship in explaining delinquency (Matsueda and Heimer, 1987; Laub and Sampson, 1988).

Family Relationships

Broken homes, large families, and working mothers seem to many persons to be obvious causes of juvenile delinquency. Research fails to show much support for this belief, however, and directs us to examine the quality of family relationships. Nye (1958) suggested that the quality of the parent-child relationship was more important than the number of parents present in the home. Parental rejection describes parent-child relationships that are lacking in warmth, love, affection, and parental appreciation for their children. Loeber and Stouthamer-Loeber found that twelve of fifteen studies measuring parent-child relations reported a significant relation between rejection and delinquency and aggression (1986: 55). Rosen (1985) found lower delinquency rates among African American youths who had more father-son interaction. Hirschi (1969) contends that delinquency is less likely among youth who have a positive "attachment" to their parent(s). More recent research supports Hirschi's belief that the quality of family life and the degree of parental attachment are more important predictors of delinquency than is family structure (Laub and Sampson, 1988; Rankin and Kern, 1994). Parents influence their children's behavior through positive interaction and emotional closeness and by gaining their children's respect. Parents are positive role models. Children who feel loved and who respect their parents and identify with them are less likely to get into trouble.

Discipline and Supervision

Parents differ greatly in parenting skills. Some parents are inconsistent in their discipline, and when they do correct their child they are nagging or too harsh. Parents who are preoccupied with their own concerns often neglect their children, fail to monitor their whereabouts, do not know their childrens' friends, or are simply too lenient or inconsistent in their discipline. Parents in "broken homes" and in large families face more difficulties administering consistent discipline and supervision. Nye (1958) found a slight causal relationship between mothers' employment and delinquent behavior of their children. Hirschi (1969) found slightly higher delinquency rates among children whose mothers were employed outside the home and suggested that such mothers were less able to supervise the children's activities and behavior closely. Inconsistent parental discipline and limited supervision are strong predictors of delinquent behavior (Patterson and Stouthamer-Loeber, 1984; Cernkovich and Giordano, 1987). Other research has noted a stronger relationship between lack of supervision and official delinquency than between lack of supervision and self-reported delinquency (Loeber and Stouthamer-Loeber, 1986:61). Wells and Rankin (1988) concluded that direct parental controls, such as close supervision and monitoring of youngsters' behavior, have as great an impact on delinquency as do "indirect controls" such as "attachments" and positive parent-child relations.

Child Abuse and Neglect

Child abuse is a serious problem in America and has a long history. It has endured because harsh discipline, corporal punishment, and cruelty to children have not always been recognized as serious problems. Dr. C. Henry Kempe first brought attention to child abuse when he reported survey results of medical and law enforcement agencies that showed high rates of child abuse. He created the term "battered child syndrome" to describe the numerous incidents of nonaccidental physical injuries of children by their parents or guardians (Kempe et al., 1962). Kempe and his associates have since dropped the term "battered child" and recommended the terms "child abuse" and "neglect," which are more inclusive terms that refer to physical abuse and failure to properly care for children's development and emotional well-being (Helfer and Kempe, 1976). The initial revelation of the problem of child abuse prompted a quantity of research in the 1960s and 1970s. Several states passed laws requiring mandatory reporting of child abuse and neglect cases, and the U.S. Congress passed the Child Abuse and Prevention Act and established the National Center on Child Abuse in 1974.

Definitions of Child Abuse and Neglect

Child abuse includes neglect and physical beating. The terms describe physical or emotional trauma to a child where no reasonable explanation, such as an accident or acceptable disciplinary practices, can be detected. Child abuse is usually a pattern of behavior rather than a single beating or act of neglect. Its effects are cumulative, and the longer it persists, the more severe are the physical and emotional effects on the child. *Neglect* refers to parental deprivation of children, such as failure to provide food, shelter, clothing, care, and nurturance. Neglect is more passive in nature than is abuse and over time results in emotional or physical problems. Abuse is a more overt, physical mistreatment of a child, often resulting in injuries requiring medical care. The two terms are often used interchangeably, and both problems often occur together in the same family (see Helfer and Kempe, 1976; Kempe and Kempe, 1978).

The Extent of Child Abuse

The American family and the home setting have been called one of the most violent institutions in the nation (Straus, Gelles, and Steinmetz, 1980). Americans face a greater risk of assault, physical injury, and even murder in their own homes, by their own family members, than they do anywhere else. Straus and his associates (1980) conducted a nationwide survey of families and found that an astounding number of parents who were interviewed in 1975 reported that they kicked, punched, bit, beat, or threatened their children with a gun or a knife. About three parents in 100 kicked, bit, or punched their children; 1 percent had beaten up their children in the past year, and 4 percent had done that at some point in the children's lives. Three of 100 children have had a parent threaten to use a gun or knife on them some time in their lives, and one in 1,000 children faced a gun or knife threat from parents during 1975. Straus and his associates estimated that between 3.1 and 4 million children have been kicked, bitten, or punched by a parent at some time in their lives; between 1 and 1.9 million were kicked, bitten, or punched in 1975 (1980: 62). The survey showed that physical abuse in these families was not a single occurrence but happened from four to nine times in the course of a year. The national survey showed that family violence was not limited to children. Straus et al. (1980) found that the extent of spousal assaults and intrafamily violence was so great that they reported on domestic abuse in general and not just child abuse. The National Center on Child Abuse and Neglect in 1982 estimated that each year 3.4 children per thousand were victims of some physical abuse in this country; 5.7 children per thousand were victims of some type of emotional, physical, or sexual abuse; and 5.3 per thousand have experienced educational, emotional or physical neglect (see Gray, 1988). The 1985 National Family Violence Survey found that each year about 1.5 million children in the United States were kicked, bitten, punched, beaten up, burned or scalded, or threatened or attacked with a knife or gun (Gelles and Straus, 1988).

The Relationship of Child Abuse to School Problems and Delinquency

Victims of child abuse and neglect suffer the worst forms of family conflict and parental rejection. Neglect and abuse have serious effects on a child's emotional development. Abused children often act out through truancy and disruptive behavior in school; run away from home; and use alcohol and other drugs. Abuse causes self-rejection and low self-esteem that youth may attempt to deal with through substance abuse, attention-getting behavior in school, or association with other deviant peers. The parent-child relationship is so damaged that parents do not have the respect of their children, so are not accepted as role models or positive authority figures. Children who have been victims of physical aggression often act out later with aggressive violent behavior against the abuser (see Zingraff and Belyea, 1986).

There is research evidence that abused and neglected children have greater difficulty in school. Kempe and Kempe believe that many abused children face academic and social problems as soon as they enter school (1978: 25). Broadhurst reviewed studies that show the detrimental effects of abuse and neglect on school performance (1980: 19–41). Bartollas (1993) reported that teachers who have worked with abused and neglected children say that these children "have difficulty in concentrating, are aloof, have little or no confidence, frequently have emotional outbursts, have not internalized rules, and are often destructive of property" (1993: 279). As a result, abused and neglected children are often labeled as disruptive in schools, are assigned to special classes, and in this way are set up for failure.

The relationship between child abuse and delinquency has been widely accepted. Curtis (1963) suggested that "violence breeds violence"—that abused and neglected children act out as juveniles and young adults with acts of violence. Researchers and professionals have described abuse and delinquency as a "cycle of violence" (Widom, 1989b: 3). Several studies document a relationship between child abuse and aggressive, delinquent, and violent behavior (see Zingraff and Belyea, 1986; Gray, 1988). Alfaro (1981) studied children in eight New York counties who had been abused and found that 10 percent of them later had records of being delinquent or ungovernable, compared to only two percent for all children in the counties during the same period. Kratcoski (1982) found no significant differences between abused and nonabused youth in the frequency of violent offenses but he found that delinquents who had been abused were more than twice as likely (45 % vs. 18 %) to engage in violence against family members, as opposed to other acquaintances or strangers. Family violence—physical fighting between parents and among siblings—is associated with youth's accepting attitudes toward violence as a part of life and with committing a violent crime in adult life (Fagan et al., 1983).

A large proportion of juvenile female offenders have been victims of physical or sexual abuse or exploitation. Bergsmann (1989) reviewed an American Correctional Association study that reported that 62 percent of female juveniles said they were physically abused. Forty-seven percent reported eleven or more incidences of abuse; 30 percent said the abuse began when they were between five and nine years of age; and 45 percent said the abuse occurred when they were between ten and fourteen years of age. Parents were the abusers in most of the cases (Bergsmann, 1989: 73). Other studies fail to show a strong relationship between abuse and later violent behavior. Fagan et al. (1983) found only a low incidence of child abuse and parental violence among violent offenders compared with nationwide rates. In most studies, in fact, the majority of abused children became neither delinquent nor violent offenders (Widom, 1989b).

In a study of street gangs on the West Coast, Fleisher (1995) found that, almost without exception, members of the Crips and the Bloods, two notorious street gangs, grew up in "dangerous family environments." Most joined gangs to escape violence at home or because they had been abandoned or neglected by their parents. They developed what Fleisher calls a "defensive world view," which he characterizes as: (1) a feeling of vulnerability and a need to protect oneself; (2) a belief that no one can be trusted; (3) a need to maintain social distance; (4) a willingness to use violence and intimidation to repel others; (5) an attraction to similarly defensive people; and (6) an expectation that no one will come to their aid (Fleisher, 1995: 103–107; see also Wright and Wright, 1994:15).

Other researchers have argued that there is a relationship between child abuse and later adult criminal behavior. Persons who have been victims of abuse or who have witnessed abusive family environments purportedly view violence and aggression as an appropriate way to deal with problems. Zingraff and Belyea (1986) reviewed a number of studies documenting cases in which offenders convicted of murder reported having been physically or emotionally abused by their parents. Many offenders convicted of first-degree murder had been severely abused by their parents; 85 percent of a group of fifty-three murderers reported that they had experienced severe corporal punishment during their early childhood; and a group of 112 felons reported significantly more abusive treatment than a comparison group of 376 noninstitutionalized male adults (Zingraff and Belyea, 1986: 52). In their study of the social histories of 18,574 inmates in North Carolina prisons, Zingraff and Belyea reported that only 9 percent reported experiencing abuse as children, and there were few statistically significant differences between abused and nonabused inmates serving time for violent crimes. These findings cast doubt on the notion that "violence breeds violence." There is some evidence that abuse breeds abuse however. Widom (1989b) reviewed studies that showed a higher likelihood of abuse among parents who were abused themselves, although the majority of abusive parents were not themselves abused as children. She estimated that about a third of the persons who were abused as children will abuse their own children (Widom 1989b: 8). A connection has also been made between abuse and neglect and delinquency. Various studies report that between 8 and 26 percent of delinquents have been abused; Widom (1989b) reported that delinquency occurs in fewer than 20 percent of those who had been abused or neglected. Widom (1989a) compared a large group of persons with histories of abuse or neglect with a matched control group and found that 28.6 percent of the abused and neglected subjects had adult criminal records, compared to 21.1 percent of the control group (1989a: 260). For both men and women, a history of abuse or neglect significantly increased one's chances of having a criminal record as an adult. However, while 29 percent of the abused and neglected subjects had adult criminal records, 71 percent did not; having a history of childhood abuse or neglect does not inevitably lead to criminal behavior as an adult (Widom, 1989a).

In summary, we know there is some connection between child abuse and neglect and later criminal behavior as juveniles or adults. We know that many abused children become abusive parents. However, most abused children do not become abusive parents, juvenile delinquents, or violent adult criminals (Wright and Wright, 1994; Widom, 1989a).

Parents, School Problems and Delinquency

There is considerable research evidence to show a relationship between parents' lack of support for education and childrens' school problems; and among school misconduct, school failure, and involvement in delinquent behavior (see Patterson and Dishion, 1985; Spivak and Cianci, 1987). Offord (1982) studied a sample of boys and girls placed on probation by the Juvenile Court of Ottawa, Canada, and found that families of delinquents with early school failure (repeating a grade, special class placement) tended to be more disorganized, nonintact, and poorer; the mothers had a history of being on welfare, and many of the fathers had been involved with the law (1982: 134, 136). Simons et al. (1991) suggest that ineffective parenting and parents' coercive, interpersonal style cause youngsters to experience difficulties with peers and authority figures at school and that these difficulties lead to negative labeling and rejection by conventional peers. School problems do not have a direct effect on delinquency, according to their explanation, but do contribute indirectly to delinquent behavior, since youth with school problems are more likely to associate with deviant peers. A coercive parenting style is important in explaining delinquent involvement; Simons and his associates found that such a style increases delinquency involvement independent of peer influences. Inept and coercive parenting includes attempts to control a child through threats, power plays, or ploys intended to make the child feel guilty and persistent complaining, nagging, and criticism (Simons et al., 1991: 652–653). The links among parenting practices, school problems, and delinquency have led to the development of school programs directed at improving parenting skills.

Family and School Involvement

Given the importance of the family in explaining delinquency, family training is logically considered by many to be a necessary step toward delinquency prevention (see Wilson and Loury, 1987). Some believe that schools are the most appropriate settings for early intervention efforts in delinquency prevention (Hirschi, 1983; Zigler and Hall, 1987; also see Patterson, 1986; and Hawkins and Lam, 1987).

Educators generally complain that in recent years schools have been expected to take on many additional responsibilities that have traditionally been the responsibility of parents. Furthermore, teachers and principals complain that many of the teaching and discipline problems they face could be alleviated if they had more support from parents. Their complaints certainly have merit. Many discipline problems could be minimized if parents would help to instill respect for teachers and support educators in disciplinary sanctions when their children have violated school regulations. Parents can help improve their children's school achievement by inquiring regularly about their required assignments, what they are studying week to week, encouraging them to complete homework, and providing a place and a quiet time in the home to complete homework.

The idea of parental involvement in the schools, however, has not been welcomed by many educators. Sara Lawrence Lightfoot (1978) noted the irony that, while families and schools share the complementary task of educating and raising young people, there is a great deal of conflict between them. According to Lightfoot, teachers tend to be defensive about their professional status, their occupational image, and their special skills and abilities. Teachers generally develop a better awareness of the educational abilities and needs of children than their parents have. Parents' fears tend to grow as they lose control of their child's daily life and as someone else becomes the expert and judge of their child's abilities. Teacher evaluations of a child's attention, study habits, discipline, or general school performance are often met with defensive reactions by parents. Teachers have difficulty with parents who do not seem to value their special competence and skills (see Lightfoot, 1978: 20–42).

Many teachers and school administrators believe that parents have no right to exert influence on the schools. Gene Maeroff (1982) suggested that some school procedures seem intentionally to exclude parents and keep them uninformed. Parents have no role in the selection of teachers for their children or the assignment of principals to schools, for example, and most schools do not involve parents in decisions regarding curriculum development and selection of textbooks (1982: 208). Other examples of schools' failure to involve parents concern setting regulations for dress and behavior; designing report cards that are either complex and unintelligible or so simple that they report little about a child's progress; and holding meetings that are scheduled during the day, with little regard for parents' work schedules (Maeroff, 1982: 208). Many schools do encourage parental involvement and have implemented a number of programs and policies to maintain close communication with parents aimed at fostering a cooperative team approach to enhance educational progress for children. In addition, parents may become involved in schools through parent-teacher organizations and through the decisions and policies of school boards.

There is evidence that parental involvement in their children's education makes a difference in school achievement. To determine why children of some low-income families were more successful in school, teams of teachers and principals visited the homes of successful students. Three common factors in the homes were: (1) the parents knew what was happening in school and kept in touch with teachers to know what was expected of their children; (2) the parents viewed school as the key to their children's upward mobility and encouraged regular attendance; and (3) in addition to the parent there was usually another adult, such as a grandparent, neighbor, or aunt, who provided addition emotional and psychological support (Maeroff, 1982: 227). The combination of these three factors resulted in a strong emphasis on regulated television viewing, completing assigned chores around the house, and doing homework. The organization and structure that began in these children's lives at home apparently carried over into the classroom.

The role of the school in promoting child-rearing practices is worth pursuing. Although schools already have many responsibilities beyond basic education, this expectation may not place many additional demands on schools. The school is already involved in child-rearing in terms of promoting social expectations, setting limits, and providing structure to students' lives. The promotion of communication and mediation skills, with opportunities for social interaction with teachers and positive peers, are important factors in child-rearing, particularly in the absence of close parental relations and supervision. Most educators' values and practices seem close to those of successful parents (Hirschi, 1983: 67). Hirschi suggests that schools have some advantages over the family in that teachers care about the behavior of children (disruption makes their lives more difficult); school monitoring of behavior is very efficient; and teachers are probably more expert than parents in recognizing deviant behavior (1983: 67). Granted, the school's role in child-rearing does have limitations. It depends on students' regular attendance and, to some extent, on parents' support for schooling. To the extent that the child and the parent are not committed to or regularly involved in the educational process, the ability of the schools to make an impact is limited. Nevertheless, the inability of schools to affect those who are less involved in education should not obscure the fact that schools do very well with many students. The difficulties in working with some students should not minimize school's potential for helping families improve their child-rearing practices (Hirschi, 1983).

J. David Hawkins and his associates (1987) have been active in developing and evaluating the effectiveness of a school-based parent-training program in Seattle. They have found that to be effective, parent training must reach the parents of children who are most at risk of delinquent behavior, and the training must involve parents before the children's misbehavior has become serious. The parent training can be implemented as early as when the children are in first grade (1987: 196–197). Others have suggested that intervention efforts may have little impact on "antisocial" families marked by criminality and family violence and that interventions with youth from such families would more effective if focused on the school and on the young person's peers (Fagan and Wexler, 1987: 665). An outstanding program designed to deal with family problems before they result in delinquency is the Oregon Social Learning Center, developed by Gerald Patterson and his associates (Patterson, 1986). They believe that many parents do not know how to deal with their children effectively and that antisocial behavior in the home and at school is associated with poor parenting skills. Children whose parents ignore their misbehavior one moment and then overreact to it another time with explosive anger are not receiving the consistent discipline that they need. The Oregon program teaches parents to use effective disciplinary techniques that emphasize firmness and consistency and encourages the use of positive reinforcement for good behavior while discouraging ineffective discipline such as yelling, making humiliating remarks, or hitting. Other programs patterned after the Oregon program have proven to be successful. The Family Teaching Center in Helena, Montana, provides a series of weekly evening classes to help parents improve their child management skills (see Siegel and Senna, 1991). The Family Teaching Center also has a school involvement program in which parents and their children participate with school teachers and social service personnel in working through problems in school discipline and academic performance (cf. Siegel and Senna, 1991: 269; National Juvenile Justice Assessment Centers, 1981).

Parent training has been among the most promising approaches for dealing with misbehavior of young people, especially very young children. There are a number of limitations to parent training as a primary means of delinquency prevention, however. Existing programs are quite expensive; they do not reach many families, some of whom could most benefit from them; many parents (some of whom most need training) are unwilling to participate; and it is not clear how long the beneficial effects of training last (Loeber, 1988). The role of government in family intervention and training has become a regular topic of discussion. Government's role in parenting training and in preventing family problems is by necessity limited, just as government efforts in crime prevention are limited. Laws and government policies have by nature been "reactive" more than preventive. Some researchers, in fact, believe that governmental interventions into family life may do more harm than good. Some social service and social welfare programs, for example, may contribute to the breakup of families that otherwise would have remained together. Government programs that may be more effective are those aimed at improving the environment in which children grow up, by improving schools, housing, and nourishment (Loeber, 1988). It is not clear whether such programs have much impact on keeping families together or on keeping children from becoming delinquent.

Peer Relationships and Delinquency

Youths' relationships with peers and the kind of friends with whom they associate are very important in predicting their school performance and behavior and in determining whether they become involved in delinquent behavior (Lawrence, 1991). As young people reach the teenage years, peer group influence often interferes with parental and family ties, encouraging alienation between youth and their parents. Next to the family, the school is the most important social institution in preparing young people for a career and a satisfying life that is free of social and legal problems. The roles of parents, peers, and the school are thus closely related in the emergence of delinquent behavior. Youth who do not have parental support and attachment are less equipped to deal with school demands and the resulting frustration of school failure. Youth are more likely to violate laws when they are with their friends, especially if ties with their parents are weak. These youth are more vulnerable to the temptations and pressures they experience from their peers. It is little wonder, then, that many youth turn to disruptive and delinquent behavior in school. When parents and schoolteachers are unable to get these young people involved in productive school performance and behavior, they often turn to delinquent friends who are experiencing similar problems. Associations with delinquent peers provide the acceptance and support that they are not getting from parents and the school.

The tendency for young people to turn away from their parents and seek closer ties with their peers has long been recognized. According to Riesman (1950), the American family began changing in the 1950s. The family was then a closely knit unit where parents had a great deal of respect and authority. Parents today have less power, less confidence, and more doubts about how to raise their children. Children are influenced by the media and by their friends, and they put pressure on their parents to go along with these norms. Riesman argued that peers were becoming a more important influence on children than their parents.

Junior and senior high schools actually play a major role in drawing youth away from their parents and other adults. Schools lump hundreds of youth together, and as a result teenagers create their own subculture, with language, behaviors, and values that are distinctly different from those of adults. In the past, American children and youth spent more time with adults; today, in contrast, children spend a large portion of their time at school, going to and from school, in school events, and with their peers. Bronfenbrenner (1970) argued that society has become age-segregated but that parents and other adults want it this way. They do not want to spend much time with their children but prefer that their children spend time with their peer group instead. Problems arise when young peer groups promote negative values and deviant behavior, and Bronfenbrenner cautioned that this alienation of youth from adults was likely to result in more violence among the younger generation (1970: 121). David Greenberg (1977) also noted the age segregation of youth and emphasized that, as youth have become excluded from adult work and leisure activities, they have been forced to associate mostly with one another. They thus are less susceptible to influence from adult role models, and the result is greater peer influence (1977: 196). As youth spend less time with their parents and other adults and much more time with their peers, their decisions and lifestyles begin to reflect the expectations of their peers. This heightened sensitivity to peers and weakened attachments to parents also explains the increased likelihood that some youth will engage in delinquent behavior (Greenberg, 1977: 196).

The nature and extent of peer influence on young people varies according to a number of factors. First of all, the influence of peers varies with the behavior or attitude in question. Peers play an important role in young peoples' alcohol and substance use, but Ronald Akers (1985) emphasized that the process is not one of peer "pressure" but of peer *influence* (p. 115). Akers found that for the majority of teenagers, peers are more likely to reinforce conforming behavior than deviant behavior; most of them reported feeling no pressure from peers to use any substances; and they said parents were more important than peers as sources of influence and knowledge in their decisions whether or not to use tobacco, alcohol, and other drugs (Akers, 1985: 117).

The importance of peer relationships tends to vary also by gender and race. Peer group influence has a greater impact on delinquency among males than among females (Johnson, 1979). Peggy Giordano, Stephen Cernkovich, and M. D. Pugh (1986) examined friendship patterns between male and female adolescents and found that females have closer relationships with peers than do males. Girls are more likely to commit a delinquent act when they are in a group of other girls and boys than when alone (Giordano, 1978: 127). The researchers also found that white females seem to have closer relationships with peers than do African American females. The African Americans felt less caring and trust and reported less pressure from their peers to behave in certain ways (Giordano et al., 1986: 1195). Merry Morash (1986) found that adolescent females belong to fewer delinquent groups than males; this helps explain their lower levels of delinquent involvement. Female characteristics such as being less aggressive and having more empathy also helps restrain girls from engaging in delinquent and violent behavior with peers (Morash, 1986). Herman and Julia Schwendinger (1985) compared groups of young people in working-class and middle-class communities in southern California and found distinct differences. Both groups were preocuupied with leisure activities and disliked or were at least indifferent to school, but the middle-class youth tended to avoid violent and aggressive roles more than the working-class youth, who were also more involved in drug use, possession, and sale. Mark Colvin and John Pauly (1983) claimed that the difference in peer relationships between working-class and middle- or upper-class youth was explained by their parents' workplace experiences. Lower-class workers tend to experience a coercive working environment, which reduces their capacity as parents to deal with their children in any way other than a repressive one, using harsh verbal or physical punishment. This coercive family environment places a strain on parent-child relations. Colvin and Pauly further argued that these children are more likely to be placed in coercive school control situations, which leads them to associate more with other peers who feel alienated from their parents and school. The resulting peer group associations increase the likelihood that these youth will become involved in delinquent activities and violent behavior (Colvin and Pauly, 1983: 542–543).

Travis Hirschi (1969) developed a social control theory of delinquency that suggests that delinquency is more likely when an individual's attachment or bond to society is weak (1969: 16). Hirschi maintained that youth who are most closely bonded to social groups such as the family, the school, and peers are less likely to commit delinquent acts (1969: 16–34). An individual's attachment to conventional others and sensitivity to other persons is related to an ability to internalize norms and to develop a conscience (1969: 18). Attachment to others also refers to the affection and respect that children have for parents, teachers, and friends; these are important considerations when youth are tempted to engage in delinquent behavior. Hirschi tested his theory on 4,077 junior and senior high school students in California, using a self-report survey along with school and police records. He found that youth with a greater attachment to parents reported less delinquent involvement. Young people with weak ties to parents reported little concern for the opinions of teachers and disliked school; these youth with less attachment to school and poor school performance were more likely to become involved in delinquent behavior (pp. 110–134). Hirschi found that attachment to peers does not imply a lack of attachment to parents. Youth in his study who were close to and respected their friends were least likely to have committed delinquent acts, but he also found that delinquents were less dependent on peers than were nondelinquents, suggesting that youths' decisions about whether or not to conform to the law affects their choice of friends, rather than the other way around (pp. 135–161).

The peer attachment-delinquency relationship as explained by social control theory has received a great deal of support among criminologists. Some have obtained findings that further specify and clarify the relationship between peer attachment and delinquency. Hindelang (1973) found a direct relationship between peer attachment and self-reported delinquency among rural males and females and concluded that this relationship appears to depend on the kinds of friends youth have and the characteristics of their peer associations. Linden and Hackler (1973) studied youths' relationships with parents, conventional peers, and deviant peers and found that youth who had closer relationships with deviant peers than with their parents and with conventional peers had the highest rates of self-reported delinquency. Liska and Reed (1985) concluded that peers can be either a positive or a negative influence and that parents, more than school, are the major sources of delinquency control (1985: 558). Burkett and Warren (1987) found that deviant peer associations, through lowered religious commitment, make youth more vulnerable to marijuana use. Positive peer influence, on the other hand, tends to reduce the likelihood that young people will use drugs. Johnson, Marcos, and Bahr (1987) found that associations with peers rather than parents seems to matter most in adolescent drug use. They disagreed with the idea of peer influence, which holds that friends' drug use makes it seem right or safe; but argued that youths use drugs "simply because their friends do" (1987: 336). Others have emphasized the interactive and reciprocal nature of peer relationships and delinquency, suggesting that association with delinquent peers leads to delinquent conduct but that delinquent conduct also increases association with delinquent peers. Thornberry (1987) proposed an interactional theory with a focus on attachment to parents, commitment to school, and association with delinquent peers:

> [A]ssociating with delinquent peers, not being committed to school, and engaging in delinquent behavior are so contradictory to parental expectations that they tend to diminish the level of attachment between parent and child. Adolescents who fail at school, who associate with delinquent peers, and who engage in delinquent conduct are . . . likely to jeopardize their affective bond with their parents. (1987: 874).

Commitment to school also affects peer relationships, so students who are committed to doing well in school are unlikely to associate with delinquent peers

(Thornberry, 1987: 875). Agnew (1991) analyzed data from the National Youth Survey and concluded that peer attachment strongly affects delinquency when an adolescent spends much time with serious delinquents, feels they approve delinquency, and feels pressure to engage in delinquency (1991: 64). Gerald Patterson and Thomas Dishion (1985) proposed a model to explain the process by which parents and peers contribute to delinquency. They suggested that during preadolescence a breakdown in family management procedures leads to an increase in a child's antisocial behavior and disrupts the development of social and academic skills, thus placing the child at risk for rejection by normal peers and for likely academic failure. During adolescence, poor parental monitoring practices and poor social skills further the likelihood of contact with a deviant peer group. The combined effects of association with deviant peers, poor parental monitoring, and academic failure contribute to the likelihood that these youth will become involved in delinquent behavior (Patterson and Dishion, 1985: 63–64).

It is clear that peer associations play an important role in delinquent behavior. Youth whose friends are positive and law-abiding are at less risk for delinquent involvement than those who associate with peers with a higher level of self-reported delinquency. Close relations with parents and the family reduce delinquent influences, but alone they are not enough. Commitment to school helps reduce delinquency, but analyses of data from the National Youth Survey show that the influence of delinquent friends is more important than school attachment in explaining delinquent behavior (Lawrence, 1991: 66). Research findings on the effects of peer associations on delinquent involvement have important implications for parents, schools, and juvenile correctional programs. Elliott, Huizinga, and Ageton (1985) suggested that treatment approaches that use adolescent peer groups or "group processes" may actually have the unintended effect of contributing to closer delinquent friendships. They believe it is not reasonable to expect prosocial values and norms to result from group processes involving serious juvenile delinquents. Incarceration of juvenile offenders together in institutional settings inevitably results in closer ties among serious young offenders; but Elliott et al. emphasized that juvenile correctional programs do not have to perpetuate this practice, and they recommended efforts to integrate high-risk youth into conventional peer groups (1985: 149–150). Gary Gottfredson (1987) reviewed studies of the effects of peer group interventions conducted in schools (e.g., Guided Group Interaction, Positive Peer Culture, peer group counseling) and arrived at a similar conclusion. He found no difference in police contacts between experimental groups (who had participated in peer group interventions) and control groups. Except for elementary school students, he found no support for the benefit of peer group treatment; and for high school students the effects even appeared harmful in that such groups may weaken students' bonds with their parents, which serve as some restraint against adverse peer group influence (1987: 709). Gottfredson suggested that "it may be useful to seek ways to avoid delinquent peer interaction entirely rather than to attempt to modify its nature" (1987: 710).

In summary, parents should be concerned about their children's friends and closely monitor what their children do, where they go, and with whom. Schools may unintentionally be promoting the development and adverse influence of deviant peer groups by the practice of tracking and placing at-risk, disruptive, and marginally performing students together (see Elliott et al., 1985: 150). Placing troublesome students together in special classes increases their association with each other and may increase discipline problems and failure. Research evidence seems to indicate that, whenever possible, dispersing problem students among different teachers and classrooms is preferable. Singling out problem students should be seen as a short-term, temporary solution, with the ultimate objective being reintegration into the regular classroom. Juvenile detention centers and training schools have for decades been viewed as "schools for crime." Association with delinquent peers is inevitable in these institutional settings. Increased emphasis on the use of community residential alternatives is clearly more appropriate for those youth who do not require a secure setting for the protection of themselves and others. Parents, schools, and correctional programs cannot entirely control or eliminate associations with delinquent peers. The evidence is clear that failure to minimize such associations promotes delinquency, however (see Lawrence, 1991: 67). The more effective delinquency prevention strategies are those that encourage stronger attachments to family, school, and nondelinquent friends. Coordinating the efforts of school and juvenile justice personnel with parents and developing community programs that accomplish collaborative efforts is a worthwhile goal for effective delinquency prevention.

Gangs & Delinquency

We have seen that peer associations take on great importance for adolescents. For most youth these friendships are positive and supportive, indeed, a normal part of adolescent development. Youth who have poor relations with their parents and family, on the other hand, are likely to experience school problems and to associate with delinquent friends. The resulting negative peer influence leads to involvement with delinquency and drugs, even to serious criminal and violent behavior. The formation of juvenile gangs is an extension of adolescent peer groups. Youth join gangs for a variety of reasons: a need for peer acceptance, belonging, and recognition; for status, safety, or security; for power; and for excitement (see Spergel et al., 1994b: 3). Youths who are especially drawn to gangs include those raised under socially depriving conditions; those who are failing in school and not involved in school activities; and those who are unemployed and who have few if any perceived job goals or opportunities.

Gangs and crime committed by gang members are evident in many American cities. A National Institute of Justice (NIJ)-sponsored survey of metropolitan police departments in the seventy-nine largest U.S. cities showed that in 1992 all but seven were troubled by gangs, as were all but five departments in forty-three smaller cities (Curry et al., 1994). In 110 jurisdictions that reported having gangs, the survey found that during the previous twelve-month period there were:

- •249,324 gang members
- •4,881 gangs
- •46,359 gang-related crimes
- •1,072 gang-related homicides (Curry et al., 1994: 1)

A gang problem of this magnitude clearly presents a challenge for law enforcement and calls for a concerted community-wide effort to respond to the problem.

Definitions and Characteristics of Gangs

Despite the existence of youth gangs since the early part of this century, delinquency experts have not been able to agree on a precise definition of a gang. The term is sometimes used (even by some youth themselves) to describe any group of teenagers who participate together in deviant and delinquent activities. Police departments and researchers generally prefer a narrower definition of gangs that includes violent behavior, group organization, leadership, and territory (see Horowitz, 1990; Curry et al., 1994; and Siegel and Senna, 1991: 281–282). Jeffrey Fagan (1989) defines gangs according to their primary purpose and activities: some are basically social groups, involved in few delinquent activities and little drug use; some gangs are involved in drug use and sales and in vandalism; other gangs have members who are serious delinquents and are extensively involved in property and violent offenses (1989: 649–651). In a study of gangs in Cleveland and Columbus, C. Ronald Huff (1989) identified three types of gangs: (1) informal, hedonistic gangs whose primary interest is in "getting high" and "having a good time"; (2) instrumental gangs that commit property crimes for economic reasons; and (3) predatory gangs that commit robberies and street muggings and are actively involved in drug use and sales (Huff, 1989: 528–529).

Gangs appear to be more structured than delinquent groups, but some loosely organized groups may still be regarded as gangs. Most gangs tend to be organized on a geographical basis, such as neighorhoods; and many are focused around racial or ethnic origin, age, or gender. Males make up the vast majority of gang membership, but female participation in gangs is increasing (see Campbell, 1990). Gangs tend to be concentrated in low-income communities, in public housing projects, and in poor black and low-income Hispanic sections of the city (Curry and Spergel, 1988: 399).

Gangs and Delinquency

Most delinquency is committed by youth who are not gang members, and gang membership is not necessarily synonymous with delinquent behavior. Huff observed that gang members spend more time in deviant adolescent behavior (skipping school, disobeying parents); only the more delinquent gangs and gang members engage in serious criminal behavior (1989: 530). Jeffrey Fagan (1990) surveyed samples of students and dropouts in Chicago, Los Angeles, and San Diego and observed that the involvement of both gang and nongang youths in delinquency and drug use suggests that gangs are only one of several deviant peer groups in inner cities; but gang members in his sample were more heavily involved in both delinquency and substance use than were nongang members (pp. 201–202, 209). City police departments in the NIJ survey reported far more gang members than gang-related incidents. The Los Angeles Police Department reported 503 gangs and 55,258 gang members but only 8,528 gang-related crimes in 1991; the Chicago Police Department reported that 29,000 gang members in forty-one gangs accounted for only 4,765 gang incidents in 1991 (Curry et al., 1994: 7). Thornberry and his associates (1993) conducted a longitudinal study to compare youths' crime patterns prior to, during, and after gang involvement. They found that gang members did not have high rates of delinquency or drug use before entering the gang, but once they became members their rates increased substantially; and the rates of delinquency decreased when the gang members left the gang. Finn Esbensen and his associates (1995) interviewed a sample of youths in high-risk Denver neighborhoods to measure the extent to which gang members differed from serious street offenders and nonoffending youth. The gang members reported more delinquency involvement than other youth, but their patterns of drug sales and use were similar to those of nongang serious offenders. What distinguished gang members and serious offenders from nonoffending youth was their associations with delinquent friends and their admitted unwillingness to listen to friends' advice not to do something that was wrong or against the law. An important and somewhat surprising finding was that gang members and nongang serious offenders were similar to nonoffenders in their involvement in conventional activities. Esbensen et al. suggest that this finding raises serious questions about the assumption that "getting 'kids' involved in after school activities will reduce their delinquent activity, or that summer jobs will reduce gang activity" (1995: 198).

Gangs and Schools

A youth gang member is likely to have done poorly in school and is not involved in school activities. Most gang members are bored with school and feel inadequate in class. They have not developed effective learning skills and therefore experience frustration and failure in school. They do not identify with teachers and tend to dislike and distrust them (see Spergel et al., 1994a: 17, 1994b: 4). Esbensen et al. found that gang members reported significantly more negative labeling by their teachers than did a comparison group of street offenders (1995: 198). Gang problems in schools often begin in the streets as students who are gang members bring gang attitudes and behaviors into the school. Gang violence generally does not occur in schools, although gang recruitment and planning of gang activities may occur on school grounds. Gang members may claim parts of the school as their turf; leave their marks with graffiti; and intimidate and assault other students (see Spergel et al., 1994a, 1994b).

Results of school crime victimization surveys indicate that there is a relationship between gang presence in schools and students' reports of fear and victimization. In 1989, 15 percent of students reported "street" gangs in their school (Bastian and Taylor, 1991). By 1993, 35 percent of students reported that "fighting" gangs were present in their schools (National Center for Education Statistics, 1993). Results of these two surveys indicate that:

- Gangs are not limited to inner-city, urban schools. Minority and white students from urban and suburban schools report gangs in their schools.

- Gang presence in schools is strongly associated with increased student reports of victimization and fear.

- Gang presence, not a student's race or ethnicity or whether the student lives in an urban area, accounts for most of the differences in students' reports of fear and victimization at school (National Center for Education Statistics, 1995).

Not all schools, even some in high crime areas, are affected by the presence of gangs. Schools that have strong leadership and a positive learning environment have been able to maintain students' commitment to education and to control gang problems and youth crime.

Responding to Gang Problems

Five strategies have been used in dealing with youth gangs: (1) neighborhood mobilization; (2) social intervention; (3) provision of social and economic opportunities, such as special school and job programs; (4) gang suppression and incarceration; and (5) special police gang units and specialized probation units (Spergel et al., 1994b: 7).

There are limits to what schools can do about family and community factors that contribute to youth gang problems, but there is much they can do in cooperation with community agencies. Public schools, especially middle schools, are among the best resources for preventing and intervening early in youth gang problems. The peak period for recruitment of new gang members occurs between the fifth and eighth grades, among youth who are doing poorly in class and are at risk of dropping out (Spergel, et al. 1994b: 10). One suggested approach is the delivery of a flexible curriculum targeted to youth gang members who are not doing well in their classes. The goal is to enhance the students' basic academic and work-related problem-solving skills (Spergel et al., 1994a: 18).

A number of components for an effective gang control and suppression strategy by schools have been recommended by experts:

- Instituting training programs to inform and prepare teachers and administrators to recognize and respond to gang problems in schools

- Making a clear distinction between gang- and nongang-related activity so as not to exaggerate the scope of the problem

•Developing clear guidelines and policies for responding to gang behavior; controlling intimidation, threats, and assaults among students; and strictly forbidding any weapons

•Enforcing rules and regulations through open communication and positive relationships among school personnel, students, and parents

•Working closely with police and probation agencies, communicating regularly and sharing information for monitoring gang activity (see Huff, 1989: 53–55; Spergel et al., 1994a: 18–19)

The most recent comprehensive effort to respond to the youth gang problem is the Gang Resistance and Education Training (G.R.E.A.T.) Program funded by the National Institute of Justice. The program was developed by the Bureau of Alcohol, Tobacco, and Firearms and the Phoenix, Arizona, Police Department. Objectives of the program are to teach youths how to set goals for themselves, how to resist peer pressure, how to resolve conflicts, and how gangs can affect the quality of their lives (Winfree et al., 1995: 11). The program is focused on the seventh-grade level, with some schools offering it also to sixth- and eighth-grade students. Extensive evaluations of the program are being conducted, including assessments of the effectiveness of the program training for police officers; the perceived effectiveness of the program; and actually implementation of the G.R.E.A.T. program in various departments (Esbensen, 1995: 17).

Female Delinquency

Most juvenile crimes known to police are committed by boys. Juvenile crimes committed by girls are much less frequent and less serious. A total of 161,117 girls under the age of eighteen were arrested in the United States in 1994 for index crimes, and girls accounted for 23 percent of all juvenile arrests for index crimes (Federal Bureau of Investigation, 1995: 222). Between 1985 and 1994, arrests of girls under eighteen for index crimes increased by 42 percent while arrests of boys eighteen and under rose by 12 percent (FBI, 1995: 222). From 1965 to 1977, arrest statistics from the Uniform Crime Reports indicated that females were not catching up with males in the commission of violent or serious crimes; but there were rising levels of female delinquency in the categories of larceny, runaway, and liquor law violations (Steffensmeier and Steffensmeier, 1980: 80). Girls' share of all juvenile arrests remained fairly steady over that time period, ranging from about 15 percent to 29 percent (1980: 66). Official measures of juvenile crime underestimate the actual involvement of young people, however, and this is even more true for females. The ratio of male to female arrests is 3.4 to 1, but self-report studies report a male-to-female ratio of only 2 to 1 (Cernkovich and Giordano, 1979; Canter, 1982). Cernkovich and Giordano (1979) found that while males report more delinquent acts than females, the difference in self-reported delinquency is considerably smaller than the difference in arrest rates. They found no significant gender differences for school problems, suspension, and expulsion; status offenses such as truancy, defying parents' authority, and running away; or drug-related offenses such as smoking marijuana, using and selling hard drugs, and driving under the influence of hard drugs.

The types of offenses for which most youth are arrested are for less serious crimes. The index crime for which most juveniles, especially girls, are arrested is larceny/theft (usually shoplifting). Besides the 600,000-plus arrests of juveniles for index crimes, 1.3 million juveniles under the age of eighteen were arrested for less serious crimes such as vandalism, drug and liquor violations, and drunkenness and disorderly conduct; girls accounted for 25 percent of these arrests (FBI, 1995: 221–222). Thus, trivial offenses are most characteristic of juveniles, and this is especially true for girls. In fact, status offenses (so-called because they are linked to the status of age and are not crimes if committed by adults) play a major role in girls' official delinquency. Status offenses accounted for 24.1 percent of all girls' arrests in 1990 but only about 8 percent of boys' arrests (Chesney-Lind, 1995:74). Arrests of juveniles for status offenses declined during the 1970s with the passage of the Juvenile Justice and Delinquency Prevention Act (JJDPA) in 1974, which called for the diversion and deinstitutionalization of youth arrested for noncriminal offenses. Arrests of juveniles, especially girls, for status offenses began increasing again in the 1980s, however. Meda Chesney-Lind (1995) suggests that girls are arrested disproportionately more than boys for such status offenses as running away and curfew violations because of a tendency to sexualize their offenses and to attempt to control their behavior under the patriarchal authority of the juvenile justice system. There is evidence that many young women run away to escape sexual victimization at home; yet once on the streets they are vulnerable to further sexual victimization (Chesney-Lind, 1995: 83).

Little attention has been paid to female delinquency, primarily because delinquency is generally associated with boys. Most research and explanations of the juvenile crime problem in fact focus on boys. Except for some early work (Lombroso, 1903; W. I. Thomas, 1923), research and writing on delinquency involving girls was virtually nonexistent until the 1950s (Pollok, 1950; Konopka, 1966). Much more attention has been given to female delinquency since a dramatic increase in arrests of girls beginning in the 1970s. Freda Adler (1975) believed that the increase in female crime could be explained by a "liberation hypothesis," that as women have become more active and taken advantage of opportunities outside the home and in the workplace, so also have they begun to engage in more crimes formerly committed almost entirely by men. Rita Simon (1975) believed that as women have become more liberated and more are working outside the home, they have had more opportunities and incentives to commit property crimes.

Other researchers have found only partial support for the liberation hypothesis to explain the increase in female delinquency. Giordano and Cernkovich (1979) surveyed girls in three high schools and two state institutions to examine their attitudes on traditional and so-called liberated feminist views. They found that the more delinquent girls were less liberated and held more traditional views of marriage and children. Rankin (1980) interviewed

385 students in several Wayne County (Detroit), Michigan, high schools to examine their attitudes toward education and involvement in delinquency. He
found that negative attitudes toward school and school performance were associated with more delinquency involvement for both boys and girls; surprisingly, however, the relationship was stronger for girls than for boys (1980:
431). The findings seem to indicate that with more women in the work force
today, the perceived occupational consequences of negative attitudes toward
education and of poor grades seem to be just as serious for girls as for boys.
Rankin suggests that school factors thus may inhibit female delinquency as
much as male delinquency (1980: 432).

John Hagan and his associates (1985) developed their power-control theory to explain variations of delinquency among males and females. The theory
examines social class, whether husbands and wives work outside the home, and
the degree of power and control men and women have in the workplace. According to the theory, in the "patriarchal" family with traditional gender role
definitions, mothers have the primary socializing role and a daughter is more
controlled than a son. Gender differences result because girls, more than boys,
are taught to avoid risks in general, particularly illegal behavior. Thus, girls appear to be more easily deterred by the threat of legal sanctions—an effect that
Hagan et al. believe is produced more through maternal than through paternal controls (1985: 1156). In an "egalitarian" family, control over daughters
and sons is more equal, and both are encouraged to be more open to risk taking. That is, daughters are encouraged to be more decisive and willing to take
control and assume responsibility, although risk taking may have unintended
consequences, such as involvement in delinquency (Hagan et al., 1987: 793).
Thus, in egalitarian families daughters are more like sons in their involvement
in risk taking, including some delinquency.

Jill Rosenbaum and James Lasley (1990) analyzed data on 1,508 adolescents from the Seattle Youth Study and found support for the power-control
theory in explaining male-female differences in the school-delinquency relationship. Positive attitudes toward school and achievement produced stronger
reductions in delinquency for boys than girls, while involvement in school activities and positive attitudes toward teachers led to more delinquency reduction for girls than for boys (1990: 510). The researchers also found social class
differences and suggested that school conformity is instilled socially in females
and in middle- and upper-class youths more strongly than in males and in lower-
class youths. Meda Chesney-Lind is critical of power-control theory as an explanation of variations in female delinquency. The argument that mothers' employment leads to daughters' delinquency in more egalitarian families is little
more than a variation on the earlier liberation hypothesis, but "now, mother's
liberation causes daughter's crime" (1995: 81–82)! She also notes methodological problems with the theory and a lack of evidence to suggest that girls'
delinquency has increased along with women's employment. A reanalysis of the
1981 National Survey of Children indicated that gender differences in delinquency were present regardless of patriarchal or egaliltarian family structures
(Morash and Chesney-Lind, 1991: 347), and female delinquency has declined

or remained stable in the last decade, as women's employment in the labor force has increased (Chesney-Lind, 1995: 82). Morash and Chesney-Lind argue for a feminist theory of female delinquency, noting that children (boys or girls) who identify with a nurturing parent who cares for others are likely to be more caring and have concern for others, rather than harm others. They believe that nurturing roles are not gender-specific. Sons can identify with a nurturing parent as readily as daughters and can learn prosocial behaviors (1991: 351). A significant amount of female delinquency can be accounted for by patriarchal tendencies of the juvenile justice system. Girls' delinquent involvement is often a result of physical and sexual abuse, since running away from victimization experiences leads to more serious criminal involvement. They are referred to juvenile court for behaviors that parents and authorities generally ignore or overlook when they are committed by boys, out of a perceived need to protect girls from engaging in more serious delinquency (see Chesney-Lind, 1995: 82–85).

Further research is needed to explain more clearly the causes of female delinquency and the extent to which girls' involvement in crime is different from boys. Boys still commit more serious and violent offenses, but girls' involvement in property and drug-related offenses is a matter of concern. Differences in how family and school factors contribute to female delinquency deserves more careful research. Finally, further research is needed to examine how the juvenile justice system responds to female delinquency, from police referral to juvenile court decisions.

Summary

Parents and families play a major role in the development of youth. Research evidence shows that the chances that young people will become involved in delinquent behavior are greater when they have experienced problems in parent-child relations, inconsistent supervision and discipline, parental rejection, and abuse. Peers have a significant influence on a youth's behavior, and association with negative peers is more likely when there are problematic relations with parents. Youth gangs often provide a feeling of acceptance and belonging for youth who lacks a positive family relationship and who is experiencing problems in school. Most research on delinquency is focused on males. Female delinquency is less prevalent than male delinquency but is characterized by a number of unique factors.

References

Adler, Freda. 1975. *Sisters in Crime*. NewYork: McGraw-Hill.
Agnew, Robert. 1991. "The Interactive Effects of Peer Variables on Delinquency." *Criminology* 29: 47–72.
Akers, Ronald L. 1985. *Deviant Behavior: A Social Learning Approach*, 3rd ed. Belmont, Calif.: Wadsworth Publishing.
Alfaro, J. D. 1981. "Report on the Relationship Between Child Abuse and Neglect and

Later Socially Deviant Behavior." In R. J. Hunter and Y. E. Walker, eds., *Exploring the Relationship Between Child Abuse and Delinquency*. Montclair, N.J.: Allanheld, Osmun.

Bartollas, Clemens. 1993. *Juvenile Delinquency*, 3rd ed. New York: Macmillan Publishing Co.

Bastian, Lisa D., and Bruce M. Taylor. 1991. *School Crime: A National Crime Victimization Survey Report*. Washington, D.C.: U.S. Department of Justice.

Bergsmann, Ilene R. 1989. "The Forgotten Few: Juvenile Female Offenders." *Federal Probation* 53:73–78.

Broadhurst. D. D. 1980. "The Effect of Child Abuse and Neglect in the School-Aged Child." In R. Volpe, M. Breton, and J. Mitton, eds., *The Maltreatment of the School-Aged Child*. Lexington, Mass.: D. C. Heath.

Bronfenbrenner, Urie. 1970. *Two Worlds of Childhood: U.S. and U.S.S.R.* New York: Russell Sage Foundation.

Burkett, Stephen R., and Bruce O. Warren. 1987, "Religiosity, Peer Associations, and Adolescent Marijuana Use: A Panel Study of Underlying Causal Structures." *Criminology* 25:109–125.

Campbell, Anne. 1990. "Female Participation in Gangs." In C. R. Huff, ed., *Gangs in America*. Newbury Park, Calif.: Sage.

Canter, Rachelle. 1982. "Sex Differences in Self-Report Delinquency." *Criminology* 20:373–393.

Cernkovich, Stephen, and Peggy Giordano. 1979. "A Comparative Analysis of Male and Female Delinquency." *Sociological Quarterly* 20:131–145.

Cernkovich, Stephen A., and Peggy C. Giordano. 1987. "Family Relationships and Delinquency." *Criminology* 25:295–321.

Chesney-Lind, Meda. 1995. "Girls, Delinquency, and Juvenile Justice: Toward a Feminist Theory of Young Women's Crime." In B. R. Price and N. Sokoloff, eds., *The Criminal Justice System and Women*. New York: McGraw-Hill.

Colvin, Mark, and John Pauly. 1983. "A Critique of Criminology: Toward an Integrated Structural-Marxist Theory of Delinquency Prevention." *American Journal of Sociology* 89:513–551.

Curry, G. David, Richard A. Ball, and Robert J. Fox. 1994. "Gang Crime and Law Enforcement Recordkeeping." *National Institute of Justice Research in Brief.* Washington, D.C.: U.S. Department of Justice.

Curry, G. David, and Irving A. Spergel. 1988. "Gang Homicide, Delinquency, and Community." *Criminology* 26:381–405.

Curtis, G. C. 1963. "Violence Breeds Violence—Perhaps?" *American Journal of Psychiatry* 120:386–387.

Datesman, Susan K., and Frank R. Scarpitti. 1975. "Female Delinquency and Broken Homes: A Re-Assessment." *Criminology* 13:33–55.

Dryfoos, Joy. 1990. *Adolescents at Risk*. New York: Oxford University Press.

Elliott, Delbert S., David Huizinga, and Suzanne E. Ageton. 1985. *Explaining Delinquency and Drug Use*. Beverly Hills, Calif.: Sage.

Esbensen, Finn-Aage. 1995. "The National Evaluation of the Gang Resistance and Education Training (G.R.E.A.T.) Program: An Overview." Paper presented at the Academy of Criminal Justice Sciences, Boston.

Esbensen, Finn-Aage, David Huizinga, and Anne W. Weiher. 1995. "Gang and Nongang Youth: Differences in Explanatory Factors." In M. W. Klein, C. L. Maxson, and J. Miller, eds., *The Modern Gang Reader*. Los Angeles: Roxbury Publishing Co.

Fagan, Jeffrey. 1990. "Social Processes of Delinquency and Drug Use." In C. R. Huff, ed., *Gangs in America*. Newbury Park, Calif.: Sage.

Fagan, Jeffrey. 1989. "The Social Organization of Drug Use and Drug Dealing Among Urban Gangs." Criminology 27:633–669.

Fagan, Jeffrey, Karen V. Hansen, and Martin Jang. 1983. "Profiles of Chronically Violent Delinquents: Empirical Test of an Integrated Theory." In J. Kleugel, ed., *Evaluating Juvenile Justice.* Beverly Hills, Calif.: Sage.

Fagan, Jeffrey, and Sandra Wexler. 1987. "Family Origins of Violent Delinquents." *Criminology* 25:643–669.

"Family Cohesiveness Is Needed" 1994. *Crime Prevention News* (No. 94–14, August 3): 12.

Federal Bureau of Investigation. 1995. *Crime in the United States, 1994.* Washington, D.C.: U.S. Department of Justice.

Fleisher, Mark. 1995. *Beggars and Thieves.* Madison: University of Wisconsin Press.

Gelles, Richard, and Murray Straus. 1988. *Intimate Violence.* New York: Simon & Schuster.

Giordano, Peggy. 1978. "Girls, Guys, and Gangs: The Changing Social Context of Female Delinquency." *Journal of Criminal Law and Criminology* 69 (1):126–232.

Giordano, Peggy C., Stephen A. Cernkovich, and M. D. Pugh. 1986. "Friendship and Delinquency." *American Journal of Sociology* 91(March):1170–1202.

Giordano, Peggy, and Stephen Cernkovich. 1979. "On Complicating the Relationship Between Liberation and Delinquency." *Social Problems* 26:467–481.

Glueck, Sheldon, and Eleanor Glueck. 1950. *Unraveling Juvenile Delinquency.* Cambridge, Mass.: Harvard University Press.

Gottfredson, Gary D. 1987. "Peer Group Interventions to Reduce the Risk of Delinquent Behavior: A Selective Review and a New Evaluation." *Criminology* 25:671–714.

Gove, Walter R., and Richard D. Crutchfield. 1982. "The Family and Juvenile Delinquency." *Sociological Quarterly* 23:301–319.

Gray, Ellen. 1988. "The Link Between Child Abuse and Juvenile Delinquency: What We Know and Recommendations for Policy and Research." In G. T. Hotaling, D. Finkelhor, J. T Kirkpatrick, and M. A. Straus, eds., *Family Abuse and Its Consequences.* Newbury Park, Calif.: Sage.

Greenberg, David. 1977. "Delinquency and the Age Structure of Society." *Contemporary Crises* 1:189–223.

Hagan, John, A. R. Gillis, and John Simpson. 1985. "The Class Structure of Gender and Delinquency: Toward a Power-control Theory of Common Delinquent Behavior." *American Journal of Sociology* 90(6):1151–1178.

Hagan, John, John Simpson, and A. R. Gillis. 1987. "Class in the Household: A Power-Control Theory of Gender and Delinquency." *American Journal of Sociology* 92(4):788–816.

Hawkins, J. D., R. F. Catalano, G. Jones, and D. Fine. 1987. "Delinquency Prevention Through Parent Training: Results and Issues from Work in Progress." In J. Q. Wilson and G. C. Loury, eds., *From Children to Citizens*, vol. 3: *Families, Schools, and Delinquency Prevention.* New York: Springer-Verlag.

Hawkins, J. D., and T. Lam. 1987. "Teacher Practices, Social Development and Delinquency." In J. D. Burchard and S. N. Burchard, eds., *Prevention of Delinquent Behavior.* Newbury Park, Calif.: Sage.

Helfer, R. E., and C. H. Kempe, eds. 1976. *Child Abuse and Neglect: The Family and the Community.* Cambridge, Mass.: Ballinger Publishing Co.

Hindelang, Michael J. 1973. "Causes of Delinquency: A Partial Replication and Extension." *Social Problems* 21:471–487.

Hirschi, Travis. 1969. *Causes of Delinquency.* Berkeley: University of California Press.

Hirschi, Travis. 1983. "Crime and the Family." In J. Q. Wilson, ed., *Crime and Public Policy.* San Francisco: ICS Press.

Horowitz, R. 1990. "Sociological Perspectives on Gangs: Conflicting Definitions and Concepts." In C. R. Huff, ed., *Gangs in America.* Newbury Park, Calif.: Sage.

Huff, C. Ronald. 1989. "Youth Gangs and Public Policy." *Crime and Delinquency* 35(4):524–537.

Johnson, Richard E. 1979. *Juvenile Delinquency and Its Origins*. Cambridge: Cambridge University Press.

Johnson, Richard E. 1986. "Family Structure and Delinquency: General Patterns and Gender Differences." *Criminology* 24:65–84.

Johnson, Richard E., Anastasio C. Marcos, and Stephen J. Bahr. 1987. "The Role of peers in the Complex Etiology of Adolescent Drug Use." *Criminology* 25:323–340.

Kempe, C. H., R. S. Kempe, F. N. Silverman, B. F. Steele, W. Droegemueller, and H. K. Silver. 1962. "The Battered-Child Syndrome." *Journal of the American Medical Association* 181:17–24.

Kempe, Ruth S., and C. Henry Kempe. 1978. *Child Abuse*. Cambridge, Mass.: Harvard University Press.

Konopka, Gisela. 1966. *The Adolescent Girls in Conflict*. Englewood Cliffs, N.J.: Prentice-Hall.

Kratcoski, Peter C. 1982. "Child Abuse and Violence Against the Family." *Child Welfare* 61:445–455.

Laub, J. H., and R. J. Sampson. 1988. "Unraveling Families and Delinquency: A Reanalysis of the Gluecks' Data." *Criminology* 26:355–379.

Lawrence, Richard. 1991. "School Performance, Peers, and Delinquency: Implications for Juvenile Justice." *Juvenile and Family Court Journal* 42(3):59–69.

Lincoln, Alan J., and Murray Straus. 1985. *Crime and the Family*. Springfield, Ill.: Charles C. Thomas.

Linden, Eric, and James C. Hackler. 1973. "Affective Ties and Delinquency." *Pacific Sociological Review* 16:27–46.

Lightfoot, Sara Lawrence. 1978. *Worlds Apart: Relationships Between Families and Schools*. New York: Basic Books.

Liska, Allen E., and Mark D. Reed. 1985. "Ties to Conventional Institutions and Delinquency: Estimating Reciprocal Effects." *American Sociological Review* 50:547–560.

Loeber, Rolf. 1988. *Crime File: Families and Crime*. Washington, D.C.: National Institute of Justice.

Loeber, Rolf, and Magda Stouthamer-Loeber. 1986. "Family Factors as Correlates and Predictors of Juvenile Conduct Problems and Delinquency." In M. Tonry and N. Morris, eds., *Crime and Justice: An Annual Review of Research*, vol. 7. Chicago: University of Chicago Press.

Lombroso, Cesare. 1920. *The Female Offender*. New York: Appleton.

Maeroff, Gene I. 1982. *Don't Blame the Kids*. New York: McGraw-Hill.

Matsueda, Ross L., and Karen Heimer. 1987. "Race, Family Structure, and Delinquency: A Test of Differential Association and Social Control Theories." *American Sociological Review* 52:826–840.

McCord, Joan. 1982. "A Longitudinal view of the Relationship Between Paternal Absence and Crime." In J. Gunn and D. P. Farrington, eds., *Abnormal Offenders, Delinquency, and the Criminal Justice System*. Chichester, UK: John Wiley.

Morash, Merry. 1986. "Gender, Peer Group Experiences, and Seriousness of Delinquency." *Journal of Research in Crime and Delinquency* 25:43–61.

Morash, Merry, and Meda Chesney-Lind. 1991. "A Reformulation and Partial Test of the Power Control Theory of Delinquency." *Justice Quarterly* 8:347–377.

National Center for Education Statistics. 1993. *National Household Education Survey*. Washington, D.C.: U.S. Department of Education.

National Center for Education Statistics. 1995. *Statistical Perspectives: Gangs and Victimization at School*. Washington, D.C.: U.S. Department of Education.

National Juvenile Justice Assessment Centers. 1981. *Juvenile Delinquency Prevention: A Compendium of Thirty-Six Program Models*. Washington, D.C.: U.S. Department of Justice.

Nye, F. Ivan. 1958. *Family Relationships and Delinquent Behavior*. New York: John Wiley.

Offord, David R. 1982. "Family Backgrounds of Male and Female Delinquents." In J.

Gunn and D. P. Farrington, eds., *Abnormal Offenders, Delinquency, and the Criminal Justice System*. Chichester, UK: John Wiley.

Patterson, Gerald R. 1986. "Performance Models for Antisocial Boys." *American Psychologist* 41:432–444.

Patterson, Gerald R., and Thomas J. Dishion. 1985. "Contributions of Families and Peers to Delinquency." *Criminology* 23:63–79.

Patterson, Gerald R., and Magda Stouthamer-Loeber. 1984. "The Correlation of Family Management Practices and Delinquency." *Child Development* 55:1299–1307.

Pollak, Otto. 1950. *The Criminality of Women*. Philadelphia: University of Pennsylvania Press.

Pope, Carl E. 1988. "The Family, Delinquency, and Crime." In E. W. Nunnally, C. S. Chilman, and F. M. Cox, eds., *Mental Illness, Delinquency, Addictions, and Neglect*. Newbury Park, Calif.: Sage.

Rankin, Joseph H. 1977. "The Family Context of Delinquency." *Social Problems* 30:466–479.

Rankin, Joseph H. 1980. "School Factors and Delinquency: Interactions by Age and Sex." *Sociology and Social Research* 64(3):420–434.

Rankin, Joseph H., and Roger Kern. 1994. "Parental Attachments and Delinquency." *Criminology* 32:495–515.

Regoli, Robert M., and John D. Hewitt. 1994. *Delinquency in Society*, 2nd ed. New York: McGraw-Hill.

Riesman, David. 1950. *The Lonely Crowd*. New Haven, Conn.: Yale University Press.

Rosen, Lawrence. 1985. "Family and Delinquency: Structure or Function." *Criminology* 23:553–573.

Rosenbaum, Jill L., and James R. Lasley. 1990. "School, Community Context, and Delinquency: Rethinking the Gender Gap." *Justice Quarterly* 7(3):493–513.

Schwendinger, Herman, and Julia Schwendinger. 1985. *Adolescent Subcultures and Delinquency*. New York: Praeger Publishers.

Siegel, Larry J., and Joseph J. Senna. 1991. *Juvenile Delinquency: Theory, Practice & Law*, 4th ed. St. Paul, Minn.: West Publishing Co.

Simon, Rita J. 1975. *Women and Crime*. Lexington, Mass.: D. C. Heath.

Simons, Ronald L., Les B. Whitbeck, Rand D. Conger, and Katherine J. Conger. 1991. "Parenting Factors, Social Skills, and Value Commitments as Precursors to School Failure, Involvement with Deviant Peers, and Delinquent Behavior." *Journal of Youth and Adolescence* 20:645–664.

Spergel, Irving, Ron Chance, Kenneth Ehrensaft, Thomas Regulus, Candice Kane, Robert Laseter, Alba Alexander, and Sandra Oh. 1994a. *Gang Suppression and Intervention: Community Models—Research Summary*. Washington, D.C.: Office of Juvenile Justice and Delinquency Prevention.

Spergel, Irving, David Curry, Ron Chance, Candice Kane, Ruth Ross, Alba Alexander, Edwina Simmons, and Sandra Oh. 1994b. *Gang Suppression and Intervention: Problem and Response: Research Summary*. Washington, D.C.: Office of Juvenile Justice and Delinquency Prevention.

Spivack, G., and N. Cianci. 1987. "High-Risk Early Behavior Pattern and Later Delinquency." In J. D. Burchard and S. N. Burchard, eds., *Prevention of Delinquent Behavior*. Newbury Park, Calif.: Sage.

Statistical Abstract of the United States, 1995. Washington, D.C.: U.S. Superintendent of Documents.

Steffensmeier, Darrell J. and Renee H. Steffensmeier. 1980. "Trends in Female Delinquency." *Criminology* 18(1):62–85.

Straus, Murray A., Richard J. Gelles, and Susanne K. Steinmetz. 1980. *Behind Closed Doors: Violence in the American Family*. Garden City, N.Y.: Anchor Press/ Doubleday.

Thornberry, Terence. 1987. "Toward an Interactional Theory of Delinquency." *Criminology* 25:863–891.

Thornberry, Terence B., Marvin D. Krohn, Alan J. Lizotte, and Denise Chard-Wierschem. 1993. "The Role of Juvenile Gangs in Facilitating Delinquent Behavior." *Journal of Research in Crime and Delinquency* 30(1):55–87.

Thomas, W. I. 1923. *The Unadjusted Girl.* New York: Harper.

Van Voorhis, Patricia, Frank T. Cullen, Richard A. Matthers, and C.Chenoweth Garner. 1988. "The Impact of Family Structure and Quality on Delinquency: A Comparative Assessment of Structural and Functional Factors." *Criminology* 26:235–261.

Wells, L. Edward, and Joseph H. Rankin. 1986. "The Broken Homes Model of Delinquency: Analytic Issues." *Journal of Research in Crime and Delinquency* 23:68–93.

Wells, L. Edward, and Joseph H. Rankin. 1988. "Direct Parental Controls and Delinquency." *Criminology* 26:263–285.

Wells, L. Edward, and Joseph H. Rankin. 1991. "Families and Delinquency: A Meta-Analysis of the Impact of Broken Homes." *Social Problems* 38:71–93.

Widom, Cathy Spatz. 1989a. "Child Abuse, Neglect, and Violent Criminal Behavior." *Criminology* 27:251–270.

Widom, Cathy Spatz. 1989b. "Does Violence Beget Violence? A Critical Examination of the Literature." *Psychological Bulletin* 106:3–28.

Wilkinson, Karen. 1974. "The Broken Family and Juvenile Delinquency: Scientific Explanation of Ideology." *Social Problems* 21:726–739.

Wilkinson, Karen. 1980. "The Broken Home and Delinquent Behavior: An Alternative Interpretation of Contradictory Findings." In T. Hirschi and M. Gottfredson, eds., *Understanding Crime: Current Theory and Research.* Beverly Hills, Calif.: Sage.

Wilson, James Q., and Glen C. Loury, eds. *From Children to Citizens*, vol. 3: *Families, Schools, and Delinquency Prevention.* New York: Springer-Verlag.

Winfree, L.Thomas, Finn-Aage Esbensen, and D.Wayne Osgood. 1995. "On Becoming a Youth Gang Member: Low Self-Control or Learned Behavior?" Paper presented at the Academy of Criminal Justice Sciences, Boston.

Wright, Kevin N., and Karen E. Wright. 1994. *Family Life, Delinquency, and Crime: A Policymaker's Guide.* Washington, D.C.: Office of Juvenile Justice and Delinquency Prevention.

Zigler, Edward, and Nancy W. Hall. 1987. "The Implications of Early Intervention Efforts for the Primary Prevention of Juvenile Delinquency." In J. Q. Wilson and G. C. Loury, eds., *From Children to Citizens*, vol. 3: *Families, Schools and Delinquency Prevention.* New York: Springer-Verlag.

Zingraff, Matthew T., and Michael J. Belyea. 1986. "Child Abuse and Violent Crime." In K. C. Haas and G. P. Alpert, eds., *The Dilemmas of Punishment.* Prospect Heights, Ill.: Waveland Press.

5

Absenteeism, Dropout, and Delinquency

I hated the school. It was overcrowded; teachers didn't care; students walked out and acted up and no one did anything to help the situation. I never knew who my counselor was, and he wasn't available to me. . . . I began spending my time sleeping in class or walking the halls. Finally, I decided to hang out on the streets. . . . That was it. End of school.—A New York student describing her dropout experience (Wehlage, 1986:20)

The school dropout rate in America has reached serious proportions. The problem is especially serious in inner-city urban schools, where as many as 50 to 70 percent of teenagers drop out of high school before graduating. Consider some of the available data on the problem:

- In 1992–93 about 382,000, or 4.2 percent, of all tenth-, eleventh-, or twelfth-grade students dropped out of high school.
- A total of 3.1 million (12.7 percent) of eighteen- to twenty-four-year olds (in 1993) were high school dropouts.
- Hispanics have the highest dropout rate (32.7 percent), and blacks have a slightly higher dropout rate than whites (16.4 vs. 12.2 percent).
- Youth in central cities drop out at a higher rate (14.9 percent) than youth in suburbs (11.0) or nonmetropolitan areas (13.1 percent) (Bruno and Adams, 1994: xiv–xv).

The dropout rate is as high as 80 percent in New York City, 50 percent in Los Angeles, and 70 percent in Chicago. The consequences of dropping out make this a national problem, not just a school problem. School dropout has an impact on unemployment, welfare, and crime.

Placed in historical perspective, the proportion of American youth who attend school and graduate is better than it was 100 years ago. Compulsory school attendance laws were introduced in state legislatures in the late nineteenth century, following the lead of Massachusetts in 1852. By 1890, twenty-seven states and territories required parents or guardians to send their children to school; by 1918, each legislature had enacted such a law (Rippa, 1980: 170). The age stipulations of early laws generally applied to children from eight to fourteen years, with some states extending the law to the age of sixteen. In some states children were allowed to leave school after completing a stated number of grades, regardless of their age. The majority of youth at the turn of the century were leaving school after age 16 and not completing high school. In advocating for more vocational training in public schools, the National Association of Manufacturers complained that 60 to 65 percent of students in 1914 had dropped out by the end of the fifth or sixth grade, with no vocational preparation or working skills (Rippa, 1980: 159).

Even though fewer youth drop out of school today and a greater percentage graduate from high school, concern about the dropout problem persists. Several explanations have been suggested for this increased concern:

1. Although the dropout rate has declined over the long term, dropout rates for recent years have remained steady and even increased, especially for some groups.
2. Minority populations, who have always had higher dropout rates than the white population, are increasing in public schools.
3. Many states have recently passed legislation to raise academic course requirements for graduation, to motivate students and improve performance, but the higher standard may push some students to drop out.
4. There is a widespread belief that the education required to obtain employment will increase in the future, leaving dropouts even more disadvantaged in the job market.
5. There is increased political pressure on schools, since state and federal education officials have begun to judge schools' performance by a series of "indicators," such as dropout rates and test scores (Rumberger, 1987: 101–102).

Studying the dropout problem is complicated by the absence of a uniform definition of dropout and of a standard system for measuring the extent of the problem. In this chapter we examine the extent of dropout and the factors associated with it and then explore the relationship between dropout and delinquency. Research evidence shows a correlation between the two, but researchers disagree whether dropout causes delinquency or delinquency causes dropout. Finally, we examine the consequences of dropping out of school and programs designed to reduce the dropout rate in American schools.

Problems of Defining and Measuring Dropout

There is no standard definition of who is a dropout, and there are at least two methods of measuring the dropout rate. Defining a dropout necessarily involves a time dimension. A student who stops attending school for a time but returns later is not considered a dropout. Some students leave school and return again. Some of those who return may stay and earn a high school diploma. Some who do not return may later complete an equivalency diploma. Thus national data sources variously report a dropout rate, a graduation rate, or a completion rate (see Pallas, 1987). They are not the same. The two major national sources of dropout statistics are compiled by the U.S. Census Bureau and the U.S. Department of Education. The methods of computing these statistics differ, so the reported dropout rates are also different, but the two sources may represent the lower and upper limits of the true rate of dropout in America.

Census Bureau Dropout Rates

The Census Bureau surveys a sample of about 60,000 households each month, representing about 150,000 persons. A School Enrollment Supplement in October each year collects data on the highest grade of school completed, current enrollment status, whether that grade was completed, and, for high school graduates ages 14–34, the year they graduated. Thus, the Bureau reports a high school *completion rate*. The sampling method used by the Bureau is considered very good, but the data are subject to some sampling error (about 1 to 2 percent). Table 5–1 reports the dropout rates by sex, race, and ethnicity for selected years.

During the one-year period from October 1992 to October 1993, about 382,000, or 4.2 percent, of all students in the tenth, eleventh, or twelfth grade dropped out of high school (Bruno and Adams, 1994: xiv). This overall dropout rate is lower than the rate of 5.2 percent reported ten years earlier, in 1983, but there have not been significant changes in recent years. There is consider-

Table 5–1
Dropout Rates by Sex, Race & Ethnicity for Selected Years, 1970–1993[a]

Group	(Percentages)					
	1970	*1975*	*1980*	*1985*	*1992*	*1993*
Total	5.7	5.8	6.0	5.2	4.3	4.2
All males	5.6	5.4	6.6	5.4	3.8	4.4
All females	5.9	6.2	5.4	5.0	4.8	4.1
White males	4.7	5.0	6.4	4.9	3.8	4.1
White females	5.3	5.8	4.9	4.7	4.4	4.1
Black males	12.6	8.3	8.0	8.3	3.3	5.7
Black females	9.9	9.0	8.5	7.2	6.7	5.0
Hispanic males	11.1[b]	10.1	16.9	9.3	5.8	4.8
Hispanic females	10.9[b]	11.6	6.9	9.8	8.6	7.7

[a]Dropout rates represent the percent of each group who are dropouts. Dropouts are defined as persons who are not enrolled in school in October of each given year and have not received a high school diploma or an equivalent high school certificate.   [b]1972 is the first year available for Hispanic students.

Sources: R. Kominski and A. Adams. (1993). "School Enrollment—Social and Economic Characteristics of Students: October 1992." Washington, D.C.: Bureau of the Census; R. Bruno and A. Adams. 1994. "School Enrollment—Social and Economic Characteristics of Students: October 1993." Washington, D.C.: Bureau of the Census.

able variation among student groups when comparing gender and race or ethnicity, as noted in the table. Dropout rates also differ significantly among students from different family income levels. Youth from families with income of less than $20,000 per year have a dropout rate of 7.5 percent; those from families who earn between $20,000 and $39,000 had a 3.5 percent rate; while the dropout rate of youth from families making $40,000 or more was only 1.5 percent (Bruno and Adams, 1993: xv; see also McMillen, Kaufman and Whitener, 1994).

Education Department Dropout Statistics

The National Center for Education Statistics (NCES) reports a variety of annual data on schools. It has the advantage over the Census data in that the dropout statistics are from all state education agencies. The Center collects data on enrollments by grade and on the number of high school graduates. The limitation of the data is that only public schools are included. The data reported are for only regular day school graduates; general equivalency diplomas (G.E.D.) or other nonregular day school credentials are excluded. Table 5–2 reports the graduation rates by states, for selected years.

Table 5–2
Graduation Rates by States[a]

	(Percentages)					
	1982	*1984*	*1985*	*1986*	*1987*	*1988*
Alabama	63.4	62.1	63.0	67.3	70.2	74.9
Alaska	64.3	74.7	67.1	68.3	66.7	65.5
Arizona	63.4	64.6	64.5	63.0	64.4	61.1
Arkansas	73.4	75.2	75.7	78.0	77.5	77.2
California	60.1	63.2	65.8	66.7	66.1	65.9
Colorado	70.9	75.4	72.2	73.1	73.7	74.7
Connecticut	70.6	79.1	80.4	89.8	80.5	84.9
Delaware	74.7	71.1	69.9	70.7	70.1	71.7
District of Columbia	56.9	55.2	54.8	56.8	55.5	58.2
Florida	60.2	62.2	61.2	62.0	58.6	58.0
Georgia	65.0	63.1	62.6	62.7	62.5	61.0
Hawaii	74.9	73.2	73.8	70.8	70.8	69.1
Idaho	74.4	75.8	76.7	79.0	78.8	75.4
Illinois	76.1	74.5	74.0	75.8	75.7	75.6
Indiana	71.7	77.0	76.4	75.2	73.7	76.3
Iowa	84.1	86.0	86.5	87.5	86.4	85.8
Kansas	80.7	81.7	81.4	81.5	82.1	80.2
Kentucky	65.9	68.4	68.2	68.6	67.4	69.0
Louisiana	61.5	56.7	54.7	61.8	60.1	61.4
Maine	72.1	77.2	78.6	76.5	79.3	74.4
Maryland	74.8	77.8	77.7	76.6	74.5	74.1
Massachusetts	76.4	74.3	76.3	76.7	76.5	74.4

Table 5–2 continued

	(Percentages)					
	1982	*1984*	*1985*	*1986*	*1987*	*1988*
Michigan	71.6	72.2	71.9	67.8	62.4	73.6
Minnesota	88.2	89.3	90.6	91.4	90.6	90.9
Mississippi	61.3	62.4	61.8	63.3	64.8	66.9
Missouri	74.2	76.2	76.1	75.6	74.4	74.0
Montana	78.7	82.1	82.9	87.2	86.2	87.3
Nebraska	81.9	86.3	86.9	88.1	86.7	85.4
Nevada	64.8	66.5	63.9	73.1	72.1	75.8
New Hampshire	77.0	75.2	75.2	73.3	72.7	74.1
New Jersey	76.5	77.7	77.3	77.6	77.2	77.4
New Mexico	69.4	71.0	71.9	72.3	71.7	71.9
New York	63.4	62.2	62.7	64.2	62.9	62.3
North Carolina	67.1	69.3	70.3	70.0	67.8	66.7
North Dakota	83.9	86.3	86.1	89.7	88.4	88.3
Ohio	77.5	80.0	76.1	80.4	82.8	79.6
Oklahoma	70.8	73.1	71.1	71.6	72.6	71.7
Oregon	72.4	73.9	72.7	74.1	72.8	73.0
Pennsylvania	76.0	77.2	77.7	78.5	78.8	78.4
Rhode Island	72.7	68.7	71.3	67.3	69.4	69.8
South Carolina	62.6	64.5	62.4	64.5	66.9	64.6
South Dakota	82.7	85.5	85.1	81.5	79.7	79.6
Tennessee	67.8	70.5	64.1	67.4	67.8	69.3
Texas	63.6	64.6	63.2	64.3	65.1	65.3
Utah	75.0	78.7	75.9	80.3	80.6	79.4
Vermont	79.6	83.1	83.4	77.6	78.0	78.7
Virginia	73.8	74.7	73.7	73.9	74.0	71.6
Washington	76.1	75.1	74.9	75.2	76.2	77.1
West Virginia	66.3	73.1	72.8	75.2	76.2	77.3
Wisconsin	83.1	84.5	84.0	86.3	85.4	84.9
Wyoming	72.4	76.0	74.3	81.2	89.3	88.3
U.S. average	69.7	70.9	70.6	71.6	71.1	71.2

[a] Graduation rates are for public schools only because data on private high school graduates were not available by state. The adjusted graduation rate was calculated by dividing the number of public high school graduates by the public ninth-grade enrollment four years earlier. Ninth-grade enrollments include a pro-rated portion of the secondary school students who were unclassified by grade. Graduation rates were also corrected for interstate population migration. Information on the number of persons of graduating age receiving G.E.D.s is not currently available.

Sources: U.S. Department of Education, Office of Planning, Budget, and Evaluation, and National Center for Education Statistics, *State Education Statistics: Student Performance, Resource Inputs, and Population.* 1986, 1987, 1989, 1990.

The Extent of Absenteeism and Dropout

Data compiled by the Census Bureau (as reported in Table 5–1) show no significant increases in the overall dropout rate from 1970 to 1993, though there have been some short-term increases among some groups and during some years. The eight-year period from 1985 to 1993 shows some significant decreases in the dropout rates for black and Hispanic students (though there was an increase from 1992–93 for black males). State-level data reported in Table 5–2 show that attrition rates decreased slightly in most states between 1982 and 1988, but there is considerable variation among states.

Variations Among Social Groups and Schools

Dropout rates are higher for some groups than for others. Students from lower socioeconomic levels and from racial and ethnic minorities and boys tend to have a higher dropout rate. The 1980 "High School and Beyond" study conducted by the National Center for Education Statistics surveyed 30,000 sophomores from more than 1,000 public and private high schools, representing 3.8 million sophomores enrolled throughout the United States. The survey reported a total dropout rate of 13.6 percent, but the rates varied from 12.2 percent for whites to 18.7 percent for Hispanics, from 12.6 percent for women to 14.6 percent for men, and from 8.9 percent for students from the highest socioeconomic levels to 22.3 percent for students from the lowest socioeconomic levels (Rumberger, 1987: 108).

Census data also show variations among social groups. Dropout rates for eighteen- and nineteen-year-olds declined from 23.8 percent in 1968 to 19.7 percent in 1984 for black males, from 24.7 percent to 14.5 percent for black females, and from 14.6 percent to 14.0 percent for white females. For white males, the dropout rate increased from 14.3 percent in 1968 to 17.9 percent in 1981, then declined to 15.8 percent in 1984. Dropout rates for Hispanics have changed little, except for a decline from 35.5 percent in 1972 to 26.2 percent in 1984 for Hispanic males ages 18 to 19 (Rumberger, 1987: 108).

Dropout rates vary as much among school systems as they do among social groups. There are differences among state educational systems, but there are also considerable differences among districts and even among schools within the same district.

Factors Associated with Dropping Out

Research studies have identified several factors associated with dropping out of school, the most prominent of which are demographic factors, family and parent factors, peer factors, school-related factors, economic factors, and individual factors (see Drennon-Gala, 1995; Dunham and Alpert, 1987; Ekstrom et al., 1986; Rumberger, 1983; and Rumberger, 1987).

Demographic Factors

Members of racial and ethnic minorities are more likely to drop out than white students, and females drop out at a slightly higher rate than males. It is not that racial or ethnic minorities are inherently likely to drop out, but these groups tend to be characterized by more of the other social factors associated with dropping out.

Family Background and Structure

Parental and family support and influence are important in determining whether a young person stays in school. Students from families of low socioeconomic status have higher dropout rates. Other parent- and family-related factors include:

- Single-parent families
- Low educational and occupation levels of parents
- Absence of learning materials and opportunities in the home
- Absence of parental supervision and monitoring
- Fewer opportunities for nonschool-related learning
- Mothers with lower levels of formal education
- Mothers with lower education expectations for their children
- Use of a language other than English in the home (Ekstrom et al., 1986: 359–360; Rumberger, 1987: 109–111)

Influence of Peers

Many students remain in school because they are encouraged to do so by their peers, and some drop out for the same reason. Many dropouts have friends who have also dropped out, but it is difficult to determine how much influence these friends have had on their decision to leave school. Dropouts often feel alienated from school life, and they tend to have friends who have lower educational aspirations and also feel alienated from school. It is not clear whether the friends influenced the decision to drop out or whether these friendships developed after the student dropped out, through associations outside school and as a means of social support.

School-Related Factors

Many students who drop out have performed poorly in school as measured by grades, test scores, and grade retention. Behavior problems in school, absenteeism, truancy, and a record of frequent disciplinary actions are also associated with dropping out. School misbehavior is a factor in dropout and is interrelated with students' school performance, whether they like school and are involved in activities, or whether they feel alienated from school. Behavior problems are closely associated with a pattern of absenteeism and truancy, which often culminates in dropping out.

Research on dropout has focused more on students' behavior and academic performance than on school structure, discipline policies, and teaching quality. School-related factors deserve more attention because many of them can be changed by improved school policies and practices. There are a number of measures that can be taken to prevent student misbehavior and increase the level of involvement of at-risk students in school. School safety, school discipline, grading policies, amount of homework assigned, and degree of student support are factors that affect the dropout rate (Toles, Schulz, and Rice, 1986). Many dropouts have left schools with poor facilities and inadequate teaching staffs, suggesting that the lack of resources has affected their performance and their decision to drop out (Fine, 1986). One student from New York described her experiences leading to dropping out:

> I hated the school. It was overcrowded; teachers didn't care; students walked out and acted up and no one did anything to help the situation. I never knew who my counselor was, and he wasn't available to me. . . . I began spending my time sleeping in class or walking the halls. Finally, I decided to hang out on the streets. . . . That was it. End of school. (Wehlage, 1986: 20)

The inability of school personnel to give more time and attention to students who are at risk of dropping out often results in failure and frustration for these students. Dropping out is a way of avoiding negative school experiences for them.

Economic Factors

About 20 percent of dropouts report that they left school because of financial difficulties and they felt that they had to work to help out their families (Rumberger, 1983: 201). It is not clear whether financial necessity really precipitated dropping out, whether they decided to work after already dropping out, or whether the pressures of working and attending school at the same time led to their dropping out. Students from lower socioeconomic backgrounds have a much higher dropout rate, and the combination of difficulties faced by lower-income families places more pressure on these youth. Mann (1987) cites studies showing that work-related reasons are cited by 21 percent of boys and 9 percent of girls who drop out. Paid employment poses a tough choice for students already at risk and frustrated with school. Working up to fourteen hours a week has little effect on schoolwork, but working fifteen to twenty-one hours a week depletes a student's time and energy and increases the dropout rate by 50 percent (Mann, 1987: 6).

Individual Factors

How students feel about themselves and whether they like school are shaped by many of the factors we have discussed. Students who stay in school generally have support and motivation from their parents and positive influence from peers, and their school performance and involvement is satisfying to them. Dropouts tend to have lower self-esteem and less sense of control over their lives than do other students. They have poor attitudes about school and low educational and occupational aspirations (see Ekstrom et al., 1986; Rumberger, 1987; Dunham and Alpert, 1987; and Wehlage and Rutter, 1986). Many students who eventually drop out see school classes as having little or no relevance for their future or for their success in life. Vocational education programs might help to retain many of these marginal students, but such programs are not available to many students who could most benefit from them. Many girls drop out because they are pregnant; some boys and girls leave school to get married; and others report dropping out because they had to help support their family (Rumberger, 1987: 110; Ekstrom et al., 1986: 363).

Consequences of Dropping Out

We have generally assumed that dropping out of school is always bad for young people and for society. High school graduation is seen as a minimal educational requirement today for entry into most jobs. A diploma is a symbol of a young person's academic success and his or her ability to meet the expectations of the workplace. There are exceptions, however. Many high school graduates have verbal and quantitative skills far below the national average and are poorly equipped for success in the workplace. Some dropouts, on the other hand, may show improvements in self-esteem and take more initiative to prove themselves in the workplace—*if* they can get a job without a high school diploma. Many dropouts later return to special classes to receive a G.E.D.

On the whole, however, the preponderance of evidence indicates that dropping out has negative consequences for the student and for society. Despite recent criticism of the quality of public school education, schools do make a difference in students' cognitive development (Alexander et al., 1985). Graduates overall are able to secure more steady jobs at better pay. Census data show that, compared to high school graduates, dropouts have significantly higher unemployment rates and lower annual earnings; this is true even when researchers control for gender and racial or ethnic group (Current Population Reports, 1984; see Rumberger, 1987: 113–114). There are individual consequences of dropping out beyond the employment and economic factors. Rumberger (1987) suggests that dropping out of school may lead to poor mental and physical health through its effects on employment and income; he cites a study that found that increased unemployment was associated with increases in total mortality, suicides, and admissions to state mental hospitals (1987: 113).

The dropout problem has social consequences beyond those that affect the individual dropout. Seven social consequences of the failure to complete high school have been identified:

1. Forgone national income
2. Forgone tax revenues for the support of government services
3. Increased demand for social services
4. Increased crime
5. Reduced political participation
6. Reduced intergenerational mobility
7. Poorer levels of health (Levin, 1972: 41–48)

As they encounter more unemployment and more financial difficulties, high school dropouts are likely to need more social services such as welfare, unemployment, and medical assistance. Unemployment and financial pressures also increase the temptation to engage in shoplifting, petty theft, and more serious criminal behavior. Since analysts predict little or no improvement in the unemployment rate and increased emphasis on education and job skills, it is likely that the social consequences of dropping out will be even greater in the future.

Delinquency and Dropout

Research during the past twenty years on the relationship between delinquency and dropout has yielded contradictory results. Historically there was nothing about leaving school before graduation that would suggest any relation to crime or deviant behavior. During the first part of this century many young people left school early, got a job, got married, and raised a family. The demands for educated and skilled workers today make that pattern quite impossible, however, and a high school diploma is a necessity to compete in the job market. Yet, not having a high school diploma does not necessarily mean a person is on the road to delinquency.

For decades many observers have believed there is a connection between dropping out of school and social problems, including unemployment and delinquency. This belief was not based on documented research, but it was assumed that dropping out of school led to unemployment, which in turn led to delinquency. The Committee on the Judiciary of the United States Senate in 1957 assumed a causal relationship in describing the dropout child as becoming a delinquent when jobs are not available: "Many of these children [school dropouts] are potential delinquents who receive little in the way of special services needed to solve the problems which caused them to drop out of school" (U.S. Senate, 1957: 8). The relationship between dropout and delinquency is not as straightforward or inevitable as some might suggest, however. Considerable research has been directed at examining the connection between dropping out of school and engaging in delinquent behavior.

Theoretical Explanations

Strain theory and control theory offer the most complete explanations of delinquency and dropout (see Chapter 3 for a more complete discussion of theoretical explanations of school problems and delinquency). *Strain theory* explains delinquency as a response to the frustrations or "strains" of school experiences. Cohen (1955) noted the frustration of working-class youths who try to meet middle-class school standards; Cloward and Ohlin (1960) held that the frustration was due to a lack of equal opportunities to attain educational and occupational goals; and Elliott and Voss (1974) posited that dropping out occurred after school failure led to alienation from school and association with other dropouts. Recent studies support strain theory in explaining school dropout. Agnew (1985) suggests that students who drop out often experience worse relationships with their parents, which may add to the likelihood of delinquency, and Farnworth and Leiber (1989) cite evidence that youths who want good, high-paying jobs but are unlikely to complete the college education required may become involved in delinquent behavior.

Social control theorists emphasize those factors that help youth avoid delinquent involvement. Hirschi (1969) maintains that delinquency takes place when young people's bonds to conventional society are weak. Youth who are attached to conventional social institutions (of which school is one of the most important) and to nondelinquent peers are less likely to become delinquent. Thus, youth who believe school has positive benefits for them, who have high educational aspirations and are involved in school, are less likely to be involved in delinquent behavior.

A number of studies have examined the relationship between delinquency and dropout. The major research questions examined are whether delinquency increases or decreases following dropout and what variables best explain dropout and delinquency.

Studies on Dropout and Delinquency

Elliott and Voss (1974) hypothesized that delinquent behavior occurs more frequently while youth are in school and declines after they drop out. The theoretical framework guiding their research was the strain theory of Cloward and Ohlin, that delinquency is a response to the frustration of limited opportunities to attain desired goals:

> Viewing delinquency and dropout as alternative responses to the strains generated by failure to achieve valued goals, we hypothesize that dropout is precipitated by aspiration-opportunity disjunctions. . . . While failure to achieve any one of these goals may be conducive to dropout, we hypothesize that dropout is primarily a response to school failure. Specifically, it is failure to achieve the goals of the youth culture, rather than academic goals, that motivtes most capable dropouts to leave school. (Elliott and Voss, 1974: 27)

They conducted a longitudinal study of 2,617 students from eight schools in California and compared rates of police contacts and self-reported delinquency for high school graduates and dropouts. Delinquency rates for the dropouts were higher and increased more while they were in school than did those for high school graduates. After the students dropped out, the rates of delinquency declined. The decrease in delinquency following dropout occurred regardless of the age of the student at the time of dropout and could not be explained by class or gender differences.

> [D]ropouts consistently have higher police contact rates than graduates for every period they are in school. . . . The dropouts reach a high level of involvement in delinquency prior to leaving school, but once they are out of school, their involvement in serious offenses declines substantially, and the total number of offenses reported declines slightly. (Elliott and Voss, 1974: 128)

Elliott and Voss conclude that their findings support the strain theory explanation that delinquency is a response to the frustration of negative school experiences and that dropping out therefore diminishes both the frustration of school and involvement in delinquency. This first major study on dropout and delinquency provoked considerable attention, and the findings raised policy questions about the wisdom of compulsory school attendance, especially for youth age 16 or older who were failing and exhibiting problem behavior in the school and the community. A weakness of the study that raises questions about the findings, however, was the failure to control for the influence of age. Previous research indicates that delinquent behavior tends to decline as persons get older, and this might explain the decline in delinquency among the sixteen- to eighteen-year-old dropouts.

Thornberry, Moore, and Christenson (1985) sought to replicate the Elliott and Voss research design to determine whether delinquency declined after dropout (strain theory) or increased after dropping out (control theory). They analyzed longitudinal data from a 10 percent sample (N = 975) of the Philadelphia birth cohort of 1945 (males born that year who lived in Philadelphia from ages 10 to 18) (see Wolfgang et al., 1972). In addition to reviewing arrest histories, they interviewed 567 (62%) of the sample. Youth who dropped out at sixteen and eighteen years of age had significantly more arrests following dropout than they had during the previous year, while they were still in school. There was a slight decrease in arrests (22%) for those who dropped out at seventeen, much less than the 55 percent decrease for all graduates.

> [R]esults of this analysis offer little support for a strain model interpretation of the association between dropping out of high school and subsequent criminal involvement; dropouts exhibit neither a short-term nor long-term reduction in criminal activity. These results are . . . quite consistent with a control perspective. (Thornberry et al., 1985: 12).

Their analyses also indicated that criminal involvement declines with youth in their early twenties, for both graduates and dropouts. Even when controlling for age, however, their results indicated that dropping out was positively associated with later criminal behavior. Thornberry et al. also controlled for social status, race, marriage, and employment and found that these variables made no difference in their finding that dropout status does have a positive impact on criminal involvement. Farrington and his associates (1986) extended the analysis of dropout, unemployment, and delinquency and found some association with criminal involvement after school dropout if youth were unemployed. Youth who stayed in school committed fewer offenses, and the research suggests that unemployment may be a more important factor in crime than school dropout. Hartnagel and Krahn suggested that unemployment and dropout may lead to criminal behavior because youth do not have enough money to buy what they need or want.

> Increased involvement in deviant behavior for unemployed dropout males may thus be a normal part of a somewhat marginalized world . . . where social controls of a job are absent, where peer group influences are strong, and where free time and boredom combine to increase the opportunities for and temptations to engage in deviant behavior. (Hartnagel and Krahn, 1989: 440)

Fagan and Pabon (1990) administered surveys to a sample of 2,467 high school students and dropouts from inner-city metropolitan areas in the East and the South and on the West Coast. Comparisons of the findings showed that delinquency and substance use were more frequent and serious among the school dropouts; but the authors could not establish a causal relationship linking substance use, delinquent involvement, and school dropout from this cross-sectional designed study.

Jarjoura (1993) analyzed data from the 1979 and 1980 National Longitudinal Survey of Youth to study delinquency and dropout. He controlled for previous offending of dropouts, which was not accounted for in the Thornberry et al. study. Previous delinquency involvement is important to consider in analyses, since dropouts have higher rates of such activity than those who graduate, and involvement often predicts dropping out. Besides controlling for gender, race, and age, Jarjoura included prior misconduct, school experiences, and performance as control variables. He found that those who dropped out because they disliked school and those who were expelled for school misconduct had the highest probabilities of involvement in theft and drugs sales after dropping out. Dropping out for personal reasons such as marriage or pregnancy had no effect on later involvement in drugs or theft but was significantly related to future violent behavior. Jarjoura suggested that this most unexpected finding of the study may be due to an aversive home environment; the violence may often be directed at a spouse or child. While youth who were expelled reported more involvement in delinquent behavior than graduates, Jarjoura found that the differences in later criminal behavior were explained by prior misconduct, not by dropping out. He noted that

> while dropouts were more likely to have higher levels of involvement in delinquency than graduates, it was not always because they dropped out. . . . In fact, if the analysis is carried out with all dropouts considered together as a group, results . . . would suggest that dropouts are not more likely to engage in delinquency as a result of leaving school early. . . . More is learned about the dropout-delinquency relationship by considering the differences based on reasons for leaving. (Jarjoura, 1993: 167–168).

This most recent major research study on dropout and delinquency is significant because it reveals more about the causes and effects, but also the complexities, of the relationship between them. As Jarjoura notes, no criminological theories to date provide an adequate explanation of dropout and delinquency. Until we understand the dropout-delinquency relationship more completely, it is unlikely that prevention programs for either of them will be effective.

Policy Implications of Delinquency and Dropout

Although there is not total agreement on the exact nature of the causal relationship between delinquency and dropout, it is clear that the two are associated. Researchers, school officials, and juvenile justice authorities have been concerned about how to select the most appropriate policies to prevent school dropout and delinquency. Dropping out of school before graduation by itself has undeniable serious consequences for the individual and for society. To the extent that dropping out is either a cause or a consequence of delinquency, the problem is further magnified. Any efforts to encourage at-risk students to stay in school through graduation that would also reduce misconduct and delinquent behavior would surely be welcomed. Four policies have been at the center of discussions concerning school dropout and delinquency: compulsory school attendance laws; school policies and "pushouts"; expulsion of disruptive students; and school reforms that raise academic requirements.

Compulsory School Attendance

There is no question that compulsory school attendance laws have been beneficial to individuals and to society in encouraging most young people to obtain a high school diploma. Many youth who dislike school and see little value in a high school education have been deterred from dropping out; only afterwards do they realize the value of their education. Retaining youth who are frustrated by their school experiences to the point of disruption and delinquency has been questioned by some, however. The presence of disruptive youth adversely affects the learning environment for students who want to learn and complete school. Worse, it may increase the probability of delinquency. Elliott and Voss (1974) questioned attempts to raise the age of compulsory attendance and efforts by probation officers and court officials to encourage delinquent dropouts to return to school. Juvenile probation requirements to attend school are based on the assumption that the school functions as a positive form of social control and assists youth in adjusting to life. The findings of Elliott and Voss are at odds with this thinking and suggest that school often aggravates the problems of some students rather than alleviating them: "Compulsory school attendance facilitates delinquency by forcing youth to remain in what is sometimes a frustrating situation in which they are stigmatized as failures. It is not surprising that these youth, trapped in our schools, rebel or attempt to escape" (Elliott and Voss, 1974: 207). The authors do not suggest that all students who are frustrated by experiences in school be encouraged to drop out, but they do maintain that the law should not restrict dropping out in cases where leaving may be the most appropriate alternative. The preferable strategy is one that would change the school structure, creating new learning environments in which competition is minimized and failure is reduced.

Jackson Toby has noted that a major factor making schools less orderly is the pressure to keep children in school longer. While acknowledging that rising educational levels is a positive side of this trend, he has maintained that compulsory attendance laws have resulted in retaining disruptive students who do not want to be in school: "The negative aspect of compulsory-school-attendance laws and of informal pressure to stay in school longer was that youngsters who didn't wish further education were compelled to remain in school. They were, in a sense, prisoners; . . . some of them became troublemakers (Toby, 1980: 29). He has suggested that compulsory school attendance laws be changed so that only younger students are required to attend. This would allow students who do not want to stay in school to drop out and would presumably diminish the extent of disruptive and violent behavior of youth who do not want to be in school. There is no denying that misbehavior and threats of violence from a small number of students create a serious disruption in schools. Allowing students simply to leave school does present a dilemma, however. While it alleviates the school problem, it creates a continuing problem for society, in terms of unemployment, loitering, and troublemaking in communities. The dilemma also raises the question of how far the school is expected to extend its educational function. Schools should be expected to create a positive learning environment that attempts to retain at-risk students who experience failure and frustration. But schools have limits in their ability to deal with disruptive and violent youth. Toby has suggested that one reason schools have become less orderly is "the decreased ability of schools to get help with discipline problems from the juvenile courts" (Toby, 1980: 30; see also Toby, 1994). School truancy and ungovernable behavior are no longer sufficient grounds for court action and incarceration in most states. Adjudicated juveniles on probation in the community are generally required to attend school and to obey school rules and regulations. Very few students are on probation, however, so tougher enforcement of probation rules is unlikely to make much difference in the extent of school disruption and crime.

School Policies and "Pushouts"

School structure, rules, or policies often result in students leaving school: "[T]he way young people experience school is the most frequently cited reason for quitting early. But what does that mean? Children who failed to learn? Or schools that failed to teach? The first are called 'dropouts,' the second are called 'pushouts' (Mann, 1987: 5).

Elliott and Voss found that a sizable proportion of students left school out of frustration after they were denied access to regular school programs.

> Since approximately one-fifth of the dropouts were pushed out of school, the phenomenon of dropout cannot be viewed strictly in terms of personal decisions on the part of youth to terminate their education. Although a substantial number of dropouts were in fact pushouts, formal expulsion was rare. Pushout resulted from the enforcement of rules prohibiting pregnant girls, married students, and troublesome 18-year-old students from attending the regular day-school program. (Elliott and Voss, 1974: 205–206).

Few of the students in their sample dropped out to go to work, and there was little evidence that dropouts rejected the benefits of a high school diploma. They suggest that restrictive school policies and the failure to accommodate all students amount to a practice of pushing some students out of school.

Mann notes that students blame the school less for their failures than might be expected. The reason given for dropping out by one-third of boys was "because I had bad grades" or "because I did not like school," while only 13 percent were expelled. "The figures underestimate the institution's willful decision not to teach all children. Referrals to special education have become a common way to solve class control problems by pushing some youth out of the mainstream" (Mann, 1987: 5). Mann acknowledges that to say schools push out some students is a harsh statement of the responsibilities and difficult decisions schools must make. If every student is given a diploma, such as with social promotion, schools will inevitably be criticized by employers and parents for not fulfilling their educational responsibilities. Maintaining minimum standards is more likely to preserve the significance of the high school diploma, but it will mean that some students may be "pushed out."

Expulsion of Disruptive Students

The most severe sanction available to the schools for dealing with disruptive students is expulsion. Few question its appropriateness for students with a history of violent behavior or for those who continue to engage in disruptive and delinquent behavior after school officials have resorted to suspensions and other sanctions short of expulsion. Toby suggests that public schools should be allowed to use expulsion more freely, especially with the small percentage of violent students who have proved that they cannot be controlled by anyone. Curtailing these students' rights to an education is justified when their behavior interferes with the rights of the majority of students to a safe educational environment.

> Expulsion is a drastic remedy. Though home instruction and alternative schools will be available for expelled students, the likelihood is that expelled students will not make much further academic progress. That is sad. Nevertheless, society must be permitted to give up on students who are threatening the educational opportunities of their classmates. (Toby, 1980: 38)

Toby's suggestions would surely help rid schools of the most troublesome students. Changing compulsory school attendance laws to apply only to younger students and allowing school officials to expell disruptive students would alleviate many school problems. Some researchers disagree with Toby on his suggested policy changes regarding compulsory attendance and expulsion, however. Gary and Denise Gottfredson (1985) express concern that such policy reforms lead in the wrong direction and do not address the fundamental problems of schools. The findings of their reanalysis of the "Violent Schools—Safe Schools Study" indicate that school disorder tends to be greatest in schools that serve communities characterized by social disorganization and largely minority populations. They are concerned that lowering the age of compulsory school attendance and expelling more disruptive students would only compound the problem of educational inequality facing minority groups and perpetuate social disorganization in their communities.

There is reason to question any drastic revisions in existing compulsory school attendance laws and expulsion policies. School failure and misconduct often result from youths' lack of attachment to school and lack of parental support for education, both of which are more common among parents who have attained less education. Parents with less education, who are disproportionately poor and minorities, often fail to support wholeheartedly their children's educational performance and may not offer enough support for school officials in attendance and conduct problems. In responding to Toby's suggestions, Wilson raises similar concerns: "Unteachable youths, or at least youths who are unteachable given the realities of most public school systems, are kept in school by a combination of compulsory attendance laws, welfare regulations, and minimum wage laws" (Wilson, 1983: 283).

Youths who do not do well in school are the ones who more frequently drop out and commit delinquent behavior. Changing state attendance laws and expulsion policies is likely to perpetuate problems of educational deficiency and delinquent conduct among those students. Kozol (1991) documented the "savage inequalities" of unequal educational opportunities facing poor and minority youth. Students in many inner-city urban schools are placed at a severe disadvantage when their schools lack adequate classroom space, textbooks, lab and computer equipment, and well-paid and qualified teachers, all of which are more common in suburban schools. These students are also more at risk of losing interest in school, dropping out, and engaging in deviant or delinquent behavior.

The issues of compulsory attendance, "pushout," and expulsion present difficult dilemmas which are unlikely to be settled in the near future. Available research studies do not offer sufficiently conclusive findings on which to develop policies for students who do not want to attend school and for those who disrupt the classroom.

> Despite evidence . . . that persistence in school pays off in terms of occupational attainment and income, there is really no evidence on which to base a policy regarding the effects of compelling young people to persist in schooling. We do not know if compelling young people to remain in school would increase their rebellion or decrease it. We do not know if compelling young people to remain in school would enhance their career prospects or decrease them. (Gottfredson and Gottfredson, 1985: 191)

Jackson Toby does make a very convincing case for taking a tougher approach with disruptive students. In schools throughout the United States, compulsory school attendance is seemingly treated as more important than promoting an orderly school environment (Toby, 1983: 43). Teachers are confronted with disruptive behavior and verbal harassment that two or three decades ago would have resulted in immediate suspension or expulsion. Many teachers complain about not being supported by principals. School administrators are often not supported in their disciplinary efforts by school board members, who frequently come under pressure from parents. Parents too often are reluctant to accept teachers' reports of their child's misbehavior, and some have gone so far as to challenge school suspensions or expulsions through court action. Legal action is certainly appropriate when a student's constitutional rights have been violated; challenging school disciplinary actions that have been administered fairly and under proper procedures, however, sends the wrong message to young people. In order to maintain an orderly and safe school environment for teachers and students, it is essential that a proper balance be maintained between students' rights and responsibilities.

Toby suggests lowering the age of compulsory attendance (to age 14 or 15) and requiring that students meet minimum behavioral standards. He believes that lowering the age of compulsory attendance would not result in a significantly higher dropout rate. Most youth do want to attend school. School attendance offers valued peer associations, and school enrollment carries a more positive status than being a dropout. Students who simply attend school but make no effort to learn present a problem for teachers and other students. Toby suggests that students who are not interested in education and who disrupt the educational process temporarily lose their enrollment status. They would be encouraged to return to school at any time, as soon as they are willing to comply with behavioral and educational expectations (see Toby, 1983: 44). Toby acknowledges that emphasizing behavioral standards instead of requiring all youth to attend school regardless of how little they learn would be a major shift in educational philosophy. The unsafe environment and disruptive conditions in some high schools certainly makes such a policy seem worth considering.

Most researchers and policymakers in the fields of education and juvenile delinquency have urged that dropout and delinquency prevention programs be tried before schools resort to a policy of excluding students. Most believe that it makes more sense to look at alternative solutions and policies, rather than simply allow more students to drop out and expel those who are disruptive. Short of excluding problem students, some changes in school structure and teaching methods may help schools retain at-risk students. We examine dropout prevention programs after we look at the effects of school reform on dropout and delinquency.

School Reform and Dropout

The 1980s brought renewed concerns in the United States about the poor academic skills of students. This in turn led to greater emphasis on the need for school reforms and higher graduation standards. As at the turn of this century, business expressed concerns about the skills and the working habits of school graduates. Mann cites a report by the Committee for Economic Development:

> If schools tolerate excessive absenteeism, truancy, tardiness, or misbehavior, we cannot expect students to meet standards of minimum performance or behavior either in school or as adults. It is not surprising that a student who is allowed to graduate with numerous unexcused absences, regular patterns of tardiness, and a history of uncompleted assignments will make a poor employee. (Mann, 1987: 224)

Most states have raised high school graduation standards, and many have instituted some form of minimum competency tests that students must pass before they can earn a diploma. School reform measures generally include a demand for higher standards in three areas: the academic content of courses; the use of time for school work; and student achievement (see McDill et al., 1987). There is general agreement that higher standards are needed for high school graduates to meet the requirements of college or the demands of business. But there are concerns about the "high costs of high standards." Such standards may not bring about the desired skills and academic performance among all students. Raising standards without also providing additional assistance for at-risk students is likely to lead to more failure and frustration: "The result for these students may not be notable increases in cognitive achievement but rather notable increases in absenteeism, truancy, school-related behavior problems, and dropping out" (McDill, Natriello, and Pallas, 1987: 11). McDill, Natriello, and Pallas believe that substantial additional assistance and resources must be provided in order to help at-risk students attain the higher standards and stay in school. While this will add to the costs of education, failure to take measures that may reduce the dropout rate will result in even greater costs to the nation.

James Rosenbaum (1989) has examined ways to improve the collaborative relationships between schools and employers. He believes that if employers placed more importance on school grades and on students' working habits in school, this would improve students' school performance and encourage more students to stay in school and complete their education. Many employers, surprisingly, do not hire applicants on the basis of high school grades, test scores, or other school information. Rosenbaum cites examples in Japan and in Boston, where high schools have developed closer relationships with employers (1989: 13–15). The benefits can be mutual, as teachers emphasize the importance to students of being prepared to compete in the job market and employers offer more job opportunities while getting better-prepared applicants. If students were required to inlude reports on grades, attendance, school behavior, extracurricular involvement, and other school information as part of a job application, there would be more incentives to stay in school and be more involved in their own education.

Dropout Prevention Programs

The problem of dropouts has grown to such serious proportions that nationwide efforts have been introduced to encourage young people to stay in school. Educators are aware that they must make special efforts to retain at-risk students and to improve the rate of high school graduation. Wehlage, Rutter, and Turnbaugh (1987) have developed a model dropout prevention program for at-risk students. The program has been implemented in several Wisconsin high schools, and the results indicate that special school interventions with at-risk youth can produce some positive benefits. Their model program has five characteristics:

1. *Administration and organization.* Schools should implement an alternative program on the school-within-a-school concept or an independent al-

ternative school. The program should be small, with twenty-five to 100 students and two to six faculty. Salient features are close teacher-student relationships, individualized instruction, control of admissions and dismissals, and authority to deal with difficult students.

2. *Teacher culture.* Teachers must believe at-risk students deserve renewed opportunity to learn. They must take an "extended role" with students, confronting problems at home or in the community, including peer group pressure or substance abuse. Teachers should work together in joint decision making and cooperation.

3. *Student culture.* The program must be voluntary. Students should apply for admission and admit that attitude and behavior changes are necessary for success; they must commit themselves to the program's rules, work expectations, standards of behavior, and consequences for breaking rules.

4. *Curriculum.* Individualization, clear objectives and evidence of progress, prompt feedback, and an active role for students are all essential.

5. *Experiential learning.* Youths need social experiences with adults who exemplify responsibility, the work ethic, and positive relationships. Experiential learning helps students to become active and reflective and introduces them to vocational opportunities. The program should involve them as volunteers in day care centers, nursing homes, hospitals, and social service agencies (Wehlage, Rutter, and Turnbaugh, 1987: 72–73).

School officials can not accomplish the task alone. It requires the collaborative efforts of parents, community organizations, businesses, churches, and social agencies. A dropout prevention plan may include a statement of expectations to parents; evening high school for students with child care or family responsibilities; and telephone and personal contacts of truants (see Hargrove, 1986). The Boston public schools and city leaders from local government, business, labor, higher education, and the community developed a collaborative effort known as the Boston Compact to tackle the student dropout and employment problems in Boston. In the first four years of the Compact, progress has been made on youth jobs and student achievement (Hargroves, 1986; see also Rosenbaum, 1989).

The high dropout rate of Hispanic students led the nation's largest Hispanic group, the League of United Latin American Citizens (LULAC), to take some action (Kemp and Moran, 1987). It created the Hispanic Education and Literacy, or HEAL, program to encourage and coordinate efforts between the community and public and private organizations to reduce the dropout rate of Hispanic students. HEAL is encouraging companies to hire students on a part-time basis on the explicit condition that the students stay in school and maintain a solid academic record. Employers are asked to donate the time of employees to tutor potential dropouts in skills where help is most needed. Companies in San Antonio have responded to the program. The Southland Corporation and the Edgewood School District began the College Pass Program. Students are given bank accounts into which the company deposits some money, which can be withdrawn only when the student graduates from high school and uses the money for higher education. Southwestern Bell employees in San Antonio serve on task forces organized by the city to prevent students from dropping out of school. The company is also financing college scholarships to needy Hispanic students and initiating basic vocational training programs to help dropouts gain the skills for jobs. The Coca-Cola Company in San Antonio is active in a program that provides counseling, gives incentive points worth monetary rewards for improved academic performance, and generates summer jobs for dropouts who return to the classroom.

Thousands of programs have been developed to help schools deal with students' underachievement and dropping out. Examples of programs in which community agencies are helping to improve academic achievement and reduce dropout include the Cities in Schools programs; incentive programs like "I Have a Dream"; university-school projects like Fordham University's Stay-in-School Partnership; business partnerships (more than 60,000 have been identified by the Department of Education); teen parent programs such as New Vistas High School in Minneapolis; and many volunteer community service programs (see Dryfoos, 1994; National School Safety Center, 1994). Cities and school districts have taken steps to reduce school truancy. During the 1993–94 school year, principals and headmasters in the Boston public schools were promised a 1 percent pay bonus if they lowered the absentee rate in their schools to 10 percent. School officials in Lawrence, Massachusetts, have reported low school attendance rates to the Lawrence Housing Authority and the public assistance office, families could have their welfare benefits reduced if their children's attendance dropped below 80 percent, and they could be candidates for eviction proceedings. Police officers on patrol in Baltimore, Maryland, search for students on the streets between 9 A.M. and 1 P.M. on school days and return truants to school. Authorities report that the practice has resulted in a reduced daytime crime rate and fewer groups of youth congregating at local hangouts. As part of the Truancy Abatement and Burglary Suppression (TABS) program of the Milwaukee Public Schools, police in 1993–94 took more than 2,100 students to TABS centers, where counselors talked to the students and contacted their parents. Authorities reported significant reductions in daytime crimes (National School Safety Center, 1995: 5). It seems clear that concerted efforts by the community, schools, and juvenile justice officials can reduce school absenteeism and dropout and thereby also reduce the number of crimes in a community.

Summary

Proportionately more Americans complete high school today than did so fifty years ago, but the dropout rate shows little improvement, particularly among minorities, those from lower socioeconomic levels, and urban inner-city youth. There are problems in defining and measuring dropout rates, and the two major national measures of school dropout differ slightly. Research studies have examined the causes and consequences of dropout and the relationship between dropout and delinquency. School dropout has serious economic and personal consequences for youth and for the future of the nation. Research has established a link between dropout and delinquency, but there is some disagreement on the exact causal relationship. The school dropout problem raises a number of social and political issues, such as the revision of compulsory attendance laws, altered school structure and policies on expulsion, school reform, and equitable funding of schools. Dropout prevention programs are being instituted throughout the country, and many show promise of effectively reducing the dropout rate.

References

Agnew, Robert. 1985. "A Revised Strain Theory of Delinquency." *Social Forces* 64: 151–167.

Alexander, D., Gary Natriello, and Aaron Pallas. 1985. "For Whom the School Bell Tolls: The Impact of Dropping Out on Cognitive Performance." *American Sociological Review* 50:409–420.

Bruno, Rosalind R., and Andrea Adams. 1994. "School Enrollment—Social and Economic Characteristics of Students: October 1993." Washington, D.C.: Bureau of the Census.

Cloward, Richard, and Lloyd Ohlin. 1960. *Delinquency and Opportunity*. New York: Free Press.

Cohen, Albert. 1955. *Delinquent Boys*. New York: Free Press.

Current Population Reports, Series 142, 1984. Washington, D.C.: U.S. Bureau of the Census.

Drennon-Gala, Don. 1995. *Delinquency and High School Dropouts*. New York: University Press of America.

Dryfoos, Joy G. 1994. *Full-Service Schools*. San Francisco, Calif.: Jossey-Bass.

Dunham, R. G., and G. P. Alpert. 1987. "Keeping Juvenile Delinquents in School: A Prediction Model." *Adolescence* 22:45–57.

Ekstrom, Ruth B., M. E. Goertz, J. M. Pollack, and D. A. Rock. 1986. "Who Drops Out of High School and Why? Findings from a National Study." *Teachers College Record* 87:356–373.

Elliott, Delbert S., and Harwin H. Voss. 1974. *Delinquency and Dropout*. Lexington, Mass.: Lexington Books.

Fagan, Jeffrey, and Edward Pabon. 1990. "Contributions of Delinquency and Substance Use to School Dropout Among Inner-City Youths." *Youth and Society* 21:306–354.

Farnworth, Margaret, and M. Lieber. 1989. "Strain Theory Revisited: Economic Goals, Educational Means, and Delinquency." *American Sociological Review* 54:263–274.

Farrington, D., B. Gallagher, L. Morley, R. St. Ledger, and D. West. 1986. "Unemployment, School Leaving, and Crime." *British Journal of Criminology* 26:335–356.

Fine, M. 1986. "Why Urban Adolescents Drop Into and Out of Public High School." *Teachers College Record* 87:393–409.

Gottfredson, Gary D., and Denise C. Gottfredson. 1985. *Victimization in Schools*. New York: Plenum Press.

Hargroves, J. S. 1986. "The Boston Compact: A Community Response to School Dropouts." The *Urban Review* 18:207–217.

Hartnagel, Timothy F., and Harvey Krahn. 1989. "High School Dropouts, Labor Market Success, and Criminal Behavior." *Youth and Society* 20:416–444.

Hirschi, Travis. 1969. *Causes of Delinquency*. Berkeley: University of California Press.

Jarjoura, G. Roger. 1993. "Does Dropping Out of School Enhance Delinquent Involvement? Results from a Large-Scale National Probability Sample." *Criminology* 31:149–171.

Kemp, Jack, and Oscar Moran. 1987. "Preventing Dropouts." *San Antonio Express-News*, June 18, A-10.

Kominski, R. and A. Adams, 1993, "School Enrollment—Social and Economic Characteristics of Students: October 1992." Washington, DC: Bureau of the Census.

Kozol, Jonathan. 1991. *Savage Inequalities*. New York: HarperCollins Publishers.

Levin, H. M. 1972. *The Effects of Dropping Out*. U.S. Senate Select Committee on Equal Educational Opportunity. Washington, D.C.: U.S. Government Printing Office.

Mann, Dale. 1987. "Can We Help Dropouts? Thinking About the Undoable." In G. Natriello, ed., *School Dropouts: Patterns and Policies*. New York: Teachers College Press.

McDill, E. L., G. Natrello, and A. Pallas. 1987. "The High Costs of High Standards: School Reform and Dropouts." In W. T. Denton, ed., *Dropouts, Pushouts, and Other Casualties*. Blommington, Ind.: Phi Delta Kappa.

McMillen, Marilyn, Phillip Kaufman, and S. D. Whitener. 1994. *Dropout Rates in the United States: 1993*. Washington, D.C.: U.S. Department of Education.

National School Safety Center. 1994. "Full-Service Schools: One-Stop Health and Social Services." *School Safety Update* (October):1–4.

Pallas, Aaron M. 1987. "School Dropouts in the United States." In W. T. Denton, ed., *Dropouts, Pushouts, and Other Casualties*. Bloomington, Ind.: Phi Delta Kappa.

Rippa, S. Alexander. 1980. *Education in a Free Society: An American History*. New York: Longman.

Rosenbaum, James E. 1989. "What If Good Jobs Depended on Good Grades?" *American Educator* (Winter):10–15, 40, 42–43.

Rumberger, Russell W. 1983. "Dropping Out of High School: The Influence of Race, Sex, and Family Background." *American Educational Research Journal* 20:199–220.

Rumberger, Russell W. 1987. "High School Dropouts: A Review of Issues and Evidence." *Review of Educational Research* 57:101–122.

Thornberry, Terence P., Melanie Moore, and R. L. Christenson. 1985. "The Effect of Dropping Out of High School on Subsequent Criminal Behavior." *Criminology* 23:3–18.

Toby, Jackson. 1980. "Crime in American Schools." *Public Interest* 58:18–42.

Toby, Jackson. 1983. "Violence in School." In M. Tonry and N. Morris, eds., *Crime and Justice: An Annual Review of Research*. Chicago: University of Chicago Press.

Toby, Jackson. 1994. "Everyday School Violence: How Disorder Fuels It." *American Educator* (Winter): 4–9, 44–48.

Toles, R., E. M. Schulz, and W. K. Rice. 1986. "A Study of Variation in Dropout Rates Attributable to Effects of High Schools." *Metropolitan Education* 2:30–38.

U.S. Department of Education. 1990. *State Education Statistics: Student Performance, Resource Inputs, and Population*. Washington, D.C.: U.S. Department of Education.

U.S. Senate. 1957. *Report of the Committee on the Judiciary—Report No. 130*. Washington, D.C.: U.S. Government Printing Office.

Wehlage, Gary G. 1986. "At-Risk Students and the Need for High School Reform." *Education* 107:18–28.

Wehlage, Gary G., and Robert A. Rutter. 1986. "Dropping Out: How Much Do Schools Contribute to the Problem?" *Teachers College Record* 87:374–392.

Wehlage, Gary G., Robert A. Rutter, and A. Turnbaugh. 1987. "A Program Model for At-Risk High School Students." *Educational Leadership* 44:70–73.

Wilson, James Q. 1983. "Crime and Public Policy." In J. Q. Wilson, ed., *Crime and Public Policy*. San Francisco: ICS Press.

Wolfgang, Marvin E., Robert M. Figlio, and Thorsten Sellin. 1972. *Delinquency in a Birth Cohort*. Chicago: University of Chicago Press.

6

School Structure and Delinquency

[D]elinquent commitments result in part from adverse or negative school experiences of some youth, and . . . there are fundamental defects within the educational system . . . that actively contribute to these negative experiences. (Walter E. Schafer and Kenneth Polk, 1967: 223).

"Growing Up Is Risky Business, and Schools Are Not to Blame"—Jack Frymier (1992)

If one were to ask a citizen, a probation officer, or a teacher which American institution is most responsible for crime and delinquency, he or she would likely answer "the family." If we asked a criminologist or someone involved in delinquency theories and research, on the other hand, he or she would likely respond that the American institution most responsible for crime is "the school" (Gottfredson and Hirschi, 1990: 159). The social institution responsible for educating children has long been criticized for the repressive environment and punitive methods of teachers, which tend to minimize the possibility of learning. Craig Haney and Philip Zimbardo (1975) highlighted this kind of criticism with an article titled "It's Tough to Tell a High School from a Prison." They noted several analogies between prisons and schools (particularly inner-city schools) and between the treatment of inmates and that of students; they also observed similarities between the two types of institutions: the stark physical appearance on the outside, surrounded by fences; the dull, endless, uniform hallways on the inside; the regimentation and controlled movement by roll calls and bells; the regulations on what students and inmates can wear, on the hair length, on when they may go to the toilet, on when they may eat, and on when they may go outside; and the use of strict discipline and corporal punishment to maintain control. Haney and Zimbardo noted that because prison guards and teachers are greatly outnumbered, by inmates and students, respectively, they often resort to techniques to divide their subjects to keep them from uniting in solid opposition to authority. Guards often turn prisoners against each other by the discriminatory use of privileges. Educators divide students into separate groups based on perceived ability and future educational or career goals and thereby set up rivalries based on rank and status within the school. Schools also promote competition between students on the premise that it will promote motivation and better performance, but it also creates barriers between students. The overall result of this prison-type school structure is to humiliate students, engendering hostility and a tendency for them either to act out disruptively or to withdraw into themselves. Haney and Zimbardo (1975: 106) emphasized that it is important to examine carefully the effects of schools because as social institutions they have a powerful influence over human behavior. Schools are expected to provide students with the critical skills and personal values necessary to function in a democratic society, including the ability to resist manipulation and dehumanization. Schools that are repressive and that typify society's worst institutions are counterproductive to the goals of education in America.

In this chapter we examine a number of questions regarding school structure, organization, and the educational process as they relate to school performance and delinquency. We first address the issues of school funding disparities and school reform measures and the relationship these may have to school performance of at-risk students. Second, we examine whether the teaching process and certain teaching strategies make a difference in students' chances for academic success. We know that teachers cannot teach students who do not want to learn, students themselves share an equal responsibility for academic success. But to what extent should school personnel be held responsible for making learning fun and for "turning on" even the resistant students to the joys of learning? Are there some things educators can do to raise students' interest in education and to help them succeed? To what extent are schools partially responsible for the success or failure of students? Third, we examine the question of whether schools cause delinquency. Are there some features of school structure and the teaching process that contribute to delinquency? Finally, if delinquency is caused more by conditions in the family and the community than by the schools, what is the role of schools in ameliorating those conditions that place students at risk of delinquent involvement? We examine some policy implications of the responsibilities of schools, students, families, and the community in reducing school failure and delinquency.

School Structure and Academic Success

Serious questions have been raised about whether schools really make much difference in the lives and attainment of students. Several writers in the 1960s and 1970s claimed that schools made little difference. A major proponent of this view was James Coleman in a report originally published in 1966, titled "Equality of Educational Opportunity" (Coleman, 1987). Jencks et al. (1972)

reanalyzed the Coleman data and other data and concluded that additional school expenditures and resources would make very little difference in students' academic performance. Titles of books illustrate the critical approach taken by many writers: *The Underachieving School, Death at an Early Age,* and *Pedagogy of the Oppressed* (Rutter, 1983: 2). Paul Copperman (1980) criticized the American educational system and charged that it had perpetuated a literacy hoax on students and their parents. Educators are giving fewer assignments, he asserted; standards are down, grades are up—and students end up with fewer skills (Copperman, 1980: 16).

Walter Schafer and Kenneth Polk (1972) have contended that several school conditions, including educational failure, perceived lack of payoff for education, and low commitment to education, contribute to delinquency. They took the position that school conditions that lead to failure also indirectly lead to delinquency. They acknowledged that one reason for low scholastic performance among lower-income children is that home influences are such that they enter school with serious deficiencies that are all but impossible for the school to overcome. Nevertheless, they argued that the school itself contributes to failure by not designing its program, curriculum, and instructional techniques so that such deficiencies are accounted for and effectively offset (1972: 182). The conditions believed to contribute to school failure and delinquency are summarized in Table 6–1.

These conditions undoubtedly continue to exist in many schools, especially those located in low-income areas of larger cities. Two questions must be raised about the arguments that schools are responsible for educational failure and delinquency. First, it has not been established that educational failure necessarily causes delinquency. There is certainly a correlation between school failure and delinquency, but it is more difficult to establish a causal relationship. We address that question, and review the available research evidence, later in this chapter. The second question is whether school administrators and teach-

Table 6–1
School Conditions Contributing to Educational Failure and Juvenile Delinquency

- Belief in limited potential of disadvantaged pupils
- Irrelevant instruction
- Inappropriate teaching methods
- Testing, grouping, and "tracking"
- Inadequate compensatory and remedial education
- Inferior teachers and facilities in low-income schools
- School-community distance
- Economic and racial segregation

Source: Walter Schafer and Kenneth Polk. 1972. "School Conditions Contributing to Delinquency." In W. E. Schafer and K. Polk, eds., *Schools and Delinquency.* Englewood Cliffs, N.J.: Prentice-Hall.

ers can be held accountable for many of the conditions that contribute to educational failure. The first four conditions summarized in Table 6–1 do describe school structures and teaching philosophies that may be altered by educators themselves, and in fact have been altered in many schools. Changes and improvements in schools in the past three decades include the introduction of special educational programs for disadvantaged students; improved teaching methods and making instruction more relevant for students; and reductions in the use of grouping and tracking. The final four conditions relate to limited resources of educational systems and are dependent upon greater taxpayer support and changes in the community. Inadequate compensatory and remedial education and inferior teachers and facilities are a direct result of the lack of resources necessary to maintain a quality school system. Citizens have been increasingly reluctant to support education with more tax dollars. They have been quick to criticize the quality of education but unwilling to pay for it, claiming that educational quality has little or nothing to do with financial resources or assuming somehow that educational quality can be had at bargain prices. Education, like most other goods and services, does cost more today than it did ten, twenty, or thirty years ago. Unfortunately, those who are most often opposed to increased taxes for schools are older citizens who no longer have children in the school system and who remember how low the school taxes were years ago, and they believe the quality of education was much better back then! Schafer and Polk were correct in describing a school-community distance. This distance is partially reflected in taxpayer resentment over the growing costs of quality education. It is also reflected in parents' reluctance to take the time to be involved in their children's school activities, often because of their already full work days. School administrators certainly must work for closer interaction and communication with the community, but parents and community leaders must show a greater interest in what happens in schools in order to reduce the distance between schools and the community.

Schools are a reflection of the community, and just as society is economically and racially segregated, so also are many schools. Schools should be expected to initiate the process of integrating communities, and in hundreds of cases they are, but without support and efforts from parents and community leaders, neither communities nor schools will be very effective in bringing together students and citizens from all social, racial, and ethnic backgrounds. In their recommendations for improving schools and reducing delinquency, Schafer and Polk placed as much emphasis on the need for additional state and federal funds as they did on specific changes required of administrators and teachers (see Schafer and Polk, 1972: 240–277). Their recommendations made more than thirty years ago, are not unlike similar recommendations made by more recent commissions on education.

Not all academics who have examined the quality of education come to such a gloomy conclusion about the effectiveness of schools. Michael Rutter (1983) reviewed a large number of studies on the effects of schools and arrived at a considerably more optimistic outlook for schooling. One reason for the critical views of schools, he found, was the narrow, limited criteria used for measuring effectiveness. Rutter argued that multiple indicators of school effectiveness are required, including scholastic attainment, classroom behavior, absenteeism, attitudes toward learning, continuation in education, employment, and social functioning (1983: 5–8). Schools vary in the effects that they have on students. Rutter noted that some of the school features that seem to have the greatest impact on students include resources and school buildings; school size and class size; organizational structure, composition of the student body, the amount of academic emphasis, classroom management, discipline and pupil conditions, pupil participation and responsibility and staff organization (1983: 15–24).

School Funding and Educational Inequality

We cannot adequately discuss school structure and teaching quality without addressing the issue of inequality of school funding, which in large part explains the vast differences between school districts in physical resources and teaching quality. The method of financing public education in America, the local property tax, is poorly suited to today's educational needs. The extreme differences in property tax bases and rates among school districts means that the quality of education that a child receives depends on where that child lives. Each state is free to develop its own method of paying for public schools. The U.S. Constitution does not mention education and does not spell out any specific guarantees for equality of education. And just as there are wide differences among states in public financing of education, there are vast differences within states: regional variations, differences between urban and rural schools, and differences between inner-city and suburban schools. The largest portion of real estate taxes goes to support the public schools, and homeowners are well aware of the differences in property tax rates and in the quality of schools in different communities. One of the first questions asked of real estate agents by persons shopping for a home relates to the quality of the school district. Home buyers usually try to buy a home in the best neighborhood and the best school district that is within their financial means. Higher tax rates do not guarantee better schools, however. Tax rates vary considerably among communities, and property tax revenues also vary according to the kind of properties included in a district. Living in a community with a large utility plant or shopping center, for example, means that schools will have much more money available to them than the schools in a neighboring community that lacks such tax-generating properties.

Inequities such as these were not recognized by the courts until the 1970s. For most of America's history, the fact that public education differed from one place to another due to differences in property taxes was considered as natural as community differences. Inferior schools were viewed as being an unfortunate but natural result of deteriorating, poor communities. The acceptance of inequities in school funding based on differences in property taxes is grounded in the importance of property as a symbol of wealth in America. Only recently have some school administrators, lawmakers, and courts begun to suggest that the present system of financing schools with local property taxes is an inequitable and impractical method of ensuring quality education for all children.

Arthur Wise (1968) was one of the first to claim that public school funding formulas deny children in poor communities equal opportunities to education. As a law school student at the University of Chicago in 1964, Wise did legal research that led him to conclude that school funding formulas based on unequal property taxes violated the Constitution. Within four years he had documented his views in a book entitled "Rich Schools, Poor Schools," in which he argued that basing school funding on property taxes denies children in poor communities "equal protection of the law" as guaranteed by the fourteenth Amendment. Thirty years later the legal theory developed by the young law school student has helped change the shape of school finance in more than half the states in this country. Jonathan Kozol (1991) renewed the challenge to unequal school funding in documenting the "savage inequalities" among selected rich and poor school districts in the nation. The issue of equality in education was initially raised in the U.S. Supreme Court case of *Brown v. Board of Education of Topeka* in 1954, in which the Court concluded that children were being deprived of equal educational opportunity because of segregation. Following the *Brown* case, there have been several federal court decisions that have affected virtually every important aspect of school policy, including the issue of unequal pupil expenditures among school districts. In *Hobson v. Hansen II* (1971) a federal court ruled that per-pupil expenditures for teachers' salaries in the Washington, D.C., school district must be equalized. Problems with equity of school funding have been apparent in several states, but court decisions have not ruled consistently against all states that have funded education inequitably. Courts in New Jersey, California, and Connecticut presumed a relationship between educational cost and quality, reasoning that disparities in funding caused disparities in quality that in turn contributed to unequal educational opportunities. Federal courts in Texas, Idaho, Oregon, and Washington, on the other hand, did not presume that costs and quality were causally related (see Reutter, 1982).

Two court cases, in California and Texas, illustrate the variations in court rulings. In *Serrano v. Priest* (1971), the California Supreme Court ruled that the state's school funding policy discriminated against pupils in property-poor districts and that therefore those students did not receive the equal protection of the laws of the state. With this precedent in mind, plaintiffs challenging unequal funding in Texas were greatly disappointed by a federal court ruling in *San Antonio v. Rodriquez* (1973) in which the court ruled that although there were inequities in the Texas school financing system, it did not violate the equal protection clause of the Fourteenth Amendment to the U.S. Constitution. The court in this case reasoned that the state's funding for local schools provided at least a minimum level of funding and that no students were deprived of educational opportunities. The fight for equitable school funding has a long history in San Antonio. The original suit was filed by Demetrio Rodriguez and other parents of students in the Edgewood School District, located on the west side of San Antonio, a property-poor area populated mostly by lower-income

Mexican-American families living in small homes and housing projects. The administrators and parents of the Edgewood district were assisted in their legal efforts by the Mexican American Legal Defense Fund (MALDEF) and were joined in a subsequent lawsuit by other property-poor districts throughout Texas. Their persistence paid off when a state district court judge declared in *Edgewood v. Kirby* (1987) that the Texas system of school financing discriminated against students in property-poor districts and was unconstitutional. Judge Clark declared that "education is a fundamental right for each of our citizens. Equality of access to funds is the key and is one of the requirements of this fundamental right" (Hall, 1987: 9), and he ordered that the current system be abandoned. Judge Clark cited the following state funding disparities in making his ruling:

- Wealthy and poor districts can be found in the same county. Edgewood, for example, had $38,854 of property value per student, while Alamo Heights, a suburban district, less than five miles away had $570,109 per student.
- Texas had three million public school children. The million in districts at the upper range of property wealth had more than two and a half times as much property wealth to support their schools as the million in the bottom range.
- The wealthiest school district had more than $14 million in taxable property wealth per student, while the poorest district had only $20,000.
- The average tax rate in the state's 100 poorest districts was 74 cents, compared with 47 cents in the 100 wealthiest districts (Hall, 1987: 8).

The fact that taxpayers in the poor districts generally pay higher tax rates than those in wealthier districts highlights the inequities of many state school funding methods. The inequality is amplified further when the lower values of taxable properties in poor districts yield less expenditures per pupil than those in wealthier districts.

Courts have closely scutinized the fairness of state school financing systems in the past decade. The disparities between rich and poor districts were considered so great that the funding methods in several states have been struck down as unconstitutional. In addition to the Texas case just cited, state school financing systems were struck down in Montana, Kentucky, and New Jersey (Katz 1991: 20), and litigation has been ongoing for the past few years in at least nineteen other states. The New Jersey Supreme Court noted disparities in educational opportunities and found that poor urban districts provided inadequate instruction in core curriculum subjects and were neglecting special educational needs. The court ruled that children in poor districts were entitled to per-pupil expenditures that were comparable to those in more affluent districts, regardless of property values or tax rates (see Katz, 1991: 21). The Kentucky Supreme Court made the most sweeping decision when it struck down not only the state's school finance system but all of its education statutes and regulations. The state legislature responded by changing the entire school system, reducing the role of the state education department, giving more control to local schools, and adding $1.3 billion to school funding over the following two years.

Equalizing funding among school districts throughout each state is not a simple, straightforward process. Taxpayers in wealthier districts are often more willing to approve higher tax rates for better school facilities and higher teacher salaries. Thus, as more state funding goes to the poorer districts, wealthier districts have increased their local funding, which has the effect of continuing the disparity in per pupil expenditures. Some states, such as Colorado, have taken the controversial step of placing a cap on expenditures by local school districts. Spending caps achieve equality among rich and poor districts, but they often do so by making the better school districts worse, since many have had to cut back on programs or reduce teacher salary increases. Forced cutbacks in funding in some of the best school districts have been questioned by some. Some policymakers argue that there ought to be districts that serve as models of quality education and that without them, wealthier families are more likely to leave the public school system and send their children to private schools (Katz, 1991).

Achieving equality of school funding by depending on extra state funding for poor districts has raised concerns, particularly because of the many demands on state funding and the tendency to shift more responsibility to local governments. Allan Odden, co-director of the Center for Policy Research in Education, thinks that states ought to be able to balance the goals of education equity and excellence. He noted, for example, that while the Midwest and the Northeast, which depend proportionately more on local revenues for school funding, have greater disparities among school districts, they also have some of the nation's best schools (Katz, 1991). Odden noted that when we have equality of dollars, we are likely to end up with a mediocre system. The dilemma in the school funding issue is whether we can have a world-class education system and equal spending across school districts (see Katz, 1991: 22).

James Coleman (1987) questioned whether equalizing school expenditures would effectively result in more nearly equal achievements among students. He noted that "(1) . . . minority children have a serious educational deficiency at the start of school, which is obviously not a result of school; and (2) they have an even more serious deficiency at the end of school, which is obviously in part a result of school" (1987: 34). He claimed that family background differences account for more variation in achievement than do school differences:

> Per pupil expenditure, books in the library, and a host of other facilities and curricular measures show virtually no relation to achievement if the "social" environment of the school—the educational backgrounds of other students and teachers— is held constant. . . . [T]he sources of inequality of educational opportunity appear to lie first in the home itself and the cultural influences immediately surrounding the home; then they lie in the schools' ineffectiveness to free achievement from the impact of the home, and in the schools' homogeneity which perpetuates the social influences of the home and its environs. (Coleman, 1987: 35).

Without question it takes more than equal educational opportunities to help students attain more nearly equal achievement levels in school. There is evidence that giving equal opportunities to persons through educational and community restructuring does make a difference. Beginning in the late 1970s, 4,000 low-income Chicago families were relocated to middle-class, often white neighborhoods throughout the city and in fifty suburbs. Early studies by the Northwestern University Center for Urban Affairs showed that more of the relocated adults were employed; the high school graduation rate of the relocated children was 95 percent, with slightly more than half of those going on to college. The students were nearly twice as likely as those who stayed in the inner city to find jobs, and they reported being happier in their new surroundings. It appears that integration and more equal educational and employment opportunities for students and their families do have the potential for helping persons make positive achievements (Alter 1992: 55).

School Reform and At-Risk Students

The issue of educational reform draws more public, legislative, and media attention than the issue of equality in school funding. In the 1950s the launching by the Soviet Union of the Sputnik satellite also launched an outcry of criticism against America's educational system, including claims that we were not adequately preparing our students to compete in the developing scientific technologies. President Ronald Reagan's National Commission on Excellence in Education echoed many of the same concerns in its 1983 report, *A Nation at Risk* which opened with this statement: "Our nation is at risk. Our once unchallenged preeminence in commerce, industry, science, and technological innovation is being overtaken by competitors throughout the world" (National Commission on Excellence in Education, 1983: 5). Other commissions, at both the federal and the state levels, have criticized the quality of public education. Some of the criticisms have related to the "liberalization" of the curriculum that allows students to enroll in a wide variety of electives at the expense of not focusing sufficiently on the core courses. Many have questioned whether schools are to blame for the academic failures of students. There certainly is some cause for concern, however, when we note that students' academic achievement has been declining. Scores on the Scholastic Aptitude Test (SAT), considered a reliable measure of overall academic achievement of college-bound high school seniors in the United States, have declined since 1966 except for small increases in 1984 and 1985. Data from the National Assessment of Educational Progress also confirms students' decreases in mathematical knowledge and in reading skills since the 1970s (Stevens and Wood, 1987: 350).

Commission recommendations for responding to the "crisis" in education, detailed in *A Nation at Risk*, are similar to other educational reform proposals dating back to the 1950s and to ideas that have come out of a number of state educational commissions calling for reforms. The commission recommended that curricula focus more on the educational basics; grading standards, entrance admissions scores for colleges and universities, and textbook rigor all be increased; more time be spent in school as well as on homework; teaching quality be increased and salaries be based on merit; and educational leaders at the local, state, and federal levels become more effective leaders for change and reform.

Mortimer Adler (1982), Ernest Boyer (1983), and John Goodlad (1984) have questioned some of these educational reform recommendations and whether it is realistically possible for schools to offer so much for all students, particularly as so much is expected of the schools. Schools have been criticized for failing to adequately educate all students in the basic educational skills, while at the same time they have been expected to take on what have traditionally been the responsibilities of families, churches, and other institutions charged with educating and socializing youth (Boyer, 1983: 63). Adler, Boyer, and Goodlad all argue that "less is better" when it comes to educational goals and objectives. Adler believes that all children are entitled to the same quality of education. Basic schooling for all students should be general and liberal, not specialized and vocational, thus preparing the students for earning livings, being good citizens, and leading good lives (Adler, 1982: 4). Boyer's proposals are similar to Adler's; he suggests four essential goals for public schools: (1) developing students' ability to think critically and communicate effectively, (2) developing an understanding of shared cultural histories, (3) preparing students for work, and (4) helping students fulfill social and civic obligations through community and social service (Boyer, 1983: 282). Goodlad, like Boyer and Adler, argues that much of what schools are currently attempting to do should be the shared responsibility of the community at large. Education is so important and so much is expected of education that Goodlad believes that the task should not be left only to the schools (Goodlad, 1984: 46). All three authors are in agreement in arguing that education should become an integral part of the community—the home, the church, the civic club, and the workplace. The community must be willing to assume many of the tasks now carried out by schools in order for schooling once again to be a primarily educative function. Their proposals have not gone without criticism: Adler for his assumption that knowledge can elevate the quality of life and Boyer and Goodlad for their failure to specify exactly how some of the school's functions can be assumed by the community (see Stevens and Wood, 1987: 353).

Educational commissions and state legislators surely have good intentions, but their recommendations for school reform and legislatively mandated policies fall far short of what is needed for real changes in education. Principals in 276 schools in eighty-five communities across the United States were interviewed using a structured interview format and were asked what state legislatures, the board of education, or the local school district had done to improve education. The "educational improvements" and the percentage of principals noting them were:

- Increased requirements for graduation   75%
- Increased requirements for teacher evaluation   72%
- Mandatory testing for students   74%
- Restrictions on participation in extracurricular activities for students who did not achieve   63%
- Required retention of students who do not achieve   44%
  (Frymier, 1992: 42–43).

A review of these improvements clearly illustrates the limitations of legislative mandates and regulations. Simply increasing the requirements for graduation and teacher evaluations, limiting extracurricular activities for failing students and requiring their retention do little to improve education. Available research evidence questions their effectiveness. And yet these are examples of educational "reforms" commonly proposed by states.

The passage of House Bill 72 (HB 72) by the Texas state legislature in 1984 is a good example of the limitations of such school reform bills and their effect on at-risk students. The legislation was a response to a real need to improve educational quality in the state and was spurred on by the National Commission on Excellence in Education report "A Nation at Risk" issued the previous year. Another incentive was the ongoing litigation over the state's system of school financing (*San Antonio v. Rodriguez*, 1973, discussed earlier, and *Edgewood v. Bynum* [1984]). The Texas school reform bill restructured the financing of education and provided for equalization of funding among school districts. Reforms to improve teaching quality included teacher competency testing and the introduction of merit pay and a career ladder. State-funded programs were to be provided for compensatory education, bilingual education, special education for handicapped children, vocational education and prekindergarten and summer preschool programs. The provisions of the legislation that seemed to get the most attention were the restriction on social promotion of students, the imposition of a limit on five days of unexcused absence before automatic course failure, and the "no pass-no play" rule, which excluded any student who earned below a 70 in any course from participating in extracurricular activities during the following grading period. This ruling provoked complaints from students, parents, and coaches; media attention; and several legal challenges (none of which have been upheld). Community reaction to the "no pass-no play" rule was that it demanded too much, too soon from students and would most hurt the marginal students for whom extracurricular activities are a major reason for staying in school.

Few would question the need for educational reforms and improvements, but there are also concerns about the unintended consequences of school reform. Simply raising standards and academic requirements without improving the quality of teaching and educational programs is likely to increase the risk that marginal students will fall further behind, failing and eventually dropping out (Smith and Hester, 1985). Reforms calling for high educational expectations are seldom accompanied by adequate programs to assist those who are struggling academically. The passage of HB 72 in Texas raised this concern. With restricted promotion of students, some educators believed dropout rates might double or triple, especially among minority students. At-risk students would be more likely to fail the exit exam, many would be eliminated from extracurricular activities, and the heightened minimum grade requirements combined with exclusion from activities would surely result in more discipline problems and dropouts (Grubb, 1985). A survey of fifty-four educational reform commissions in thirty-two states revealed that fewer than one-third had adequately considered the plight of at-risk students in making their recommendations (Smith and Hester, 1985: 6). In an effort to assess the initial effects of the Texas school reform bill, a survey was conducted on a sample of 1,407 high school students in San Antonio in 1986 (Lawrence, 1986). He found that most of the students had a fairly high regard for the job being done by their teachers and the school in general, but a sizable proportion (25 to 50 percent) also reported some problems and complaints about the teaching process and school requirements. At-risk students, primarily those from minorities whose parents were not well educated and were unemployed or underemployed, were of lower socioeconomic status; had a greater rate of school failure; had difficulty meeting the higher grading standards; participated less in tutoring programs; and participated less frequently in extracurricular activities. Results of the survey showed that there were more at-risk students in school districts that had a smaller per-pupil expenditure for education. Legislators who passed HB 72 promised to provide additional school funding to improve the quality and equality of public education in Texas, in addition to raising academic requirements; but there were concerns among citizens and legislators whether there would be adequate state funding to pay for the provisions of the educational reform bill. Meanwhile, at-risk students have suffered from the reform provisions that were easiest to implement—higher academic standards and restrictions on participation in activities. It will take years before the additional state funding results in measurable improvements in educational programs for the poorest school districts. Those are among the unintended consequences of educational reform.

Do Schools Cause Failure—and Delinquency?

In addition to criticizing disparities in school funding, unequal educational opportunities, and school reforms that result in underachievement and the failure of many students, some observers charge that schools cause delinquency. Articles titled "Schools and the Delinquency Experience" (Polk, 1982) and "How the School and Teachers Create Deviants" (Kelly, 1977) drew more negative attention to the schools and raised the question whether there are in fact "delinquent schools" that significantly influence delinquency rates among youth (Wenk, 1975). It has been suggested not that schools are direct causes of delinquency but that the failure of schools to actively involve all youth in the educational process, particularly marginal, at-risk youth, results in their failure to become socialized and prepared for life and work. Schools, according to some, do not offer equal educational opportunities, resulting in the academic failure of disproportionate numbers of inner-city, lower-class students. School failure is linked to behavioral problems in the school and to delinquency in the community. "Because misconduct in school generally precedes misconduct in the community, the manner in which schools react to misconduct may determine whether it will be followed by official delinquency" (Wenk, 1975: 9).

Kenneth Polk (1982) described a process by which delinquency results from some students' school experience, depending on social class, academic performance, and the degree of family support. Polk emphasized the "gatekeeping" function of schools, by which elite positions and credentials are conferred on some students while others are assigned lower status and lower credentials. Because the educational system is competitive, there are necessarily both winners and losers. Unfortunately, the wins and losses are not randomly distributed but are greatly dependent on family background factors. Family background factors of students who are more likely to be losers in school include belonging to a lower social class or a minority group, speaking a different language, or living in the wrong part of town (1982: 228). Family background also means that some students come to school more prepared and equipped with greater competencies to face the competitive academic environment.

Polk argued that the gatekeeping function carries over to the school authorities' responses to student deviance and disruption in school. Teachers and principals often respond differently to incidents of student disruption and rule violations. Deviant behavior by "good" students is often overlooked; even when students who are doing well are caught for disruption or school rule violations, future problem behavior is generally minimized by the threat that future misconduct could jeopardize their future academic careers. Promising students are also rewarded with more opportunities for involvement in school activities. Students who perform poorly may be singled out for disruptive behavior and are also excluded from school activities, which reduces their bond with the school even more. Polk supported his claims with data that he believed provided evidence of a connection among family background, school performance, and deviance; between school performance and adult success; and between the labels attached by schools and juvenile courts and the likelihood of juvenile and adult criminality (1982: 229–230).

Arguments about schools as a cause of delinquency tend to fall into one of two categories of criminological theories: labeling theory and strain theory (introduced in Chapter three). According to Albert Cohen's (1955) strain theory, a lower-class boy becomes frustrated (experiences strain) because he is not prepared to meet the middle-class standards and demands of school. Cohen believes that successful school performance is based on such middle-class values as punctuality, neatness, ambition for achievement and success, individual responsibility, delay of gratification, and self-control. According to Cohen, students from the lower class do not have these values and therefore experience frustration or strain in the school environment. They respond to this frustration by associating with peers who are similarly frustrated and act out with disruptive behavior, truancy, and often delinquent behavior.

Labeling theorists focus on the practice of tracking students in schools. It is a common practice in schools to classify students according to their perceived learning ability and to place them into groups, or "tracks," of students who supposedly perform at a similar level. Such tracking ideally makes it possible for teachers to direct their efforts at the appropriate ability level for slower and faster learners. Labeling theorists believe that the practice of placing students in tracks on the basis of perceived ability or career or academic potential unfairly labels students. Through the practice of tracking, they argue, schools promote failure and ultimately delinquency by treating some students differently within the school structure. The practice of tracking unfairly limits the potential of many students, particularly along gender, class, ethnic, or racial lines. Teachers and administrators often selectively label students in lower tracks as troublemakers. Labeling theorists present some evidence that students often take on or live up to the negative labels given them. The impact of school tracking affects a student's "(1) *personal identity* (i.e., how the individual views self); (2) *public identity* (i.e., how others view the individual); and (3) *self-image* (i.e., how the individual evaluates self) (Kelly and Pink, 1982:55). Teachers, peers, parents and others come to expect less from students in low-ability tracks, while more is expected of students in high-ability tracks. The expectations are often fulfilled. Misconduct and behavior problems are also often expected of students in lower tracks.

> When such a student engages in school crime, he or she is probably not only living up to teacher, peer, parental, and self expectations, but . . . may also be striving to obtain some measure of success and well-being. . . . [T]he misbehavior serves to confirm the initial diagnosis and labeling as a potential troublemaker. (Kelly and Pink, 1982: 55)

The practice of tracking in schools has been criticized as a cause of academic failure and often of dropout and delinquency, for at least three reasons: (1) more minority and lower-income students are in the basic or low-ability tracks; (2) placement in the tracks tends to be permanent, with little movement up or down in spite of students' learning and progress; and (3) tracking has a labeling and stigmatizing effect; teachers expect less of the lower-track students, and frequently their expectations are correct.

To understand better the connection between labeling theory and school tracking, it may help to recall that labeling theory is based on the sociological theory of "symbolic interactionism." Simply put, proponents of that view remind us that there is nothing inherent in an act that makes it deviant. Rather, an act becomes deviant only as a label is applied to it by others. Proponents of the symbolic-interaction theory stress the importance of interactions between individuals and the formation of a self-image through social interactions. Howard Becker believed that deviance is created by society, that "*social groups create deviance by making the rules whose infraction constitutes deviance,* and by applying those rules to particular people and labeling them as outsiders. . . . The deviant is one to whom that label has successfully been applied" (1963: 9). Walter Schafer (1972) described how certain school behavior becomes labeled deviant through interactions: "It is our thesis that *underachievement, misbehavior and early school-leaving are properly and most usefully to be seen as adverse school-pupil interactions* and not simply as individual acts, carried out by students as natural responses to damaged psyches or defective homes" (1972: 146). Thus, whether student behavior is labeled deviant and whether and how teachers respond to the behavior depend on several factors, such as the particular norms and values of the school and how frequently it enforces the norms; the nature of the student population (e.g., middle- or lower-class, inner-city or suburban), which affects the tolerance limits; and characteristics of the students, such as whether the student is college-prep, an athlete, or a club leader and has a reputation for good behavior (Schafer, 1972: 150–151). Schafer noted that some students are disruptive or perform poorly in school because of low innate ability, low commitment to school goals, or low acquired capabilities, including social skills (1972: 156). These deficits are attributable to the child's family background and home environment, but they are reenforced or altered by school experiences. Academic skills and classroom and study habits can be improved with quality education. Social skills affect students' relations with school personnel and with their peers; students must be able to interact with teachers and other students in ways that do not disrupt the learning process. Schafer contended that students in difficulty very often differ little if at all from nondeviant students and are equally concerned about succeeding in school and in life.

> What we are stressing is the importance of recognition by those on the firing line that probably more of their students care than they realize and that wise use of responses—those which support manifestations of existing commitment and which serve to develop necessary means or skills—can vitally affect the student's orientation toward school and thus his likelihood of success. (Schafer, 1972: 159)

Labeling theory has not received much support through research and data, and those who argue that schools cause delinquency through the practice of tracking likewise fail to support their claims with much solid research evidence. Few studies have been conducted on the subject since the 1970s and 1980s, and the ones that have been done tend to suffer from methodological weaknesses. The relatively few studies that do show evidence of negative effects of tracking deserve our careful review, however. Few would disagree that there are unequal educational opportunities in our schools or that the students who suffer what Jonathan Kozol calls "savage inequalities" come from schools with primarily lower-class, minority student populations.

Schafer, Olexa, and Polk (1972) examined data that showed some relationship between track position and academic achievement, extracurricular activities, dropout rate, misbehavior in school, and delinquency. They acknowledged that it may not be the track position itself but initial differences in educational ability or commitment to school that explains those effects; thus, the data do not establish a definite causal link between track position and misbehavior. They did find that even when IQ and previous ability factors were controlled, blacks and low-income students were still more likely to be found in the basic or low-ability tracks, and they contended that the differences were caused partly by students' position in the tracking system. They also found that track assignment was virtually *irreversible*, operating much like a rigid caste system.

Kelly (1977) reported on research to test his belief that guidance counselors and teachers base many of their academic decisions regarding placement of students on nonacademic criteria. A comparison of teachers' selections of students for a remedial reading program with the school reading specialist's evaluations indicated that only 28 percent actually met the criteria for place-ment in the special program. He concluded from his analysis that students who exhibit certain attributes, such as prior contact with remedial or "stigmatizing" institutions and programs, can expect to be singled out for special processing and treatment, even though they do not qualify academically for such treat-ment (Kelly, 1977: 205). Kelly and Grove (1981) analyzed the same data and found evidence that students are routinely assigned to a low-ability track not on the basis of IQ or current ability and performance but often because of their past academic record. Their findings also suggested that race, social class, and other nonacademic factors (such as the father's occupation and student mis-conduct) were criteria for tracking.

Nijboer and Dijksterhuis (1983) administered a questionnaire to 1,202 stu-dents in Holland to examine the relationship between secondary school per-formance and delinquency. Questions assessed the students' self-reported delin-quency; their experiences within the school system; and the peer, teacher, and parental reactions that their behavior had elicited. They found evidence of poor school achievement and self-fulfillment of negative labels. Poor achievers often are considered failures by teachers, and the researchers suggested that this view often resulted in negative student attitudes toward school, loss of motivation, and mental stress. As a result of being labeled a failure, some students resort to rebellion against the school, initially through unruly behavior and truancy. Nijboer and Dijksterhuis concluded that it appears that the educational process does have an effect on the development of juvenile delinquency, but they ac-knowledged that it is still unclear how this process evolves.

One of the most striking findings of this survey is the devastating effect of nega-tive labeling on the juvenile psyche. Applied seemingly innocently to a poor aca-demic achiever, a negative label can destroy motivation and lead to a student's be-wilderment about where he belongs. Personal values become distorted, hopes are crushed, and (partially) self-imposed alienation from the mainstream ensues. Affil-iation with similarly segregated individuals (or groups) follows, and the seeds of predelinquent behavior are sown. (Nijboer and Dijksterhuis, 1983: 4)

Michael Wiatrowski, Stephen Hansell, Charles Massey, and David Wilson (1982) analyzed data from a nationally representative longitudinal sample of more than 1,600 high school boys to test whether placement in a noncollege curriculum track causes losses in self-esteem and increased delinquency. Results of their analysis raise doubts about the causal relationship between tracking and delinquency in high school, but the authors suggest that research should focus more on possible causes of delinquent behavior in junior high school, where most tracking occurs; there is evidence that peer group influences on adoles-cents peak in junior high school. Wiatrowski et al. have suggested that the de-terminants of delinquency may have already exerted their influence by high school and may have been set in motion before the sophomore year. They also noted that the absence of major effects of tracking on delinquency in their analysis may reflect the fact that students eventually accept their placement in a given curriculum (87 percent of the sample were satisfied with their curriculum). They believe it is unlikely that delinquency was caused by alienation from or dissatisfaction with curriculum placement. Young peoples' attitudes and behavior are certainly influenced and molded through their associations in schools, their families, and their peers, but Wiatrowski and his associates believe that more research needs to be done to identify how these processes work and what factors are most influential. Kenneth Polk (1982) questioned the methodology and data interpretation of the study by Wiatrowski et al. and insisted that there is empirical evidence that forms of school stratification such as grades, school attachment, self-esteem, and tracking are in fact interrelated and that school experiences are significantly related to delinquency.

There seems to be no question that poor grades, low-ability tracking, and maladaptive behavior in school are associated with disruptive and delinquent behavior. It is highly questionable, however, whether there is a causal relationship. In his review of several papers on labeling presented at the third Vanderbilt Sociology Conference in 1974, Walter Gove concluded that evidence does not support the position of the labeling perspective that being labeled deviant is the major cause of deviant identities and lifestyles. Rather,

> it is the behavior or condition of the person that is the critical factor in causing someone to be labelled a deviant. . . . [T]he evidence reviewed consistently indicates that labelling is not the major cause of the development of stabilized deviant behavior. In fact, labelling often appears to have the opposite effect. For example . . . with crime and drug addiction labelling appears to have a deterrent effect. (Gove, 1975: 295)

This is not to deny that school tracking is often based on nonacademic criteria and often does limit the learning potential of some students. Most evidence shows, however, that students' academic abilities and performance are the foremost criteria for grouping in the school setting. There is little evidence to indicate that labels are applied to students independent of some behavioral differences or that it is the labels that cause disruptive and delinquent behavior (see also Gottfredson and Hirschi, 1990: 160). The relationship of school tracking, performance, and delinquency has raised differing opinions, but the issue certainly directs our attention to school structure and the educational process and the effects that these have on school experiences and delinquency.

Are Schools to Blame for Delinquency?

We have noted earlier in our discussion that schools are a reflection of society. As important social institutions, schools are a part of the community, and they reflect both the best and often the worst aspects of any community. They give the community pride and identity—and some schools reflect the divisiveness, segregation, and inequality that unfortunately characterize some communities. The nature of the community, its people, and its leaders, can limit the potential of schools; in spite of the professionalism and determination of some very dedicated school administrators and teachers, it is often difficult to overcome some of the obstacles that stand in the way of creating a positive learning environment.

Jack Frymier (1992) and his associates at Phi Delta Kappa have studied this issue of whether schools are to blame for the difficulties children face in growing up, getting an education, and becoming productive citizens. They reviewed volumes of studies dealing with educational problems, the difficulties facing children at risk, and how the problems children face outside school limit their ability to learn once they are in the classroom. They studied 21,706 students and 9,652 teachers in 276 different schools throughout the United States to determine some of the problems that place children at risk and some of the strategies used by teachers in the educational process. The survey research results reported by Frymier are very helpful in answering the question of whether schools are in fact to blame for educational failure, and for delinquency.

> Everyone "knows" . . . that schools have not caused all or even most of the problems with which children have to deal. The school does not cause some children to come to school hungry every day. The school did not cause an increase in the divorce rate or alcohol consumption or parental conflict or adolescent suicide. The school did not promote the inanity of much of television programming today. The school did not push the National Rifle Association's agenda of no restrictions on gun sales and no registration of handguns. Those problems have all resulted from conditions in the home and circumstances in the larger culture. (Frymier, 1992: vi)

Frymier acknowledges that schools are *not* doing a perfect job, and they emphasize that it would be wrong for teachers and administrators either to not attempt to improve schools or to give up because so many students come to school unmotivated and unprepared to learn because of family and community problems. Educators must do the best they can, in spite of difficulties they and students face and must develop new and better ways of making schools positive learning environments where teachers can teach effectively and where students are positively involved.

Factors That Make Learning Difficult

Children and youth face several difficulties that tend to interfere with their ability to concentrate on the numerous tasks required to perform successfully in school. Factor analysis conducted by Frymier revealed five factors that impede learning: personal pain, academic failure, family tragedy, family socioeconomic situation, and family stability (1992: 26). These five factors and the individual items that constitute each of them are summarized in Table 6–2.

The cross-sectional design of the survey research conducted by Frymier et al. made it impossible to determine the exact causal relationship of the five factors. Intercorrelations of the at-risk factors make it difficult to determine which are causes and which are effects. Parents' educational and employment status are related, and together they may partially explain frequent moves and childrens' changes in schools. Lack of stability in children's residence and school

Table 6–2
Factors Placing Students At Risk of School Failure and Delinquency

Personal Pain	*Academic Failure*	*Family Tragedy*
Suspended from school	Low grades	Parent sick
Attempted suicide	Failed courses	Parent died
Involved in pregnancy	Overage in grade	Parent lost job
Student sold drugs	Retained in grade	Friend died
Student used drugs	Excessive absences	Student ill
Student used alcohol	Low self-esteem	Sibling died
Parent was alcoholic	Referred to Spec. Ed.	
Student arrested	Low reading scores	
Student abused		
Socioeconomic Situation	*Family Instability*	
Father unemployed or in low-level job	Broken home	
Father not H.S. grad.	Moved frequently	
Mother unemployed or in low-level job	Changed schools frequently	
Mother not H.S. grad.	Parents divorced last year	
Parents' negative attitude to education		
English not primary language		

Source: Frymier, 1992. *Growing Up Is Risky Business, and Schools Are Not to Blame.* Bloomington, Ind.: Phi Delta Kappa.

status weakens the possibility of stable peer relations and partially explains the use or selling of drugs and the arrest risk. All of these factors place students at risk of academic failure. It is clear that family problems and parents' lack of support for education precede children's problems and potential failure in school. The opposite (students' school problems causing parental and family problems) is highly unlikely. The causal order is not as clear with school performance and behavioral problems, however. Some researchers have concluded from their evidence that school failure leads to delinquency, which then leads to dropping out; they note that delinquency rates decrease during summer vacations and after students drop out of school (see Elliott and Voss, 1974; and see Chapter 5). Others argue that association with delinquent peers and involvement in delinquency lead to absenteeism, school failure, and dropout (see Thornberry et al., 1985; and Jarjoura, 1993; also discussed in Chapter 5). Thus, we can not determine with certainty which of the factors are independent, dependent, or intervening variables, that is, which are causes of the others and which are effects.

    School variables are one of the most significant correlates in any study that examines youths' self-reported delinquency. Youth involved in delinquency also misbehave in school. They do not like school, they do not do well in school, and they are frequently truant. Michael Gottfredson and Travis Hirschi (1990) attribute the school-delinquency correlations to the school's system of rewards and restraints and the student's abilities and level of self-control:

> The school restrains conduct in several ways: it requires young people to be at a certain place at a certain time; it requires them to do things when they are not under its direct surveillance; and it requires young people to be quiet, physically inactive, and attentive. . . . At the same time, the school rewards punctuality, the completion of homework, and proper deportment; it also rewards demonstrations of academic competence, providing in return affection from teachers, advancement within the system, and ultimately educational certification and occupational success. . . . The school, in other words, is a sanctioning system implicated in the socialization of children. (Gottfredson and Hirschi, 1990:162–163)

These school rewards and sanctions, however, depend equally on parents for their implementation. The school cannot very well sanction youth for not complying with its behavioral expectations or reward students for good school work without parents and families who are supportive of educational goals and means. Gottfredson and Hirschi acknowledge that school sanctions do not affect the behavior of all children equally. Students who do poorly in school do not experience the rewards of academic accomplishments and are unlikely to be restrained by threats of suspension or expulsion for misbehavior. Delinquents therefore "tend to avoid and eventually to leave school in favor of less restricted environments" (Gottfredson and Hirschi, 1990: 163).

Problems characteristic of at-risk students are variously both causes and effects of negative school experiences. They are associated with difficulties in school, often with school failure, and sometimes with delinquent behavior. Unfortunately, most of these problems are beyond the power of the school to change. The school cannot be blamed for family problems and for the personal problems of students. The school is charged with the responsibility for providing a quality educational opportunity for all students. Teachers and administrators are charged with the responsibility for providing a positive educational environment in which students may learn and obtain skills and knowledge commensurate with their level of ability and the effort expended.

> Schools have an obligation to improve the quality of life for young people, and educators work hard to make that come about. But when people outside the schools mouth platitudes about family and home and parents, then blame the school for children's failure to learn what they need to learn, their act of blaming is unconscionable.
>
> Schools reflect society, they do not lead it. Schools are not doing as much as they can, nor are they as effective as they ought to be. . . . But the problems that most children face lie outside the school rather than inside, on the street rather than on the playground, and in the living room rather than in the classroom. (Frymier, 1992: 32)

In summary, it is difficult to support the argument that schools are to blame for failure and delinquency. There are characteristics of school structure and the teaching process that seem to be associated with positive or negative learning environments, however. These characteristics are of course within the power of administrators and teachers to change—given that sufficient resources and support exist from the community and the taxpayers. We direct our attention to these next.

What Teachers Can Do

As part of the Phi Delta Kappa study, teachers were asked what they did to help specific students and how they worked with students who were at risk. Thirteen examples of special teacher and school efforts were identified and are summarized in Table 6–3.

Teachers at the fourth-grade level reported that they used more instructional procedures to help students than did teachers at the seventh- or tenth-grade levels. The differences suggest that teachers at the elementary level knew their students better; they had more time with each students; they were more responsive to students' needs; or that the secondary teachers may not have known what instructional provisions were being made for students, who typically had six or more different teachers (Frymier, 1992: 34–35).

The 9,652 teachers in the study were asked whether they used some of thirty different teaching strategies, and how effective they seemed to be. The teaching strategies and the teachers' responses are summarized in Table 6–4. These strategies are naturally limited by whether the school districts have the available programs and resources. Teachers who are assigned to classrooms with thirty or more students and who have very limited educational support services available in their school districts must struggle to help a wide variety of students with individualized teaching strategies, with only limited outside help. Unfortunately, the greatest number of at-risk students who are most in need of educational support services are in rural or inner-city schools, where resources are often stretched the thinnest (see, e.g., Kozol, 1991).

Teachers were asked to indicate who was most responsible for helping students to acquire the learning or behavior in ten different areas. The teachers thought that they (teachers) were responsible for reading, mathematics, writ-

Table 6–3
School and Teacher Efforts for At-Risk Students

•Placed in a smaller class	•Provided with extra homework
•Offered computerized instruction	•Given extra opportunities for parental involvement
•Referred to Special Education	
•Placed in lower group or track	•Offered extra instruction in basic skills
•Given individualized instruction	
•Allowed flexible scheduling	•Referred child to psychologist
•Given tutoring or special assistance	
•Provided with special instructional materials	•Provided with special teachers

Source: Frymier 1992. *Growing Up Is Risky Business, and Schools Are Not to Blame.* Bloomington, Ind.: Phi Delta Kappa.

Table 6–4
Teaching Strategies for At-Risk Students

	Use Regularly	Think Effective		Use Regularly	Think Effective
Smaller classes	49%	87%	Extra homework	23%	26%
Computerized instruction	23	50	Emphasize study skills	86	83
Special teachers	67	85	Restrict from sports	33	38
Peer tutoring	63	81	Refer to psychologist	60	71
Retain in grade	44	48	Refer to social worker	54	70
Special education	73	84	Confer with parents	94	81
Vocational courses	50	79	More time on basic skills	84	87
Alternative school	37	69			
Special study skills	69	83	Eliminate art and music	6	9
Special textbooks	48	71			
Place in low group	55	55	Notify parents	94	81
Emphasize coping skills	68	83	Chapter 1 program	95	79
			Teacher aides	48	77
Flexible scheduling	48	69	Say "leave at 16"	10	15
Individualize instruction	79	91	Before-school programs	23	47
			After-school programs	42	63
Home tutoring	24	62	Summer school programs	56	71

Source: Frymier 1992. *Growing Up Is Risky Business, and Schools Are Not to Blame.* Bloomington, Ind.: Phi Delta Kappa.

ing, listening, and higher-order thinking skills. Teachers thought that parents were responsible for students' daily attendance and attitude toward school; that students and teachers were responsible for attention in class; and that parents and students were responsible for completion of homework and general behavior in school (Frymier, 1992: 37).

According to this recent research conducted on a fairly representative cross-section of teachers from 276 schools, there seems to be clear evidence that teachers provide students who are at risk with more instructional efforts than they offer other students who are not at risk. Teachers seem to take responsibility for providing the best possible education for students and are committed to helping students who are in need of special help. At the same time, they are also saying that some of the responsibility for school success lies with students themselves and with their parents. Teachers are trained to apply their skills on educational problems and to come up with appropriate solutions. They have less influence and less responsibility for dealing with problems that originate in society or in the home. Many of these problems affect how well students attend to and master basic educational skills. There are limits to what teachers and schools can do, but the data from this study indicate that many of the teachers work very hard to help students who have special problems.

School Programs and Teaching Strategies

There are wide variations among schools in the kinds of programs and teaching strategies used and in the intensity with which the teaching staff apply different efforts. Evaluation research on ability grouping at the secondary level indicates that it is ineffective and that there may be some negative effects; assigning students to different levels of the same course has no consistent positive or negative effects on students, whether of high, average, or low ability (Slavin, 1990: 494). Promoting students who have not made satisfactory achievement has received criticism, and yet research indicates that there is no evidence that retention is more beneficial than promotion (Jackson, 1975). Holmes and Matthews (1984) concluded from a meta-analysis of forty-four studies that retention is not helpful; promoted students did better in school achievement than the retained group, and nonpromotion actually had negative effects on students (1984: 89). Robert Slavin and Nancy Madden (1989) reviewed research on programs for students at risk and found that while special remedial programs that were diagnostic and prescriptive may keep students from falling further behind, they are not really effective. They found that special education programs seldom bring students up to an acceptable level of school performance, but early intervention, continuous progress, cooperative learning, remedial tutoring, and computer-assisted instruction programs have been effective (Slavin and Madden, 1989). Some special programs for at-risk students are effective at the preschool and elementary levels but not at the secondary levels. At the secondary level, dropout prevention programs that have been successful generally are characterized by student success in school; positive student/adult relationships; relevance of school experience; and reduction of outside interference from gang-related activities and drug use (McPartland and Slavin, 1990). McLaughlin et al. (1990) found that a "personalized school environment" that included an "ethic of caring" made a difference in at-risk students' achievement. They noted that a personalized school environment is a matter of organizational design in schools and is not limited to individual teachers' practices and values.

J. David Hawkins and Tony Lam (1987) tested a model of classroom-based instructional strategies designed to assist in delinquency prevention. Their model consisted of three instructional strategies: proactive classroom management, interactive teaching, and cooperative learning (1987: 250–251). Implementation of the strategies after one year did not lead to consistent differences in the perceptions of experimental and control students, but there was evidence of some promising trends. Students were more likely to engage in learning activities and less likely to be off-task in the classroom; they spent more time on homework; they developed greater educational aspirations and expectations for themselves; and they were less likely to be suspended or expelled from school when their teachers used these instructional strategies (1987: 268). Hawkins and Lam believe the experimental teaching strategies "may create an environment of greater opportunity for involvement and skill development in classrooms for a larger proportion of students" (1987: 268).

We have emphasized throughout this book the important role that parents play in helping their children achieve in school and avoid delinquent behavior. Sara Lawrence Lightfoot (1978), in her book *Worlds Apart: Relationships Between Families and Schools,* noted that cultural developments had separated the home and the school—the two main social institutions important in children's lives. She observed parents and teachers carrying out their separate roles with little contact with each other. She further noted that the division extended to researchers in education and child development, who tended to focus their scholarly efforts on the child either in the school or in the home. This barrier between parents and teachers has not gone unnoticed by teachers and school administrators, who frequently complain about the lack of interest and support shown by parents for their children's school performance. There is evidence, however, that educators do little to cultivate a closer working relationship with parents. Henry Becker and Joyce Epstein (1982) surveyed 3,700 teachers in Maryland regarding their involvement with parents. According to their findings, only a few teachers initiated interactions with parents beyond what was minimally expected of them; they did not seem to know how to work with parents; and many avoided using strategies that involved informal learning activities for students in the home, believing they would be too difficult for parents. Fewer than 10 percent of the teachers in this sample requested parental cooperation (Becker and Epstein, 1982).

Much more can, and should, be done by educators to elicit parental involvement in their children's education. Part of the problem seems to be the failure to recognize the changes that are occurring in the American family. Fewer children are living with both biological parents. Some share time with both parents, individually and at different residences, following a divorce settlement that involves joint custody. A study cosponsored by the National Association of Elementary School Principals and the Charles F. Kettering Foundation concluded that schools play an important role in the lives of single parents and their children and that they must be recognized as a valid family unit (see Maeroff, 1982: 212). Gene Maeroff cited findings of a survey of 1,200 single parents in forty-seven states conducted in 1980 by the National Committee for Citizens in Education. According to survey results, in fewer than 5 percent of the cases did the parent without custody receive information about school activities from the school, and in fewer than 7 percent of the cases did that same person get a copy of the youngster's report card from the school (Maeroff, 1982: 212). Maeroff suggested that educators stop using the term "broken home" and discard their assumptions related to single-parent families and their children (i.e., that the children will automatically have problems in school performance and in behavior). Schools should maintain records on names and addresses of both parents following divorce, and identical reports should be sent to both of them (Maeroff, 1982: 213).

A separate but related issue is that of parents' and citizens' involvement in school decisions regarding curriculum, activities, and policies. As with school performance, there is little parental or citizen involvement in school policy-making decisions. Maeroff is critical of parents who tend to sit back and let their school board members get involved for them. He contended that tax-payers are simply too willing to delegate all responsibility for the schools to the few people who are willing to take on the burden of school board service (Maeroff, 1982: 213). Few nonboard members attend the school board meetings, and there is little communication between the public and board members. The result is that few taxpayers have any idea of what is happening in the schools.

Teachers and administrators complain about parents' lack of interest and involvement in their children's school performance and about parents' lack of support for educators in dealing with students' attendance and behavior problems. The idea of parental involvement in school policies and decisions is not welcomed by educators, however. Many teachers and school administrators do not believe that parents have the right to exert influence on the schools (Maeroff, 1982: 208). Most schools do not make any effort to involve parents in the selection or assignment of teachers or principals; curriculum development; textbook selection; or dress and behavior regulations. Nancy Chavkin and David Williams (1987) surveyed parents and school administrators in six southwestern states and reported that parents expressed interest in participating in more school decisions than educators believed would be useful. Many educators may avoid parents' input on hiring, curriculum, and textbook selection out of a belief that few parents have the qualifications and background to contribute meaningfully in such decisions. Most school districts generally make an effort to inform students and their parents about regulations regarding dress and behavior and about the consequences for violating school rules. Students and parents are seldom involved in the process of developing school codes and sanctions, however. There is ample evidence that codes of conduct are more likely to be supported when the persons affected have a role in their development. This is a point that cannot be underscored enough. Since some of the teachers' most vocal complaints relate to students' dress styles and behavior in school—and to the lack of parental support for school discipline—it stands to reason that every effort to gain student and parental support is to the teachers' and principals' advantage. Most parents will still be reluctant to become more involved, because of time constraints and because they view education as the primary responsibility of the paid professionals—teachers and principals.

School Performance: Whose Responsibility?

Frymier (1992) concluded that schools must provide quality educational programs that are geared to the learning abilities and skills, past experience, and motivation and interest level of students. The ultimate responsibility for successful school achievement lies with the individual student, however.

> Teachers must do what they can to incite energy output, and . . . must time things so that curiosity will peak at the moment stimulus material is available and in a form to be perceived. But the energy for learning comes from the learner, and the responsibility for learning must be assumed by the student. The student must reach out . . . and grasp or grapple with information that the teacher presents. . . . That

interaction between student and content must be nurtured, reinforced, practiced, and reflected upon to bring about understanding and meaningfulness, but the student has to lead that charge. (Frymier, 1992: 68)

This is surely not debatable—no learning can happen unless the student is receptive and responsible. But the question still arises as to why so many students have difficulty learning or refuse to take education seriously and become actively involved in school. It is one thing to insist that students be responsible for active involvement in the educational process, but in reality too few students have been encouraged by their parents to pursue education seriously. Too few parents are positive role models for the value of education. Books, newspapers, and informative magazines are increasingly rare in too many homes. Television viewing has taken the place of reading and has replaced lively and informative conversations over the dinner table (and today few families even sit down for meals together). It is unlikely that we will see many changes in families' active support for education, so the primary responsibility for motivating students will fall upon the schools. One promising strategy is for schools to implement programs to improve family-school relationships. Bruce Ryan and Gerald Adams (1995) have recommended a family-school relationships model that takes into account different family patterns and contexts and encourages within-the-family learning processes, support and encouragement for learning and homework, monitoring of attendance and homework, and open discussion of about school concerns and problems (1995: 6, 10).

Most persons do want to learn, and most aspire to succeed. Even students who are at risk in school are interested in learning and in succeeding in a job or career in the future. The problem is that they often do not see the school curriculum as relevant to what they need to know in order to succeed, and many youth have unrealistic career expectations that exceed their current level of skills and academic performance. But is this the fault of students? Or have schools failed to convey clearly the relevance of school course material for life and job success? A reasonable explanation for some children's difficulty in learning or refusal to learn is that

> what we require them to learn is perceived as threatening or irrelevant or meaningless. Our bureaucratic approach to schooling has an aura of rationality that makes it difficult for professionals to question either the what or the how of education. From the child's point of view . . . either the what or the how . . . may not be in harmony with the life force of the individual. Our logic of curriculum may not match the psychology of their learning preferences or styles or needs. We are good at convincing ourselves as adults that what we are doing is noble and worthwhile, but it may not square with children's needs, or at least not with some children's needs. (Frymier, 1992: 68–69)

We must also recognize that children's educational needs vary considerably. There are certain basic skills (such as reading, writing, and arithmetic!) that all persons need to function well. Beyond those basic skills, however, there is considerable variation in what must be learned to be a machinist, an office assistant, a retail sales representative, a teacher, or a medical specialist. What a person needs to learn to be a well-functioning, self-directed, independent and rational individual also varies and depends on skills and understanding for which elementary and secondary education only begin to provide the basic foundation. What a person needs in order to appreciate historical events and sites, art, music, and the traditions of other cultures experienced through travels and everyday life is quite different from the skills needed to meet the demands of everyday life.

We expect a lot from our schools—possibly too much. Educators are criticized for failing to provide all students with some degree of historical and cultural awareness and some social and personal skills in addition to basic educational skills. That criticism is not without foundation. Thousands of students graduate from high school each year with skills and knowledge that would hardly place them at a ninth-grade level. College professors and employers decry the sad level of preparation of many of the high school graduates they see. In the study of teachers and students in 276 high schools throughout the country, Frymier report that never did as many as 50 percent of the at-risk students get the special assistance they needed (1992: 69).

> In one sense, teachers and schools were making mighty efforts to help those who were at risk. In another sense, they were not even beginning to make a dent on the problem. Their heart was in the right place—teachers helped students who were at risk more than students who were not at risk—but most students who were at risk were not provided with special efforts of any kind, and most students who were not at risk got even less assistance. (Frymier, 1992: 69)

Are schools failing? Are schools to blame for students' lack of interest in learning and for the underachievement of so many? One hundred years ago, fewer than 10 percent of Americans finished high school; today more than 80 percent of young people graduate (Frymier, 1992: 16). We are succeeding in retaining more students, but our success in this area means that there are more young people in school who do not want to be there, some who have special difficulties in learning, and some who disrupt the educational process for teachers and those students who want to learn.

There is room for improvement in American education. Educators can reassess school structure and the educational process. We can develop more and better ways to assess students, what they need to know, and how best to teach them. We can develop better ways to use time, materials, and teaching methods. More collaboration with industry and business may help. More support from parents and community leaders would also help. Surely the future of our young people, and the future of our country deserve our best efforts in improving our educational system.

Summary

The way in which schools are structured and organized and the strategies used by teachers in the educational process both affect the quality of students' educational experiences. In this chapter we addressed the related issues of inequality in school funding, school reforms, and their effect on at-risk students. Many criminologists have contended that schools are partially to blame for students' failure and the resultant delinquency of some. Educational researchers, on the other hand, have emphasized the many problems in the home, the community, and among peers that affect school success or failure and that are beyond the schools' control or influence. There are some teaching strategies that are effective in helping at-risk students perform better academically and avoid involvement in delinquent behavior.

References

Adler, Mortimer. 1982. *The Paideia Proposal.* New York: Macmillan.

Alter, Jonathan. 1992. "The Body Count at Home." *Newsweek* 120 (Dec. 28):55.

Becker, Henry J., and Joyce L. Epstein. 1982. "Parent Involvement: A Survey of Teacher Practices." *Elementary School Journal* 83:85–102.

Becker, Howard. 1963. *Outsiders.* New York: Free Press.

Boyer, Ernest. 1983. *High School: A Report on Secondary Education in America.* New York: Harper and Row.

Chavkin, Nancy F., and David L. Williams. 1987. "Enhancing Parent Involvement: Guidelines for Access to an Important Resource for School Administrators." *Education and Urban Society* 19:164–184.

Cohen, Albert K. 1955. *Delinquent Boys: The Culture of the Gang.* New York: Free Press.

Coleman, James S. 1987. "Equal Schools or Equal Students?" In E. Stevens, Jr. and G. M. Wood, eds., *Justice, Ideology, and Education.* New York: McGraw-Hill.

Copperman, Paul. 1980. *The Literacy Hoax.* New York: William Morrow.

Elliott, Delbert S. and Harwin H. Ross. (1974). *Delinquency and Dropout.* Lexington, Mass.: Lexington Books.

Frymier, Jack. 1992. *Growing Up Is Risky Business, and Schools Are Not to Blame.* Bloomington, Ind.: Phi Delta Kappa.

Goodlad, John. 1984. *A Place Called School.* New York: McGraw-Hill.

Gottfredson, Michael R., and Travis Hirschi. 1990. A General Theory of Crime. Stanford, Calif.: Stanford University Press.

Gove, Walter, Ed. 1975. *The Labelling of Deviance: Evaluating a Perspective.* New York: John Wiley.

Grubb, W. Norton. 1985. "The Initial Effects of House Bill 72 on Texas Public Schools: The Challenge of Equity and Effectiveness." Lyndon B. Johnson School of Public Affairs Policy Research Project Report No. 70. Austin: The University of Texas.

Hall, Ginger. 1987. "State School Fund Plan Ruled Illegal." *San Antonio Express-News,* April 30, 1,8–9.

Haney, Craig, and Philip G. Zimbardo. 1975. "It's Tough to Tell a High School from a Prison." *Psychology Today* (June): 26, 29–30, 106.

Hawkins, J. David, and Tony Lam. 1987. "Teacher Practices, Social Development, and Delinquency." In J. D. Burchard and S. N. Burchard, eds., *Prevention of Delinquent Behavior.* Newbury Park, Calif.: Sage.

Holmes, C. Thomas, and Kenneth M. Matthews. 1984. "The Effects of Nonpromotion on Elementary and Junior High School Pupils: A Meta-Analysis." *Review of Educational Research* 54:225–236.

Jackson, G. B. 1975. "The Research Evidence on Grade Retention." *Review of Educational Research* 45:613–635.

Jarjoura, G. Roger. 1993. "Does Dropping Out of School Enhance Delinquent Involvement? Results from a Large-Scale National Probability Sample." *Criminology* 31:149–171.

Jencks, C., M. Smith, H. Acland, M. J. Bane, D. Cohen, M. Gintis, B. Heyns, and S. Michelson. 1972. *Inequality: A Reassessment of the Effect of Family and Schooling in America.* New York: Basic Books.

Katz, Jeffrey L. 1991. "The Search for Equity in School Funding." *Governing* (August): 20–22.

Kelly, Delos H. 1977. "How the School and Teachers Create Deviants." *Contemporary Education* 48(4):202–205.

Kelly, Delos H., and Winthrop D. Grove. 1981. "Teachers' Nominations and the Production of Academic 'Misfits.' " *Education* 101:246–263.

Kelly, Delos H., and William T. Pink. 1982. "School Crime and Individual Responsibility: The Perpetuation of a Myth?" *Urban Review* 14(1):47–63.

Kozol, Jonathan. 1991. *Savage Inequalities.* New York: Harper Perennial.

Lawrence, Richard. 1986. "School Reform and Student Problems: An Evaluation of Texas House Bill 72 and Its Effects on At-Risk Youth." Paper presented at the Annual Meeting of the Midwest Criminal Justice Association, Chicago.

Lightfoot, Sara Lawrence. 1978. *Worlds Apart: Relationships Between Families and Schools.* New York: Basic Books.

Maeroff, Gene I. 1982. *Don't Blame the Kids.* New York: McGraw-Hill.

McLaughlin, Milbrey W., and Joan Talbert. 1990. "Constructing a Personalized School Environment." *Phi Delta Kappan* 72(3):230–235.

McPartland, James M., and Robert E. Slavin. 1990. *Policy Perspectives: Increasing Achievement of At-Risk Students at Each Grade Level.* Washington, D.C.: U.S. Department of Education.

National Commission in Excellence in Education. 1983. *A Nation at Risk: The Imperative for Educational Reform.* Washington, DC: U.S. Government Printing Office.

Nijboer, J. A., and F. P. H. Dijksterhuis. 1983. "Education and Delinquency: The Relationship Between Performance at School and Delinquency." *International Summaries.* Washington, D.C.: National Institute of Justice.

Polk, Kenneth, 1982. "Curriculum Tracking and Delinquency: Some Observations." *American Sociological Review* 47:282–284.

Polk, Kenneth. 1982. "Schools and the Delinquency Experience." In D. Rojek and G. Jensen, eds., *Readings in Juvenile Delinquency.* Lexington, Mass.: D.C. Heath.

Reutter, E. Edmund, Jr. 1982. *The Supreme Court's Impact on Public Education.* Bloomington, Ind.: Phi Delta Kappa and National Organization of Legal Problems of Education.

Rutter, Michael. 1983. "School Effects on Pupil Progress: Research Findings and Policy Implications." *Child Development* 54:1–29.

Ryan, Bruce A., and Gerald R. Adams. 1995. "The Family-School Relationships Model." In B. A. Ryan, G. R. Adams, T. P. Gullotta, R. P. Weissberg, and R. L. Hampton, eds. *The Family School Connection: Theory, Research and Practice.* Thousand Oaks, Calif.: Sage.

Schafer, Walter E. 1972. "Deviance in the Public School: An Interactional View." In K. Polk and W. E. Schafer, eds., *Schools and Delinquency.* Englewood Cliffs, N.J.: Prentice-Hall.

Schafer, Walter E., Carol Olexa, and Kenneth Polk. 1972. "Programmed for Social Class: Tracking in High School." In K. Polk and W. E. Schafer, eds., *Schools and Delinquency.* Englewood Cliffs, N.J.: Prentice-Hall.

Schafer, Walter E., and Kenneth Polk. 1972. "School Conditions Contributing to Delinquency." In K. Polk and W. E. Schafer, eds. *Schools and Delinquency.* Englewood Cliffs, NJ: Prentice-Hall.

Slavin, Robert E. 1990. "Achievement Effects of Ability Grouping in Secondary Schools: A Best-Evidence Synthesis." *Review of Educational Research* 60(3):471–499.

Slavin, Robert E., and Nancy A. Madden. 1989. "What Works for Students at Risk: A Research Synthesis." *Educational Leadership* 46:4–13.

Smith, R. C., and E. L. Hester. 1985. *Who's Looking Out for At-Risk Youth?* Chapel Hill, N.C.: MDC.

Stevens, Edward, Jr., and George H. Wood. 1987. *Justice, Ideology and Education.* New York: McGraw-Hill.

Thornberry, Terence P., Melanie Moore, and R. L. Christensen. 1985. "The Effect of Dropping Out of High School on Subsequent Criminal Behavior." *Criminology* 23:3–18.

Wenk, Ernst A. 1975. "Juvenile Justice and the Public Schools: Mutual Benefit Through Educational Reform." *Juvenile Justice* 26:7–14.

Wiatrowski, Michael D., Stephen Hansell, Charles R. Massey, and David L. Wilson. 1982. "Curriculum Tracking and Delinquency." *American Sociological Review* 47:151–160.

Wise, Arthur E. 1968. *Rich Schools, Poor Schools.* Chicago: University of Chicago Press.

7

School Law and
Students' Rights

It can hardly be argued that either students or teachers shed their constitutional rights . . . at the schoolhouse gate. . . . In our system, state-operated schools may not be enclaves of totalitarianism. School officials do not possess absolute authority over their students. Students in school as well as out of school are "persons" under our Constitutions. They are possessed of fundamental rights which the State must respect. . . .—Justice Abe Fortas, *Tinker v. Des Moines Independent Community School District*, 309 U.S. at 506, 511, (1969)

The issue of students' rights has emerged as a focus of attention in discussions about misconduct in schools.[1] Many school officials and citizens are convinced that the growing problems of student disruption and general lack of respect for authorities are attributable directly to an overemphasis on students' rights. Some believe that the balance has shifted from teachers' authority to students' rights. We address those issues in this chapter and outline the disciplinary procedures and sanctions that have been upheld by the courts as acceptable for schools to use in enforcing rules, including the use of corporal punishment. Students do have rights. They do not (in the words of Justice Abe Fortas) "shed their rights at the schoolhouse gate." The U.S. Supreme Court in *Tinker v. Des Moines* reminded educators and school boards that schools may not be operated in a totalitarian manner, with absolute authority over students. In this chapter we discuss the authority of school boards and officials in developing and enforcing school rules and students' rights and responsibilities relating to school rules. Most of the focus in this chapter is on what the courts have determined to be reasonable and fair enforcement of rules and on various court decisions that protect students against school sanctions that have been found to be unreasonable and unconstitutional.

The increase in violence, drugs, and weapons in schools has directed our attention to the need to take all reasonable steps to ensure a safe learning environment for students and teachers. Rather than view students' rights as impeding school officials' authority, we must see the rights and responsibilities of students and educators in a broader context. An emphasis on the proper balance of rights of both students and teachers is especially appropriate in an educational setting. Treating students as young citizens of the community, with rights and responsibilities, teaches an invaluable lesson in preparation for life in a democratic society.

Given the demands for equal rights among disadvantaged groups such as minorities and women over the past few decades , it should not be surprising that students have also exerted their rights under the U.S. Constitution. Most school administrators and many teachers will at some time in their career be involved in a lawsuit or legal challenge (see Chandler, 1992). Although there is evidence that many educators lack sufficient knowledge of Supreme Court decisions that affect them (Reglin, 1992), most school districts have worked to develop clear policies and regulations and to communicate them to teachers, parents, and students. Certainly one of the benefits of the increase in litigation involving schools is the development of clear policies and guidelines and the efforts to communicate them to students and parents.

School teachers and principals are given wide authority and power in supervising students and regulating their conduct. The authority of school officials is not absolute, however, and actions taken to enforce school rules and discipline students must at all times be reasonable. The courts have given school boards and officials considerable discretion in establishing and enforcing regulations, but they have also closely examined school policies to ensure reasonableness and fairness. School rules are considered reasonable if they contribute to advancing the educational process, and they are generally considered fair and sufficiently clear "if they provide students with adequate information as to what is expected of them and are so stated that persons of common intelligence are not required to guess at their meaning" (Alexander and Alexander, 1992: 279). In addition to relating directly to the educational process, school rules are usually upheld by courts if they use terminology that parents and students can be expected to understand. School regulations do not have to be formally adopted and published, and the absence of formally adopted rules may not limit formal action by school officials, but the formal adoption and publication of rules is certainly more convincing to courts when schools seek to prove that a given rule was necessary and was enforced fairly.

Common Law and the Student

Various court decisions over the years have established what is referred to as a "common law of the school" (see Alexander and Alexander, 1992: 279f.). Under the common law as defined through various court decisions, teachers and students both have certain rights and responsibilities. These rights and responsibilities have their basis in what is necessary in order for schools to fulfill their educational objectives and meet the expectations that society places on them. The courts generally have recognized that teachers have a great responsibility to educate students and therefore have given teachers considerable latitude in controlling student conduct in order to maintain a positive learning environment in the classroom. Teachers have what has been referred to as "inherent authority" in their role as educators. "Inherent" means that the teacher's authority is not limited to what is spelled out literally in school policies, regulations, and handbooks. By virtue of the special teacher-student relationship, the teacher also has an obligation "to promote the harmony of the school by requiring discipline while protecting and advancing the interest of the child" (Alexander and Alexander, 1992: 280). In a ruling more than a century ago, the Wisconsin Supreme Court enunciated the extent of the teacher's authority.

> While the principal or teacher in charge of a public school is subordinate to the school board . . . and must enforce rules and regulations adopted by the board . . . he does not derive all his power and authority in the school and over his pupils from the affirmative action of the board. He stands for the time being *in loco parentis* to his pupils, and because of that relation, he must necessarily exercise authority over them in many things concerning which the board may have remained silent. (*State ex rel. Burpee v. Burton*, 45 Wis. 150, 30 Am. Rep. 706 [1878])

Students also have a responsibility to conduct themselves in a manner that allows school officials to fulfill the educational function of the school. Thus, while students enjoy their rights to a public education, they are expected at the same time to conduct themselves in a way that does not interfere with the educational goals of teachers or other students. This means that individual student rights in the school are subordinate to the right of teachers and other students to pursue educational goals uninterrupted and in a safe environment. Students' responsibilities were defined by the Wisconsin Supreme Court in the same case just cited.

> In the school, as in the family, there exist on the part of the pupils the obligations of obedience to lawful commands, subordination, civil deportment, respect for the rights of other pupils and fidelity to duty. These obligations are inherent in any proper school system, and constitute . . . the common law, and is subject, whether it has or has not been reenacted by the district board in the form of written rules and regulations. Indeed it would seem impossible to frame rules which would cover all cases of insubordination and all acts of vicious tendency which the teacher is liable to encounter daily and hourly. (State ex rel. Burpee v. Burton, 45 Wis. 150, 30 Am. Rep. 706 [1878])

The school is often referred to as a community, and indeed the rights and responsibilities of students and teachers are very similar to those of citizens in society. Some reduction of individual rights and freedoms may be necessary in order for the community to harmoniously meet its objectives. Political philosophers such as Thomas Hobbes and Jean-Jacques Rousseau have referred to the "social contract" whereby individual and community rights and duties are balanced for the common good of the community. The same concept may be correctly applied to the balance of rights and responsibilities of teachers and of students in public schools. An early ruling by a court in Missouri illustrates this balance of rights and responsibilities.

The teacher of a school as to the children of his school, while under his care, occupies, for the time being, the position of parent or guardian, and it is his right and duty not only to enforce discipline to preserve order and to teach, but also to look after the morals, the health and the safety of his pupils; to do and require his pupils to do whatever is reasonably necessary to preserve and conserve all these interests. (State v. Randall, 79 Mo. App 226 [1899])

Reasonableness of School Rules

School rules must be reasonable, that is, they must be related to educational objectives, and the discipline or sanctions for violation of the rules must not be unfair or excessive. "Reasonableness" is a central concept in the law and is a major test of whether rules and regulations will stand up in court. Reasonableness generally refers to "that which is proper, rational, and fair; and precludes conduct that can be characterized as immoderate, excessive, and unsuitable to the particular conditions or circumstances (Alexander and Alexander, 1992: 281). The authority of teachers and school officials in responding to a multitude of different behaviors and examples of misconduct under a variety of circumstances cannot possibly be spelled out exactly in written rules and regulations. Courts have therefore allowed for considerable flexibility in determining what is reasonable as teachers and school officials take disciplinary actions.

In Loco Parentis

The English translation of the Latin term *in loco parentis* is "in the place of the parent." The concept originated in English law that gave schoolmasters parent-like authority over students. Teachers' and school officials' roles as authorities and guardians of students are limited to school functions and activities and must be limited to what is considered reasonable. While there are limitations, the intent of the *in loco parentis* doctrine under the law has been to help define the school-student relationship and to help maintain an orderly environment that is conducive to meeting educational goals.

Constitutional Due Process

The Fourteenth Amendment to the U.S. Constitution provides that no state shall deprive a person of life, liberty, or property without due process of law. This post–Civil War amendment has come to be of special importance, since it applies the rights guaranteed to citizens under the federal constitution to actions of state and local agencies of government. Thus, for example, the Fourth Amendment right against unreasonable search and seizure, the Fifth Amendment protection against self-incrimination, and the Sixth Amendment guarantee of the right to legal counsel and to a fair and impartial hearing are all applied to the state government agencies through the Fourteenth Amendment. Stated in a positive way, a state *may* deprive a person of life, liberty, or property as long as the individual is given due process.

There are two kinds of due process: *procedural* and *substantive due process.* Procedural due process requires that a constitutionally prescribed procedure must be followed before a person may be deprived of life, liberty, or property. The U.S. Supreme Court has identified three components that make up procedural due process. First, the person must be given proper notice that he is about to be deprived of life, liberty, or property; second, the person must be given an opportunity to be heard and to present his side of the issue or case; third, the person must receive a fair hearing. The procedures prescribed for and expected to be followed by all police and court officials, including probation officers, all routinely include careful measures to ensure that no persons are stopped, questioned, temporarily detained, or taken into custody for law violations unless these three procedures are provided for in the process. It is now (or should be) common practice for school officials to follow these three mandates when any student is deprived of the liberty to attend school or deprived of property such as illegal substances or weapons.

The second type of due process is called substantive due process. To satisfy this constitutional requirement, before a state may deprive someone of liberty or property, it must show that the objective and methods used have been reasonable and appropriate for accomplishing the objective. An Arizona court defined substantive due process:

> The phrase "due process of law," when applied to substantive rights . . . means that the state is without power to deprive a person of life, liberty or property by an act having no reasonable relation to any proper governmental purpose, or which is so far beyond the necessity of case as to be an arbitrary exercise of governmental power. (Valley National Bank of Phoenix v. Glover, 62 Ariz. 538, 159 P.2d 292 [1945])

Substantive due process is a major factor in court decisions relating to corporal punishment in schools. Courts have upheld the right of school authorities to use physical punishment as a means of discipline. Corporal punishment in schools has not been found to violate the Eighth Amendment against cruel and unusual punishment, as long as school officials can show that the punishment is not excessive and that it reasonably relates to educational objectives. We discuss corporal punishment in more depth later in this chapter.

Suspension and Expulsion

Courts have applied the due process clause of the Fourteenth Amendment to school disciplinary actions that include suspension or expulsion of students. "Expulsion" refers to action taken by a school board to prohibit a student from attending a given school for up to the remainder of that school year. "Suspension" refers to action taken by a school board to prohibit a student from attending school for a shorter period of time, generally no longer than ten school days. Under substantive due process, the school policy should clearly state the grounds for dismissal, and the school board should be able to show that dismissal of any student in a given case is justifiable and appropriate in order to fulfill educational objectives of the school and that the dismissal is not excessive in light of the circumstances of the case. Procedural due process requires written notice to the student giving the grounds for the suspension or expulsion, describing the hearing process, and including a statement summarizing the school officials' decision and the evidence or facts on which the decision was based.

The Supreme Court on Suspensions

The United States Supreme Court ruling in *Goss v. Lopez* (419 U.S. 565, 95 S.Ct. 729 [1975]) detailed the procedural due process requirements for temporary suspension of students. Administrators of the Columbus, Ohio, Public School System (CPSS) appealed the judgment of a federal court that had ruled that various high school students in the CPSS (including the principle appellee, Dwight Lopez) were denied due process of law contrary to the Fourteenth Amendment because they were temporarily suspended without a hearing. Ohio law provided that a principal could suspend a pupil for up to ten days for misconduct or expel the student. In either case, the student's parents were to be notified within twenty-four hours and given reasons for the action. In the case of expulsion (but not suspension), the pupil or his or her parents could appeal the decision to the school board and receive a hearing. Neither the CPSS nor the individual high schools involved had written procedures regarding suspensions. At the time of the case they had only a regulation that referred to the state statute. The suspension procedure was limited to a formal or informal description of the conduct for which suspension could be imposed. Six of the nine students who had appealed the school system's decisions to the federal court had been suspended for disruptive or disobedient conduct; another one student had been immediately suspended for attacking a police officer who was attempting to remove him from the auditorium where he had been demonstrating. One student was arrested along with other students for demonstrating at a high school, taken to the police station, and released without being formally charged. Before that student returned to school the following day, she was notified that she had been suspended for a ten-day period. No one from the school testified regarding the incident, and there was no record detailing the basis on which the principal had made the decisions on suspension. Dwight Lopez was suspended in connection with a disturbance in the lunchroom that involved some physical damage to school property. Lopez testified that he was not a party to the destructive conduct but was an innocent bystander. No one from the school testified regarding the incident, and there was no recorded evidence indicating the official basis for concluding that Lopez was lying. Lopez never had a hearing. On the basis of the evidence, the federal court declared that the students were denied due process of law because they were suspended without a hearing prior to the suspension or within a reasonable time after being suspended. The U.S. Supreme Court upheld the ruling of the federal court.

School officials in *Goss* had argued that because there is no constitutional right to an education at public expense, the due process clause does not protect against expulsions from a public school system. The Court drew upon previous rulings to refute that argument, noting that the due process clause forbidding deprivations of liberty applies where "a person's good name, reputation, honor, or integrity is at stake because of what the government is doing to him" (*Wisconsin v. Constantineau*, 400 U.S. 433, 437; 91 S.Ct. 507, 510 [1971]). The Court in *Goss* noted that misconduct charges and suspension could "seriously damage the students' standing with their fellow pupils and their teachers as well as interfere with later opportunities for higher education and employment" (419 U.S. 565 at 567; 95 S.Ct. 729 at 731 [1975]).

School officials had also argued that the due process clause comes into play only when the state subjects students to a "severe detriment or grievous loss" and that a ten-day suspension is neither severe nor grievous. The Court noted that because "education is perhaps the most important function of state and local governments" (*Brown v. Board of Education*, 347 U.S. 483, 493; 74 S.Ct. 686, 691 [1954]), exclusion from the educational process for even a ten-day period is a serious sanction in the life of a child.

The Court required a written notice and a hearing as part of the suspension and expulsion process in order to avoid unfair or mistaken exclusion from the educational process. The Court noted in the *Goss* case that the due process clause does not shield students from suspensions that are imposed properly, and the justices noted the reasons for and the importance of a fair hearing and decision process.

> The concern would be mostly academic if the disciplinary process were a totally accurate, unerring process, never mistaken and never unfair. Unfortunately, that is not the case, and no one suggests that it is. Disciplinarians, although proceeding in utmost good faith, frequently act on the reports and advice of others; and the ... facts and the nature of the conduct under challenge are often disputed. The risk of error is not at all trivial, and it should be guarded against if that may be done without prohibitive cost or interference with the educational process. (419 U.S. 565 at 568; 95 S.Ct. 729 at 732 [1975])

The Court noted that suspensions are necessary to maintain order in schools and that they may be a valuable educational device, if the process is done fairly and there is communication between school officials and students: "(I)t would be a strange disciplinary system in an education institution if no communication was sought by the disciplinarian with the student in an effort to inform him of his dereliction and to let him tell his side of the story in order to make sure that an injustice is not done" (419 U.S. 565 at 568; 95 S.Ct. 729 at 732 [1975]). The Court required that schools, in order to meet due process requirements, provide the student with oral or written notice of the charges against him and an explanation of the evidence to be presented by the authorities, as well as an opportunity to present his side of the story. The Court did not require a delay between the time of the notice and the hearing; an informal hearing could be held minutes after the alleged misconduct had occurred. Instead, emphasis was placed on telling the student what he is accused of doing and the basis for the accusation and on giving the student an opportunity to explain his version of the facts. Exceptions were allowed in cases where a student's presence poses a continuing danger to persons or property or presents an ongoing threat of disrupting the educational process. In such cases the notice and hearing should follow the student's removal as soon as possible.

In *Goss v. Lopez* the Court did not impose due process requirements on school officials that were unrealistically formal, time-consuming, or inappropriate in an educational setting. The requirements were no more than what a fair-minded school board and principal might expect of themselves in enforcing school regulations. In this case the Court addressed only suspensions of ten days or less; it stopped short of requiring the right to counsel, and of granting students the right to confront and cross-examine witnesses or to calling their own witnesses. Expulsions or longer suspensions would likely require more formal procedures.

Grounds for Expulsion or Suspension

The U.S. Supreme Court has noted that suspension and expulsion are not minor sanctions to be taken lightly but instead serious actions that may have significant consequences for a pupil's future educational and employment endeavors. School boards and officials should therefore be certain that dismissal of a student has a direct relation to furthering educational goals and that they have made a good-faith effort to provide an alternative educational program for the offending student. The "Pupil Fair Dismissal Act" of Minnesota provides an example of such a program:

> No school shall dismiss any pupil without attempting to provide alternative programs of education prior to dismissal proceedings, except where it appears that the pupil will create an immediate and substantial danger to self or to surrounding persons or property. Such programs may include special tutoring, modification of the curriculum for the pupil, placement in a special class or assistance from other agencies. (Minn. Stat. Ann., Sec. 127.29, Subd.1)

The grounds for dismissal should be clearly stated in writing and distributed to all students and parents along with clear explanations of the expectations and the possible consequences for violations of school rules. In Minnesota a pupil may be dismissed on the following grounds:

1. Willful violation of any reasonable school board regulation. Such regulations must be clear and definite to provide notice to pupils that they must conform their conduct to its requirements.
2. Willful conduct that materially and substantially disrupts the rights of others to an education.
3. Willful conduct that endangers the pupil or other pupils or the property of the school (Minn. Stat. Ann., Sec. 127.9 Subd.2).

Suspension Procedures

School boards and officials must follow at least the minimum procedures detailed by the the U.S. Supreme Court in the case of *Goss v. Lopez*. These include at least an informal conference with the student and a written statement of the facts and the grounds for the suspension decision. The period of suspension may not exceed ten school days.

Expulsion Procedures

Before school officials can expel a student for the remainder of a school year, there must be a written notice of its intent; a statement of the facts; and a formal hearing, to include witnesses, and the student must have the right to legal counsel, to confront and cross-examine the witnesses, and to present evidence of his or her own; there must also be a formal record of the hearing. The suspension and expulsion procedures required in the state of Minnesota are summarized in Table 7–1.

Corporal Punishment

Corporal punishment in the schools has been defined as "the infliction of pain or confinement as a penalty for an offense committed by a student" (Hyman 1990: 10). Corporal punishment is not, by definition, self-defense by teachers and principals against attacks by students. Proponents of corporal punishment argue that it is often necessary to control students and to maintain order and discipline in schools. Without the use or threat of corporal punishment, proponents argue, teachers would be powerless to control students, especially those who might otherwise threaten them. Opponents counter this claim by noting that most corporal punishment is not used in situations where a teacher is personally threatened by a potentially assaultive student or with students who pose a threat to the safety of teachers or other students, or to school property. It is more often used against students who have talked in class without permission or disobeyed a school rule. Far from threatening a teacher or principal, students who receive corporal punishment are often so compliant as to bend over in order to "get their licks."

Corporal punishment is not the same as self defense. States that forbid the use of corporal punishment do allow the use of force in specific situations, such as to quell a disturbance; to protect oneself, property, or another person; or to protect a student from self-injury (see Hyman 1990: 14). All states and school districts that forbid corporal punishment do recognize the right of teachers to protect themselves against assaults by students.

In states and schools that still use corporal punishment, the wooden paddle is the most common method of administering it. Several other methods and "weapons" have been used however: rubber hoses, leather straps and belts, switches, sticks, rods, ropes, and plastic baseball bats. Punching, slapping, kicking, shaking students and grabbing them while pushing them hard up against a wall or locker are other popular methods of "getting students' attention" (see Hyman 1990: 11).

Table 7–1
Procedures for Suspension and Expulsion of Students

Suspension Procedures

1. No suspension from school shall be imposed without an informal administrative conference with the pupil, except where it appears that the pupil will create an immediate and substantial danger to him/herself or other persons, or to property.
2. A written notice containing the grounds for suspension, a brief statement of the facts, a description of the testimony, a readmission plan, and a copy of the statute shall be given to the pupil at or before the suspension is to take effect.

Expulsion Procedures

1. No expulsion shall be imposed without a *hearing* (unless waived by the pupil and parent or guardian).
2. Written notice of the intent to expell shall:
   • Be sent to the pupil and parent or guardian by certified mail;
   • Contain a complete statement of the facts, a list of the witnesses, a description of their testimony; state the date, time, and place of the hearing; and include a copy of the statute;
   • Describe alternative educational programs available to the pupil prior to beginning expulsion proceedings;
   • Inform the pupil and parent/guardian of the right to have legal counsel; examine the pupil's records before the hearing; present evidence; and confront and cross-examine witnesses.
3. The hearing shall be scheduled within ten days at a time and place reasonably convenient to pupil and parent/guardian; and shall be closed unless the pupil or parent/guardian request an open hearing.
4. The pupil shall have a right to representation, including legal counsel; and if financially unable to retain counsel, the school board shall advise the pupil's parent/guardian of available legal assistance.
5. The hearing shall take place before an independent hearing officer; a member or committee of the school board; or the full school board, as determined by the school board.
6. The proceedings of the hearing shall be recorded and testimony shall be given under oath.
7. The pupil, parent/guardian, or representative shall have access to all school records or employee who may have evidence upon which the action may be based; they may confront and cross-examine any witness testifying for the school system; and shall have the right to present evidence and testimony. The pupil cannot be compelled to testify.
8. The recommendation of the hearing officer or school board member or committee shall be based solely upon substantial evidence presented at the hearing, and given within two days.
9. The decision by the school board shall be rendered within five days after the recommendation, and shall be in writing, giving the facts upon which the decision is made.

Source: Minnesota Stat. Ann. 127.30, 127.31

History of Corporal Punishment

Corporal punishment has been common in American schools since the colonial period. Its use to discipline students has been justified by the belief that physical means are necessary to get students' attention and to win their compliance with school rules. Schoolteachers and parents were pretty much in agreement that to "spare the rod" was to "spoil the child"—an Old Testament biblical statement attributed to Solomon in the book of Proverbs (13:24).

Falk (1941) traced the history of corporal punishment in America, noting its widespread use through the colonial period and the nineteenth century and into the twentieth century. The use of corporal punishment in schools was a legal sanction in every state except New Jersey (Falk 1941: 1, 124). Support for corporal punishment is a reflection of a view of government as an authority figure and of students as amenable to order and control only through fear and physical threats. The use of corporal punishment has diminished significantly in most parts of the country. Proponents generally argue that the threat of corporal punishment is often necessary, however; removing the possibility of corporal punishment in schools would surely mean trading social order for chaos! Corporal punishment has been considered synonymous with school discipline and order in most schools in America.

Current Policies and Practices

Maurer (1981) conducted a survey of corporal punishment practices in California and found that teachers and principals reported 46,022 instances of the use of a paddle or strap during the 1972–73 school year. Most of the recipients of the reported punishment were younger children; fewer than 5 percent of the blows were directed against high school students large enough to pose any real threat to the teachers. During that year 535 parents complained that the punishment was too severe or was not deserved or that their child had been seriously injured (Maurer 1981: 4). Corporal punishment is illegal in all continental European countries, including former Communist states, as well as in Israel, Ireland, and Puerto Rico. In the United States, on the other hand, it is estimated that more than 1 million children are hit by teachers and principals annually; 10,000 to 20,000 students sustain injuries serious enough to require medical attention (Goodlad, 1984; Regoli and Hewitt, 1994). Boys and African Americans are hit the most. Nationwide, while 25 percent of students are African American and 51 percent of students are boys, 37 percent and 80 percent, respectively, of corporal punishment cases involve members of these groups (Shaw and Braden, 1990: 378–383). Ten percent of the children in Alabama, Arkansas, Mississippi, and Tennessee schools were corporally punished during the 1986 school year (Hyman, 1990: 240–42). Presently, twenty-one states and the District of Columbia prohibit corporal punishment in public schools (Regoli and Hewitt, 1994). Prohibitions against corporal punishment stem at least in part from the belief that while physical punishment may produce short-run conformity, it increases the probability of problem behavior, such as delinquency, in the long run (Straus, Kurz, Loseke, and McCord, 1991: 133–154).

There is now under way a movement in the United States to ban corporal punishment in schools entirely, but sponsors of such a ban face stiff resistance. In one national opinion poll 48 percent of Americans answered affirmatively when asked: "Do you agree with teachers being allowed to inflict corporal punishment?" Forty-four percent of the sample disagreed; 8 percent registered no opinion (Hyman, 1990).

The message behind corporal punishment is that physical force, infliction of pain, and violence are acceptable ways to solve problems. This message is certainly not lost on children. Kempe et al. (1962) have suggested that parents who were beaten as children end up beating their own children. Teachers who attended schools in which corporal punishment was an accepted practice may likewise find it natural to turn to physical force themselves.

Constitutionality of Corporal Punishment

The U.S. Supreme Court considered the constitutionality of corporal punishement in the 1977 case of *Ingraham v. Wright* (97 S.Ct. 1401 [1977]). The Court held that the punishments administered to students at Drew Junior High School, in Dade County, Florida, in October 1970 did not violate the Eighth Amendment to the Constitution against cruel and unusual punishment. Fourteen-year-old James Ingraham, an eighth grader, was paddled so severely that a resulting hematoma required doctor's care, and prescription pain pills, a laxative, sleep pills, ice packs, and a week's bedrest were required. The Court also held that the due process clause of the Fourteenth Amendment to the Constitution does not require notification of charges and an informal hearing prior to the infliction of corporal punishment.

Petitioners in the case argued that

> public school children may be savagely beaten and whipped by teachers acting under color of state law, yet they will have no Constitutional redress. But hardened criminals suffering the same beatings at the hands of their jailers will have Constitutional claims. Neither the Constitution nor common sense condones that conclusion. (cited in Lee 1979: 180)

Justice Lewis Powell, writing for the majority in a five-to-four decision, supported the use of corporal punishment in schools on the basis of common law and traditional societal attitudes, noting that there is a long tradition of corporal punishment in schools. He acknowledged that corporal punishment has been abandoned as a means of punishing criminal offenders but noted that "the practice continues to play a role in the public education of school children in most parts of the country. . . . Professional and public opinion is sharply divided on the practice. . . . Yet we can discern no trend towards its elimination" (*Ingraham v. Wright*, 97 S.Ct. at 1407).

Since the Ingraham case, several more states have passed legislation banning the use of corporal punishment in schools. Nevertheless, the practice continues in some schools, particularly those in the southern United States. Lee (1979) suggested that students and their parents cannot look to the courts for meaningful protection against the abuses of corporal punishment in schools. She suggested they assess the political climate in their communities and organize around discipline issues, pushing for elimination of corporal punishment from their school systems and for the substitution of more humane alternatives.

Research on Corporal Punishment

There is not, nor is there ever likely to be, any available research evidence on the effectiveness of corporal punishment in controlling student behavior. Ethical limitations on testing the effects of corporal punishment on students preclude such research. In order to examine the effectiveness of corporal punishment as a disciplinary tool, it would be necessary to randomly assign misbehaving students to paddling and nonpaddling groups and to take pre- and post-measures of behavior (see Hyman and Wise, 1979: 349). The problems with this methodology are obvious. While a majority of Americans are supportive of corporal punishment as one means of school discipline, it is unlikely that research on the subject would receive widespread support or funding. Steps taken to protect the human subjects in such research would preclude research support by funding agencies and research organizations. Much of the available research on corporal punishment is therefore limited to survey research and analysis of existing discipline records.

Bongiovanni (1979) concluded from a review of the research on corporal punishment in schools that the weight of the evidence indicates that it is not only ineffective but probably counterproductive.

> Corporal punishment is ineffective in producing durable bahavior change; it is potentially harmful to students, school personnel and property; it is highly impractical in light of the controls required for maximal effectiveness. . . . When we consider the stated role of school personnel in education the use of corporal punishment appears to be time-consuming and contrary to the best interests and welfare of the students. The potential for negative side-effects, especially that of social disruption, constitutes the greatest danger. In light of this danger the possible reduction in any undesirable behavior should be secondary in importance. (Bongiovanni 1979: 367–368)

Welsh (1979) observed many juvenile delinquents through clinical observations. His observations led him to suggest the following propositions:

1. The level of reported aggressive behavior in males is a function of the severity of their corporal punishment histories.
2. Severity of corporal punishment in the home is more important than socioeconomic class as a precursor to delinquency.
3. Corporal punishment produces both fear and anger; when the fear habituates, anger is left in its place.
4. The more aggressive a culture, the more probable the members of that culture will be found to utilize corporal punishment as their chief socialization technique (Welsh 1979: 132–3).

The findings of some of the available studies on corporal punishment are summarized in Table 7–2. There are only a few studies that support the use of corporal punishment as an effective disciplinary technique (Reardon and

Table 7–2
Corporal Punishment: Findings of Selected Studies

Reported Findings	Author	Date	Method
The level of reported aggressive behavior in males is a function of the severity of corporal punishment histories. "Belt Theory of Juvenile Delinquency"	Welsh	1979	Clinical observations N = 48, N = 77
Supported by majority of subjects; it *does* change behavior; students learn self-discipline; less harmful than humiliation; necessary for some students; no harmful effect	Reardon & Reynolds	1979	Survey, 292 Pennsylvania school districts (558 parents, 972 teachers; 1,278 principals
Support for CP correlated with: lower expenditures; fewer school support personnel; percent school dropouts; percent illiteracy	McDowell & Friedman	1979	Newspaper editorial opinions (N = ?)
Characteristics of users of CP: close-mindedness, neuroticism; fewer years experience; impulsive; also a subject of CP when a student	Rust & Kinnard	1983	Personality Scales; N = 114 teachers, princ., Tennessee schools
Majority of principals believe CP is effective in: maintaining general discipline; reducing specific behavior problems; teacher morale; support for teachers	Rose	1984	Survey of principals (N = 232); rep'g 10 school districts in 18 states
Evidence of some race and gender bias in administration of CP, but not as strong as many educators would hypothesize	Shaw & Braden	1990	Analyses of discipline files (N = 6,244), 16 Florida schools
Symptoms of CP: memory, concentration problems; sleep disturbances; somatic complaints; habit disorders	Hyman	1990	Surveys; N = 81 teachers, 35 college students
CP may produce conformity in immediate situation; tends to increase deviance and delinquency in the longer run	Straus	1991	National Family Violence Survey (N = 3,300 children, 6,000 couples)

Reynolds, 1979; Rose, 1984). We have noted the methodological difficulties associated with assessing whether corporal punishment is effective in changing behavior or whether it may result in some negative side effects. In the majority of studies, the authors conclude that corporal punishment is more likely to produce only short-term conformity and may increase deviance and delinquency (Straus, 1991); aggressive behavior in males (Welsh, 1979); and problems with memory and concentration, sleep disturbances, and somatic complaints (Hyman, 1990).

Given the rising level of violence among youth in communities and schools, allowing school officials to use corporal punishment seems to be an inappropriate means of responding to school rule violations. We are trying to teach youth to avoid violence as a way of problem solving and are teaching them that communication, mediation, and nonconfrontational means are better alternatives for settling differences. Surely it is time for school officials throughout America to recognize that physical force and infliction of pain is not the way to solve school problems.

Search and Seizure

The Fourth Amendment to the U.S. Constitution provides for "the right of people to be secure in their persons, houses, papers, and effects" and for the right "against unreasonable searches and seizures." School officials are frequently confronted with the question of whether to search a student's pockets, book bag, purse, locker, or automobile. Educators often must make an instant decision whether to initiate a search, particularly in cases of bomb threats and dangerous weapons, in order to protect the safety of students and teachers. The Fourth Amendment as applied to persons conducting searches generally pertains to law enforcement, court, and security officers. The right of school officials to search students depends on whether any illegal evidence seized may be turned over to law enforcement officers and used as evidence in juvenile or criminal prosecution. In such cases, a search warrant is required.

There are three parts to the Fourth Amendment that apply to students. First, students have a right to privacy ("to be secure in their persons, papers and effects"); second, they have a right against unreasonable searches and seizures; third, any search must be specific as to the location of the search and what is being sought. The courts have not required school officials to show probable cause for searches or to obtain search warrants from a judge before initiating a search. They must have "reasonable suspicion" before conducting a search, but this requirement is less rigorous than the requirement of "probable cause," which is required for police to obtain a search warrant (see Alexander and Alexander, 1992: 339). "Reasonable suspicion" means that school officials must have some facts or knowledge that provide reasonable grounds to search, and a school search may be conducted only if it is necessary to fulfill educational objectives. Thus, a student's freedom from unreasonable search and seizure must be weighed against the need for school officials to maintain order, discipline, and a safe learning environment.

The U.S. Supreme Court in the case of *New Jersey v. T.L.O.* (105 S.Ct. 733 [1985]) defined students' Fourth Amendment rights and provided guidelines for officials in conducting school searches. The case originated when a teacher at a New Jersey high school found two girls smoking in the restroom. The teacher took them to the principal's office because smoking in restrooms was in violation of a school rule. When questioned by the assistant vice principal, T.L.O., a fourteen-year-old freshman, denied that she had been smoking and claimed that she did not smoke at all. The vice principal demanded to see her purse, and upon opening it he found a pack of cigarettes and also noticed a package of cigarette rolling papers, which are commonly associated with the use of marijuana. A further search of the purse produced some marijuana, a pipe, plastic bags, a substantial amount of money, an index card containing a list of students who apparently owed her money, and two letters that implicated her in marijuana dealing. The evidence was turned over to the police, and she was charged with delinquent conduct. The juvenile court denied her motion to suppress the evidence found in her purse, held that the search was reasonable, and adjudged her delinquent. The state appellate court affirmed the juvenile court's finding, but the New Jersey Supreme Court reversed, ordered that the evidence found in her purse be suppressed, and held that the search was unreasonable.

On appeal, the U.S. Supreme Court ruled that the Fourth Amendment prohibition against unreasonable searches and seizures does apply to school officials, who are acting as representatives of the state; students do have expectations of privacy when they bring to school a variety of legitimate, noncontraband items. The Court noted, however, that school officials have an equally important need to maintain a safe and orderly learning environment. In balancing students' Fourth Amendment rights and school officials' responsibilities, the Court ruled that school officials do not need to obtain a warrant before searching a student as long as the search was reasonable in light of educational objectives and not excessively intrusive in light of the student's age and sex and the nature of the violation (105 S.Ct. at 736 [1985]).

The Court cited two considerations in determining whether a warrantless search was "reasonable" or not. First, "one must consider whether the . . . action was justified at its inception"; second, "one must determine whether the search . . . was reasonably related in scope to the circumstances which justified the interference in the first place" (105 S.Ct. at 744 [1985]). The first involves the justification or grounds for initiating the search, while the second relates to the intrusiveness of the search (see Alexander and Alexander, 1992: 339–340). In one case, a school administrator had heard reports that a student was involved in drugs. A search of the student's locker and car revealed drugs and was found reasonable and constitutional (*State v. Slattery*, 56 Wn.App. 820, 787 P.2d 932 [1990]). In another case, a student's car was searched, and cocaine was found, after the assistant principal noticed that the student smelled of alcohol, walked unsteadily, and had slurred speech, glassy eyes, and a flushed face. The court found that the observations were sufficient to support reasonable suspicion (*Shamberg v. State*, 762 P.2d 488, Alaska App. [1988]). School officials must also be able to justify the extensiveness and the intrusiveness of searches and show that there was reasonable suspicion. In one case in which money was missing from a schoolroom, a teacher searched the books of two students and then required them to remove their shoes. The court found the search to be reasonable and not excessively intrusive, because the two students had been alone in the room where the stolen money disappeared (*Wynn v. Board of Education of Vestabia Hills*, 508 So. 2d 1170, Ala. [1987]).

In summary, the courts have recognized the need for school officials to maintain a positive and safe learning environment in schools and therefore have required only "reasonable suspicion" rather than demanding the more stringent standard of "probable cause" for student searches. Courts, nevertheless, do hold firmly to the need for officials to show that reasonable grounds existed to justify a search. Alexander and Alexander (1992) have offered some guidelines for school officials in determining whether a search is justified:

1. Students do have a right to privacy of their persons, papers, and effects.
2. The courts will consider the seriousness of the offense and the extent to which a search intrudes on a student's privacy.
3. Reasonable suspicion requires that the school official have some evidence regarding the particular situation, including the background of the student, to justify a search for items that are in violation of school rules.
4. While a warrant is not required, a school official must have knowledge of the alleged violation, where illegal contraband is presumed to be located, and the identity of the student alleged to be in violation (1992: 341).

Locker Searches

The U.S. Supreme Court recognizes that even a limited search of students "is a substantial invasion of privacy," although the Court has not addressed the question of whether students have a reasonable expectation of privacy in their lockers or desks (*New Jersey v. T.L.O.* 105 S.Ct. at 741 [1985]). A number of state courts have considered the issue of locker searches, and the majority of them have held that students have a legitimate expectation of privacy in regard to their lockers (see Bjorklun, 1994; and see note 1). This would suggest that a locker could be searched only when school officials have reasonable suspicion that an individual student may have concealed illegal contraband in a locker, under the standard set forth in the *T.L.O.* decision. Random locker searches, according to this decision, would be in violation of the Fourth Amendment.

The Massachusetts Supreme Court held that students have an expectation of privacy in their school lockers, but only if there is no "express understanding to the contrary" (*Commonwealth v. Snyder*, 413 Mass. 521, 597 N.E. 2d 1363, 1366 [1992]). This condition has implications for random locker searches without prior individualized reasonable suspicion. It was applied in a ruling by the Wisconsin Supreme Court in 1993 (*In Interest of Isaiah B.*, 176 Wis.2d 639, 500 N.W. 2d 637 [1993]); (see also Bjorklun, 1994: 1070). A random locker search was conducted at Madison High School in Milwaukee after six incidents involving guns had been investigated by school officials within a one-month period in the fall of 1990. In one incident, students reported that they were shot at as they left the school following a basketball game. In another incident multiple gunshots were heard by students as they were leaving school grounds following a near riot after a school dance. The following week school officials received reports of guns in the school and on school buses, and the rumors that a shootout was inevitable. Because of the fear and tension and the risk to students' safety, the principal ordered a random search of school lockers. About seventy-five to 100 of the school lockers were searched, including that of Isaiah B., where school security officials found a handgun and a packet of cocaine in Isaiah B.'s coat pocket. On the basis of the evidence, he was adjudicated delinquent in juvenile court. He challenged the adjudication on the basis of the absence of individualized suspicion for the search of his locker; he had no history of prior weapons violations, nor was there any evidence of his involvement in the recent gun incidents at the school. The Wisconsin Supreme Court ruled that the random locker search was not in violation of the Fourth Amendment, because the Milwaukee Public School System had a written policy and students had been informed that the school system had ownership and control of school lockers. The policy in the *Milwaukee Public School Handbook* states:

> School lockers are the property of Milwaukee Public Schools. At no time does the Milwaukee school district relinquish its exclusive control of lockers provided for the convenience of students. Periodic general inspections of lockers may be conducted by school authorities for any reason at any time, without notice, without student consent, and without a search warrant. (cited in Bjorklun, 1994: 1071)

The court noted that students might have a reasonable expectation of privacy in their lockers if schools do not have a policy explicitly stating otherwise. Schools may adopt such a policy; when they do and clearly inform students of the policy, random searches of school lockers are not in violation of the Fourth Amendment.

The U.S. Supreme Court implied (in a footnote) in the *T.L.O.* decision that individualized suspicion is not always a prerequisite to a search if less than ordinary conditions exist. Since *T.L.O.* the Court has upheld random drug testing of railway employees and border guards when no individualized suspicion was present. The rationale in these rulings was that the government's interest in public safety and the need to discover potential threats to safety made such searches permissible. Bjorklun (1994) believes that the presence of weapons and drugs in schools is a less than ordinary condition, and the need to make schools safe justifies random locker searches without individualized suspicion. This is not unlike the justifiable searches, using metal detectors, of all persons entering an airplane boarding area, a courtroom, or a school building. The prevalence of weapons in society and the resulting threat to public safety has unfortunately infringed on everyone's freedom. In response to weapons and drug problems, Zirkel (1994) has noted, society has moved "to a warlike view of alcohol, drugs, and violence in the schools. Reflecting this change, courts have started to sacrifice the individualized aspect of reasonable suspicion" (Zirkel, 1994: 729). Sanchez (1992) analyzed eighteen cases dealing with searches of students in schools. Only three of the searches were declared invalid by the courts, and fifteen led to criminal or delinquency proceedings.

Sanchez concluded that as school officials are increasingly faced with students who are carrying weapons and dealing in drugs, state courts have expanded the power of school officials to conduct searches. It is apparent that more school systems will adopt policies in this area and announce to students that lockers are school property and may be opened and searched whenever school officials believe it is necessary.

Canine Searches

Because of an increase in the possession and use of drugs in schools, officials have turned to "K-9" police officers, who bring their dogs into the school to sniff out drugs. The practice has generally been limited to urban schools, and many officials are hesitant to resort to this intrusive type of drug detection. Robert Rubel, the author of several books and articles on school crime, has advised some principals on a tactic by which drug-sniffing dogs may help get rid of drugs in schools and has reported at least one incident in which the tactic was successful in getting drugs out of the school. In this case, the principal announced over the school intercom just before the lunch hour that a K-9 officer and his drug-sniffing dog would be at the school after the lunch hour, "just for a visit and to sniff out some student lockers." Immediately after the lunch bell rang, there was a flurry of activity, with some students rushing to their lockers, then to the restrooms, followed by a flushing of toilets. When the officer and his dog arrived later, no drugs were found, but they had a nice visit with the students—and the principal had the satisfaction of knowing that, at least for the rest of that day, the school was very likely free of drugs.

This strategy would not have resulted in the seizure of evidence that is admissible in court. It may, however, accomplish the overall goal of school officials: to rid schools of drugs. As a simple deterrent strategy, it also avoids the legal question of admissibility of evidence gained through canine searches. Courts have expressed some reservations in accepting evidence from canine searches in schools (see Alexander and Alexander, 1992: 341–342).

The Tenth Circuit Court of Appeals in *Zamora v. Pomeroy* (639 F.2d 662 [1981]) ruled that using dogs for an exploratory sniffing of lockers was permissible. At the beginning of the year the schools had given notice that the lockers were joint possessions of the school and the student and that they might be periodically opened. That notice and the need for officials to maintain a proper educational environment led the court to determine that locker inspections were not unreasonable under the Fourth Amendment.

The Seventh Circuit Court held in *Doe v. Renfrow* (631 F.2d 91; 635 F.2d 582 [1980]) that school officials stood *in loco parentis* and could use dogs to sniff out drugs, because there was less expectation of privacy in the public schools and because officials had a duty to maintain a positive educational environment. Alexander and Alexander (1992: 341) note that this decision may be contrary to the U.S. Supreme Court decision in *New Jersey v. T.L.O.* which limited the application of *in loco parentis*.

Courts have been reluctant to accept canine searches in schools under some circumstances. A federal district court ruled in *Jones v. Latexo Independent School District* (499 F. Supp. 223 [E.D. Tex. 1980]) that using dogs to sniff both students and automobiles was in violation of the Fourth Amendment. The court ruled that without individual suspicion the sniffing of students was too intrusive and not reasonable; because students did not have access to their automobiles during the school day, the school officials' interest in sniffing the cars was minimal and not reasonable.

The Fifth Circuit Court addressed two questions in *Horton v. Goose Creek Independent School District* (690 F.2d 470 [5th Cir. 1982]): first, whether the sniff of a drug-detecting dog was a "search" under the Fourth Amendment; second, whether the Fourth Amendment protects students against searches by school officials who are trying to maintain a safe educational environment that is conducive to learning (690 F.2d at 475). The court ruled, first, that a dog sniffing lockers and cars did *not* constitute a search and that no further inquiry needed to be made as to its reasonableness (690 F.2d at 477). Regarding the second question, the court held that school officials may search students if they have reasonable cause. A personal canine search of students, however, was considered to be overly intrusive on a student's "dignity and personal security" and could not be justified under the Fourth Amendment without prior individualized suspicion (690 F.2d at 481–2).

Strip Searches

The courts have determined that strip searches require more than just "reasonable suspicion" that a student is in possession of something illegal. Because of the intrusive nature of strip searches, school officials should have "probable cause" that the student is in possession of illegal substances or a weapon that may threaten the safety of other students. The Second Circuit Court of Appeals ruled in *M.M. v. Anker* (607 F.2d 588 [2d Cir. 1979]) that as the intrusiveness of a search intensifies, a higher level of justification for the search should be required—that probable cause be present (which is the same standard as that required for criminal prosecution). A New York court held that a teacher violated the Fourth Amendment rights of students who were strip-searched after some money was missing in a classroom. The search did not meet the test of even individualized reasonable suspicion, since there was no observed act or evidence to indicate which student, if any, might have taken the money. Further, a strip search was considered an excessively intrusive type of search when the expressed purpose was to locate a missing three dollars (*Bellnier v. Lund* 438 F.Supp. 47 [N.D.N.Y. 1977]).

Combining canine searches and strip searches has also come under critical scrutiny. The Seventh Circuit Court held that school officials violated a student's constitutional rights when they used dogs to detect drug odors and then strip-searched the student. The officials did not have reasonable suspicion or probable cause to justify the intrusive search. The court condemned this nude search of a thirteen-year-old child and considered it worse than a violation of his constitutional rights:

It is a violation of any known principle of human decency. Apart from any constitutional readings and rulings, simple common sense would indicate that the conduct of the school officials in permitting such a nude search was not only unlawful but outrageous under settled indisputable principles of law. [*Doe v. Renfrow*
631 F.2d 91 [7th Cir. 1980])

Metal Detector Searches

Schools are part of the community, and they reflect what is going on in
the community. Youth have carried drugs and weapons from the streets into
the school hallways. In a 1993 survey of 16,000 students by the national Centers for Disease Control and Prevention, more than one in ten high school
students (11.8 percent) said they carried a weapon on school property; about
7.3 percent said they were threatened or injured with a weapon in school;
and 4.4 percent said they had skipped school at least one day in the past
month because they felt unsafe (Levy, 1995: 12A). School officials in many
urban schools have initiated the use of metal detectors as a response to the
problem.

There are legal and policy questions involved in the use of metal detectors
or scanning devices in schools (see Johnson, 1993). Federal courts have approved suspicionless searches using handheld and walk-through metal detectors in airport boarding areas and courthouses, but neither the U.S. Supreme
Court nor the lower federal courts have made a specific ruling on suspicionless
searches of students using metal detectors. A New York state appellate court
in *People v. Dukes* (151 Misc. 295, 580 N.Y.S. 2d 850 [1992]) approved the
use of metal detectors to search students at random as they entered the lobby
of a Manhattan public high school, reasoning that "the governmental interest
underlying this type of search is equal to if not greater than the interest justi-
fying the airport and courthouse searches." The court noted that a fatal shooting in a Brooklyn high school a few months earlier and the confiscation of more
than 2,000 weapons from students during the 1990–91 school year underscored the validity of its decision. Special police officers from a school safety
task force set up several metal detector scanning posts in the lobby of Washington Irving High School one morning in May 1991. Signs announcing a
search for weapons were posted outside the building, and students had been
informed at the beginning of the school year that searches would take place.
The officers conducted the search in a uniform manner under written guidelines adopted a few years earlier by former Chancellor Richard E. Green. The
stated purpose of the search was to prevent students from bringing weapons
into the schools. All students who entered the school were subject to the search,
although the officers could choose to limit the search by a random selection
of students. Officers explained the scanning process and asked the students to
place any bags on a table and remove all metal objects from their pockets. The
officer passed a metal scanner over the bags and from the students' feet to their
heads, without touching the student's body. Students were searched by officers of the same sex. If any metal activated the scanning device, the student
was again asked to remove any metal objects from the bag or his or her per-

son. If the device was activated after a second scan, the student was escorted to a private area. Before conducting a pat-down search, the officer asked the student for a third time to remove any metal objects (580 N.Y.S. 2d at 850-51 [1992]).

Courts consider metal detector searches in airports and courthouses to be "administrative searches" and have held them to be reasonable when the intrusion on an individual's privacy is no greater than necessary to justify the governmental interest in public safety. An administrative search is not connected with probable cause or the issuing of a warrant. It is designed to protect the public and is directed at a group or class of people, rather than at a particular person. The state court acknowledged that an administrative search of a student at school differs from that of a passenger in an airport in that the subject has consented to the airport search and may walk away and not board the plane, but the student is required by law to attend school. The New York court nevertheless ruled that "consent is hardly a necessary component of a valid administrative search" and was "satisfied that the guidelines are minimally intrusive despite the absence of a consent provision" (*People v. Dukes*, N.Y.S. 2d at 851-53 [1992]).

The Superior Court of Pennsylvania upheld metal detector searches in a 1995 case involving students at University High School in Philadelphia (*In the Interest of F.B.*, 658 A. 2d 1378). Because of a high rate of violence in the local schools, the Philadelphia school district resorted to metal-detector scans and publicized the search policy through letters to parents and students. The court ruled that the searches did not violate students' Fourth Amendment rights because they were given prior notice. No individualized suspicion was necessary because the searches were part of a regulatory plan to ensure the safety of students; the searches were announced by signs posted on the front door; and all students or a randomly selected number of students were subjected to the searches, which were conducted in a uniform manner.

Only a relatively small number of urban schools have resorted to the use of metal detectors, generally in response to growing problems with violence and students carrying guns into school. There are a number of considerations that should be weighed carefully by school boards before it initiates a metal detector policy (Johnson, 1993: 4–5). First, metal detectors in schools are likely to raise public relations problems and costly litigation; second, in addition to legal expenses, metal detector searches require expenditures for public information materials, staff training, detection equipment, and some administrative overhead; third, some parents, students, and staff are likely to strongly oppose the intrusion on students' dignity and privacy; fourth, most school districts will find it difficult to demonstrate any convincing need for metal detector searches. Johnson (1993) noted that the Texas Association of School Boards has not developed a model policy for using metal detectors for searching students for weapons, and the legal division of the state board does not recommend that a school district adopt a metal detector policy except in schools with a documented problem of several weapon-related incidents that seems to justify such a program.

As a senior staff attorney for the Texas Association of School Boards, Johnson has several recommendations for districts that decide to proceed with a metal detector policy:

•Collect factual documentation regarding weapon-related incidents involving students in or around schools.

•Work to gain student, staff, and community agreement on the need for such a policy and to secure their participation in its development.

•Develop search procedures that are as economical and as unintrusive as possible.

•Develop a policy that incorporates the features of the search program in *People v. Dukes*, and with consultation from the school district's attorney.

•Before implementing the search policy, give plenty of notice to students, parents, and staff about the purpose of the policy and the techniques to be used, along with the district's plans for disciplining (or reporting to law enforcement authorities) students found to be in violation of the district's policy against carrying weapons.

•Provide training and precise written instructions for all administrators and school officials who will be conducting the search procedures (Johnson, 1993: 6–7).

Drug Testing

Alcohol and substance abuse continue to be serious problems in society. In 1990 the National Institute on Drug Abuse surveyed more than 30,000 randomly selected individuals in a sample of households across the United States. Results of the survey showed that about 23 percent of youth ages 12 through 17 reported having used one or more illegal drugs at some time, and 48 percent had used alcohol; 8 percent of youth (about 1.6 million people) reported using drugs within the past month, and 24 percent had used alcohol within the past month (National Institute on Drug Abuse, 1991: 13–14). Drug and alcohol abuse has become a problem in many schools. The Centers for Disease Control and Prevention in Atlanta conducted a national survey of 16,000 high school students in 1993, and nearly one-fourth (24 percent) of the students said they had been offered, sold, or given drugs on the school campus (Levy, 1995: 12A).

School officials are concerned about drugs in the school and about their effects on students, and some have begun to resort to drug testing programs to control the problem. Some private businesses and state and federal government agencies have used drug testing to deter drug use among employees, particularly where job safety was clearly at risk. In 1989 the U.S. Supreme Court ruled on two cases, *Skinner v. Railway Labor Executives Ass'n* (489 U.S. 602, 109 S.Ct. 1402) and *National Treasury Employees Union v. Von Raab* (489 U.S. 656, 109 S.Ct. 1384), which involved drug testing of railway employees and customs service employees, respectively. The court ruled that a drug or alcohol test, whether it is a blood, urine, or breath test, is a search, but the tests were upheld because of the government's interest in protecting public safety (by preventing accidents among railway workers or those caused by improper use of firearms by customs officers). Because of the public safety interest, no individualized suspicion was required before mandatory drug tests of these workers could be required (see Alexander and Alexander, 1992: 342–343). The *Skinner* and *Von Raab* cases involved drug tests of employees, but the rulings have been extended to public school situations involving students. The Seventh Circuit Court of Appeals ruled in the 1988 case of *Schaill v. Tippecanoe County School Corporation* (864 F.2d 1309) that random drug testing of students who participated in interscholastic programs did not violate their Fourth Amendment rights. An important factor in the decision was the procedure for ensuring due process for the student if the test results were positive. The student and his or her parent or guardian could obtain a second lab test at a laboratory of their choice and could present evidence and an explanation for the positive results, such as the student's use of other, legal medications.

Similar testing procedures were upheld in *Brooks v. East Chambers Consolidated Independent School District* (730 F.Supp. 759 [S.D.Tex 1989]; 930 F.2d 915 [5th Cir.1991]) and in the 1995 U.S. Supreme Court case of *Vernonia School District v. Acton* (115 S.Ct. 2386). In both cases, all students who participated in extracurricular activities were tested at the beginning of the school year and by random selection the rest of the year.

In the *Vernonia* case, the parents of James Acton filed suit after he was denied participation in football because they refused to sign consent forms for mandatory drug testing. Vernonia is a small logging community in Oregon where school sports are important in the town's life and student athletes are admired in the schools and the community. School district officials had resorted to the drug testing policy to curb a growing drug problem in the schools. School officials had begun to notice a sharp increase in drug use among students, accompanied by an increase in disciplinary problems. Students were rude during class, and outbursts of profanity became more common. The number of disciplinary referrals increased, and several students were suspended (115 S.Ct. at 2388). Many of the problem students were athletes. Administrators and coaches were concerned about student athletes' drug abuse, and evidence was presented on the effects of drugs on coordination, performance, and safety among athletes. The school district initially responded to the drug problem by offering special classes, speakers, and presentations. When those efforts had little effect, district officials proposed the drug testing policy to parents for their input and feedback. Parents who attended a meeting gave their unanimous approval, and the school approved the policy, under which all students participating in interscholastic sports would be tested at the beginning of the season for their sport, and a 10 percent random selection of student athletes would be tested weekly. The expressed purpose of the policy was to "prevent student athletes from using drugs, to protect their health and safety, and to provide drug users with assistance programs" (115 S.Ct. at 2389). The U.S. Supreme Court upheld the policy with a 6–3 decision handed down June 26, 1995.

The Supreme Court has used a number of criteria to determine the legality of drug testing programs: (1) whether there is a compelling need; (2) whether the drug testing programs has a limited scope and achievable goals; (3) whether less intrusive methods in schools have been tried; (4) whether students have diminished expectations of privacy; (5) whether there are limitations on officials' discretion in selecting students for testing; and (6) whether the testing is intended to enforce school rules and not to produce evidence for criminal prosecution (see Bjorklun, 1993: 918–923). The Court determined that the Vernonia School District policy met these criteria. The increase in students' drug use, the disciplinary problems, and the threats to safety in athletics presented a compelling need. The Court in both the *Schaill* and the *Vernonia* cases noted that students who voluntarily participate in athletics have a diminished expectation of privacy for a variety of reasons, including "communal undress" in locker rooms and showers, required physical examinations, and state high school athletic rules that prohibit smoking, drinking, and drug use (Bjorklun, 1993: 921). The drug testing policy had been instituted only after less intrusive methods proved unsuccessful, and the testing policy was limited in its scope and intended only to prevent students' drug abuse, not to gather evidence for criminal prosecution.

Justice Sandra Day O'Connor, joined by Justices John Paul Stevens and David Souter, wrote a dissenting opinion, noting that "millions of . . . students who participate in interscholastic sports, an overwhelming majority of whom have given school officials no reason whatsoever to suspect they use drugs at school, are open to an intrusive bodily search" (115 S.Ct. at 2397). The majority decision of the Supreme Court clearly goes beyond the Court's decision in *T.L.O.* that school officials must have individualized suspicion that a student search would likely reveal evidence of the student's violation of the law or school rules. Justice Antonin Scalia, writing for the majority, justified drug testing without individualized suspicion by noting that

> deterring drug use by our Nation's schoolchildren is at least as important as enhancing efficient enforcement of the Nation's laws against the importation of drugs. . . . And . . . the effects of a drug-infested school are visited not just upon the users, but upon the entire student body and faculty, as the educational process is disrupted. (115 S.Ct. at 2395)

Other School Responsibilities and Student Rights

Child Abuse Reporting

The 1974 federal Child Abuse Prevention and Treatment Act includes a provision stating that medical personnel and other professionals, including schoolteachers and officials, are required to report suspected instances of child abuse and neglect. State statutues also require the reporting of child abuse. Teachers were concerned about being sued for reporting suspected abuse if the reports turned out to be unfounded. The statutes therefore grant immunity from criminal and civil liability to reporters of child abuse and neglect "if the report *is made in good faith*" (Alexander and Alexander, 1992: 315). In a 1985 Oregon case, *McDonald v. State, By and Through CSD* (71 Or.App. 751, 694 P.2d 569), the state court dismissed the parents' complaint after their child was removed from their custody on the basis of reports by a teacher and a principal of suspected child abuse. Child abuse allegations were later found to be groundless, and the parents regained custody of their child. The court ruled that the principal and the teacher had acted in good faith and had reasonable grounds to report the suspected child abuse.

In order to ensure that medical professionals, law enforcement officials, lawyers, and teachers comply with statutes that require them to report suspected child abuse or neglect, most state laws include a criminal penalty or civil liability for failure to report. Statutes that require the reporting of suspected abuse include statements such as "reason to believe," so a teacher who may be charged with failure to report suspected child abuse should be prepared to show that there was not "reason to believe" that child abuse or neglect had occurred (Alexander and Alexander, 1992: 316).

Freedom of Speech and Expression

The First Amendment rights relating to freedom of speech and expression are more misunderstood and less clear than, for example, the Fourth Amendment relating to unreasonable search and seizure. The U.S. Supreme Court has used the test of "material and substantial disruption" to determine whether a school can deny a student the right of freedom of expression. In the case of *Tinker v. Des Moines Independent Community School District* (393 U.S. 503, 89 S.Ct. 733 [1969]), the Supreme Court ruled that students wearing black armbands to protest the Vietnam War did not pose a substantial disruption to the educational process and that the school officials violated the students' right to freedom of expression when they banned the armbands. In the more recent case of *Bethel School District No. 403 v. Fraser* (478 U.S. 675, 106 S.Ct. 3159 [1986]) the Supreme Court supported school officials' suspension of a student who made a lewd speech full of sexual innuendos that offended the teachers and other students at the school. The Court thus made a distinction between the "political message" in the *Tinker* case and expression that includes vulgar and offensive terms (see Alexander and Alexander, 1992: 317). The two cases also serve as contrasting examples of how the First Amendment right to freedom of expression may have positive educational value. In the *Tinker* case, the silent protest against the Vietnam War presented an opportunity for organized class discussions that might have had positive educational value. School officials, teachers, and students could also choose not to recognize the students making the silent protest, whose actions did not interfere with the educational process or the rights of other students. In contrast, the delivery of an indecent speech containing vulgar and offensive terms can hardly be said to have any positive educational value, so the Bethel School District was justified in curtailing the student's right to freedom of expression.

Student appearance issues that involve freedom of expression include the question whether school officials may regulate students' dress and personal appearance, including haircuts. Students and parents have relied on the First Amendment and the equal protection clause of the Fourteenth Amendment to contest school regulations regarding student attire, and available court cases reveal a lack of consensus as to whether various dress styles pose a "material and substantial disruption" of the educational process. Students who wear gang colors and paraphernalia in some schools pose a potential risk and disruption, and some schools have considered policies that ban the wearing of gang-related clothing. No court cases to date have tested the legality of any bans, however.

School regulations banning unkempt or long hair have been challenged in some court cases, but school officials are hard-pressed to prove that the length or style of students' hair significantly disrupts the school educational process. A federal appellate court refused to become involved in haircut disputes, saying that "we refuse to take our judicial clippers to this hairy issue" (Alexander and Alexander, 1992: 318). Federal circuit courts of appeals have been involved in considerable litigation regarding school regulations on student hairstyles, but the rulings are not consistent. Some courts have determined that hairstyles may be a distraction in schools and can be regulated; other courts have ruled that hairstyles are constitutionally protected. Some federal judges have expressed indignation at having to rule on matters relating to hairstyles, in light of court calendars full of weightier criminal and civil matters. Despite ruling in favor of one school district's good-grooming rule, the federal court nevertheless noted: "The entire problem seems minuscule in light of other matters involving the school system" (cited in Alexander and Alexander, 1992: 318).

Summary

Students do not (in the words of Justice Abe Fortas) "shed their constitutional rights at the schoolhouse gate." As citizens, students enjoy the same constitutional rights as all other Americans. The courts have also determined, however, that school officials may develop and enforce policies with the intent to make schools safe and healthy places with positive educational environments where all students can pursue their education. Constitutional rights embodied in the First and the Fourth Amendments guaranteeing students freedom of expression and freedom from unreasonable search and seizure have therefore been applied in a manner that balances students' rights and responsibilities against the responsibility of school officials to provide a safe learning environment for teachers and students.

Note

1. The assistance of Gene Bjorklun, Professor of Education at St. Cloud State University, was invaluable in doing the legal research for this chapter. Allowing me to search and seize from his personal library, providing copies of court decisions and his publications, and sharing his knowledge and insights on school law made the task easier for this nonjurist. Thanks also to Circuit Court Judge Kristena LaMar, Multnomah County, Portland, Oregon, for her helpful comments on an earlier draft of this chapter.

References

Alexander, Kern, and M. David Alexander. 1992. *American Public School Law*, 3rd ed. St. Paul, Minn.: West Publishing Co.

Bjorklun, Eugene C. 1994. "School Locker Searches and the Fourth Amendment." *Education Law Reporter* 92:1065–1073.

Bongiovanni, Anthony F. 1979. "An Analysis of Research on Punishment and Its Relation to the Use of Corporal Punishment in the Schools." In I. Hyman and J. Wise, eds., *Corporal Punishment in American Education*. Philadelphia: Temple University Press.

Chandler, Gary L. 1992. "Due Process Rights of High School Students." *High School Journal* 75:137–143.

Falk, Herbert A. 1941. *Corporal Punishment*. New York: Columbia University Press.

Goodlad, John. 1984. *A Place Called School*. New York: McGraw-Hill.

Hyman, Irwin A. 1990. *Reading, Writing, and the Hickory Stick*. Lexington, Mass.: D.C. Heath.

Hyman, Irwin A., and James H. Wise, eds. 1979. *Corporal Punishment in American Education*. Philadelphia: Temple University Press.

Johnson, Robert S. 1993. "Metal Detectors in Public Schools: A Policy Perspective." *Education Law Reporter* 80(March 25): 1–7.

Kempe, C. H., et al. 1962. "The Battered Child Syndrome." *Journal of the American Medical Association* 18:17–24.

Lee, Virginia. 1979. "A Legal Analysis of Ingraham v. Wright." In Hyman and Wise, *Corporal Punishment in American Education*. Philadelphia: Temple University Press.

Levy, Paul. 1995. "Today's Lesson: Safety at School." *Minneapolis Star-Tribune*, September 3, 12A.

Maurer, Adah. 1981. *Paddles Away: A Psychological Study of Physical Punishment in Schools*. Palo Alto, Calif.: R & E Research Associates.

National Institute on Drug Abuse. 1991. *National Household Survey on Drug Abuse: Highlights 1990*. Washington, D.C.: Government Printing Office.

Reardon, F. J. and R. N. Reynolds. 1979. "A Survey of Attitudes Toward Corporal Punishment in Pennsylvania Schools." In I. A. Hyman and J. H. Wise, eds., *Corporal Punishment in American Education*. Philadelphia: Temple University Press.

Reglin, Gary L. 1992. "Public School Educators' Knowledge of Selected Supreme Court Decisions Affecting Daily Public School Operations." *Journal of Educational Administration* 30(2):26–31.

Regoli, Robert M., and John D. Hewitt. 1994. *Delinquency in Society*, 2nd ed. New York: McGraw-Hill.

Rose, Terry L. 1984. "Current Uses of Corporal Punishment in American Public Schools." *Journal of Educational Psychology* 76:427–441.

Rust, James O. and Karen Q. Kinnard. 1983. "Personality Characteristics of the Users of Corporal Punishment in the Schools." *Journal of School Psychology* 21:91–105.

Sanchez, J. M. 1992. "Expelling the Fourth Amendment from American Schools: Students' Rights Six Years After *T.L.O.*" *Journal of Law and Education* 21(3):381–413.

Shaw, Steven R., and Jeffery P. Braden. 1990. "Race and Gender Bias in the Administration of Corporal Punishment." *School Psychology Review* 19:378–383.

Straus, Murray A., Demie Kurz, Donileen Loseke, and Joan McCord. 1991. "Discipline and Defense: Physical Punishment of Children and Violence and Other Crime in Adulthood." *Social Problems* 38:133–154.

Welsh, Ralph S. 1979. "Severe Parental Punishment and Aggression: The Link between Corporal Punishment and Delinquency." In I. Hyman and J. Wise, eds., *Corporal Punishment in American Education*. Philadelphia: Temple University Press.

Zirkel, Perry A. "Another Search for Student Rights." *Phi Delta Kappan* 75:728–230.

8

Juvenile Justice, Police, and the Court

Under our Constitution, the condition of being a boy does not justify a kangaroo court.—U.S. Supreme Court Justice Abe Fortas, *In re Gault*, 387 U.S. 1, at 28 (1967)

The Juvenile Justice System

Juveniles have not always been processed through a separate system of justice. American judicial procedures in the nineteenth century followed those of England, subjecting children to the same punishments as adult criminals. Some punishments were very severe. Youth who committed serious offenses could be subjected to prison sentences, whipping, and even the death penalty. During the nineteenth century, criminal codes applied to all persons, adults and children alike. No provisions were made to account for the age of offenders. There were no separate laws or courts and no special facilities for the care of children who were in trouble with the law.

During the nineteenth century a number of developments paved the way for a separate system of justice for juveniles: urbanization, the child-saving movement, the reform school movement, and the concept of *parens patriae* (Siegel and Senna, 1991: 379). An increase in the birthrate and an influx of immigrants to America brought a new wave of growth to American cities. With this growth came an increase in the number of dependent and destitute children. Many urban youth and children of immigrants were perceived to be prone to deviant and immoral behavior. Some community leaders pushed for state intervention to "save" these children through shelter care and educational programs. The result of this "child-saving movement" was to extend government intervention in youth behaviors, which had previously been the responsibility of parents and families. The leading advocates in the child-saving movement believed that such youth problems as idleness, drinking, vagrancy, and delinquent behaviors threatened the moral fabric of society and must be controlled; if parents could not or would not control and properly supervise their own children, then the government should intervene. They pushed for legislation that would give courts jurisdiction over children who were incorrigible or runaways and who committed crimes. These children could be committed to Houses of Refuge and similar institutional care facilities (see Siegel and Senna, 1991: 379). Reform schools were also created by state and local governments to care for vagrant and delinquent youths. State reform schools opened in Massachusetts in 1848, in New York in 1849, in Ohio in 1850; these were followed soon after by youth institutions in Maine, Rhode Island, and Michigan in 1860 (U.S. Department of Justice, 1976). The child-saving movement and the reform schools did provide services for children, but they were considered by some to be unnecessarily intrusive. Institutional life was detrimental to many youths. The harsh working conditions and the strict discipline were unable to stop juvenile delinquency. It became apparent to many that the early reform schools were not caring adequately for the growing number of troubled youths and were becoming a financial burden for the public.

The legal basis for court jurisdiction over wayward children and the origin of the juvenile court may be traced back to an early English legal doctrine known as *parens patriae*. Under this doctrine, a court could declare a child a ward of the state when it was established that the parents had failed to properly care for and supervise the child. The doctrine was central to the juvenile court philosophy, because children who violated laws were not to be treated as criminals. Because children were considered less mature and less aware of the consequences of their actions, they were not to be held legally accountable for their behavior as were adults. Under the juvenile justice philosophy, youthful offenders were designated as delinquent rather than as criminal, and the primary purpose of the juvenile justice system was not punishment but rehabilitation (see Mennel, 1972; and Davis, 1980).

The first juvenile court was established in Cook County (Chicago), Illinois, in 1899. This first step in processing juvenile offenders separately from adults was the culmination of the reform efforts just discussed. The juvenile reform efforts were also based on the growing optimism that application of the social sciences was more appropriate for handling juvenile offenders than the law. Delinquency was viewed more as a social problem and a breakdown of the family than as a criminal problem. Thus, social workers, probation officers, and psychologists took the place of lawyers and prosecutors. They examined the background and the social history of the child and evaluated the family environment to assess the child's needs; they then developed a treatment plan to remediate the problems. The juvenile court judge was expected to be more like a father figure than a legal jurist (Davis, 1980). The purpose of the juvenile court was to protect and treat the child, not to punish; therefore, the juvenile proceeding was more civil than criminal. Since the juvenile legal process was purportedly "in the best interests of the child" and not intended to punish, the hearing was more informal, unlike the more formal, adversarial criminal court process. It was believed that children did not need the same formal procedural legal rights as adults in criminal court; thus, children were denied many of the legal rights of adults, such as formal notice of the charges and the right to legal counsel.

The main features that have distinguished juvenile court proceedings from adult criminal court proceedings may be summarized as follows (see Greenwood, 1988):

• *Absence of legal guilt.* Because juveniles are generally less mature and often unaware of the consequences of their actions, they are not held legally responsible for their actions to the same extent as adults. Legally, juveniles are not found guilty of crimes but are "found to be delinquent." Juvenile status—generally, being under eighteen years of age—is a defense against criminal responsibility, much like the insanity defense. Exceptions are made in cases of more mature juveniles who have committed serious offenses. The juvenile court may waive jurisdiction and transfer the case to criminal court.

• *Treatment rather than punishment.* The stated purpose of the juvenile court is treatment of the child and community protection, not punishment as it is for adult felony offenders in criminal court.

• *Informal, private court proceedings.* Juvenile court hearings are more informal, and in many states they are not open to the public, with usually only the child, parents, attorneys, and probation officer present. Hearings are often held in the judge's chamber. The majority of hearings are informal, uncontested, nonadversarial proceedings that take less than ten minutes. This practice is rooted in the original child-saving philosophy that the purpose of the court was for treatment, not punishment. Proceedings for more serious juvenile offenders are now often open to the public.

• *Separateness from adult offenders.* Juvenile offenders are kept separate from adult offenders at every stage of the juvenile process, from arrest (or "taking into custody") to detention, pretrial and court proceedings, to probation supervision and institutional corrections. All juvenile records are also maintained separately from adult criminal records, including in computerized information systems.

• *Focus on a juvenile's background and social history.* A juvenile's background and the need for and amenability to treatment are considered of equal importance with the offense committed when making decisions on handling each case. This is consistent with the stated purpose of treatment rather than punishment. The assumption that court officers can assess and treat juveniles' needs is open to question. The practice of basing the length of "treatment" on the child's needs as well as on the offense has come under criticism. Children who commit relatively minor crimes but have "greater needs for treatment" are often supervised for longer periods of time than are more serious offenders who have been determined to be less "in need of treatment."

• *Shorter terms of supervision and incarceration.* The terms of probation supervision, confinement in a detention center, or commitment to a correctional facility are usually shorter in duration than for adult offenders—generally not much longer than one to two years, on average. In recent years many states have revised their juvenile statutes, extending their jurisdiction and length of incarceration over violent juvenile offenders.

• *Distinctive terminology.* Consistent with the need to treat juveniles differently from adults because of their immaturity and their limited legal accountability, different terms are used when handling juveniles at each stage of the process. Juveniles are "taken into custody," not arrested and transported to a detention center, not booked into jail; a petition for delinquency is filed with the court, rather than a criminal indictment; the result is an adjudication of delinquency, rather than conviction of a felony or misdemeanor crime.

Police and Juvenile Offenders

Police are the first contact that most young people have with the juvenile justice system. Police are charged with preventing crime and enforcing the law. They are given the authority to arrest and to use physical force. Society entrusts a great deal of authority to police, but it also expects a lot from them—from community protection to apprehension of all offenders. In reality, traditional police patrol does little to prevent crime. Police react to crime only after it has already happened, responding to citizen calls, reporting to crime scenes, conducting investigations, and tracking and apprehending offenders. The fact that police are called upon for many services besides law enforcement makes their job even more difficult.

Juvenile crime presents a difficult challenge for police. Police officers encounter a wide variety of deviant and delinquent behavior among children and youth, ranging from minor status offenses to serious crimes. Juveniles are often less predictable than adults and often exhibit less respect for the authority of officers. The immaturity of many children and youth means that they are more vulnerable to the "dares" of other youth, and they often engage in deviant behavior when in the company of their peers. Many youth view the policeman on patrol not as a deterrent to delinquent behavior but as a challenge to their ability to avoid detection and confrontation while loitering at night or engaging in behaviors ranging from petty mischief to property damage (vandalism) to the more serious crimes of theft and assaults. The immaturity of many youth, coupled with limited parental supervision and negative peer influence, presents special problems for police, who frequently encounter juveniles with little respect for law and authority. Juveniles also present a special problem for police because they are less aware of the consequences of their actions or do not care about the consequences to their victims, or the legal consequences to themselves.

Police handle many noncriminal matters referred to as *status offenses,* such as incorrigibility (disobeying parents), running away, curfew violations, and truancy, as well as nondelinquent juvenile matters such as neglect, abuse, and missing-persons reports. Most urban police departments have special police units or juvenile bureaus for handling the increasing number of juvenile cases. Duties of special juvenile officers include taking missing children reports; ex-

amining runaway cases; investigating juvenile crimes; contacting and inter-
viewing juveniles, their parents, school officials, and complainants regarding the
circumstances of an offense; maintaining juvenile records; and appearing in juvenile court.

Police Officers in Schools

Police have played an important role in assisting schools with law enforcement responsibilities. Officers on routine police patrol are involved in incidents
ranging from truancy to juvenile crimes, such as drug and weapon possession,
to student fights and assaults. Officers regularly drive by schools during night
and weekend patrols, to prevent burglary and vandalism to school property.
Police departments have taken an active role in developing delinquency prevention programs since the early part of this century. The Police Athletic League
(P.A.L.) has established activities and programs in cities throughout the United
States. Many police departments take great pride in their efforts to prevent
youngsters from getting into trouble. One of the most recent and well-known
prevention programs is the Drug Abuse Resistance Education (D.A.R.E.) program, which has been implemented in schools throughout the United States.
Originally begun by the Los Angeles Police Department, D.A.R.E. programs
have been established in large and small cities throughout the country. Special
juvenile officers undergo several weeks of training in order to be D.A.R.E. officers, who present a structured curriculum of educational materials to primarily fifth- and sixth-graders. Research on D.A.R.E. programs show mixed results
in terms of long-term drug and delinquency prevention, but the programs are
widely supported by educators and by police departments.

Many school administrators who have witnessed an increase in juvenile
crime activity have chosen to employ police officers full-time during school
hours. The costs are generally shared with the local police department, and the
specific duties and responsibilities are agreed upon by the police department
and the school system. The origin of police-school liaison officers has been
traced to Liverpool, England, in 1951. The concept was soon introduced to
North America; the Flint, Michigan, school district hired police officers in 1958,
and schools in British Columbia, Canada, began placing police-school liaison
officers in many schools in 1972 (LaLonde, 1995: 20). School police officers
in the United States generally focus on traditional police functions. They patrol school grounds, parking lots, hallways, stairways and bathrooms; check student identification; handle trespassers, class cutters, and truants; investigate
criminal complaints; handle disruptive students; and prevent disturbances at af-
ter-school activities (see Blauvelt, 1990: 6). In the United States, school police officers are usually armed, although not all officers may be in uniform.

Police assigned to schools also provide services beyond traditional law enforcement functions. They are available to counsel students and faculty on crime
and security issues, and they improve school safety and prevent crime through
educational programs. School liaison officers in Canada are not armed and place
more emphasis on the crime prevention and educational role than on law enforcement and patrol functions (LaLonde, 1995). School administrators should

carefully assess the frequency and seriousness of crime and disruption in their schools before determining whether to hire police or security professionals (see Blauvelt, 1990). School administrators and police officials should then develop mutually agreeable policies governing the specific duties and responsibilities of the school liaison officers. Police school liaison officers are valuable resources in preventing school crime and in responding to crime incidents when they occur. School police officers' activities are not limited to working directly with students. They may provide crime prevention education and advice to school staff, parents, and students. In summary, school liaison officers may:

•counsel, advise, and talk informally with students

•teach classes on alcohol and drug use prevention

•advise school personnel and students on security precautions

•offer safety and crime prevention education to students, staff, and parents

•work to improve the safety and security of the school

•gain students' trust and be aware of bullying behavior, harrassment, alcohol and drug use, and gang activities

•investigate, document, and record critical incidents

•serve as a liaison between the school and the criminal justice system (see LaLonde, 1995)

Police school liaison officers have proven to be effective in helping to control school crime and in responding appropriately when it occurs. Officers may be instrumental in helping to reduce the number of crime incidents in the neighborhood around schools during school and nonschool hours. Police officers who work in schools have been able to obtain valuable information from students that has helped in the investigation of crimes in the community. The most effective programs emphasize close working relationships among police, school staff, and students and emphasize clear communication regarding the police role, policies, and actions to be taken in crime incidents.

Police Discretion

Police have considerable discretionary power in handling juvenile matters, ranging from reprimand and release to transporting a juvenile to detention and making a referral to juvenile court. Discretion is important in police work, for the officer's decision to intervene in any suspected law violation is the first stage in the juvenile justice process. Officers use their discretion in deciding whether to take official actions with offending juveniles or simply to order them to "move on," "break it up," or "get on home." Most police contact with juveniles is nonofficial, and police take official actions in only 10 to 20 percent of their encounters with juveniles (Bartollas, 1993: 395).

Police discretion has been criticized, however, because some believe that police abuse their broad discretionary powers and tend to base their decisions on factors other than the offense. Factors such as sex, race, socioeconomic status, and individual characteristics of the offender have been shown to make a difference in police officers' decisions whether or not to take official actions. Girls are less likely than boys to be arrested and referred to juvenile court, but they are often referred more than boys for status offenses such as running away or disobeying parents (Armstrong, 1977; Chesney-Lind, 1977). Researchers have reported varying results from studies on the importance of race in discretionary police actions. Some studies report few differences when offense seriousness and prior record are controlled for. African Americans and other minority youths seem to be involved in more frequent and serious offenses than whites, so it is difficult to determine whether they are singled out unfairly by police for official action. There is some evidence of racial bias, however, as minority youths have often been targeted by police for official intervention (Wolfgang et al., 1972: 252). Some critics also contend that lower-class youths are processed into the justice system for offenses for which middle- or upper-class juveniles are simply reprimanded and released to their parents. Police and juvenile officers justify this use of discretion by saying that middle- and upper-class youth are more likely to be corrected without referral to the justice system because their parents have the resources to provide their children with the necessary supervision and corrective services (Bartollas, 1993: 398). Merry Morash (1984) found that an older juvenile with a prior record who fits the image of a serious delinquent is more likely to be referred by police to the juvenile court. A juvenile's demeanor and attitude make a difference in a police officer's use of discretion. A youth who is polite and respectful is more likely to get off with a reprimand, while a negative and hostile attitude is likely to result in a court referral (Piliavin and Briar, 1964; Lundman, Sykes, and Clark, 1990). In addition to the characteristics and demeanor of the juvenile, police are also influenced by public pressure and press coverage. Newspaper articles that emphasize youth gangs and violence tend to heighten public fears and concern about juvenile crime, resulting in pressure on police to arrest and process juveniles to court.

Police discretion is necessary, and the juvenile justice system could not function without it. Juvenile courts in urban areas have a backlog of cases, probation officers' caseloads are too high for them to provide adequate supervision, and correctional facilities are becoming overcrowded. The system must concentrate on those juvenile offenders who pose the greatest risk and need official intervention to prevent further offending.

Police Diversion and Alternatives to Detention

Diversion of minor juvenile offenders and deinstitutionalization of status offenders have been promoted as effective delinquency prevention strategies by federal legislation during the past two decades. The Juvenile Justice and Delinquency Prevention (JJDP) Act of 1974 promoted the diversion of juvenile offenders from the justice system and the referral of those youth who require intervention to community-based programs. Diversion had been recommended by the 1967 President's Commission on Law Enforcement and Administration of Justice as a process for referring minor juvenile offenders to community treatment programs in lieu of formal juvenile justice processing. Criminologists argued that processing minor offenders through the justice system had a stigmatizing effect that was likely to perpetuate rather than reduce the chance of further delinquent behavior. Many experts noted that too much was expected of the juvenile court system, and some believed that court referrals should be made only for juvenile offenses that would be crimes if committed by adults; status offenders, they suggested, should be diverted to agencies outside the formal justice process, which would provide services to meet the needs of at-risk children. Youth Service Bureaus (YSBs) were among the diversion agencies that were developed through federal funding to provide an alternative source for police referral of minor status offenders. These programs offer counseling, job treatment, educational help, job assistance, and recreational opportunities for youth.

The deinstitutionalization of status offenders (DSO), provided for in the JJDP Act, was a major emphasis. The act required states to place juveniles who were charged with offenses that would not be criminal if committed by an adult not in juvenile detention or correctional facilities but rather in shelter facilities. Amendments to the original act (in 1977, 1980, and 1992) required that states receiving JJDP Act grant funds provide assurance that they were taking action to remove status offenders and nonoffenders from detention and correctional facilities and not detaining juveniles in adult jails (see Holden and Kapler, 1995). Solomon Kobrin and Malcolm Klein (1982) conducted a national evaluation of DSO programs and found mixed results. One problem was the definition of status offenders. They found that "pure" status offenders were relatively rare; most status offenders had prior delinquent experiences. Some areas limited their programs to pure status offenders, so many otherwise eligible youth were not served by the programs. Another problem was "net widening." In some areas, the number of juveniles referred to court actually increased, and many youngsters whose behavior did not justify police intervention were referred to diversion programs. Thus, many status offenders who would have previously been handled by police or intake probation officers through a "reprimand and release" were drawn into diversion or DSO programs.

Diversion and alternatives to detention programs have for the most part been effective in reforming the juvenile justice system. Anne Schneider (1985) conducted a comprehensive national evaluation of DSO programs and found that they were successful in significantly reducing the number of status offenders in detention and institutions. Diversion and deinstitutionalization of status offenders are not a panacea for delinquency prevention, but shelters and foster care are as effective and much less expensive than detention and juvenile institutions (see Holden and Kapler, 1995; and Raley, 1995).

Police Decisions in Handling Juvenile Offenders

A police officer may refer a minor offender to a youth services bureau, a community agency such as a Big Brother or Big Sister program, or a similar delinquency prevention program. In the majority of cases where police have reason to believe that a juvenile has committed an offense, the youth is taken to the police department juvenile bureau for questioning, may be fingerprinted and photographed, and is then taken to the intake unit of the juvenile probation department, where a decision is made to detain the youth or release to the parents. The options available to the unit are these:

• *Questioning, warning, and release in the community.* The least severe sanction is to have an officer question a youth for a possible minor offense and give a warning and reprimand on the street without taking formal actions.

• *Station adjustment.* Police may take a youth into custody and to the station, record the alleged minor offense and actions taken, give the youth an official reprimand, and release the youth to the parents. The parents are generally contacted first and may be present when the youth is reprimanded. In smaller cities the youth may be placed under police supervision for a short period of time.

• *Referral to a diversion agency.* Police may release and refer a juvenile to a youth service bureau (YSB), a Big Brother/Big Sister program, a runaway center, or a mental health agency. Diverting minor offenders from the juvenile justice system to a YSB that provides counseling and social services is considered preferable for many first-time offenders and troubled youth.

• *Issuing a citation and referring to juvenile court.* The police officer can issue a citation and refer the youth to juvenile court. The intake probation officer accepts the referral, contacts the parents if the police have not already done so, and releases the youth to the parents on the condition that they will report to the court when ordered to do so. The intake officer then determines whether a formal delinquency petition should be filed (in some states this decision is made by the prosecuting attorney assigned to the juvenile court).

• *Taking to a detention center or shelter home.* The police officer can issue a citation, refer the youth to the juvenile court, and take him or her to a detention center. The intake officer at the detention center then decides whether to hold the juvenile or release him or her to the parents. Juveniles are detained when they are considered dangerous, when there is a lack of parental supervision, or when there is a high probability that he or she will not report to the court when ordered to do so. If a detention center is felt to be too restrictive and an appropriate parent or foster home is not available, the youth may be placed in a shelter care facility, which can be either a private home or a group home. Most states now provide for a detention hearing within a day after the youth's referral at which a judge or referee must determine whether there is sufficient reason to continue to detain the juvenile. In cities without a separate juvenile detention center, juveniles who cannot be released to their parents are confined in a separate section of the county jail or may be transported to a juvenile facility in another county. There has been a national effort to remove juveniles from adult jails. Removing juveniles from their homes and detaining them in juvenile centers is considered a last resort.

Police and Juveniles' Legal Rights

The law of arrest or taking into custody is generally the same for juveniles as for adults. A police officer must have probable cause to believe that the suspected juvenile has committed an offense. "Probable cause" means more than mere suspicion, but absolute certainty is not required. Juveniles, like adults, have certain procedural rights after being taken into custody. Under the U.S. Supreme Court case of *Miranda v. Arizona* (384 U.S. 436), police officers are required to notify suspects of their rights before interrogation—their right to remain silent, since anything they say may be held against them in court, and their right to speak with an attorney. The 1967 Supreme Court case of *In re Gault* (387 U.S. 1) made the right against self-incrimination and the right to counsel applicable to juveniles but failed to specify whether a juvenile could waive the Miranda rights intelligently and knowingly. The 1979 Supreme Court case of *Fare v. Michael C.* (442 U.S. 23) applied the "totality of circumstances" standard to the interrogation of juveniles. The case involved a juvenile who asked for his probation officer, but not an attorney, while being interrogated by police. When his request was denied, he continued to willingly talk to police, implicating himself in the crime. The Supreme Court ruled that Michael C. appeared to understand his rights, and his conviction was upheld.

Thomas Grisso (1981) conducted research on a sample of juveniles who had been questioned by police in St. Louis. Although most of them had waived their Miranda rights, Grisso found that most of the youth sixteen years of age or younger did not adequately understand their Miranda rights and therefore could not make an informed, intelligent waiver. Many jurisdictions now require that a parent, legal guardian, or attorney be present during any police questioning for any confession to be admissible in court. The Supreme Court ruling in the *Gault* case also required that the parents must be immediately informed when a juvenile is taken into custody, by the officer who took the juvenile into custody, the juvenile bureau officer, or by the court intake officer.

The Fourth Amendment right against unlawful search and seizure also applies when a police officer stops a juvenile for questioning as a suspect in a crime. We discussed in Chapter 6 the procedures that are required for police officers and school officials to conduct a search of student's book bags or pockets for unlawful drugs or weapons. The legal procedures governing search and seizure of a juvenile who is a suspect in a crime are essentially the same as those for adults. A police officer is allowed to conduct a pat-down search for weapons that a suspect in a crime may be carrying. If other illegal substances such as drugs are found during a search for weapons, the search and seizure will generally be held admissible in court. In circumstances where a juvenile is not a suspect in a crime and has not consented to have his or her person or property searched, then police must obtain a valid search warrant. Exceptions in the case of school searches for drugs and dangerous weapons were noted in Chapter 6.

Fingerprinting, Photographing, and Records

Postarrest procedures that are standard for adult suspects are sources of controversy when applied to juveniles. Some state juvenile codes require that judges approve the fingerprinting and photographing of juveniles, particularly before the court has entered an adjudication. Some juvenile statutes limit these procedures to juveniles arrested for felony crimes; others leave the decision to individual police department policy. The National Advisory Commission on Criminal Justice Standards and Goals (1977) recommended that juvenile fingerprints and photographs be taken only for evidence and investigation of specific crimes; that they be used and recorded only by the local police department and not sent to a central records depository such as the Federal Bureau of Investigation; and that they be destroyed once the investigation is complete or when the juvenile is no longer under juvenile court supervision. Some of the original precautions against treating juveniles differently from adults and keeping all juvenile records separate are currently being examined and questioned, since many juvenile justice procedures are becoming "criminalized" (see Feld, 1993).

The Juvenile Court

The original intentions of the juvenile court—to act in the best interests of the child, in an informal, caring environment—often led to arbitrary decisions. Under the guise of treatment and rehabilitation, juveniles often received sentences that were longer and more punitive than those given to adults who had committed comparable offenses. The practice continued for more than fifty years, until the procedural informality of the juvenile court was questioned by the United States Supreme Court in the case of *Kent v. United States*, 383 U.S. 541, 566 (1966), which noted that a child receives "neither the protections accorded to adults nor the solicitous care and regenerative treatment postulated for children," and the informal procedures were condemned in the case of *In re Gault* (387 U.S. 1, 1967). The Court mandated several legal procedures common to the criminal court, such as formal written notice of the charge against the young offender. The court must determine if a juvenile who waived the rights stated in the police officer's Miranda warning fully understood the rights and was capable of making an informed, voluntary waiver.

Court Intake Procedure

Referrals to the juvenile court are usually made by a police officer, but they also may be made by school officials and truant officers. The intake unit of the court serves as a preliminary screening process. The intake procedure is done by one or more probation officers, who determine whether a petition should be filed for adjudication of delinquency. In some jurisdictions the decision whether to file a delinquency petition is made in consultation with the prosecutor. The intake procedure is important in the juvenile court process, because many courts have promoted the policy that it is in the best interests of the juvenile and the community to place the youngster under "informal adjustment," a type of short-term unofficial supervision, or to make a referral to social services or a community agency. Many court officials believe that unless the juvenile has committed a serious offense or has a prior record, it is better to handle the case informally, short of adjudication and formal probation.

When a case is referred to the intake unit of the juvenile court, the intake officer must verify the juvenile's age to determine that the court has jurisdiction over the case. The officer also reviews the report of the police officer or other referring agency, to ascertain that it is an appropriate referral to the court. The next step is to conduct a preliminary investigation to determine whether the case may be processed informally or should be petitioned to the court. The officer generally interviews the juvenile and the parent(s) or legal guardian and may contact the complainant in the case, school officials, or other parties that may provide relevant information about the juvenile and the particular case. In many jurisdictions, the prosecuting attorney makes the legal decision whether the alleged offense should be adjudicated in court and whether there is sufficient evidence to do so. The case is dismissed if the court does not have jurisdiction, if the case is weak, or if the intake officer's preliminary investigation raises questions about the need to file a petition for delinquency. Informal adjustment is recommended for status offenders and for juveniles charged with minor offenses. The intake officer may require a short period of supervision or payment of restitution for damaged or stolen property or may refer the juvenile to a social agency or youth services bureau for guidance and supervision. The case may be dismissed at that point, or it may remain open pending the juvenile's positive adjustment.

Adjudication Hearing

The adjudication hearing is the fact-finding part of the hearing. The judge first determines if the juvenile understands his or her rights, and the charges are read by the prosecuting attorney. The judge asks the juvenile if he or she understands the charges, wishes to be represented by legal counsel (if an attorney is not already representing the juvenile), and wants a full hearing or is willing to waive that right and accept the adjudication of delinquency (similar to a guilty plea). Many urban juvenile courts require the appearance of officers and witnesses only for full hearings, in order to streamline the court docket. If the juvenile wants a full hearing, the adjudication is then rescheduled so that the police officer, complainant, and any witnesses can be present to testify. The adjudication hearing is also rescheduled for juveniles who request a jury trial, although few states provide for the right to a jury trial for juveniles. The U.S. Supreme Court ruled in the 1971 case of *McKiever v. Pennsylvania* (403 U.S. 528) that it was not a constitutional right in juvenile proceedings, and jury trials are rare even in those states that provide for them.

In the 1967 *Gault* decision, the Supreme Court held that juveniles and their parents must be given adequate notice in writing of the charge, the right to legal counsel, and written notice of when they are to appear in court. The ideals stated in this prominent case have yet to make a significant impact on juvenile court practices throughout the nation. Feld (1988a) studied legal representation in six midwestern states, and reported that in three of them only about one-half or fewer of the juveniles charged and adjudicated were represented by legal counsel. The American Bar Association-Institute of Judicial Administration recommended that juveniles should have the right to effective counsel at all stages of the proceedings and that this right should be mandatory and not waivable (1980: 81). Juveniles are allowed to waive their right to legal counsel in many jurisdictions. The Minnesota statute (Sec. 260.155), for example, states that "Waiver of any right . . . must be an express waiver intelligently made by the child after the child has been fully and effectively informed of the right being waived."

Serious questions have been raised concerning whether juveniles can make an informed, intelligent and voluntary waiver of their fifth and sixth Amendments rights not to incriminate themselves, to have legal counsel, and to receive the due process of a full hearing. We noted in the first part of this chapter the concerns regarding juveniles' waiver of their Miranda rights during police questioning. In a sample of St. Louis youth who had been questioned by police, Grisso (1981) found that most of those fourteen and under and one-third to one-half of the fifteen- and sixteen-year-olds lacked the necessary competence to waive their rights to silence and counsel (1981: 194). In a replication of part of Grisso's research, Lawrence (1983) collected data and interviewed a sample of forty-five youths and their parents immediately following their appearance in juvenile court. A third of the juveniles had only a poor understanding and fewer than one-half had only a fair understanding of their right to remain silent and to have legal counsel. There was no significant difference in legal understanding between the juveniles and their parents, which raises questions whether parents can make an intelligent, informed waiver of their child's legal rights. The study was conducted in an urban juvenile court in a southwestern state that requires that all juveniles who appear in court be accompanied by an attorney. Lawrence assessed the role of attorneys and probation officers and found that probation officers often play a more important role in explaining juveniles' legal rights, primarily because they had spent more time with the youth before the court hearing and were more aware of the youths' fair to poor legal understanding. On the basis of the finding that attorneys seemed to overestimate the extent of juvenile clients' understanding of their legal rights and the court process, these recommendations were made:

> the appointment of legal counsel at an earlier point in the juvenile justice process is recommended as a means of enhancing juveniles' understanding of the law and the legal process, and ensuring that any waiver of their legal rights is an informed waiver with a full understanding of the possible consequences of the waiver. Earlier appointment of legal counsel would also reduce the wide variation in the quality of legal counsel and the amount of time attorneys are able to spend in case preparation. (Lawrence, 1983: 57)

Barry Feld (1989) examined a sample of juveniles against whom petitions were filed for delinquency and status offenses in Minnesota in 1986 and found that more than half of the juveniles did not have lawyers. He was particularly concerned that nearly one-third of juveniles who received out-of-home placement and more than one-fourth of those incarcerated in secure institutions were not represented by legal counsel (1989: 1323). The U.S. Supreme Court in the

1979 case of *Scott v. Illinois* (440 U.S. 367) and the Minnesota Supreme Court in the 1967 case of *State v. Borst* (154 N.W. 2d 888) held that it was not proper to incarcerate an adult offender without legal representation or without a valid waiver of counsel. In many cases, juveniles are clearly receiving less justice and more punishment than adult offenders. "Whether the typical *Miranda* advisory and the following waiver of rights under the 'totality of the circumstances' is sufficient to assure a valid waiver of counsel by juveniles is highly questionable" (Feld, 1989: 1323). The issue is further complicated by the finding that juveniles who are represented by counsel tend to receive more severe dispositions than unrepresented juveniles (Bortner, 1982; Feld, 1988a). A number of possible explanations have been suggested for this finding (see Feld, 1988a: 419–20), but clearly more research is needed on the question of legal representation for juveniles.

Disposition Hearing

Once the juvenile has been adjudicated delinquent, the next stage in the court process is the disposition, comparable to the sentencing phase in adult criminal court. Juvenile court proceedings are considered "bifurcated" in the sense that the adjudication and the disposition hearings are separate. Separating the hearings allows time for the probation officer to write a social history or predispositional report to assist the court in its decision making. It has been common practice in many courts for the disposition hearing to proceed immediately following adjudication. In this case, the probation officer has completed the predisposition report prior to both hearings. The disposition hearing is more informal than the adjudication hearing. The judge asks for the probation officer's report, which is based on interviews with the child and the parents and may include information from school officials, other social service agencies, and mental health professionals. The report examines such factors as the child's family structure and quality of parental supervision; peer relationships; attendance, grades, and behavior in school; participation in school and community activities; degree of maturity and responsibility; attitude toward authority figures; and previous court or police involvement. The disposition hearing may include testimony and cross-examination of the probation officer and any other persons who have provided information in the report. Juveniles may have legal counsel and may challenge the facts and information presented in the predisposition report. The most important factors in the disposition hearing are the seriousness of the offense and the juvenile's prior record (which are most important), the social information contained in the probation officer's report, and the dispositional options available to the court (see Bartollas, 1993: 437–439).

The dispositional alternatives available to juvenile courts vary considerably, with urban courts having more options available. The primary alternatives include:

1. *Dismissal.* Even though there may have been sufficient evidence to adjudicate a juvenile, a judge can dismiss the case if there is insufficient evidence that the child needs formal supervision by the court.

2. *Court diversion alternatives.* Many state juvenile codes now include provisions that allow for suspension of the formal adjudication or disposition process, and the juvenile may be supervised under "informal adjustment" by a community agency (preadjudication) or by a probation officer (predispositional). The case may be terminated after six months of successful adjustment or may be returned to court for adjudication and disposition.

Mediation is an alternative for resolving conflicts and disputes outside the courtroom. Mediation can take place as an alternative to trial and adjudication or, after a finding of guilt, to determine the disposition and often to establish restitution conditions. Mediation sessions are arranged for victims who are willing to meet with the offender and are facilitated by a trained mediator. The Victim Offender Reconciliation Program (VORP) is a form of mediation that has operated in a number of courts for more than a decade. If a settlement is reached, the mediator writes out the terms of the agreement, and both parties sign it. If the parties cannot make an agreement, the case may be referred back to the court. There are several benefits of mediation: (1) victims have an important role in the process, with an opportunity to express feelings about the crime and the impact of the damages and costs of the crime; (2) the offender is confronted with the responsibility for the crime and its impact on the victim and has an opportunity to make restitution for the wrongful actions; (3) court backlogs can be reduced, and judges have an additional sentencing tool that is often more effective than court-ordered conditions. There is some evidence that offenders involved in mediation are more likely to satisfactorily fulfill restitution conditions and are less likely to re-offend. (Mediation has been implemented in many schools as a student conflict management program; this is discussed more in Chapter Ten.)

3. *Probation.* The child may be released to the parents with orders to report to a probation officer. Probation supervision includes several conditions and rules that must be followed, including an order to attend school regularly and to obey all school rules and regulations. Juveniles with a history of behavioral or academic performance problems in school may be ordered to attend an alternative school. The juvenile may be ordered to pay restitution, complete community service restitution, or participate in counseling or treatment programs for specific identified needs.

4. *Placement in community residential programs.* The court may order placement in a residential facility or foster care if there is evidence of inadequate parental supervision or poor parent-child relations. Such placements are short term and in nonsecure residential programs. The court may also order temporary placement in a mental health facility or a residential drug and alcohol treatment facility.

5. *Institutional commitment.* Juveniles who are considered a risk to the community may be committed to more secure facilities, often called "training schools." These are generally administered and operated by the state and range from minimum-security schools with open campuses and cottage-like settings to medium- or maximum-security correctional facilities for juveniles or young adults. The latter are generally considered the last resort and are reserved for

youths who have committed serious crimes or who failed to adjust in a number of other juvenile programs. Institutional commitment may be for a fixed term or for an indefinite term up to the juvenile's twenty-first birthday. Recent legislation in some states allows courts to extend their jurisdiction over juveniles. Under an "extended juvenile jurisdiction" statute, youth who are convicted of violent crimes may be transferred to an adult correctional facility at a given age (usually eighteen or twenty-one).

Waiver and Transfer

Juveniles who commit serious or violent offenses may be tried as adults in criminal court. All juvenile cases must initially be filed in juvenile court, which has exclusive, original jurisdiction over minors. The juvenile court alone has the authority to waive jurisdiction and transfer a juvenile to adult criminal court. The waiver decision essentially is a choice between punishment in adult criminal court or rehabilitation in juvenile court (Podkopacz and Feld, 1996). The juvenile court must determine whether the seriousness of the present offense and the juvenile's prior record justify transferring the case to criminal court. There are three ways by which a juvenile case may be transferred to criminal court: judicial waiver, prosecutorial discretion, and statutory exclusion (Sickmund, 1994; Feld, 1993: 233–243). All states provide for the transfer of more serious juvenile offenders by one or more of these methods.

Judicial waiver (also called certifying, remanding, or waiver and transfer) is usually requested by the prosecuting attorney and takes place after a hearing, in accordance with two U.S. Supreme Court cases. In the 1966 case of *Kent v. United States* (383 U.S. 541), the Supreme Court reversed the conviction of a sixteen-year-old youth who had been tried as an adult. The waiver to adult court was ruled invalid because the juvenile had been denied a hearing with assistance of legal counsel, and no written statement had been made giving reasons for the waiver to criminal court. In *Kent*, the Supreme Court expressed concerns that the *parens patriae* philosophy of the juvenile court had led to questionable legal practices that were arbitrary and unfair: "There is evidence . . . that there may be grounds for concern that the child receives the worst of both worlds: that he gets neither the protection accorded adults nor the solicitous care and regenerative treatment postulated for children" (383 U.S. 541, at 556 [1966]).

In the 1975 case of *Breed v. Jones* (421 U.S. 519), the Court ruled that it was in violation of the double jeopardy clause of the Fourteenth Amendment to prosecute a juvenile in criminal court following adjudicatory proceedings in juvenile court. The purpose of the hearing in juvenile court therefore is not to determine guilt or innocence but to assess the juveniles' threat to public safety and amenability to treatment under the juvenile justice system. Under most waiver statutes, the juvenile court judge considers such factors as the circumstances and seriousness of the alleged offense, prior adjudications, and the age and maturity of the youth. Although judicial waivers accounted for only 2 percent of juvenile court cases in 1992, an estimated 11,700 juvenile delinquency cases were waived and transferred to criminal court in 1992, and waivers increased 68 percent from 1988 to 1992 (Sickmund, 1994: 1).

Some states provide for *prosecutorial discretion*, allowing prosecutors to file certain juvenile cases in either juvenile or criminal court. Concurrent jurisdiction statutes are generally limited to serious, violent, or repeat crimes. Donna Bishop and her associates (1989) examined the practice of prosecutorial waivers in Florida and found that few of the juveniles transferred were dangerous repeat offenders for whom the waiver would be justified. They found that a lack of statutory guidelines and the ease of prosecutorial waiver without judicial oversight accounted for the transfer of many inappropriate cases to criminal court (Bishop et al., 1989: 198).

Juveniles are transferred to criminal court in many states by *statutory exclusion*. Although this is not generally thought of as a form of juvenile transfer, many juveniles under eighteen years of age are tried in adult criminal court because some state legislatures have set the maximum age for juvenile court jurisdiction at sixteen or fifteen, rather than at seventeen as in most states (see Sickmund, 1994: 4; and Szymanski, 1994).

With the recent trend to "get tough" on youths involved in crime, more juveniles are being transferred to the adult court (Sickmund, 1994). There is evidence, however, that many juveniles waived to adult court are not the most dangerous or serious offenders. Bortner (1986) examined 214 remanded juveniles and found that they were not more dangerous or intractable than nonremanded juveniles. Her analysis suggested that their remand did not enhance public safety, and she concluded that political and organizational factors accounted for the increased number of remands. There is evidence that criminal courts have given less severe sentences to waived juveniles than were likely if those young offenders had been tried in juvenile court. Donna Hamparian and her associates (1982) found that most of the juveniles transferred to adult court in 1978 received fines or probation; the small number who were incarcerated received sentences of one year or less. More recent research indicates that juveniles waived to criminal court are receiving more severe sentences than if they had been retained in juvenile court, but there are significant disparities in the sentences for property and personal offenses and between adult and juvenile courts (Rudman et al., 1986; Podkopacz and Feld, 1996).

Research evidence suggests that judicial waiver may have little more than symbolic value, relaying a message to the public that something is being done about violent juvenile crime. Waiver and transfer, however, may not accomplish much in terms of reducing the growing number of serious and violent juvenile offenders. It does remove more serious offenders from the juvenile system, but there are questions whether the adult system is equipped to handle a growing number of youthful offenders. Rudman et al. (1986) believe that waiver creates new problems for adult corrections, and it may be counterproductive to send juvenile offenders for several years of punishment with adult offenders rather than a few years of treatment in the juvenile system.

The quality and effectiveness of juvenile justice system responses to violent youth will be improved not by removing them but by evolving broader dispositional responses to the juvenile court. Measures such as increasing the age of juvenile corrections jurisdiction and improving the quality of services in secure institutions may have more immediate impacts on violent juvenile crime than simply transferring the "problem" to the overburdened criminal courts. (Rudman, Hartston, Fagan, and Moore, 1986: 94)

In summary, the waiver and transfer of juveniles to adult court is likely to increase in frequency as officials respond to public pressure for tougher measures against juvenile crime. This is an issue that demands further evaluative research to determine its appropriateness in responding to juvenile crime. It is important for legislators to consider policies for responding to juvenile crime that are most effective in producing long-term benefits for the protection of the community and change for juvenile offenders.

Current Juvenile Court Trends and Reforms

The juvenile court has come under criticism from both conservatives and liberals. Conservatives contend that the court is "soft on crime" when the primary goal is to treat juvenile offenders rather than to hold them accountable for their crimes. Giving serious and repeat offenders too many chances through diversion programs and community treatment alternatives sends a message to them and to the community that we do not take juvenile crime seriously. Juvenile training schools are criticized for their open, private school-like setting, and conservatives believe some juveniles should be confined for longer sentences in a more punitive setting.

Liberal critics express concern about the social problems that confront youth and place many at risk of involvement in gangs, drug use, and delinquency. Liberals claim that formal processing through the juvenile justice system often aggravates the problems, and institutional confinement in detention centers and training schools only serves to further criminalize juveniles. Judicial critics denounce the lack of procedural safeguards and uniformity in the informal juvenile court process, with many juveniles receiving more punitive sanctions than adults for minor offenses that would result in no more than a fine in adult court.

Practitioners in the juvenile system also express dissatisfaction, and they often disagree among themselves. Police and prosecutors want tougher sanctions for juvenile offenders and fewer "second chances" through diversion programs and community alternatives. Probation officers contend that a large group of juvenile offenders have special needs that can be met through treatment and supervision in the community. Given their knowledge of the social and family background of referred juveniles, probation officers are reluctant to take a punitive approach except as a last resort after treatment alternatives have failed.

The juvenile court is currently undergoing significant changes and reforms. The reform movement began with U.S. Supreme Court decisions of *Kent, In re Gault*, and *In re Winship* in the 1960s, in which the Court required that juveniles receive most of the same due process protections provided for adults in criminal courts. Juveniles were provided notice of the charges, given the right to counsel, and afforded protection against self-incrimination and unlawful searches. The high court stopped short of giving juveniles the right to bail and a jury trial, however. Another step in juvenile court reform involved efforts to remove status offenders from formal adjudication and commitment to detention centers and juvenile institutions. Juvenile lockups and training schools housed many youths whose only "crime" was disobeying their parents, running away, or being truant. Advocates of such practices argued that involvement in status offenses was the first step toward more serious delinquency and that early intervention might prevent serious delinquency. Opponents noted the unfairness of punishing youths for minor deviant behavior and voiced concerns about the adverse effects on status offenders from being housed with older, hard-core juvenile offenders. The President's Commission on Law Enforcement and Administration of Justice (1967) recommended narrowing the range of offenses going before the juvenile court, and groups such as the American Bar Association-Institute of Judicial Administration (1982) called for an end to adjudicating and incarcerating status offenders in juvenile institutions.

The current focus of discussion concerning juvenile court reform is the very purpose of juvenile courts: punishment or treatment. Barry Feld has noted that about a fourth of the states have redefined their juvenile codes' statements of purpose, deemphasizing rehabilitation and placing more importance on public protection and safety (1988b: 842; 1993: 245). These statutory changes represent significant departures from the original juvenile justice philosophy of treatment "in the best interests of the child." Courts have reasoned that a "just deserts" approach may be more effective in changing and correcting the juvenile offender. The Washington Supreme Court reasoned that "sometimes punishment is treatment" and upheld the state legislature's conclusion that "accountability for criminal behavior . . . and punishment . . . does as much to rehabilitate, correct and direct an errant youth as does the prior philosophy of focusing on the particular characteristics of the individual juveniles" (*State v. Lawley*, 591 P.2d 772,773 [1979]); (see Feld, 1993: 245–246). Arguing along the same lines, Judge Charles E. Springer (1986) has argued for the adoption of the justice model for the juvenile court, placing emphasis upon the crime committed and holding juveniles morally and legally accountable for law violations.

> The message of the juvenile court that should be heard by the community and, most importantly, by the delinquent youth is this: "Young citizen, you must obey the law; if you violate the law, you are accountable for your deeds. You are to be blamed and punished for it; still, we will do the best we can to help you so that it does not happen again." . . . Putting justice first is not to demean or diminish the role of education and rehabilitation in the juvenile court process. The . . . single most effective rehabilitative factor in the lives of most juvenile offenders is their being held accountable, being punished, being blamed, and being warned of the consequences of future law violations. (Springer, 1986:82–83)

Some have questioned the feasibility of "rehabilitating" the juvenile court and suggest that it is time to abolish it. Barry Feld (1993) argues that judicial and legislative changes have "criminalized" the juvenile court, as they have altered the court's jurisdiction over status offenders, who are diverted from the system, and over serious offenders, who are increasingly transferred to adult criminal court. There are fewer differences between criminal courts and juvenile courts; the latter now tend to "punish youths for their offenses rather than treat them for their 'real needs' " (Feld, 1993: 197). Beyond being punished for their crimes, however, he argues, juveniles would benefit from the procedural safeguards that are standard in criminal courts.

> As long as young people are regarded as fundamentally different from adults, it becomes too easy to rationalize and justify a procedurally inferior justice system. The gap between the quality of justice afforded juveniles and adults can be conveniently rationalized on the grounds that "after all, they are only children," and children are entitled only to custody, not liberty. (Feld, 1993: 267)

Abolition of the juvenile courts is unlikely in the near future, but the courts are clearly undergoing considerable reforms. Feld was a member and committee chair of the Minnesota Juvenile Justice Task Force, which recommended major revisions in Minnesota's juvenile code (see Feld, 1995). He is convinced that, rather than weakening the role of the juvenile court, the new Minnesota laws have strengthened it.

American citizens look to the police and the courts to solve the nation's juvenile crime problem. As juvenile crime has become more rampant and as a disproportionate number of young people commit violent crimes, citizens have demanded tougher laws from their legislators. In an effort to show that "something is being done," legislators have enacted more severe punishment for juvenile offenders. It is well to remember, however, that there are "limits to the criminal sanction" (Packer, 1975). Police and the courts can not prevent crime or eliminate the root causes of juvenile delinquency. They can only respond to criminal violations after they occur. Focusing all of our attention on laws and their enforcement is not an adequate approach for combatting the social and family problems that lead to juvenile delinquency (see Feld, 1995: 980–982, 1128). The Minnesota Task Force that recommended changes in juvenile laws emphasized that

> juvenile crime is directly related to the quality of life in a community—not to the degree of punishment handed out by the government. . . . The inter-relationships among family, religion, health care, education, housing, employment, community values, and crime mean that all segments of the community must play an active role in combatting juvenile delinquency. (Advisory Task Force on the Juvenile Justice System, 1994: 16)

As long as society relies solely on tougher laws and their enforcement to respond to juvenile crime, we are unlikely to see any changes in the current trend of increasing numbers of young people who are committing crimes. Legal institutions will continue to respond to the juvenile crime problem, but social institutions—the family, schools, community agencies—are essential in helping to prevent the problem before it occurs.

Summary

The juvenile justice process differs from the legal process for adults in a number of key areas. Police respond differently to younger, minor juvenile offenders and are actively involved in a variety of delinquency prevention programs. The separate system of justice for juveniles was originally developed to identify and treat the youngsters' needs rather than to punish. That philosophy has come under question recently as some critics claim that the treatment approach has been ineffective in stemming the recent growth in juvenile crime. Others have condemned the lack of procedural fairness in juvenile court proceedings and contend (along with the U.S. Supreme Court) that juvenile offenders often get the worst of both worlds: they receive neither the treatment originally intended nor the legal safeguards received by adults in the criminal court. The juvenile justice process is undergoing a number of changes throughout the nation in response to these criticisms.

References

Advisory Task Force on the Juvenile Justice System. 1994. *Final Report.* St. Paul, Mn.: Minnesota Supreme Court.

American Bar Association-Institute of Judicial Administration. 1982. *Juvenile Standards Relating to Noncriminal Misbehavior.* Cambridge, Mass.: Ballinger.

American Bar Association-Institute of Judicial Administration. 1980. *Juvenile Justice Standards Relating to Pretrial Court Proceedings.* Cambridge, Mass.: Ballinger.

Armstrong, Gail. 1977. "Females Under the Law—Protected but Unequal." *Crime and Delinquency* 23:109–120.

Bartollas, Clemens. 1993. *Juvenile Delinquency,* 3rd ed. New York: Macmillan Publishing Co.

Bishop, Donna M., Charles E. Frazier, and John C. Henretta. 1989. "Prosecutorial Waiver: Case Study of a Questionable Reform." *Crime and Delinquency* 35:179–201.

Blauvelt, Peter D. 1990. "School Security: 'Who You Gonna Call?'" *School Safety* (Fall): 4–8.

Bortner, M. A. 1982. *Inside a Juvenile Court: The Tarnished Ideal of Individualized Justice.* New York: New York University Press.

Bortner, M. A. 1986. "Traditional Rhetoric, Organizational Realities: Remand of Juveniles to Adult Court." *Crime and Delinquency* 32:53–73.

Chesney-Lind, Meda. 1977. "Judicial Paternalism and the Female Status Offender." *Crime and Delinquency* 23:121–130.

Davis, Samuel M. 1980. *Rights of Juveniles: The Juvenile Justice System,* 2nd ed. New York: Clark Boardman Co.

Feld, Barry C. 1988a. "*In re Gault* Revisited: A Cross-State Comparison of the Right to Counsel in Juvenile Court." *Crime and Delinquency* 34:393–424.

Feld, Barry C. 1988b. "Juvenile Court Meets the Principle of Offense: Punishment, Treatment, and the Difference it Makes." *Boston University Law Review* 68:821–915.

Feld, Barry C. 1989. "The Right to Counsel in Juvenile Court: An Empirical Study of

When Lawyers Appear and the Difference They Make." *Journal of Criminal Law and Criminology* 79:1185–1346.

Feld, Barry C. 1993. "Criminalizing the American Juvenile Court." In M. Tonry, ed., *Crime and Justice: An Annual Review of Research.* Chicago: University of Chicago Press.

Feld, Barry C. 1995. "Violent Youth and Public Policy: A Case Study of Juvenile Justice Law Reform." *Minnesota Law Review* 79:965–1128.

Greenwood, Peter. 1988. *Crime File: Juvenile Offenders.* Washington, D.C.: National Institute of Justice.

Grisso, Thomas. 1981. *Juveniles' Waiver of Rights: Legal and Psychological Competence.* New York: Plenum Press.

Hamparian, D. M., L. K. Estep, S. M. Muntean, R. R. Priestino, R. G. Swisher, P. L. Wallace, and J. L. White. 1982. *Youth in Adult Courts: Between Two Worlds.* Washington, D.C.: U.S. Department of Justice.

Holden, Gwen A., and Robert A. Kapler. 1995. "Deinstitutionalizing Status Offenders: A Record of Progress." *Juvenile Justice* (OJJDP Journal) 2(Fall/Winter): 3–10.

Kobrin, Solomon, and Malcolm W. Klein. 1982. *National Evaluation of the Deinstitutionalization of Status Offender Programs: Executive Summary.* Washington, D.C.: U.S. Department of Justice.

LaLonde, Mark. 1995. "The Canadian Experience: School Policing Perspective." *School Safety* (Fall): 20–21.

Lawrence, Richard. 1983. "The Role of Legal Counsel in Juveniles' Understanding of Their Rights." *Juvenile and Family Court Journal* 34:49–58.

Lundman, Richard J., Richard F. Sykes, and John P. Clark. 1990. "Police Control of Juveniles: A Replication." In R. A. Weisheit and R. G. Culbertson, eds. *Juvenile Delinquency: A Justice Perspective*, 2nd ed. Prospect Heights, Ill.: Waveland Press.

Mennel, Robert M. 1972. "Origins of the Juvenile Court: Changing Perspectives on the Legal Rights of Juvenile Delinquents." *Crime and Delinquency* 18:68–78.

Morash, Merry. 1984. "Establishment of a Juvenile Police Record." *Criminology* 22:97–111.

National Advisory Commission on Criminal Justice Standards and Goals. 1977. *Juvenile Justice and Delinquency Prevention.* Washington, D.C.: U.S. Department of Justice.

Packer, Herbert L. 1975. *The Limits of the Criminal Sanction.* Stanford: Stanford University Press.

Piliavin, Irvin, and Scott Briar. 1964. "Police Encounters with Juveniles." *American Journal of Sociology* 70:206–214.

Podkopacz, Marcy R., and Barry C. Feld. 1996. "The End of the Line: An Empirical Study of Judicial Waiver." *Journal of Criminal Law and Criminology* 86:449–492.

President's Commission on Law Enforcement and Administration of Justice. 1967. *Task Force Report: Juvenile Delinquency and Youth Crime.* Washington, D.C.: U.S. Government Printing Office.

Raley, Gordon A. 1995. "The JJDP Act: A Second Look." *Juvenile Justice* (OJJDP Journal) 2(Fall/Winter): 11–18.

Rudman, Cary, Eliot Hartstone, Jeffrey Fagan, and Melinda Moore. 1986. "Violent Youth in Adult Court: Process and Punishment." *Crime and Delinquency* 32:75–96.

Schneider, Anne. 1985. *The Impact of Deinstitutionalization on Recidivism and Secure Confinement of Status Offenders.* Washington, D.C.: U.S. Department of Justice.

Sickmund, Melissa. 1994. "How Juveniles Get to Criminal Court." *OJJDP Update on Statistics.* Washington, D.C.: U.S. Department of Justice.

Siegel, Larry J., and Joseph J. Senna. 1991. *Juvenile Delinquency*, 4th ed. St. Paul, Minn.: West Publishing Co.

Springer, Charles E. 1986. *Justice for Juveniles.* Washington, D.C.: U.S. Department of Justice.

Szymanski, Linda. 1994. *Upper Age of Juvenile Court Jurisdiction Statutes Anslyses.* Pittsburgh: National Center for Juvenile Justice.

U.S. Department of Justice. 1976. *Two Hundred Years of American Criminal Justice: An LEAA Bicentennial Study.* Washington, D.C.: Law Enforcement Assistance Administration.

Wolfgang, Marvin F., Robert M. Figlio, and Thorsten Sellin. 1972. *Delinquency in a Birth Cohort.* Chicago: University of Chicago Press.

9

Juvenile Corrections

We need to begin a national movement founded on a basic human concern about justice for juveniles and the conditions of their confinement. . . . It is time that we begin to do the right thing by working together to achieve lasting improvements in the conditions of confinement for juveniles in this country.—John J. Wilson, Acting Administrator, Office of Juvenile Justice and Delinquency Prevention (1994)

Major guiding principles of the juvenile justice system have been to make judicial decisions that are "in the best interests of the child" and to use the "least restrictive" dispositional alternatives that can appropriately offer correctional treatment for the child and protection of the community. Juvenile corrections is made up of institutional and residential facilities as well as various forms of community supervision, the foremost being probation. Juvenile corrections has a long history in America, beginning with the development of houses of refuge and probation in the nineteenth century. Juveniles are confined in separate correctional facilities from adults, but many of the "training schools" in which thousands of children are confined differ very little from prisons for adult criminals. The goal of juvenile corrections is to prevent young offenders from becoming adult criminals, but juvenile correctional institutions have had the unintended effect of becoming "schools for crime." Many incarcerated adult felons report that they were institutionalized as youths. Severe punishment of young offenders appears to have little effect in deterring them from crime but may in fact promote more criminality as young adults. Major efforts in the 1970s led to a movement to deinstitutionalize young offenders and to remove all status offenders from juvenile institutions. There has been a nationwide effort over the years to develop a variety of community treatment programs for juvenile offenders. Those efforts seem to have stalled somewhat in the 1990s, however, with public demands for a "get tough" approach for what is perceived to be a youth crime plague.

The juvenile court judge decides on the most appropriate dispositional alternative after adjudicating a young offender. The choice of available alternatives varies in different jurisdictions, but the majority of juvenile offenders are placed under some form of community supervision, the most common being probation. Probation supervision may be combined with orders of restitution, temporary placement in a residential facility, or participation in a treatment program. More secure placement is the more appropriate disposition for serious offenders, those with a history of repeated delinquent involvement, and those for whom placement at home with their parents is ill advised because they pose a risk to public safety. Such youth may be sent to facilities ranging from semi-secure group homes to secure training schools. A variety of "intermediate sanctions" have been developed to provide more public safety than regular probation can offer, while being less intrusive and expensive than correctional institutions. These alternatives to incarceration include intensive probation supervision, electronic monitoring, and home detention.

Juvenile Probation

Probation is the most common form of community supervision and treatment in the juvenile justice system. The concept of probation was originally developed through the efforts of John Augustus, a Boston bootmaker who persuaded a judge in 1841 to release an offender to him for supervision in the community rather than sentence him to prison. Augustus worked with hundreds of offenders and set the stage for probation as we know it today. As the first probation officer, Augustus developed many of the probation strategies that continue to be used in probation today: investigation and screening, supervision, educational and employment services, and guidance and assistance.

The state of Massachusetts followed up on the work of Augustus and established a visiting probation agent system in 1869 (Bartollas, 1993: 453). Probation was developed statewide in Massachusetts by 1890, and many other states adopted probation statutes soon after that. What began as a volunteer movement became the most common correctional alternative, funded and administered by the courts or by state or local government. Today juvenile probation is administered by the juvenile court or a group of courts in the jurisdiction or by a state or local department of youth services, a department of social services, or some combination of these (see McShane and Krause, 1993: 67). In either organizational context, the juvenile court judge and the probation staff have a close working relationship. Today virtually all counties in the nation have juvenile probation services, though in some remote rural counties a single probation officer may serve multiple counties and have the responsibility of covering a wide geographical area. Juvenile probation departments in cities are administered by a chief probation officer, with one or more assistants overseeing specialized units within the department. Larger departments may have units specializing in intake services; investigation and preparation of the predisposition report, or social history; a field supervision unit; and detention services.

There are four components of juvenile probation:

•As a *legal disposition* juveniles are under court supervision with conditions and rules with which they must comply before being released.

•As an *alternative to incarceration* probation is a nonpunitive disposition that emphasizes correctional treatment and reintegration of juvenile offenders.

•Probation is a *subsystem* of the juvenile justice system.

•As a *court service agency*, probation officers conduct investigations for the court, supervise juveniles, and provide services that are helpful to youth, their families and the community (see National Advisory Commission on Criminal Justice Standards and Goals, 1973: 312).

In practice, probation is basically an agreement between the juvenile court and the young offender. The adjudicated delinquent agrees to comply with the court orders and probation conditions and is released to his or her parents. In cases where the probation officer's investigation has indicated that parental supervision is lacking, the youth may be placed with a legal guardian or foster parents or in a group home. In either case, the placement is less punitive than commitment to a juvenile institution. Probation supervision may continue for an indefinite period of time, but it usually does not exceed two years. Each probation case is usually reviewed periodically to ensure that some progress is being made and treatment goals are being met and to guarantee that the juvenile is not kept on probation unnecessarily. If a juvenile is not complying with probation conditions, then the probation officer is expected to take the case before the judge, who may choose to revise the probation conditions or order the youth referred to a different placement, including commitment to a more secure setting if he or she seems to present a danger to himself/herself or to the community.

Probation Officer Duties and Responsibilities

Intake

The intake officer is responsible for accepting referrals from the police and, in some cases, from the schools, parents, or other social agencies. The intake officer must verify that the department has jurisdiction in each case. This involves determining from a written report from the referring officer that the child is allegedly in violation of a provision in the state juvenile code. The range of forbidden juvenile behavior is quite broad, ranging from status offenses such as disobeying parents and running away to felony offenses. The intake officer must also verify the child's date of birth, to ascertain that the department has jurisdiction. State juvenile codes vary, but most legal definitions of a juvenile include youth between the ages of ten and seventeen. The intake officer must immediately inform the parents of the referral and decide whether to turn the youth over to the parents pending further action or to temporarily detain the child. Options available include a "reprimand and release"; diversion and referral to a community agency for informal supervision and intervention; and efforts, in cooperation with school officials, to place students with learning and/or behavioral problems in alternative schools. These referrals are informal and voluntary, but they may be accompanied by the threat of more formal action if the youth is not cooperative. Under the "least restrictive" philosophy of the juvenile justice system, the goal of probation agencies is to divert minor juvenile offenders from processing through the juvenile court and refer them to other agencies for short-term intervention and guidance. Diversion is considered most appropriate for status offenders and youth who have alledgedly committed minor property crimes. The intake officer serves a screening function, separating those cases that seem appropriate for diversion from cases that should be petitioned to juvenile court. The decision whether to file a petition for adjudication is made in consultation with the county or state prosecuting attorney.

Investigation

Delinquency petitions are filed in cases of juveniles referred for violent crimes, for more serious property offenses, and for persistent minor offenses. When the decision has been made to take a case to court, it is referred to an investigation unit pending appearance in the juvenile court. In juvenile courts that use a bifurcated hearing (separate adjudication and disposition stages) the probation officer conducts an investigation and writes a social history report after the child has been adjudicated in the fact-finding part of the hearing. Many courts combine the adjudication and disposition parts of the hearing, so the report must be prepared beforehand and ready for the judge to read if the youth was found delinquent in the adjudication stage of the hearing. In either case, the probation officer generally has at least thirty days to complete the social history report. As part of the investigation, the probation officer interviews the youth and his or her parents; reviews current and past arrest records; may request a psychological evaluation; and may review reports or interview officials from social agencies and schools. As a rule, the probation officer's investigation involves at least one interview with the youth and parents in the probation office and includes at least one visit to the home and often a visit or a phone call to the child's school.

Considerable importance is placed on the social history report, as it represents the primary source of background information on the juvenile. The importance accorded to the report does vary with different judges, however. Some judges request a complete report from the probation officer, which may include a risk assessment, a recommended supervision and treatment plan with specific goals, and possibly a recommended contractual agreement between the youth (which may include the parents) and the court. Other judges prefer a brief summary statement of the youth's background and place equal or greater importance on the legal circumstances of the case. Since probation officers serve the court, they understandably write the kind of report that the juvenile court judge prefers. Probation officers also come to know the particular legal philosophy of the judge and whether he or she leans more toward a punitive or toward a treatment philosophy for juvenile offenders. There is evidence that presentence reports reflect probation officers' attitudes (Katz, 1982); some analyses of the judicial process suggest that officers' recommendations simply reflect what the writer believes the judge wants to hear (Blumberg, 1973: 283; Carter and Wilkins, 1967). Social history reports do present an accurate picture of the youth and the family background, but the recommendations often reflect what the judge has been known to prefer in similar cases. Probation officers have thus been referred to as "judicial civil servants" who are not given full recognition by judges and attorneys in the courtroom, but they are now acquiring professional status through more specialized education and training, and their investigative services are recognized as being invaluable in most courts (Lawrence, 1984).

Supervision

The third major function of a probation officer is to provide supervision of offenders in the community. When a juvenile court judge sentences a youth to probation, the probation officer generally meets with the youth and his or her parents to explain the rules and conditions of probation, to answer any questions about the term of probation and the court's expectations, and to ensure that they understand the importance of complying with the probation conditions. The length of time that a juvenile is on probation varies from state to state. It may be for an indefinite period of time until the youth reaches the age of majority, usually seventeen or eighteen years, but some states limit the period of juvenile probation to two years or less (Bartollas, 1993: 458).

The probation officer performs an important role in clarifying and emphasizing the statements and any warnings made by the judge during the hearing. This is particularly true when a child and his or her parents are hesitant to ask the judge or attorney any questions during the tense moments of a court hearing. Most hearings are brief, perfunctory proceedings, often lasting five to ten minutes or less, and thus the full significance of the legal proceeding may not be grasped by the juvenile and the parents. The probation officer is often more helpful than a defense attorney in explaining the significance of the juvenile court hearing (Lawrence, 1983). The officer explains the rules and conditions of probation and emphasizes the importance of complying with each of them, including reporting regularly to the probation office. Special probation conditions require additional explanation, especially if the court has ordered restitution payments to victims or community service restitution; avoidance of drinking or drug use, and participation in drug treatment programs. Juvenile probation officers face a special challenge in supervising delinquents, because they usually receive little assistance and support from the parents and family. Most juvenile offenders do not have a very good relationship with their parent(s), and they show little respect for their parents' authority. Families of delinquents are often characterized by parental negligence or abuse, inconsistent discipline, poor communication, and poor parenting skills. Probation supervision is more difficult without solid parental and family support. When such support is available, a rare but ideal condition, parents can play an important role, helping a youth comply with probation conditions, closely supervising their child, and communicating regularly with the probation officer. Parental support is especially important in closely monitoring the child's school attendance and behavior, peer associations, and compliance with curfew requirements. Probation officers must perform a dual role: they must encourage, help, and assist the young offender to make a positive adjustment but also must act as an authority figure who will report probation violations to the court.

In carrying out the supervision responsibility, probation officers function in one of three roles: casework management, treatment, and surveillance (Bartollas, 1993: 458–459). *Casework management* involves maintaining current files on each juvenile in a caseload that averages fifty to 100 cases. In addition to the police offense reports and social history report, the file includes contact reports on every personal visit and telephone call regarding the juvenile. Contacts are made with each juvenile once a week to once a month or less, depending upon the intensity level of supervision needed. The casework task may include a risk assessment and treatment plan, and the contact reports documents the degree of progress toward meeting the treatment goals. Documentation in the juvenile's file is important. Cases may be managed by more than one caseworker or may be transferred to another officer who is less familiar with the case. If the probation officer files a court petition for revocation of probation, he or she may be called to testify as to the violations of probation conditions, including the exact dates, circumstances, and details of the violations. Paperwork and file management are sources of frustration and complaints among probation officers, but they are an important part of the job responsibilities (see Lawrence, 1984).

The *treatment* function of a juvenile probation officer focuses on his or her role as a caseworker or counselor. We have noted the importance of working with the parents and families of juvenile delinquents. Among the difficulties faced by probation officers is the significant number of juveniles from dysfunctional families. Parents have lost control and the respect of their child. The parent-child relationship has deteriorated to the point that the youth has become incorrigible, refusing to comply with the parents' demands. The parents have either given up on or have never used effective communication and management strategies. Juvenile probation officers commonly say that they work with as many delinquent parents as they do delinquent children. Because a poor parent-child relationship is one of the major problems faced by probation officers in working with delinquents, some educational background in family counseling, social work, or general counseling skills has traditionally been one of the job requirements for juvenile probation officers. Training seminars in family intervention and guidance are provided for many juvenile officers around the nation, and probation conferences often include at least one session on the subject. Since the minimum educational requirement for probation officers is a four-year college degree, they are not expected to provide professional counseling services, however, nor are they qualified to do so. One of their responsibilities, therefore, is to identify problems that require more professional treatment and then refer the child and family to mental health services for family counseling and guidance.

Recognition in the 1970s that juvenile probation officers had neither the expertise nor the time to provide professional counseling and treatment led to an emphasis on the probation officer as *resource broker* or *manager*, rather than counselor. As a resource broker, the officer's responsibility is to assess the juvenile's needs and then make appropriate referrals to other social agencies that can best provide the needed services. The resource broker model of probation is most appropriate in metropolitan jurisdictions where there are many available agencies and resources for referral. Juveniles on probation in smaller communities with fewer available resources, however, are likely to receive only the counseling and guidance that the probation officers themselves are able to provide.

The *surveillance* function requires the probation officer to closely monitor juveniles to make certain that they are complying with the probation conditions. This may be accomplished through questions directed at the juvenile during office visits; when suspicions arise, the officer generally verifies the juvenile's compliance through telephone calls or personal visits to the juvenile's home or school. The surveillance function is much like that of a police officer, and probation officers have the authority to take probationers into custody for violating conditions of probation. Some probation officers carry a badge, handcuffs, and even a handgun, although the latter is more common among adult probation officers with high-risk caseloads in metropolitan areas.

The surveillance function is not emphasized as much in juvenile probation as it is in adult probation. Juvenile probation officers generally focus on youths' compliance with probation conditions and depend on police officers to arrest, investigate, and report the commission of a new crime by the juvenile. For juveniles suspected of continued illegal drug use, however, probation agencies may require drug testing. Violation of probation conditions is considered a "technical violation," and in such cases officers have more latitude in deciding whether to file for revocation of probation than they have when a youth is rearrested by police for a new crime. In either case, probation revocation is not automatic, however, and the juvenile is entitled to a revocation hearing under due process guidelines established by the U.S. Supreme Court in the 1972 case of Morrissey v. Brewer (408 U.S. 471, 92 S.Ct. 2593). If the judge finds that there is sufficient evidence that probation conditions have been violated, he or she may revoke probation and commit the juvenile to a state training school, or the judge may choose from a range of less punitive alternatives, including more intensive probation supervision with more restrictive conditions or temporary placement in a semisecure group home placement.

The multiple roles and responsibilities of probation officers are often quite at odds with each other, and officers may experience "role conflict" (see Lawrence, 1984). It is difficult for a probation officer to be a counselor or advocate for a juvenile one day and then an officer enforcing probation rules and threatening revocation as a consequence for violations the next. Attention to both responsibilities is necessary, however, and it is important that juvenile probationers understand that while the probation agency is there to help them adjust to problems at home, school, and in the community, they are also responsible for complying with probation rules and avoiding any more delinquent involvement. Some criticism has been leveled at juvenile officers who empha-size the advocacy or counseling function and fail to enforce probation condi-tions. Many probation departments have taken a balanced approach to proba-tion supervision, utilizing a logical consequences model whereby juveniles are held accountable for antisocial behavior. Dennis Maloney, Dennis Romig, and Troy Armstrong (1988) noted that the purpose of the balanced approach to juvenile probation is to protect the community from delinquency, to make of-fenders accountable for delinquent acts, and to ensure that juvenile offenders leave the system with more skills for living productively and responsibly in so-ciety than they brought to it (Maloney et al., 1988: 10). Many juvenile pro-bation agencies throughout the United States have adopted the balanced ap-proach, giving equal attention to the community, the victim, and the juvenile offender (Maloney et al., 1988). Probation officers like the balanced approach and an emphasis on the logical consequences model, because it helps to allevi-ate much of the role conflict experienced by officers in the past. Adopting a logical consequences approach in probation supervision reminds juveniles to take probation seriously and encourages them to be less resistant and more open to a cooperative working relationship with their probation officers. The balanced approach places emphasis on three programming priorities: offender accountability, competency development, and community protection (Baze-more and Umbreit, 1994: 3). Through restitution and community service, of-fenders are required to make amends to victims and the community. Commu-nity protection is increased through closer surveillance and by directing juvenile offenders' time and energy into more productive activities during nonschool hours. The goal of competency development recognizes the need to help ju-venile offenders develop skills, get work experience, interact with conventional adults, earn money, and take part in productive activities. Advocates of the bal-anced approach emphasize the importance of having community organizations work together with juvenile justice professionals and offenders (Bazemore and Umbreit, 1994).

Recent Innovations in Juvenile Probation

The juvenile court judge traditionally had only two primary options when sen-tencing adjudicated delinquents: probation or commitment to a juvenile insti-tution. There have been a number of innovations in juvenile corrections that offer more intensive supervision and that hold juvenile offenders more ac-countable than traditional probation. Intensive probation supervision, electronic monitoring, and restitution programs are recent developments within proba-tion agencies that many observers claim are more successful than regular pro-bation supervision and have advantages over institutional commitment in that they are less expensive and avoid severing ties between the juvenile's family and the community. The use of volunteers is another development in probation, though it is less an innovation than a return to the origins of probation, which began as a volunteer movement.

Volunteers in Probation

We noted that probation began as a volunteer movement under John Augustus in Boston in 1841. Juvenile justice professionals have long recognized that probation officers with caseloads of fifty to 100 juveniles cannot offer the amount of time and attention that many troubled juveniles need. Judge Keith Leenhouts initiated a court-sponsored volunteer program in Royal Oak, Michigan, and pushed for the development of similar programs throughout the United States. More than 2,000 juvenile court-sponsored volunteer programs are in operation, and more than 10,000 volunteers are giving their time to assist juvenile probation officers in several ways (Bartollas, 1993: 464). Volunteers are carefully screened and receive several hours of training. Many probation agencies have a volunteer coordinator who attempts to match each volunteer with a juvenile client. After meeting with the probation officer to become familiar with the youth's needs and probation goals, the volunteer is encouraged to meet weekly with the juvenile. Activities may include tutoring, meeting after school for a soda, and participating jointly in activities such as bowling, skating, or attending a movie or ballgame. Participation in entertaining activities with a volunteer offers juvenile probationers an opportunity to develop a positive relationship with a supportive adult role model.

Intensive Probation Supervision

Probation has been criticized by many for being too lenient and for providing only minimal supervision. There is no question that many juveniles need more supervision than a probation officer with a large caseload can provide. Intensive supervision programs have been adopted by many probation agencies as an alternative to sending high-risk juveniles to a correctional institution (Byrne, 1986). A small number of cases (usually no more than fifteen to twenty-five) are assigned to a probation officer, who is expected to make daily contacts and to closely monitor their daily activities. The recidivism rate of juveniles who have received intensive probation supervision is often higher than that for juveniles on regular probation, but that is due at least in part to the high-risk juveniles who participate in the programs and to the fact that the officer's close surveillance often detects probation violations that might have gone unnoticed with regular probation supervision. Even if intensive supervision is no more effective in reducing recidivism of high-risk juvenile offenders, the cost benefits (about one-third that of confinement) make it a desirable alternative to incarceration (Latessa, 1986).

Electronic Monitoring and House Arrest

Juveniles may be placed on probation under special conditions that require them to remain in their homes at all times except for school, employment, or medical reasons. House arrest may be supplemented with frequent random phone calls, personal visits, or electronic monitoring, in which probationers are fitted around the ankle with a nonremovable monitoring device that signals the probation department's computerized monitoring station if the offender leaves the house (see Ball and Lilly, 1986; Petersilia, 1986; Schmidt, 1986; and Charles, 1989). The monitoring device is connected to the telephone in the house and makes random phone calls to verify the probationer's presence. Some monitoring devices can detect through a voice analysis if someone other than the probationer responds to the call, and some have a breath analyzer to detect whether the subject has been drinking alcohol. Electronic monitoring has the advantage of operating as an effective alternative to incarceration in a detention center, at less than half the cost. Joseph Vaughn (1989) conducted a survey of eight juvenile electronic monitoring programs and found that most were successful in reducing the number of days that juveniles spent in detention, and the youth were able to participate in school and work activities during the time they were not confined to their homes. Vaughn found, however, that the treatment benefits of electronic monitoring programs still remain in question.

Restitution Programs

Another innovative program in juvenile probation is restitution. Restitution can take two forms: monetary or service, either to the victim or to the community (Schneider, 1985; Schneider and Warner, 1989). In monetary restitution, the probationer may be ordered to reimburse the victim of the crime for property damages or for the medical costs of personal injury. In the second form, a juvenile may be required to provide some service directly to the victim or the community. Four goals of restitution programs have been identified:

•Holding juveniles accountable
•Providing reparation to victims
•Treating and rehabilitating juveniles
•Punishing juveniles (Schneider, 1985:1)

Victim restitution is done with the consent of the victim, and service restitution is usually done under the supervision of a probation officer. Juvenile restitution programs exist in more than 400 jurisdictions throughout the nation, and by 1985 most states had legislation authorizing such programs as part of probation (Schneider, 1985).

Restitution programs are usually a part of probation and are ordered as a probation condition. They may also be implemented at other stages of the juvenile justice process, for example, as part of a diversion program or as a method of informal adjustment at probation intake. In support of the goals identified by Schneider (1985), restitution offers alternative sentencing options for the court (see Newton, 1979: 435–468). It directs attention to the forgotten persons in the justice process, the victims, and provides monetary compensation or service to them. It is rehabilitative in that the juvenile has an opportunity to compensate the victim for injury or damages, and it encourages the offender to be accountable for wrongful actions and to become a productive member of society. Restitution is not the same as "retribution" (or "just deserts"), which is the belief that offenders must be made to pay for their crimes through punishment. It does meet the dual objectives of rehabilitation and retribution, however, and may improve the public's attitude toward offenders and the justice system, since offenders literally pay something back to the victim and to the community, taking responsibility for their actions (Galaway, 1989). Restitution has been criticized as being an unfair and unrealistic expectation for juvenile offenders at a time when unemployment rates are high for all youth (Staples, 1989). For that reason, community service restitution programs, under the supervision of a probation officer or volunteer worker, are more widely used than monetary restitution. Evaluations of restitution programs indicate that they are quite effective as a treatment alternative. Schneider (1986) evaluated programs in four states and found that the program participants had lower recidivism rates than did control groups of youths placed on regular probation. The differences were not dramatic (only a difference of 10 percent in recidivism rates in some comparisons), but the restitution programs did seem to result in more positive attitudes among many juveniles (Schneider, 1986: 550). The National Center for Juvenile Justice studied 6,336 probation cases in Utah, which has a statewide restitution program (Butts and Snyder, 1992). In more than half (3,215 or 51 percent) the cases, restitution was ordered as part of probation. Results of the study showed a significant relationship between the use of restitution and recidivism. Restitution combined with probation was associated with lower recidivism rates one year later; 32 percent of restitution cases recidivated, whereas 38 percent of those not paying restitution were involved in new court referrals within one year (Butts and Snyder, 1992: 4). The results of the study suggest that the use of restitution as part of probation is associated with significantly less recidivism among some juvenile offenders.

Residential Programs and Institutional Corrections

Juvenile institutions have existed in the United States since 1824, when the first house of refuge opened for females in New York; the first school for males opened in that city a year later. Several more houses of refuge were opened for boys in Boston, Philadelphia, Cincinnati, Chicago, and other cities, with more than fifty private or state-administered houses established in the 1830s and 1840s (Bartollas, 1993: 484–485). The cottage system was developed later in the nineteenth century as a more humane improvement over the crowded houses of refuge in the cities. The cottage system housed smaller groups of juveniles in separate buildings in a rural campus setting. These facilities later came to be known as training schools or industrial schools, and they exist today as the primary form of juvenile corrections in the United States. It was assumed that removing juvenile offenders from the criminogenic conditions of the cities would reform them through exposure to a simple rural lifestyle. Required attendance in school classes and vocational training were intended to teach the wayward youths work skills and habits. Several changes have taken place in juvenile institutions in this century:

- Custodial care had become the primary purpose of training schools, leading reformers to push for expanded treatment efforts.
- Reception centers were developed to diagnose and classify new admissions, and a variety of therapy programs were directed at juvenile residents' needs.
- Accredited educational programs were developed, complemented by better vocational programs, including automobile repair, welding, woodworking, and printing.
- The types of juvenile correctional facilities were expanded to include forestry and wilderness programs, ranches and farms, in addition to the prison-like training schools (Bartollas, 1993: 485).

Juvenile training schools came under criticism in the 1960s and 1970s as reformers highlighted the inhumane conditions in them and claimed that housing minor juvenile offenders with more serious and violent offenders made the facilities nothing more than "schools for crime." Jerome Miller received national attention in the early 1970s when, as director of the Massachusetts juvenile corrections agency, he closed all the training schools and placed juveniles in alternative public and private residential programs. Research that evaluated the effects of closing the state schools indicated that the reform did not result in an increase in delinquency in the state (see Schwartz, 1989: 100; and Coates, Miller, and Ohlin, 1978). Barry Krisberg and James Austin (1993) reported that a cost analysis that compared the Massachusetts system with other state juvenile corrections systems indicated that the Massachusetts system was cost-effective while providing public safety and offender rehabilitation (1993: 163). The Massachusetts experience has been closely followed, and many other states have considered reforms similar to those initiated by Jerome Miller.

Incarceration of juvenile offenders is very costly and does little to reduce crime rates. Krisberg and Austin suggest that a better use of tax dollars might be to fund neighborhood-based crime prevention efforts that are directed at reducing child abuse, school dropout rates, youth unemployment, and drug dealing (1993: 163). The tremendous increase in the number of offenders who are being sentenced to correctional institutions has placed enormous demands on state and federal budgets. The cost of building and operating correctional institutions means that many states have had to cut back on other expenditures. From 1960 to 1985, state and local spending per capita increased 218 percent for corrections, significantly more than the increase for hospitals and health care (119 percent), police (73 percent), or education (56 percent) (Bureau of Justice Statistics, 1988:120). Spending a higher proportion of taxpayer dollars on corrections than on education raises an alarming question of whether we are taking dollars from school classrooms and putting them into prison cells (Lawrence, 1995a). Research evidence indicates that a better use of taxpayer dollars is to invest in educational programs that have been shown to be effective in reducing delinquency and to concentrate correctional spending on community-based programs that are more cost-effective than incarceration, while still providing for public safety.

Detention Centers

Juvenile detention centers, also called juvenile halls or shelters, were established around the turn of this century to serve as an alternative to placing juveniles in adult jails. They are administered by city, county, or state governments, though most are run by counties in conjunction with child welfare departments or juvenile courts. Detention centers serve as a temporary holding facility for juveniles who need to be held for their own safety or for that of the community or who may be held temporarily after arrest and referral to the probation intake unit pending release to their parents. Juveniles are usually detained for a week or less, with exceptional cases being held up to three or four weeks. The juvenile codes of most states require that a detention hearing be held before a child may be held more than one or two days. The physical environment of many metropolitan juvenile detention centers resembles many adult jails. The facilities are usually adjacent to the probation offices and hearing rooms of the juvenile court but are usually of concrete and steel construction, with small individual cells or rooms containing a bed, toilet, and sink. If the cell has a window, it is only a small opening that allows some natural light into the tiny room. Detention centers are built and programmed almost entirely around custody and security concerns. Educational, recreational, and treatment programs are secondary. This emphasis is justified by the short-term nature of detention and the focus on custody and security. Several county and regional detention centers built in the past few years feature a modular living arrangement that is less institutional in appearance, with space designed for educational, recreational, and treatment programs.

Correctional Institutions for Juveniles

Violent juvenile offenders and those who have a record of repeated involvement in crime may be committed to state training schools. This is the most severe sanction available to young offenders within the juvenile justice system. According to the latest available Children in Custody (CIC) census of 1991, a total of 36,278 juveniles were held in long-term public facilities on February 15, 1991 (Snyder and Sickmund, 1995: 167). Nearly all the youth (98 percent) were committed for law violations; two percent were status offenders and nonoffenders; and 90 percent were male (Snyder and Sickmund, 1995: 165). There were other major findings reported in the 1991 CIC census of long-term public facilities, including:

•The number of juvenile admissions in 1990 was 97,732.

•Minorities accounted for more than two-thirds of the juveniles in long-term facilities.

•Blacks accounted for 49 percent of institutional residents.

•White Hispanics accounted for 17 percent of institutional residents.

•The number of minorities held in public long-term facilities increased 37 percent from 1983 to 1991.

•The number of non-Hispanic white juveniles dropped 23 percent from 1983 to 1991.

•Most juveniles (67 percent) were in institutional rather than open settings.

•The number of juveniles held for violent personal offenses accounted for 39 percent.

•The number of juveniles helf for serious property crimes accounted for 38 percent.

•The number of juveniles held for alcohol and drug offenses accounted for 12 percent. (Snyder and Sickmund, 1995: 164–167).

Larger states such as California, Illinois, Ohio, New York, and Texas have several training schools each, and account for nearly half of all juveniles held in public long-term facilities (Snyder and Sickmund, 1995: 168). Many states have developed coeducational facilities, with separate cottages for girls and boys but with shared participation in education, vocational, and treatment programs.

The physical structure of juvenile training schools varies from cottage settings to open dormitories, and maximum security facilities may house residents in individual cells. The secure training schools have an institutional appearance inside and out, with high fences surrounding them, locked doors, and screens or bars on windows. Residents' movements throughout the facility are restricted and closely supervised by the staff. The living quarters of the medium-security cottage and dormitory-style facilities are more homelike, but they offer little privacy for residents. Even these medium-security training schools are usually surrounded by fences. Few juvenile training schools are minimum security, because most juveniles are sent to a training school because they need restricted confinement (Bartollas, 1993: 497).

Juvenile training schools represent the most punitive sanction available in the juvenile justice system. Removing youth from their families, communities, and public schools is a significant punishment for many of them. They live under close twenty-four-hour supervision, with strict rules and discipline. Serious violations of the rules, especially fighting and assaultive behavior, result in short-term commitment to disciplinary segregation, which is a secure detention setting within the training school. Staff maintain discipline among the residents by withholding privileges or extending the length of stay for those who violate any rules.

Many training schools do have some good programs, including medical and dental care; an accredited school; vocational training; recreation; and treatment programs. Rehabilitation is still the primary purpose of juvenile training schools. The treatment methods that are used most widely are behavior modification, guided group interaction, transactional analysis, reality therapy, and positive peer culture. Efforts are made to prepare the juveniles for return to their families and communities. Juveniles who have made satisfactory adjustment and are within a few weeks of their release may be allowed to make home visits or take part in work-release programs in the community. The goal of rehabilitation is seldom achieved in most juvenile training schools. Studies indicate that few of the programs being used in training schools are effective in preventing future delinquency, although there is some evidence that institutional treatment may work with some youth. Carol Garrett (1985) reviewed more than 100 studies conducted between 1960 and 1983 on juvenile corrections treatment programs such as counseling, behavior modification, and life-skill improvement. Garrett found no single treatment strategy that was most effective, but she concluded that the majority of interventions did produce positive change. On the other hand, Steven Lab and John Whitehead (1988) analyzed juvenile correctional research done from 1975 to 1984 and concluded that treatment has little impact on recidivism. One problem seems to be that the programs themselves are not being used effectively (see Whitehead and Lab, 1989). The staff of juvenile training schools face the dilemma of trying to adapt programs to a diverse and varied juvenile offender population. Most juvenile institutions today house a significant proportion of minority youth who have become involved in criminal activities because of problems at home, at school, and in their communities. It is likely that competency-based education and employment skills may be more relevant for them than traditional counseling programs (Siegel and Senna, 1991: 586).

Despite the goals of treatment, juvenile training schools remain institutional settings marked by oppressiveness and fear. As states confine dangerous juvenile offenders together with younger, smaller, or less serious offenders in the same institution, even the closest supervision and the best programs have little positive effects. Training school staff are often powerless to prevent incidents of inmate abuse by other inmates (Feld, 1977). Clemens Bartollas, Stuart Miller, and Simon Dinitz (1976) examined victimization in a maximum-security juvenile institution in Columbus, Ohio. In this training school, which the inmates called a "jungle," 90 percent of the residents were involved in abuse, either as abusers or as victims of abuse. In a reexamination of the same institution nearly two decades later, Bartollas and his associates (1993) found conditions to be no better: it was overcrowded (thirty-five youth jammed into rooms designed for twenty-four); the strong still victimized the weak, stealing food, clothing, and toiletries; consensual sexual behavior appeared to be widespread; and treatment had all but disappeared from the institution. One social worker was quoted as saying, "We don't do anything in here," and a youth leader said, "This place is a warehouse for children" (Bartollas, 1993: 505).

Juveniles who are confined in training schools find the institutional environment oppressive and stressful. Despite any good intentions of treatment or "training," staff must first be concerned about maintaining security and close supervision among the residents. Thus, juvenile training schools resemble adult prisons, with security precautions such as restriction of movement throughout the facility, regimented schedules, and occasional strip searches for contraband. Adaptation to the institutional setting becomes a higher priority for the juvenile residents than treatment; gaining acceptance from their peers in the institution is of more immediate importance than working toward a positive adjustment to the community. The inmate subculture in training schools presents a serious problem, with the introduction of youth gangs in many juvenile institutions throughout the nation.

Coeducational training schools have been developed in many states as a way to humanize and normalize juvenile institutions. They have been effective in some respects, but training school staff must still deal with close supervision and security issues while trying to implement treatment programs among a juvenile population more concerned about adapting in an oppressive institutional environment. Unfortunately, there is little that can be positively stated about juvenile training schools. Punishment does not work to change juvenile offenders, and the punitive setting of most training schools is more likely to make juveniles worse than to result in any positive change. Bartollas has noted that "all confined juveniles must deal with the loss of freedom, the oppressiveness of institutional life, and a highly stressful environment. Of the various ways to cope with confinement, it is disturbing that adopting prosocial attitudes and using the present experience to prepare for the future is the least popular adaptation" (1993: 509). Training school staff face limitations in correcting juvenile offenders because they cannot make any impact on those factors in the community where juvenile crime originates: in the home, among peers, and in the schools. The least-restrictive model remains the more appropriate correctional strategy. Policymakers must balance public safety concerns with the need to reintegrate wayward juveniles into the community and social institutions such as the schools.

An outstanding example of an excellent juvenile correctional program is the Hennepin County Home School, a state-licensed residential correctional treatment facility for adjudicated delinquents (Hennepin County Home School, 1993; and assorted undated brochures). Originally developed in 1909, the Home School is located on a 190-acre site in a suburban area nineteen miles west of downtown Minneapolis. The facility can house a maximum of 168 juveniles in seven separate cottages. The Home School employs about 140 staff in a variety of positions, including cooks, nurses, social workers, juvenile correctional workers, maintenance workers, teachers, supervisors, and administrators. Counting only staff members who work directly with residents, the staff-to-resident ratio is about one staff to eight residents. There are programs for male and female offenders, including a juvenile sexual offender program and a special educational program. Treatment program components include intensive therapy groups, individual therapy, and family counseling. Education is provided by specially certified teachers from the nearby Hopkins Public School District. The "Beta" school program focuses on tutoring and assisting students who have been attending public school or providing remedial instruction in basic skills for youth who had not been actively involved in school prior to their commitment. In addition to providing a treatment emphasis, the Home School closely supervises residents twenty-four hours a day, and a county sheriff's deputy patrols the grounds each night. The progress of each resident is regularly monitored, and individual residents must develop a plan for their release, outlining their goals and expectations. The plans are reviewed by the staff, who work closely with the courts and probation departments in the community reintegration process. The Hennepin County Home School has been successful in helping to change hundreds of young offenders. According to a brochure on the "Beta" school program, statements and letters from probation officers, parents, and former residents themselves attest to the success of this residential correctional program.

Community Residential Programs

The main types of community-based programs are group homes, foster care, day treatment programs, and survival or wilderness programs. *Group homes,* also referred to as halfway houses, are small residential facilities in the community that are designed to house about ten to twenty-five youths. Group homes serve as an alternative to incarceration, provide a short-term community placement for youth on probation or after-care supervision, and serve as a halfway house for youth needing semisecure placement but less than the supervision offered by a training school (Bartollas, 1993: 469).

Foster care programs offer temporary placement for juveniles who must be removed from their own homes. Foster parents provide shelter, food, and clothing for neglected, abused, or delinquent children. They are subsidized by local or state governments to cover their expenses. It is difficult to get enough persons who are willing to serve as foster parents, especially for delinquent youth. Foster care places considerable stresses on a home, because many delinquent youth have experienced abusive parental relationships and are therefore distrustful and often rebellious toward foster parents. Foster care is a better placement alternative to institutional life for youth who must be removed from their biological parents. Foster parents are able to provide temporary shelter with more consistent, firm supervision than troubled juveniles may have been receiving in their own homes. Short-term placement with foster parents gives more time for probation officers to seek other placement alternatives.

Day treatment programs are nonresidential programs that offer delinquent youth a variety of educational, counseling, and training activities. They are less expensive to operate because they are nonresidential and require fewer staff members. Project New Pride is an outstanding example of such a program (see Bartollas, 1993: 471; and Siegel and Senna, 1991: 552–553). It was begun in Denver, Colorado, in 1973 and has served as a model for similar programs around the country. The program is for serious or violent youthful offenders from fourteen to seventeen years of age. The project's goals are to reintegrate hard-core youths back into their communities and to reduce the number of re-arrests. Successful reintegration means reenrolling youths in school, getting them jobs, or both. The program utilizes alternative schooling, vocational training and job placement, and family counseling. The Denver program has served as a model for similar programs in Chicago, Los Angeles, Boston, San Francisco, Kansas City, Providence, Washington, D.C., and other cities.

Associated Marine Industries (AMI) runs a group of nonresidential programs in Florida that use various marine projects to motivate and challenge delinquent youths (Greenwood and Zimring, 1985). The youth attend the program during the day, five days a week for six months. They attend remedial classes; learn scuba diving, safety procedures, and marine biology; and work on a project such as restoring an old boat or doing landscaping work.

Survival Programs and Wilderness Camps

An approach that has been a viable institutional alternative for serious juvenile offenders is the type of outdoor education and training programs most widely known as Outward Bound (Greenwood and Zimring, 1985). The goals of Outward Bound are to use the "overcoming of a seemingly impossible task to gain self-reliance, to prove one's worth, and to define one's personhood" (Bartollas, 1993: 472). Outward Bound programs attempt to accomplish these goals through backpacking in wilderness areas, high-altitude camping, mountain hiking, rock climbing, and rappeling. Participants first receive training in basic skills, then participate in an expedition, and are tested in a solo experience. The wilderness experience lasts from three to four weeks.

VisionQuest is a survival program based in Tucson, Arizona. The program contracts with juvenile courts and takes juveniles who are committed to the program from California, Pennsylvania, and several other states. VisionQuest programs, which last from twelve to eighteen months, include wilderness camps, cross-country travel on a wagon train, and a voyage on a large sailboat. The youth are closely supervised and rigorously challenged emotionally, intellectually, and physically. VisionQuest has drawn some controversy for its confrontational style with juveniles who do not perform up to expectations, slack off, or act out (Greenwood and Zimring, 1985).

Thistledew Camp is an example of an effective wilderness program for correcting juvenile offenders (Minnesota Department of Corrections, 1992). Thistledew is located between two lakes in a remote forest area of northern Minnesota. It features a unique educational facility intended to serve delinquent youth who have experienced failure in the home, school, and community. Education is provided for youths at all levels, and all classroom teachers are certified in learning disabilities (LD) or emotional/behavioral disorders (EBD) to provide optimum services for students with special needs. About a third of the time at Thistledew Camp is devoted to Challenge, an outdoor wilderness survival program similar to Outward Bound. Challenge is a high-adventure wilderness experience designed to build individual self-confidence, develop leadership abilities, and teach the importance of a group effort. Residents receive training and instruction in the use of equipment and in basic wilderness techniques. Expeditions are conducted throughout the year and are geared to the seasons. Treks include canoeing, backpacking, rock climbing, cross-country skiing, and traveling by snowshoe. Expeditions are planned to be rugged and difficult in order to build self-confidence and to teach the importance of teamwork. "Solo camping" is a final phase of Challenge. Camping alone in an isolated area for three days and nights, residents experience loneliness, hunger, and cold, and they learn how to handle those situations in a self-reliant manner (Minnesota Department of Corrections, 1992).

Wilderness programs are also used in conjunction with probation supervision. Staffed by probation officers and lay volunteers, wilderness probation involves juveniles in outdoor expeditions to give them a sense of confidence and purpose (Callahan, 1985). Counseling and group therapy are combined with day hikes and a wilderness experience. The programs provide an opportunity for juveniles on probation to confront difficulties in their lives and to attain some personal satisfaction (Siegel and Senna, 1991:540).

Juvenile Corrections Issues and Policy Implications

Dramatic changes have taken place in juvenile corrections in the past two decades. Juvenile corrections policies have gone from deinstitutionalization to a "get-tough" approach, with a return to greater use of institutions over this twenty-year period. Juvenile justice administrators and corrections officials recognized two decades ago that committing delinquents to isolated training schools away from the community was not an effective long-range answer to juvenile crime. Thus began a trend toward deinstitutionalization or "decarceration" and a greater use of community correctional alternatives. That trend has been curtailed or even reversed in the 1990s, as policymakers have been pressured by public demands to "do something" about youth involvement in drugs, gangs, and violent crime. The usual response has been to "get tough" on crime and criminals, which usually means a return to incarceration of offenders. The Children in Custody (CIC) survey was conducted on more than 3,200 public and private facilities nationwide that provide custody and care for more than 92,000 children daily who are wards of juvenile courts, juvenile corrections, or private agencies (Allen-Hagen, 1991: 1). Statistics indicate that after a decade of decarceration efforts, the number of juveniles being incarcerated has started to increase. From 1985 to 1989 the average daily population and total census count of juveniles in public facilities increased 14 percent, and the juvenile custody rate per 100,000 increased 19 percent (Allen-Hagen, 1991: 2). The increasing number of adjudicated youths being sent to juvenile corrections facilities does not include the growing number who are waived to criminal court, tried as adults, and often sent to adult institutions. Juvenile corrections policies in the 1990s are being dominated by a conservative, control-oriented philosophy.

Serious juvenile offenders are not the only youth being targeted for institutionalization. Minor offenders who engage in status offenses such as running away, truancy, alcohol consumption, and parental disobedience are increasingly subjected to a "hidden" system of juvenile control. According to the Juvenile Justice and Delinquency Prevention Act of 1974, status offenders could no longer be committed to juvenile institutions. There is evidence that the act is being subverted by a practice of placing youth in private hospitals. Ira Schwartz (1989) has noted that there is a "hidden" system of juvenile control in which troubled youth are put in private mental hospitals and substance-abuse clinics. Hospitals have developed psychiatric and chemical dependency units that compete for the availability of patient admissions covered by medical insurance. Many have used scare tactics and appealed to parents' worries, suggesting that youths' misbehavior is a sign of depression, emotional disturbance, or alcohol or drug abuse that can be treated through inpatient care at the clinics. A total of 16,735 juveniles were admitted to private psychiatric hospitals in 1980; by 1985 the number was up to 35,000 (Schwartz, 1989: 137). Juvenile admissions to psychiatric units in the Minneapolis-St. Paul area more than doubled in eight years, going from 88 admissions per 100,000 in 1977 to 199 in 1985; in 1985 nearly $14 million was collected by Minneapolis-St. Paul hospitals for inpatient psychiatric services for juveniles (Schwartz, 1989: 136–138). Schwartz questioned whether most of the admissions were appropriate and noted that many of the programs used punitive behavior modification techniques that were typically found in juvenile training schools. It is highly questionable whether this "hidden" system of juvenile corrections is an effective treatment alternative or merely a profit-generated addition for hospitals.

Limitations of Juvenile Corrections in Delinquency Prevention

Considerable debate has developed around the question of whether correctional programs have been effective in changing offenders (Martinson, 1974). Charles Murray and Louis Cox Jr. (1979) have argued that juvenile institutions have a "suppression effect" and have been a more effective deterrent to delinquency than have community-based corrections programs. Further analyses have raised questions about that conclusion, however, with evidence indicating that community-based treatment may be as effective as institutionalization (Lundman, 1986). There is still much to be learned about the effectiveness of juvenile corrections programs in changing the delinquent.

There is little question that juvenile corrections has several limitations as a primary source of delinquency prevention. There are several reasons for this:

1. It is always a "reactive" approach, not "proactive" or preventive. The juvenile court can intervene only after a juvenile's delinquent involvement is serious or persistent enough to warrant police arrest and referral. Delinquency prevention is generally more effective at an early age, before the onset of more serious behavior.
2. Correctional agencies may actually promote rather than prevent delinquency by bringing offenders together and isolating them from the community. Frank Tannenbaum (1938) claimed that juvenile correctional institutions were "schools for crime," where young offenders' delinquent tendencies often became worse. Criminologists today also have suggested that group interventions, such as Positive Peer Culture and Guided Group Interaction, used in juvenile institutions may actually maintain and enhance delinquent behavior of the youth (Elliott, Huizinga, and Ageton, 1985: 149; Gottfredson, 1987: 710).
3. The factors that generate and influence delinquent behavior—factors that are for the most part beyond the power of correctional agencies to change— usually lie within the community, the family, and the school.

True delinquency prevention requires a coordinated and consolidated effort of the entire community. A proactive approach to delinquency prevention must include community-wide efforts to address unequal educational opportunities, unemployment, poverty, and racism. This requires the combined efforts of legislative bodies with the support of citizens. Delinquency prevention also requires some long-range, expensive legislative programs that many voters would not accept. Many voters prefer to spend billions of dollars on building and operating correctional institutions, believing that incarceration and punishment are the best means to crime control.

Some evidence suggests that we may be taking money from school classrooms and pouring it into prison cells. Comparisons of state and federal expenditures for corrections and for education indicate that there have been significant increases in funds going to corrections, while the amount of state and federal dollars going to education has remained stable or actually declined in recent years (Lawrence, 1995a). Corrections does need to expand. Most state prison systems do need to provide additional space and hire more officers to house and supervise the growing numbers of sentenced offenders. Cutting back on educational funds while spending more money for prisons or training schools, however, is not the answer to crime prevention. Institutions are only a short-term, reactive approach to juvenile crime. Young people with inadequate schooling who are faced with the grim realities of unemployment and poverty are tempted by drug dealing, gang involvement, and other criminal activities. The threat of punitive sanctions has little deterrent effect on desperate youth who foresee little future for themselves. True delinquency prevention must offer more opportunities for at-risk youth to experience positive alternatives and to succeed in productive social and economic roles (see Regoli and Hewitt, 1994: 445–446). The African saying "It takes a whole village to raise a child" has never been more true than when applied to the need for total community involvement in delinquency prevention.

Reexamining Community Corrections Models

Community corrections has undergone many changes in the past two decades. The emphasis on rehabilitation, which focused on offenders' needs and problems, has given way to greater concerns for public safety and attention to victims. The changes are due in part to increases in crime and and in the number of high-risk offenders being sentenced to community corrections programs. Questions have been raised about the effectiveness of rehabilitation and whether it is even a realistic or primary goal of corrections. Community corrections was founded on three models that distinguished it from institutional corrections: diversion, advocacy, and reintegration (see Lawrence, 1991). *Diversion* of less serious or first-time offenders from formal judicial processing to alternative community programming was considered more appropriate for the child and the community. Youth received helpful intervention without the stigma and adverse effects of more punitive sanctions and at less cost to taxpayers. Community corrections agents adopted an *advocacy* role in assisting young offenders through referrals to community resources, educational programs, and employment opportunities. *Reintegration* was the ultimate goal of community corrections, in recognition of the reality that many offenders are persons who have been alienated from mainstream society and social institutions. Many delinquents are school dropouts or have been "pushed out" of school because of misbehavior and poor performance. Many young offenders lack the education, job skills, and labor market credentials to compete in main-stream society. Reintegration is directed at change in both offenders and the community, through opportunities and resources such as alternative schools, job training, and employment (see O'Leary and Duffee, 1971; Smykla, 1981; Lawrence, 1991).

We have witnessed a demise of the original community corrections models. Although many treatment programs have shown positive results, the role of rehabilitation has been questioned (Lipton, Martinson and Wilks, 1975; Allen, 1981). A growing public intolerance of crime, coupled with the belief that community corrections cannot control crime, has resulted in demands for greater use of jails and prisons. Politicians have rushed to embrace punishment rather than community interventions. "Getting tough on crime" has become a sure way to gain voter approval. Probation and community corrections have become identified as too lenient and "soft on crime." The readiness of politicians to increase prison sentences but not allocate sufficient funds to corrections departments has resulted in overcrowded prisons and overflowing probation caseloads that render meaningful supervision impossible. The emphasis in corrections is now more on controlling and punishing the offender than on reintegrating him or her into the community.

The original community corrections models have given way to emphases on just deserts, adversarial proceedings, and restitution (Lawrence, 1991: 453). Court sanctions based on "just deserts" are now more important than diversion from the system. Sentencing guidelines in many states are based on a just deserts model, focusing more on the crime than on the criminal (von Hirsch, 1976). Community corrections agents now view themselves more as *adversaries* of the offender than as advocates, in large part because probation has been criticized for being too lenient and is often viewed as "getting off" rather than as a judicial sanction in its own right. Excessively large probation caseloads have placed unrealistic demands on officers and make probation supervision meaningless, and corrections departments have responded by developing intensive supervision probation (ISP) programs (Byrne, 1986; Petersilia, 1990) in which the probation officer's role is on control, surveillance, and monitoring. Offender *restitution* is now more important than offender reintegration. Restitution is a means by which victims and the community may be repaid for the wrongs suffered at the hands of offenders. Proponents of restitution have argued for the rehabilitative and reintegrative effects of restitution. But many states with little previous commitment to community corrections have turned to restitution programs as a means of reducing prison commitments and making offenders share in the cost of corrections. Texas, for example, has diverted more than 800 offenders from prison each year and collected more than $2 million annually to cover costs of the program and to compensate victims (Lawrence, 1990). Restitution programs have been a welcome addition to community corrections, but they will be most effective when they incorporate goals of offender change and reintegration.

I have argued that community corrections programs would be more effective if they integrated the old and new community corrections models

(Lawrence, 1991). Integrating diversion and deserts, advocacy and adversary roles, and reintegration and restitution is difficult but not impossible. Crime control and offender reintegration are both necessary ingredients of effective community corrections. Community corrections programs must ensure protection for the general public and also offer chances for offenders to free themselves from a no-win criminal lifestyle. We must develop intermediate sanctions that offer the necessary degree of control, but we must also place equal importance on reintegrating the offender in the community. An effective corrections policy would strive for a balance between punishment and rehabilitation, between emphasis on community protection and offender change. Crime control strategies and punitive sanctions alone are short-term solutions that further alienate offenders from the community. On the other hand, treatment programs that fail to address offender accountability or the realities and demands of a productive, crime-free lifestyle will not reduce criminal involvement.

"Reintegrative Shaming" in Community Corrections

Community corrections should continue to focus on reintegration but also must adopt strategies whereby offenders are confronted with the wrongfulness of crime and the damage done to victims and the community. There must be more emphasis placed on making the juvenile justice and corrections processes more meaningful and consequential. I have argued for a community corrections model that incorporates internalization, shaming, and reintegration (Lawrence, 1991: 459–461). *Internalization* is the strategy of behavior change on which one reintegration correctional policy was based (Kelman, 1958; O'Leary and Duffee, 1971). Efforts to reform offenders by force and threats of punishment require constant surveillance and place unrealistic demands on corrections agents. True behavior change, on the other hand, means that offenders have internalized community standards and values. To accomplish true reintegration requires changes in the offender and in the community. In addition to offender change, reintegration seeks community support to provide opportunities and resources for offenders. Under a reintegration policy, community corrections agents would be involved with community institutions such as schools, businesses, churches, and civic organizations. Equal emphasis would be placed on offender accountability, community protection, and opportunities for education, training, and employment.

"Reintegrative shaming" was first described by Braithwaite (1989) as one way of criminal punishment. It is a process by which the community may express disapproval of law violations, followed by their reacceptance into the community of law-abiding citizens. More common is stigmatization, whereby the offender is labeled for lawbreaking, and the person, rather than the behavior, is rejected (Braithwaite, 1989: 55). By stigmatizing law violators, we treat them as outcasts, which generally results in high crime rates. Reintegrative shaming, in contrast, is based on a "family model" in which punishment is administered by supportive family members. Braithwaite argues that his theory of offender punishment explains crime variations better than other theories and suggests

that it explains the lower crime rates in countries like Japan that emphasize public shaming and acknowledgement of responsibility followed by reacceptance of the wrongdoers (1989: 84–97, 164–165).

There are clearly dangers with advocating a shaming strategy for corrections in America. Images come to mind of historic colonial sanctions such as the ducking stool, the scarlet letter, the stocks and pillory. Many persons today support public shaming practices as effective crime deterrents, but they omit the reintegrative element of acceptance and support by the community. For example, ordering persons convicted of driving while intoxicated to display bumper stickers announcing their conviction may be a well-intended effort to shame them into compliance but is actually stigmatization that may lead to community alienation. Requiring law violators to make public apologies in a newspaper is a better example of reintegrative shaming if it is accompanied by an opportunity to make restitution and by community forgiveness and acceptance. Present-day advocates of paddling in schools justify its use as an effective device for shaming misbehaving students and deterring further misconduct. Beyond the questionable practice of using physical force to change behavior, paddling as punishment is more stigmatization than reintegrative shaming. Gaining compliance from persons, in society or in schools, requires more than stigmatizing punishment. Reintegrative shaming seeks to encourage offenders to accept responsibility and to internalize laws and community expectations and then works toward acceptance and support of them. Under a reintegrative shaming approach, getting offenders to internalize laws and societal expectations is accompanied by efforts to involve them positively in the community. Juvenile probation officers might bring together representatives of the offender's school, employer, and other concerned groups to attend the court hearing and to offer opinions of how they might be able to contribute to monitoring the offender's behavior and assist in his or her rehabilitation (Braithwaite, 1989: 173). The objectives are to increase the level of informal social control and to achieve reintegration of the offender and community organizations.

Reintegrative emphases in community corrections are embodied in restitution programs that involve "paying for crime" and encouraging reacceptance by the victim and the community. Victim-Offender Reconciliation Programs (VORPs) combine the concept of restitution and traditional justice principles that dictate that when a person wrongs another, he or she has a responsibility to make amends to the victim and to society. VORP extends this principle by actually bringing the victim and the offender together in a face-to-face meeting. The goals of VORP include humanizing the justice process through face-to-face mediation, emphasizing offender accountability, providing for victim restitution, improving community understanding of crime and justice, and providing an alternative to incarceration (Coates, 1990: 126). Findings from a survey of 240 juvenile justice agencies that have a victim-offender mediation program indicated that the programs are widespread and functioning well; are supported well by the community and those working with the juveniles; and are considered very successful (Hughes and Schneider, 1989).

The concept of "restorative justice" is emerging as a viable means of attaining offender accountability and change and is viewed as a way to involve offenders, victims, and the community together in responding to crime (Galaway and Hudson, 1990; Bazemore and Umbreit, 1995). Restorative justice presents an alternative to the traditional retributive justice approach that views crime as a violation against the laws of the state and places total responsibility on the state for punishing and correcting the offender. Restorative justice is neither punitive nor lenient. Crime is viewed as an act against another person or the community, and victims and the community are equally important in helping to resolve the crime problem (Bazemore and Umbreit, 1994: 6–7). According to Gordon Bazemore and Mark Umbreit, "restorative justice sanctions could meet the need of communities to provide meaningful consequences for crime, confront offenders, denounce delinquent behavior, and relay the message that such behavior is unacceptable" (1995: 302).

A comprehensive community corrections approach is one that facilitates change in offenders, the justice process, and the community. Correctional programs that include community service, restitution, and victim-offender reconciliation are meaningful sanctions that avoid stigmatization but make offenders accountable while still being reintegrated with the community.

Juvenile Corrections and Schools

Schools play an important role in delinquency prevention and can support the objectives of community corrections agencies. School officials and juvenile probation officers are responsible for dealing with many of the same youth, and yet few efforts have been made to improve the interorganizational relations between them. Many schools rely on police and security officers to patrol school grounds and the hallways; police respond to incidents of drug and weapon possession in schools or investigate other criminal incidents. There is less communication and cooperation between juvenile probation and school officials, however. This is unfortunate, because schools and corrections agencies rely on each other to achieve common objectives. Students who have been adjudicated delinquent are generally ordered to attend school and obey school regulations. School attendance and participation in school activities can be beneficial in helping delinquent youth refrain from further delinquent involvement.

Delinquency is a community problem whose solution requires a total community effort. Trying to get different organizations to work together in delinquency prevention efforts however, has traditionally faced difficulties. Walter Miller (1958) noted that a major barrier to delinquency prevention was conflict and disagreement among institutions. Miller's description of one community's concern about juvenile gang violence more than thirty years ago rings true in many cities today. Though most community organizations agreed there was a problem, they disagreed on how to deal with the problem. The police, courts, probation, social welfare agencies, churches, and schools all disagreed and accused one another of improper actions. Differences revolved around the causes of delinquency and the methods for dealing with it (Miller, 1958:

22–23). Reid (1964) concluded that interagency coordination in delinquency prevention and control is more likely when there are shared goals and complementary resources and when the time and effort put into coordination is seen as worthwhile to each agency (1964: 421–427). Agencies that deal with problem youth frequently have less than optimal interorganizational relations. Social welfare and probation agencies were found to have the highest level of conflict and the lowest level of coordination in one study that compared relations among juvenile probation, police, social welfare, mental health, and school officials (Hall, Clark, Giordano, Johnson, and Van Roekel, 1981). Results of a study of school teachers, principals, and probation officers in three different cities revealed significant conflict over goals and methods of delinquency prevention (Lawrence, 1995b). School officials and probation officers expressed sharply divided opinions on matters pertaining to judicial procedures, sharing of school and court records, and appropriate probation supervision strategies for delinquent students in schools (Lawrence, 1995b: 10–12).

There clearly is a need for school and probation officials to develop better interorganizational relations. Schools and community corrections agencies would improve their ability to deal with delinquent students if they improved working relationships. Steps might include:

• Informal personal meetings between school and probation officials
• Exchange of resources such as meeting rooms, offices, or personnel
• Joint planning for programs and activities for at-risk and delinquent students
• Written agreements and policies regarding the sharing of school and court records, students' probation status and educational progress, and supervision and disciplinary policies (see Lawrence, 1995b: 5; and Oliver, 1991:950)

Several juvenile probation and school partnerships have been developed around the United States. The Yuba County (Marysville, California) Probation Department developed the Truancy Intervention Program and the Probation and Schools Success Program (PASS) with the local school district and has probation officers located in various community schools. The Community School Program was developed in Monterey County, California, by the probation department and school district to address the educational needs of youth who have dropped out or been expelled. A probation officer works with teachers in the Community School Program. A contract that specifies expectations for attendance, proper attire, conduct, and productivity is developed among each student, the parents, and school personnel. The Clark County (Jefferson, Indiana) Probation Department has a volunteer school liaison officer to provide some services and keep lines of communication open between the probation agency and the school (see National School Safety Center, 1995).

The Pennsylvania Commission on Crime and Delinquency has supported a School-Based Probation Services Program through grants to probation agencies and schools. The Lehigh County Probation Department worked with the Allentown School District to place full-time juvenile probation officers in public schools. The goals of the program are to:

•strengthen cooperation and communication between schools and the probation department

•inform teachers about the duties, functions, and limitations of the juvenile justice system

•provide an alternative approach for suspended students and behavioral problems

•act as a liaison among the school district, juvenile probation agency, police departments, and the youths' families

•confront drug abuse by having juvenile justice officials train teachers on signs of abuse (National School Safety Center, 1995: 1)

The duties of the school-based probation officer include providing the school with a list of the students who are on probation supervision, monitoring the attendance and behavior of probation clients, and intervening in behavioral problems of probation clients.

Funding for the program has come from the Pennsylvania Juvenile Court Judges' Commission and the Pennsylvania Commission on Crime and Delinquency. More than $885,000 was provided in 1993 to seventeen counties (including Lehigh County) for developing and operating school-based probation programs. As of 1995 the commission has provided a total of nearly $3.5 million in federal funds from the Office of Juvenile Justice and Delinquency Prevention to support thirty-five school-based probation programs throughout the Commonwealth of Pennsylvania.

Evaluations of this School-Based Probation Services Program indicate that it has been successful. Details on the methods of evaluation and data collection were not specified, but officials report dramatic changes in the school behavior and performance of the middle-school youths served by the program: detentions and suspensions dropped 4 percent; tardiness dropped 9.5 percent; absenteeism was down 15 percent; dropouts were reduced by 29 percent; and grade averages increased 4.1 percent. School officials and students have responded positively to the program. Although the probation officers work directly only with students assigned to school-based probation, school officials reported that their presence has reduced the incidence of behavioral problems among the student body in general (National School Safety Center, 1995: 2).

One of the concerns in developing the school-based probation program was the ability of the school district and the probation department to share relevant information and records while maintaining confidentiality of sensitive information. The school and juvenile court records are kept separately by schools and probation agencies in order to maintain confidentiality and to ensure that a child is not unfairly labeled or stigmatized. Information is shared only on an as-needed basis between teachers and probation officers, and the sharing of information is specified in written agreements between the school district and probation departments.

Another concern of the school-based probation program was the role definition of the probation officer. Precautions were taken to ensure that the officers' role was limited to working directly only with juveniles who were under the jurisdiction and supervision of the juvenile court. There is a concern that officers in the schools may observe more delinquent behavior, resulting in additional referrals to the justice system. The Pennsylvania Commission addressed this concern by requiring school-based probation officers to work only with those youths already on juvenile probation and not allowing them to serve as discipline officers for the entire student body.

Schools and probation agencies clearly stand to benefit by better interagency relations and sharing of goals and resources. Schools contribute to probation objectives through special efforts and programs aimed at retaining probation clients in school. School involvement and educational attainment are major factors in crime reduction, as young offenders receive the education and skills that are essential for employment and a productive lifestyle. Probation agencies contribute to safer schools where teachers and students have less fear of crime when court orders and school rules are strictly enforced. The development of better working relations between school and probation officials is a necessary first step in getting the whole community involved in correcting young offenders.

Summary

Juvenile corrections is charged with carrying out the sentence imposed by the court. Corrections encompasses a wide variety of programs, ranging from traditional training schools and probation supervision to innovative programs such as restitution, mediation, and "restorative justice," emphases that incorporate offender accountability and concern for the victim. Corrections agents often experience role conflict in supervising delinquents as they exercise their authority enforcing court orders, while at the same time attempting to be change agents for young offenders. Effective corrections programs must work closely with parents and families, school officials, and community agencies in a collaborative effort to help change delinquent youth and reintegrate them into society.

References

Allen, Francis A. 1981. *The Decline of the Rehabilitative Ideal.* New Haven: Yale University Press.

Allen-Hagen, Barbara. 1991. *Children in Custody 1989.* Washington, D.C.: Office of Juvenile Justice and Delinquency Prevention.

Ball, Richard, and J. Robert Lilly. 1986. "A Theoretical Examination of Home Incarceration." *Federal Probation* 50:17–25.

Bartollas, Clemens. 1993. Juvenile Delinquency, 3rd ed. New York: Macmillan.

Bartollas, Clemens, Stuart J. Miller, and Simon Dinitz. 1976. *Juvenile Victimization: The Institutional Paradox.* New York: Halsted Press.

Bazemore, Gordon and Mark S. Umbreit. 1994. *Balanced and Restorative Justice: Program Summary.* Washington, D.C.: Office of Juvenile Justice and Delinquency Prevention.

Bazemore, Gordon, and Mark Umbreit. 1995. "Rethinking the Sanctioning Function in Juvenile Court: Retributive or Restorative Responses to Youth Crime." *Crime and Delinquency* 41:296–316.

Blumberg, Abraham. 1979. *Criminal Justice: Issues and Ironies*, 2nd ed. New York: New Viewpoints.

Braithwaite, John. 1989. *Crime, Shame and Reintegration*. Cambridge: Cambridge University Press.

Bureau of Justice Statistics. 1988. *Report to the National on Crime and Justice*, 2nd ed. Washington, D.C.: U.S. Department of Justice.

Byrne, James. 1986. "The Control Controversy: A Preliminary Examination of Intensive Probation Supervision Programs in the United States." *Federal Probation* 50:4–16.

Butts, Jeffrey A. and Howard N. Snyder. 1992. *OJJDP Update on Research: Restitution and Juvenile Recidivism*. Washington, D.C.: U.S. Department of Justice.

Callahan, Robert. 1985. "Wilderness Probation: A Decade Later." *Juvenile and Family Court Journal* 36:31–35.

Carter, Robert M., and Leslie T. Wilkins. 1967. "Some Factors in Sentencing Policy." *Journal of Criminal Law, Criminology, and Police Science* 58:503–514.

Charles, Michael. 1989. "The Development of a Juvenile Electronic Monitoring Program." *Federal Probation* 53:3–12.

Coates, Robert B. 1990. "Victim-Offender Reconciliation Programs in North America: An Assessment." In B. Galaway and J. Hudson, eds., *Criminal Justice, Restitution, and Reconciliation*. Monsey, N.Y.: Criminal Justice Press.

Coates, Robert B., A. D. Miller, and Lloyd E. Ohlin. 1978. *Diversity in a Youth Correctional System: Handling Delinquents in Massachusetts*. Cambridge, Mass.: Ballinger.

Elliott, Delbert S., David Huizinga, and Suzanne S. Ageton. 1985. *Explaining Delinquency and Drug Use*. Newbury Park, Calif.: Sage.

Feld, Barry C. 1977. *Neutralizing Inmate Violence: The Juvenile Offender in Institutions*. Cambridge, Mass.: Ballinger.

Galaway, Burt. 1989. "Restitution as Innovation or Unfilled Promise." *Federal Probation* 52:3–15.

Galaway, Burt, and Joe Hudson, eds. 1990. *Criminal Justice, Restitution, and Reconciliation*. Monsey, N.Y.: Criminal Justice Press.

Garrett, Carol. 1985. "Effects of Residential Treatment on Adjudicated Delinquents: A Meta-Analysis." *Journal of Research in Crime and Delinquency* 22:287–308.

Gottfredson, Gary D. 1987. "Peer Group Intervention to Reduce the Risk of Delinquent Behavior: A Selective Review and a New Evaluation." *Criminology* 25:671–714.

Greenwood, Peter, and Franklin Zimring. 1985. *One More Chance: The Pursuit of Promising Intervention Strategies for Chronic Juvenile Offenders*. Santa Monica, Calif.: RAND Corp.

Hall, Richard H., John P. Clark, Peggy C. Giordano, Paul V. Johnson, and Martha Van Roekel. 1981. "Patterns of Interorganizational Relationships." In O. Grusky and G. A. Miller, eds., *The Sociology of Organizations*. New York: Free Press.

Hennepin County Home School. 1993. *Juvenile Sex Offender Program*. Minneapolis, Minn.: Hennepin County Home School.

Hughes, Stella P., and Anne L. Schneider. 1989. "Victim-Offender Mediation: A Survey of Program Characteristics and Perceptions of Effectiveness." *Crime and Delinquency* 35:217–233.

Katz, Janet. 1982. "The Attitudes and Decisions of Probation Officers." *Criminal Justice and Behavior* 9:455–475.

Kelman, Herbert. 1958. "Compliance, Identification, and Internalization: Three Processes of Attitude Change." *Journal of Conflict Resolution* 2:51–60.

Krisberg, Barry, and James F. Austin. 1993. *Reinventing Juvenile Justice*. Newbury Park, Calif.: Sage.

Lab, Steven, and John Whitehead. 1988. "Analysis of Juvenile Correctional Treatment." *Crime and Delinquency* 34:60–83.

Latessa, Edward. 1986. "The Cost Effectiveness of Intensive Supervision." *Federal Probation* 50:70–74.

Lawrence, Richard. 1983. "The Role of Legal Counsel in Juveniles' Understanding of Their Rights." *Juvenile and Family Court Journal* 34(4):49–58.

Lawrence, Richard. 1984. "Professionals or Judicial Civil Servants? An Examination of the Probation Officer's Role." *Federal Probation* 48(4): 14–21.

Lawrence, Richard. 1990. "Restitution as a Cost-Effective Alternative to Incarceration." In B. Galaway and J. Hudson, eds., *Criminal Justice, Restitution, and Reconciliation*. Monsey, N.Y.: Criminal Justice Press.

Lawrence, Richard. 1991. "Reexamining Community Corrections Models." *Crime and Delinquency* 37(3):449–464.

Lawrence, Richard. 1995a. "Classrooms vs. Prison Cells: Funding Policies for Education and Corrections." *Journal of Crime and Justice* 18:113–126.

Lawrence, Richard. 1995b. "Controlling School Crime: An Examination of Interorganizational Relations of School and Juvenile Justice Professionals." *Juvenile and Family Court Journal* 46(3):3–15.

Lipton, Douglas, Robert Martinson, and Judith Wilks. 1975. *The Effectiveness of Correctional Treatment: A Survey of Treatment Evaluation Studies*. New York: Praeger.

Lundman, Richard J. 1986. "Beyond Probation: Assessing the Generalizability of the Delinquency Suppression Effect Measures Reported by Murray and Cox." *Crime and Delinquency* 32:134–147.

Maloney, Dennis, Dennis Romig, and Troy Armstrong. 1988. "The Balanced Approach to Juvenile Probation." *Juvenile and Family Court Journal* 39:1–49.

Martinson, Robert. 1974. "What Works? Questions and Answers About Prison Reform." *Public Interest* 35:22–54.

McShane, Marilyn D., and Wesley Krause. 1993. *Community Corrections*. New York: Macmillan.

Miller, Walter B. 1958. "Inter-Institutional Conflict as a Major Impediment to Delinquency Prevention." *Human Organization* 17:20–23.

Minnesota Department of Corrections. 1992. *Thistledew Camp*. St. Paul, Minn.: Minnesota Department of Corrections.

Murray, Charles, and Louis Cox Jr. 1979. *Beyond Probation*. Beverly Hills, Calif.: Sage.

National Advisory Commission on Criminal Justice Standards and Goals. 1973. *Corrections*. Washington, D.C.: U.S. Government Printing Office.

National School Safety Center. 1995. "School-Based Juvenile Probation: Everyone Benefits." *School Safety Update* (December): 1–4.

Newton, Anne. 1979. "Sentencing to Community Service and Restitution." *Criminal Justice Abstracts* (September): 435–468.

O'Leary, Vincent, and David Duffee. 1971. "Correctional Policy Models: A Classification of Goals Designed for Change." *Crime and Delinquency* 17:373–386.

Oliver, Christine. 1991. "Network Relations and Loss of Organizational Autonomy." *Human Relations* 44:943–961.

Petersilia, Joan. 1986. "Exploring the Option of House Arrest." *Federal Probation* 50:50–56.

Petersilia, Joan. 1990. "Conditions that Permit Intensive Supervision Programs to Survive." *Crime and Delinquency* 36:126–145.

Regoli, Robert M., and John D. Hewitt. 1994. *Delinquency in Society*, 2nd ed. New York: McGraw-Hill.

Reid, William. 1964. "Interagency Co-ordination in Delinquency Prevention and Control." *Social Service Review* 38:418–428.

Schmidt, Annesley. 1986. "Electronic Monitors." *Federal Probation* 50:56–60.

Schneider, Anne L. 1985. *Guide to Juvenile Restitution*. Washington, D.C.: U.S. Department of Justice.

Schneider, Anne L. 1986. "Restitution and Recidivism Rates of Juvenile Offenders: Results from Four Experimental Studies." *Criminology* 24:533–552.

Schneider, Anne L., and Jean Warner. 1989. *National Trends in Juvenile Restitution Programming.* Washington, D.C.: U.S. Department of Justice.

Schwartz, Ira. 1989. *(In)Justice for Juveniles.* Lexington, Mass.: Lexington Books.

Siegel, Larry J., and Joseph J. Senna. 1991. *Juvenile Delinquency,* 4th ed. St. Paul, Minn.: West Publishing Co.

Smykla, John. 1981. *Community-Based Corrections: Principles and Practices.* New York: Macmillan.

Snyder, Howard N., and Melissa Sickmund. 1995. *Juvenile Offenders and Victims: A National Report.* Washington, D.C.: Office of Juvenile Justice and Delinquency Prevention.

Staples, William. 1986. "Restitution as a Sanction in Juvenile Court." *Crime and Delinquency* 32:177–185.

Tannenbaum, Frank. 1938. *Crime and the Community.* Boston: Ginn and Company.

Vaughn, Joseph B. 1989. "A Survey of Juvenile Electronic Monitoring and Home Confinement Programs." *Juvenile and Family Court Journal* 40:1–36.

Von Hirsch, Andrew. 1976. *Doing Justice.* New York: Hill & Wang.

Whitehead, John, and Steven Lab. 1989. "Meta-Analysis of Juvenile Correctional Treatment." *Journal of Research in Crime and Delinquency* 26:276–295.

10

School-Based Programs
for Delinquency Prevention

The real answers to violence and vandalism in schools cannot be provided by the Government in Washington or by government at the State or local level. State, Local and Federal agencies can work together to insure that schools are receiving all the resources and assistance they need, but the ultimate solutions can only be found in the students, parents, teachers and administrators who make up the educational community of a school—U.S. Senator Birch Bayh, 1977:47

Juvenile delinquency is a pervasive social problem that has a significant impact on communities and schools. Many persons are affected when young people engage in disruptive and delinquent behavior . The fear of victimization in schools grips many students and teachers. Disruptive and threatening behavior creates an adverse environment that makes learning difficult if not impossible. We noted in Chapter 9 that juvenile corrections programs face a number of limitations in delinquency prevention; the same may be said of the entire juvenile justice system. There have traditionally been two ways to deal with juvenile crime: prevention and control (Hawkins and Weis, 1985: 74). Prevention refers to actions taken to stop illegal behavior before it ever occurs; control refers to reactions to violations of the law and takes place only after delinquent behavior has occurred. Police, juvenile courts, probation departments, community corrections agencies, juvenile detention centers, and correctional institutions constitute the juvenile justice system, and all are concerned with control, not prevention. The system is primarily reactive, not preventive in nature. Preventive actions within the justice system are limited primarily to police interventions with status offenders—children and youth who have engaged in noncriminal behaviors such as running away and school truancy. Police do have the authority to take status offenders into custody and refer them to the juvenile court. Status offenders may not, however, be adjudicated delinquent, and under most state juvenile statutes they may not be committed to a juvenile institution.

The Juvenile Justice and Delinquency Prevention Act of 1974 established a dual function philosophy for juvenile justice that separated formal legal control from prevention (Hawkins and Weis, 1985: 74). Federal, state, and local governments are interested in delinquency prevention. The federal Office of Juvenile Justice and Delinquency Prevention (OJJDP) is the arm of the U.S. Department of Justice that is responsible for disseminating information about delinquency prevention and control. Under the 1974 Act, the juvenile court is limited in its role of delinquency prevention and formally deals only with juveniles who have engaged in delinquent acts that are considered crimes if committed by adults. The 1974 Act called for deinstitutionalization of status offenders and removal of status offenders from the juvenile court. The role of crime prevention is not the primary role of the juvenile court, but it is considered the responsibility of the community, which includes families and the schools.

Limiting the juvenile court to a control function does not mean that delinquency prevention is less important. Rather, the division of responsibility is an acknowledgement that delinquency prevention is more appropriately accomplished by social institutions such as families and schools. Delinquency prevention has long been recognized as the most important means of dealing with crime. The Task Force Report on Juvenile Delinquency of the President's Commission on Law Enforcement and Administration of Justice (1967) focused on the importance of prevention and noted that

> the most promising and . . . important method of dealing with crime is by preventing it. . . . The Commission doubts that even a vastly improved criminal justice system can substantially reduce crime if society fails to make it possible for each of its citizens to feel a personal stake in it—in the good life that it can provide and in the law and order that are prerequisite to such a life. . . .
>
> Clearly it is with young people that prevention efforts are most needed and hold the most promise. It is simply more critical that young people be kept from crime, for they are the Nation's future, and their conduct will affect society for a long time to come. They are not yet set in their ways; they are still developing, still subject to the influence of the socializing institutions that structure . . . their environment: Family, school, gang, recreation program, job market. But that influence, to do the most good, must come before the youth has become involved in the formal criminal justice system (President's Commission on Law Enforcement and Administration of Justice, 1967: 41).

Some preventive efforts do exist within the juvenile justice system. Examples include police D.A.R.E. programs, the Police Athletic League (PAL), and diversion programs for minor offenders. Preventive efforts within components of the juvenile justice system, however, are not likely to have much impact in reducing the rates of juveniles' initial delinquency involvement. Delinquency prevention must begin in the community, the home, and the schools. It is there that delinquent behavior originates, and that is where delinquency prevention must begin.

Theoretical Foundation for Delinquency Prevention

Delinquent behavior is associated with academic failure and school problems. In Chapter 3 we noted several theoretical explanations of delinquency that include school factors. Some students disrupt class and engage in delinquent behavior in response to frustration and "strain" at not being able to meet academic expectations and demands of schools (Cohen, 1955). Students from the lower socioeconomic class often are denied equal access to goals and opportunities in society, and the resulting frustration results in rejection of society's goals or in illegal means of attaining the goals (Cloward and Ohlin, 1960). According to strain theory, the school may be seen as a middle-class institution with expectations and demands that lower-class students feel they cannot successfully meet. Many youths turn to delinquency out of frustration, feelings of failure, and low self-esteem. School absenteeism, truancy, and dropout are often indicators of students' frustration and perceived inability to meet educational demands. Researchers have established an association linking poor academic achievement, disruptive behavior, delinquency, and dropout (Elliott and Voss, 1974). There is some disagreement on the causal ordering of dropout and delinquency and on whether dropping out actually causes more delinquent involvement, but there clearly is a relationship between dropout and delinquency (Thornberry et al., 1985; Jarjoura, 1993).

A second school factor that is related to delinquency is attachment to school and commitment to education (Hirschi, 1969). Students who do not like school, who do not feel an "attachment" to it, and who are not involved in school activities are more likely to become involved in delinquent behavior. Students who did not participate in school activities were found to have significantly more self-reported delinquent involvement than students who were more actively involved in school (Lawrence, 1985). Likewise, students who are not committed to educational goals and do not see the value of education have a greater probability of delinquent involvement. Criminologists seek to explain the causes of delinquent behavior in order that rational policies and effective interventions may be developed to prevent the problem. The explanations of delinquency point to a number of school-related interventions that have been shown to be effective in preventing delinquency among some at-risk youth.

School-Based Prevention: Some Observations

Several factors have been identified which are associated with school crime, according to the *Safe School Study* and more recent analyses of the school crime problem (National Institute of Education, 1978: 111–113; Gottfredson and Gottfredson, 1985). First, the amount of *crime in the neighborhood* around the school is a factor. The presence of gangs, drug dealing, and violence in the school's attendance area tends to increase the level of disruption and violence within the school. The more crime and violence to which students are exposed outside the school, the greater the problems in the school. A school's proximity to students' homes can make the school a convenient target for vandalism. The presence of nonstudent youths around the school also increases the risk of property loss. School administrators can do very little to change the conditions and criminal incidents in the neighborhood surrounding the school. They can, however, take security precautions to make school grounds a safe zone and develop firm and consistent disciplinary policies that will reduce the level of disruption and delinquent behavior inside school buildings. Regular communication and coordination with local law enforcement agencies will help to keep police informed about law violations and concentrate police patrols in trouble spots around schools.

School size and structure are also factors in crime and disruption. The probability of victimization is greater if the teacher has large classes of more than thirty students (NIE, 1978: 111). Larger schools, and schools with larger classes, tend to have more violence and vandalism. Marcus Felson (1994) compared urban schools in the past ("convergent city schools") with the present "divergent metropolitan schools" (1994: 93–95). City schools in the past, for example, had perhaps 600 secondary school students, with twenty teachers supervising twenty homerooms of thirty students each. About 300 of the students were boys. Youths from outside the school would likely be recognized as such, and any student who committed a crime would be recognized by name or described to teachers to find out his name. About 1 percent, or six students, would be most difficult to control, but they were not too numerous for school teachers to control.

In contrast, the larger divergent metropolitan school of 3,000 students has some 300 teachers supervising 100 homerooms of thirty students each. With 1,500 boys it becomes difficult for teachers and other students to recognize who does and does not belong and equally difficult to recognize and identify students who commit crimes in school. The 1 percent of students who are most difficult to control numbers at least thirty students, a formidable number who can easily interfere with education and present serious security risks, especially when they form gangs. The physical size and setting of smaller schools present fewer problems with security and control. The buildings are more compact, and the fewer halls and stairwells are easy to watch. Large school buildings that are spread out present special difficulties in controlling entry points. Longer hallways, the number of them, and the many stairwells connecting two and three stories present security risks for students and teachers.

Larger schools also are characterized by lower levels of student involvement in school activities. Roger Barker and Page Gump (1964) conducted research on big and small schools and noted an interesting paradox. Although large schools offer more opportunities for extracurricular activities than do small schools, a significantly greater proportion of students in smaller schools participate. The authors explained this paradox in terms of "undermanning." Because a smaller school's activities are short of students, they actively recruit more students to participate. For example, a school of 500 students has to recruit 5 percent, or twenty-five male students, to fill a football roster. This means that more students, regardless of their abilities, will participate. A large school with 3,000 students can field a football team with fewer than 1 percent of the students. The smaller schools cannot compete with larger schools and may not win many championships, but by involving more students they win out on what is undoubtedly more important for students: involvement and overall school achievement (Barker and Gump, 1964: 64–74; and Felson, 1994: 96).

Schools are built today to accommodate a growing number of students and designed with efficiency in mind. It is more efficient for school districts to build a smaller number of large schools. Smaller schools cannot provide teachers and students with as many learning resources as efficiently as larger schools. Given taxpayers' concerns about the cost of education, it is unlikely that we will see any trends toward building smaller schools. An alternative to physically re-structuring schools is the "schools-within-a-school" concept (Gottfredson and Gottfredson, 1985: 172; Hawkins and Weis, 1985: 85). Under this plan, large schools are divided into smaller units. The schools may be subdivided by edu-cational structures, with students, teachers, guidance counselors, and adminis-trators in separate units, or by separating academic and extracurricular activi-ties. The schools-within-a-school plan aims to provide more attention to individual students and to increase opportunities for students to take initiative and get recognition. Proponents believe this type of school restructuring will increase and improve student-teacher interaction and result in more active par-ticipation among students. The plan supports the control theory of delinquency prevention, since it is expected to result in greater involvement in school, greater commitment to education, and positive attachments between students and teachers.

A third factor in preventing school disruption is the *quality of school gov-ernance and the existence of clear and consistent* discipline policies. A firm, fair, and consistent system for running a school seems to be a key factor in reduc-ing violence. Where the rules are known and where they are firmly and fairly enforced, less violence occurs. Good coordination between the faculty and ad-ministration also promotes a better school atmosphere. Schools that are run with clear, explicit rules that are firmly and uniformly enforced are marked by much less disruption. Schools in which there is coordination between teachers and principals have more consistent discipline policies; teachers feel more con-fident that the school administrators will back them up, and they get along bet-ter with the administration. School principals must be clear and firm in en-forcing rules, especially as they face questions and lack of support from parents of problem students. When teachers are confused about school policies or when administrators do not uniformly enforce the policies, students are given mixed signals and respond by testing the limits of educators through disruptive be-havior. Firm enforcement of school policies does not mean that schools should be run in authoritarian ways, however, or use sanctions that deny students their dignity. Sanctions can be effective without being harsh, and rewards can be as effective as punishments in getting students to conform (Gottfredson and Got-tfredson, 1985: 173). Students should be disciplined and corrected but not alienated from the school community. Experience shows that if students per-ceive a hostile or authoritarian attitude on the part of the teachers and principals, disruption and vandalism may result. There are differences of opinion, but some observers believe that student involvement in setting school policies and discipline procedures may be effective in reducing disruption and rule violations (Hawkins and Weis,1985: 87). It is hypothesized that student involvement in school policies and governance will increase student attachment to school and promote positive peer pressure to reduce disruption and create a positive and safe learning environment.

Another important factor is the *degree of student commitment to education*, which determines whether students comply with teacher expectations or engage in disruptive behavior. Perceived irrelevance of education is one of the key factors that has been identified as important in the school-delinquency connection (Schafer and Polk, 1967: 231–232). Many students do not understand the importance of reading, writing, and math skills in getting a job and doing well in the workplace. Schools and the business community can do more to impress upon students the importance of education for life and work. Simply telling them that education is important is not enough for many students. Teachers can include work-related problems and examples in school lesson plans, and they can invite a variety of employers to speak to their classes about the skills required for the workplace. Many employers do not in fact recognize school performance as being important in screening job applicants. Surveys of employers have shown that grades and test scores are important when hiring college graduates, but not high school graduates; many employers do not even request school transcripts, and some consider participation in extracurricular activities more important than grades (Rosenbaum, 1989). James Rosenbaum (1989) has emphasized that students who are not motivated by personal standards or parental pressure to excel in school have little incentive to do well, since schoolwork does not really affect the jobs they will get after high school. When students perceive that school tasks, demands, and rewards have no payoff for them in the future, the school experience becomes meaningless for them. They feel no commitment to education, no incentives for achieving academically, and they have little to lose by disrupting the classroom environment. Students need to feel that their courses are relevant and that school attendance and performance will make a difference for their immediate and future employment prospects. Disruptive students are often those who have given up on school, do not care about grades, find courses irrelevant, and feel that nothing they do makes any difference. Some students take out their frustration by disrupting the classroom or acting violently toward teachers or other students. Caring about grades and seeing relevance in education is an important step toward commitment to school and to each student's own future.

Developing Student Commitment to Education

A major function of schools is the development of youths' cognitive and social skills. Many school-based prevention programs focus on student skill development. Life skills training helps young people in communication skills, decision making, and conflict resolution. Developing these skills will help them improve interpersonal relations with family members, teachers, and peers (Hawkins and Weis, 1985: 88). Some believe that schools should help young people develop social skills just as they do cognitive skills. Young people with better social skills find that interactions with conventional others are more rewarding, and they are more likely to develop attachments to positive persons. Social skills also contribute to students' academic success and commitment to schools (Hawkins and Weis, 1985: 88).

School and Business Cooperation in Education

Schools and the business community can enhance students' perception of the relevance of education by placing more emphasis on preparing students for the work world. Offering students career and employment information would help improve their commitment to and their expectations of attaining legitimate employment. Improving students' commitment to gainful employment will in turn help increase their commitment to schooling as a necessary step toward employment. One method for including this information in the school curriculum is "experiential prevocational training and exploration," in which students are introduced to several career options and the required skills and training for them (Hawkins and Weis, 1985: 89). The training can begin in classrooms and includes field trips to various work sites. Improving students' social and vocational knowledge and skills has significant potential for increasing their commitment to education and reducing the likelihood of their delinquent involvement.

James Rosenbaum (1989) has examined the Japanese model of school-employer relationships, and he has identified several ways in which schools and employers can work together in the United States. To motivate students and bolster teachers' authority, employers can:

•Show students that some desirable jobs are available to them

•Hire students before they leave school

•Hire students on the basis of their grades

Schools can help to better prepare students for employment and bolster teachers' authority by adopting similar practices. They can:

•Maintain strong ties to employers

•Advise employers and students and help to match qualified students with employers

•Make student evaluations, grading systems, and transcripts available to employers in a clear and understandable form (see Rosenbaum, 1989: 40)

Collaborative efforts between schools and employers will help to prepare students with skills needed for the workplace; demonstrate a direct relationship between school performance and employment; and increase the incentives for students to attend school regularly and apply themselves. The Boston Compact is an example of high schools working together to improve student achievement by developing linkages with employers. Boston businesses promised to hire more youth if the Boston public schools worked to improve student academic achievement. Employers did increase job opportunities for Boston's high school graduates, but the schools have not done so well at improving students' attendance or school achievement (Rosenbaum, 1989: 15). Some Boston high schools and employers have extended the original Boston Compact initiative, however, and have informally agreed to use grades, teacher evaluations, and attendance to select students for some jobs (Rosenbaum, 1989).

Assessment of School Climate and Safety

Before school administrators introduce any policies relating to discipline and crime prevention, it is important to conduct a thorough assessment of school climate, orderliness, and safety. Time, effort, and valuable resources may be wasted if policies and programs are instituted before a careful assessment of existing needs and problems. Measuring the extent and the nature of school disruption is a clear indicator that administrators care about school safety and orderliness (Gottfredson and Gottfredson, 1985: 197). Schools have come under pressure from parents, politicians, and the media to "do something" about the problems of disruption and crime. The extent and seriousness of the problems vary considerably from school to school, however. Periodic assessments will help to pinpoint any problem areas so that appropriate policies can be instituted. Schools regularly assess students' academic performance and overall educational achievement, and teachers are assessed as to their effectiveness in the classroom. Schools could benefit greatly by including regular measures of school climate, orderliness, and safety. There are a number of ways that schools can closely monitor the number and types of disruptive incidents. Measures can also include teachers' and students' perceptions of school climate and safety (see Gottfredson and Gottfredson, 1985).

Assessment of school climate and safety requires the full support of school administrators, who are sometimes hesitant about collecting data that may place the school in a negative light and that could be used against them in litigation. Gottfredson and Gottfredson suggest that legislative action may be necessary to mandate periodic assessment of school climate, with the added provision that the required monitoring implies no private right of action (1985: 196). Legislation may also be necessary to ensure that schools have sufficient resources to conduct periodic assessments and develop programs to improve school safety.

Robert Rubel and Peter Blauvelt (1994) have recommended that school administrators make a careful assessment of school security needs and discipline policies. A physical security assessment of school grounds and buildings should include the number and location of entrances and exits; lighting around the buildings and parking lot; detailed recording of all incidents of assault, theft, and vandalism; and inventory control of all school supplies and equipment. School administrators must determine if law enforcement or security personnel should be hired to patrol the school buildings and grounds and, if so, how they are to be selected and trained. Developing sound discipline policies and procedures requires that all school personnel be clear as to their rights and duties in enforcing school rules and that discipline policies be clearly communicated to students and their parents.

Teachers and administrators should work together to help identify school safety and discipline issues that are in need of improvement and then implement policies and activities specifically to address those needs. Through cooperative efforts in developing specific policies and procedures directed at identified needs, teachers will see that administrators are serious about improving school safety and discipline. Developing consistent expectations for student behaviors and clear policies and procedures for responding to rule violations will help to improve the school climate. Students are more likely to view school policies as being fair and equitable and see that administrators are serious about maintaining a safe and orderly school environment (see Hawkins and Weis, 1985: 89–90; and Rubel and Blauvelt, 1994).

School-Based Prevention: Some Model Programs

A large number of school-based delinquency prevention programs have been developed and implemented during the past few decades. These programs range from early interventions for at-risk students in elementary schools to curricular additions that include all students to programs aimed at students who have been identified as being at high risk for delinquency. An excellent review of educational programs conducted through the mid-1980s was done by J. David Hawkins and Denise M. Lishner (1987b). Joy Dryfoos (1994) reviewed school-based programs and presented information on programs that provide health and social services as well as recreational opportunities in local schools. The Office of Juvenile Justice and Delinquency Prevention has also documented a number of delinquency prevention programs throughout the United States, many of which are school-based programs (see Howell, 1995; and Office of Juvenile Justice and Delinquency Prevention, 1995). I have selected a limited number of some of the more outstanding programs directed at delinquency prevention for review in this section. Unfortunately, complete information on the specific design and method is not available for every program, and many programs have failed to conduct or report on any efforts to monitor and evaluate program outcomes.

The Perry Preschool Project

One of the oldest school-based delinquency prevention programs is the Perry Preschool Project in Ypsilanti, Michigan (Berrueta-Clement, Schweinhart, Barnett, and Weikart, 1987). Originally developed in 1962, the project was designed to prevent educational failure among students who were identified as being at risk of school dropout. The program concentrated on a lower socioeconomic, predominantly black, neighborhood in Ypsilanti, Michigan.

Fewer than one in five of the parents of the students in the program had completed high school, compared to one in two nationally. About half of the families were headed by a single adult. In two out of five families no parent was employed, and those who were employed worked in jobs classified as unskilled labor. Half of the families received welfare assistance, compared to only one in twenty families nationwide.

The Perry preschool program was an organized educational program that was directed at the intellectual and social development of young children. Teachers on the staff had received in-service training and worked in teams with extensive managerial support. The staff-child ratio was about one adult for every five to seven children in the program. Children attended preschool for two school years at ages three and four. Classes were conducted for two hours and thirty minutes each morning, five days a week; the school year ran from October through May. In addition, teachers visited mothers and children in the home for one and a half hours each week (Berrueta-Clement et al., 1987: 224). The program is based on the premise that a major link between early preschool intervention and avoiding later misbehavior and delinquency is the prevention of school failure. Through the Perry Preschool Project, children who are at risk of educational failure have an opportunity to achieve success in early schooling. Early school success is linked to later success and higher attainment in school, which in turn is related to reduced involvement in misbehavior and delinquency.

The program has been evaluated annually among students ages 4 to 11 and those fourteen, fifteen, and nineteen years of age. The measures collected for the last three age groups included school records, interviews, and juvenile and adult arrest and court records. Outcome measures were collected on students from the preschool program and a matched control group. Overall, the preschool program resulted in a significant reduction in the number of youths who were later arrested or charged with crimes (31 percent of those in the program compared to 51 percent of those in the control group), and the program resulted in lower numbers of self-reported offenses. Participants in the preschool program were more likely to graduate from high school and to undertake some kind of postsecondary education or vocational training; more likely to be working at age 19; and less likely to have received some form of welfare assistance later as adults (Berrueta-Clement, 1987: 231–234). The Perry Preschool Project is clear evidence that early preschool intervention with an at-risk population of children can have very significant results in delinquency prevention.

Cities in Schools Program

The Cities in Schools (CIS) program is a public-private partnership that has operated in more than thirty cities. The program was developed to reduce school violence, prevent students from dropping out, and provide more successful school experiences among inner-city students who often fail in school (Murray et al., 1980; and see Hawkins and Lishner, 1987b; Office of Juvenile Justice and Delinquency Prevention, 1995: 82–83). Students are referred to

CIS programs because of low academic achievement, poor attendance, disruptive behavior, or family problems. Students were offered academic support, counseling, cultural enrichment activities, and other human services. Caseworkers monitored each student's progress and well-being. Students and school staff were grouped into school "families" to provide positive support networks. A three-year study compared treatment and control students at three different sites. Outcomes at two of the sites showed mostly negative results, but students in one site showed positive results, including more personal control, increased attention and effort in the classroom, more success in interpersonal relations and in learning situations, better reading skills, and better attendance (Murray et al., 1980). Although program evaluations have shown mixed results, the Cities in Schools concept has produced some excellent programs that have made a difference for many high-risk youth.

School Action Effectiveness Study

A project that evaluated seventeen alternative education programs for sixth- to twelfth-grade students in high-crime communities was conducted by Gary and Denise Gottfredson (1986). The alternative education programs were based on the assumption that school structure and organization contribute to the failure of many students and that school failure reduces students' commitment to conventional values, which in turn increases the liklihood of delinquent involvement. Project developers believed that some changes in school organization might help reduce disruptive classroom behavior, absenteeism, dropout, and delinquency. Interventions varied among the alternative education programs but included peer counseling, leadership training, parent involvement, skills classes, token economies, vocational education, and school climate improvement. Positive results, including better school safety, less teacher victimization, slightly less delinquency, decreases in student alienation, and improved self-concept, were noted in some of the alternative programs (Gottfredson and Gottfredson, 1986; and see Hawkins and Lishner, 1987a).

Project P.A.T.H.E.

This project, the title of which stands for "Positive Action Through Holistic Education," was a three-year delinquency prevention program implemented by the Charleston County, South Carolina, public schools between 1980 and 1983 (Denise Gottfredson, 1986). The program combined an environmental change approach with direct intervention for high-risk youths to reduce delinquent behavior and increase educational attainment. The program involved school staff, students, and community members in planning and implementing a comprehensive school improvement effort; changed disciplinary procedures; and enhanced the school program with activities that were directed at improving achievement and creating a more positive school climate. The program was implemented in four middle schools and three high schools. One middle school and one high school were included in a study as comparisons to assess year-to-year differences in the program. The program resulted in small but measurable reductions in delinquent behavior and misconduct. Students in the program were suspended less often and reported less involvement in delinquent behavior and drug-related activities. School attendance increased in the high schools but dropped slightly in the middle schools. The PATHE program improved general school climate and discipline management, and school safety improved in all the schools. The program increased the academic success experiences of the students, and significantly more students in the program graduated from high school. Denise Gottfredson noted that the improved school climate in the PATHE programs seemed to be responsible for students' increased sense of belonging in the school and (in the middle schools) for students' greater level of attachment to the school (1986: 726). School climate was defined as teachers' perceptions of the way the school was managed, teacher and student perceptions of school safety, staff morale, and improved discipline management. The program did not result in reduced delinquent behavior among the high-risk students but did increase students' commitment to education as indicated by the rates of dropout, retention, and graduation and by achievement test scores.

> The PATHE experience implies that altering the school organization can be an effective approach to delinquency prevention. Involving the school staff, students, and community members in planning and implementing change; . . . retraining school staff when necessary; making changes in the curriculum and discipline procedures in the school, and creating clear standards for implementing performance is a collection of accomplishments difficult to achieve. But, taken together, these activities reduce the risk of involvement in delinquent activities for the general school population. (Gottfredson, 1986: 728)

Law-Related Education

A recent delinquency prevention approach that has gained widespread acceptance throughout the United States involves a variety of additions to the regular school curriculum to promote prosocial attitudes and behaviors. The most prominent of these curriculum approaches and the one most evaluated is law-related education (LRE). LRE seeks to help students understand rights and responsibilities that are part of everyday life. The program teaches youth about good citizenship, encourages them to become more accountable for their actions, and attempts to develop respect for the law. LRE added a drug component to the curriculum in 1988 to stress to youth that they will be held accountable for illegal drug use. Since 1978, the Office of Juvenile Justice and Delinquency Prevention (OJJDP) has funded a national LRE effort through grants to five organizations: the American Bar Association, the Center for Civic Education, the Constitutional Rights Foundation, the National Institute for Citizen Education in the Law, and the Phi Alpha Delta Public Service Center. In 1989–90 LRE was active in forty-three states. The National Training and Dissemination Program (NTDP) provides coordination for statewide LRE programs, but the success of LRE depends on the initiative of local citizens, educators, and justice professionals. Since 1984, LRE programs have been conducted in 670 school districts, training some 52,000 teachers and resource persons, to reach an estimated 2.4 million students (Office of Juvenile Justice and Delinquency Prevention, 1990:4).

Law-related education is based on the premise that helping young people to recognize that they have a stake in their future is crucial if they are to become law-abiding, responsible citizens (Office of Juvenile Justice and Delinquency Prevention, 1990). One way to do this is to teach them about the law, the legal system, and their rights and responsibilities as citizens. LRE aims to help young people grasp the importance of laws and their relationship to everyday life and problems. The programs include a curriculum for elementary through high school students. LRE is intended to help students understand why rules exist and why it is important that rules are obeyed. The curriculum also teaches them how the courts work and why citizens who break the law must be held accountable for their illegal activities. The educational focus of LRE is on civil, criminal, and constitutional themes relating to such familiar topics as consumer protection, housing law, voting rights, child custody, spouse and child abuse, and traffic laws. LRE curricula include scenarios that illustrate key constitutional issues such as search and seizure, indentured servitude, political asylum, and freedom of speech, the press, and religion. The programs engage students in debating issues that directly involve them and require careful application of the Constitution, such as drunk driving, drug testing on the job and in the schools, handgun registration, environmental protection laws, and computer crimes. Effective LRE programs engage students in lively debates about school locker searches for drugs or weapons; about freedom of the press in student publications; or in mock trials for drunk driving, theft, assault, and murder. LRE directs students' attention to the necessity of a balance between rights and responsibilities and how rule violations and weapon and drug possession disrupt the school environment and threaten the safety of all students. By teaching students about the law through active, personal engagement, it is hoped that they will gain a deeper understanding that will in turn promote positive attitiudes toward the law and prosocial behavior.

James W. Fox, Kevin Minor, and William Pelkey (1994) examined the perceptions of juvenile offenders who participated in Kentucky's LRE diversion program. The state Juvenile Services Division received funds in 1990 from the National Training and Dissemination Program to introduce law-related education as a diversion option. All delinquents and status offenders ages 12 to 17 who meet the criteria for diversion are eligible to participate in LRE. The Kentucky program consists of the LRE curriculum noted earlier, and coverage is also given to drug education and community issues. Trained staff also rely on active learning techniques, field trips, and interactive presentations from resource persons such as law enforcement officers, attorneys, and judges. Fox and his associates examined pretest and posttest data for thirty-three juvenile offenders diverted into a LRE program and for a control group of twenty-eight public school students (total N = 61). Information was gathered on the number of LRE subjects who were referred for a new offense within one year following completion of the program. Data were also collected on juveniles' perceptions of themselves, their parents, their neighbors, their best friends, judges, teachers, and the police. The LRE group had significant pretest-to-posttest improvements in perceptions of police officers, themselves, parents, and teachers, but the posttest perceptions of LRE subjects did not significantly differ from the perceptions of the control subjects on any scale. Only six (10.5 percent) of the LRE participants were referred for one offense each in the year following the program. The researchers acknowledge that the quasi-experimental design does not allow definite cause-effect conclusions to be drawn, but the results do suggest that LRE may be a viable addition to a juvenile diversion program.

Drug Abuse Resistance Education (D.A.R.E)

Drug abuse prevention has received considerable attention as an addition to the school curriculum, especially as alcohol and drug use are increasingly seen as being among the biggest problems faced by schools and communities. In 1986 the U.S. Congress passed the Drug-Free Schools and Communities Act to promote drug abuse education and prevention throughout the nation. Millions of federal dollars have been allocated to assist in state and local drug prevention efforts. In many states, schools are required by law to have drug education programs.

Drug Abuse Resistance Education (D.A.R.E.) is the best known and most widely disseminated school-based drug prevention program in the United States. It was originally developed in 1983 by the Los Angeles Police Department in cooperation with the Los Angeles Unified School District. D.A.R.E. programs now operate in all fifty states and in six foreign countries (Rosenbaum et al., 1994: 6). D.A.R.E. is unique for its collaborative effort between education and law enforcement and for its use of trained, uniformed police officers in the classroom to teach a highly structured drug prevention curriculum. The program targets students in their last years of elementary school, usually the fifth or sixth grade. The D.A.R.E. program is focused on this age group because it is assumed that these students are most receptive to antidrug messages and are entering the drug experimentation phase where intervention may be most beneficial. D.A.R.E. officers receive eighty hours of instruction in classroom management, teaching strategies, communication skills, adolescent development, drug information, and the D.A.R.E. lessons. The D.A.R.E. officers are closely observed by the classroom teacher, and there are periodic visits from an experienced D.A.R.E. officer to ensure that the curriculum is being delivered consistently and well. The law enforcement agency pays for the officer's training and salary and for the instructional materials, which include student workbooks, visual aids, and graduation certificates. Officers teach the D.A.R.E. curriculum in one-hour sessions for seventeen weeks. Teaching strategies include lectures, workbook exercises, question-and-answer sessions, audiovisual materials, and role-playing sessions. The strategies support the objective of D.A.R.E., to teach peer resistance skills by offering students several ways to say no to drugs. D.A.R.E. is a comprehensive program that includes a wide variety of teaching objectives, including:

•Harmful effects from misuse of drugs

•Consequences of using alcohol, marijuana, and other drugs

•Sources and types of pressure to use drugs

•Media influences on behavior and advertising techniques for tobacco and alcohol

•Strategies for resisting peer pressure to use drugs

•Developing assertiveness skills

•Decision making and risk taking

•Older student leaders as role models who do not use drugs

•Forming friendships as support systems (Rosenbaum et al., 1994: 8)

D.A.R.E. programs have received wide support from parents, school teachers, and principals. A statewide evaluation of D.A.R.E. programs in Ohio included a survey of nearly 400 teachers and principals in the spring of 1994. The educators gave high marks to the D.A.R.E. program: nine out of ten felt D.A.R.E. had made a positive difference in students' attitudes about drugs, and three out of four believed that D.A.R.E. had delayed students' use of illegal substances. The educators felt that the students responded positively to the D.A.R.E. officer as a teacher, and most recommended that the D.A.R.E. program be continued in their schools ("A Model for Evaluating D.A.R.E.," 1995).

The results of empirical studies evaluating the effects of D.A.R.E. programs do not show that the programs have a consistent or significant impact on students' drug use, however. Michele Harmon (1993) examined the effectiveness of the D.A.R.E. program in Charleston County, South Carolina, using a quasi-experimental design. A sample of 341 D.A.R.E. students and 367 comparison students were administered pre- and posttests to compare the effects of the program on such variables as school attachment and commitment, belief in prosocial norms, self-esteem, assertiveness, attitudes about substance use, beliefs regarding the police, and drug use. Students in the D.A.R.E. group used alcohol less, had higher levels of belief in prosocial norms, reported less association with drug-using peers, showed an increase in attitudes against substance use, and were more assertive. However, no significant effects were found for self-reported cigarette, tobacco, or marijuana use in the last year; frequency of any drug use in the past month; coping strategies; atittudes about police; school attachment and commitment; or rebellious behavior.

Susan Ennett, Nancy Tobler, Christopher Ringwalt, and Robert Flewelling (1994) conducted a meta-analysis of several D.A.R.E. program outcome evaluations. Eight evaluation studies representing six states and one Canadian province met their criteria of studies that used a control group, pretest-posttest design, and quantitative outcome measures. Each of the studies had evaluated a statewide or local D.A.R.E. program and included at least ten schools with sample sizes of from 500 to 2000 students. The meta-analysis examined six outcome measures, including knowledge about drugs, attitudes about drug use, social skills, self-esteem, attitude toward police, and drug use. The outcomes of the D.A.R.E. programs were compared with school-based drug use prevention programs in a control group of schools. The results of the meta-analysis indicated that the D.A.R.E. programs had very little effect on the outcome variables measured and that its impact was smaller than other drug prevention programs using interactive techniques. Except for tobacco use, the effects of the D.A.R.E. programs were slight and not statistically significant. Ennett and her associates noted that some features of D.A.R.E. may be more effective in school districts where the D.A.R.E. curricula for younger and older students are in place, and its impact on community law enforcement relations may have important benefits. The results showing D.A.R.E.'s limited influence on adolescent drug use behavior contrasts with the popularity and prevalence of the program. The authors cautioned that expectations that the D.A.R.E. program would significantly change adolescent drug use should not be excessive (Ennett et al., 1994: 1399).

Dennis Rosenbaum and his associates (1994) evaluated the D.A.R.E. program in twelve urban and suburban schools in Illinois, involving 1,584 students. A matched group of twenty-four schools was selected for the study. Twelve schools were randomly assigned to receive D.A.R.E., and twelve served as controls for comparison. The D.A.R.E. program had no statistically significant overall impacts on students' use of alcohol or cigarettes about one year after completion of the program. The only statistically significant main effect of D.A.R.E. was on perceived media influences regarding the portrayal of beer drinking: more of the D.A.R.E. students recognized the media's portrayal of beer drinking as desirable. The program appeared to have some effect in encouraging girls to quit using alcohol but seemed to have the opposite effect for boys. The apparent failure of D.A.R.E. to produce any measurable differences in students' drug attitudes and use raises questions about the value of using D.A.R.E. programs to spend time on issues that are not directly related to substance use. Rosenbaum and his associates suggested that greater attention should be given in drug prevention programs to changing students' inaccurate perceptions concerning the extent to which drugs are used and sanctioned by peers. The overall decline in the prevalence of drug use among the school-age population raises the question of whether factors other than school-based drug prevention programs are responsible for the decline or whether the evaluation measures are simply not precise enough to detect the effectiveness of school programs (Rosenbaum et al., 1994: 27). It is possible that the decline in drug use may be attributable to the current emphases on the health risks of drug use, declining social acceptance, and the fact that youth are getting these messages from multiple sources, including the media, parents, family members, and their peers. Rosenbaum and his associates conclude that "apparently we, as a society, are doing something right in preventing drug abuse among youth, but the specific impact of school-based drug education is not clearly discernible" (1994: 28).

Gang Resistance Education and Training (G.R.E.A.T.)

The newest delinquency prevention program is based on an enhancement of the regular school curriculum, much like the D.A.R.E. program. G.R.E.A.T. and D.A.R.E. in fact have many features in common, from their origins in police departments to their delivery by uniformed police officers in the school classroom. In 1991 the Phoenix, Arizona, Police Department initiated a pilot project with seven school districts in the Phoenix metropolitan area to provide youth in the lower grades with the skills necessary to resist becoming gang members. After a pilot study involving nearly 4,000 students, the police department took the program to the entire Phoenix area, targeting fourth- and seventh-grade students. After about a year of operation, the police department entered into a collaborative agreement with the Bureau of Alcohol, Tobacco, and Firearms (ATF) to sponsor and train the police instructors for national distribution of the program, called G.R.E.A.T. (Gang Resistance Education and Training). Police officers are currently trained for the program at the Federal Law Enforcement Training Center at Davis-Monthan Air Force Base (Winfree, Esbensen, and Osgood, 1995).

The G.R.E.A.T. program is designed to teach youths how to set goals for themselves, how to resist peer pressure, how to resolve conflicts, and how gangs can affect the quality of their lives. The program is taught by uniformed police officers over nine consecutive weeks during the school year. The program targets seventh-grade students, though some schools have offered it to sixth- and eighth-graders, and there is a third- and fourth-grade component and a summer program component. These age groups were targeted because many observers believe that many youth are predisposed toward gang membership at those levels, and much gang recruitment occurs in the middle school and even in the later elementary school levels (McEvoy, 1990). The program curriculum consists of eight parts, covering such topics as:

- Crimes, victims, and their impact on the school and neighborhood
- How cultural differences affect the school and the neighborhood
- Conflict resolution
- Meeting basic needs without joining a gang
- How drugs affect the individual, the school, and the neighborhood
- Responsibilities of students in the school and the neighborhood
- Setting short- and long-term goals (Winfree et al., 1995: 12)

Police officer-instructors are provided with detailed lesson plans that have clearly stated purposes and goals and serve as instructional guides. Classroom teachers are also provided a copy of the curriculum and are expected to remain in the classroom during the officer's instructional presentation. Students who complete the program receive a certificate at the tenth week. Since its development in 1991, the G.R.E.A.T. program has been adopted by many other law enforcement agencies. As of September 1994, a total of 954 police officers in forty-three states had completed training under the direction of the Bureau of Alcohol, Tobacco, and Firearms (Esbensen, 1995). A comprehensive multisite evaluation of the G.R.E.A.T. program is currently being conducted, and results of the program are forthcoming.

Other Educational Models for Preventing Delinquency

Enhanced Methods of Classroom Instruction

Teachers make a difference in the lives of young people. Some teachers are more effective than others in maintaining discipline and order in the classroom and in nurturing a positive learning environment. To accomplish this task in some school settings takes more patience and perseverance than many persons (including many parents!) are able to muster. Teachers are faced daily with overwhelming challenges. Many students do not want to learn; maintaining discipline among students often requires more time and energy than teaching; and many students are increasingly reluctant to respect teachers' authority. The skillful and experienced teacher must constantly decide how best to get students engaged and involved in learning and must use a variety of techniques to maintain an orderly classroom that is conducive to learning. Techniques including behavior modification, psychodynamic and humanistic interventions, and the teaching of prosocial values and behaviors have been promoted as means by which educators can reduce disruption, aggression, and violence in the schools and in the community (Goldstein, Apter, and Harootunian, 1984).

J. David Hawkins and his associates have developed, implemented, and tested the effects of classroom-based instructional practices that are intended to improve student academic achievement and bonding to school and positive peers and reduce disruption and delinquent behavior (Hawkins and Weis, 1985; Hawkins and Lam, 1987; Hawkins and Lishner, 1987a and 1987b). Three general principles for delinquency prevention were identified by Hawkins and Weis (1985):

1. To be effective, prevention efforts should focus on the causes of delinquency.
2. There are multiple correlates and causes of delinquency that derive variously from the family, school, peers, and community.
3. Delinquency results from experiences during the process of social development in the family, in school, and with peers, so different prevention efforts are required at different stages in youths' social development (1985:77–8).

The *social development model* is an integration of control theory (Hirschi, 1969) and social learning theory (Akers, 1985; and see Hawkins and Weis, 1985). According to the model, the development of social bonds to conventional persons inhibits delinquent involvements. There are three conditions that seem to be necessary for development of social bonds: opportunities for involvement, skills, and reinforcements (Hawkins and Lishner, 1987a; Hawkins and Lam, 1987). According to the model, delinquency can be prevented only when youth have the opportunities to interact with conventional peers and adults and to be involved in conventional activities. Such interactions and involvements are expected to lead to positive social bonds when youth experience them positively and gain the necessary skills and when there are rewards for positive involvement in the community and in schools.

The social development model has been applied and evaluated in school settings. Hawkins and Lam (1987) examined what effects teaching practices have on classroom behaviors, academic achievement, school bonding, and school-related delinquent and antisocial behavior. The project involved 1,166 seventh-grade students in Seattle in 1981–82 (513 experimental and 653 equivalent control subjects). Three classroom-based instructional strategies were implemented and evaluated in the project: proactive classroom management, interactive teaching, and cooperative learning (see Hawkins and Lam, 1987: 250–251). *Proactive classroom management* is aimed at establishing a learning environment that is conducive to learning, promotes appropriate student behavior, and minimizes student disruption. Teachers give clear instructions for student behavior and recognize and reward cooperative student efforts. *Interactive teaching* is based on the premise that all students can and will develop the skills that are necessary to succeed in the classroom. Components include developing a mental set, setting clear objectives, checking for understanding, undergoing remediation, and performing assessment. Students must master learning objectives before proceeding to more advanced work. Grades are determined by mastery and improvement over past performance, rather than by comparison with other students. Interactive teaching seeks to expand opportunities for students' success and enhance their perception of their own competence and commitment to education. *Cooperative learning* involves small groups of students of differing abilities and backgrounds working together. Team scores are based on individual students' improvement over past performance, so each student contributes to the team's overall achievement. Students in cooperative classrooms seem to exhibit better mastery of learning tasks, are motivated, and have more positive attitudes toward teachers and schools than students in competitive or individualistic classrooms (see Hawkins and Lam, 1987: 251). Using cooperative learning aims to develop more interaction among students across racial and social class lines, reduce alienation, and reduce attachments to delinquent peers.

The teaching practices used in this project revealed some positive results. Students in the experimental group did engage in more behaviors associated with academic success and in fewer behaviors associated with academic failure. No significant differences were found, however, in student bonding to school or to peers, and there were no differences in students' self-reported truancy, stealing from desks or lockers, or incidence of getting in trouble at school for drugs or alcohol. The teaching practices did result in lower rates of classroom misbehavior resulting in suspensions and expulsions. Students in the experimental group appeared to benefit from the special teaching practices. They were more likely to engage in learning activities and less likely to be off task in the classroom; spent more time on homework; liked math classes better; and developed greater educaitonal aspirations and expectations for themselves (Hawkins and Lam, 1987: 268). The authors acknowledged that two important questions remained unanswered from this study. First, it is unclear whether many schools and teachers will adopt and consistently support these special teaching practices. Second, it is not clear whether the positive results observed among students after one year will continue. More research is needed to determine the long-term effects of special teaching practices on the classroom environment and on students.

Alternative Education Programs

Alternative education has become widely accepted as a means for preventing school dropout and delinquency. School districts throughout the nation have recognized the need to develop alternative educational programs for students who are not achieving in the regular classroom and who often disrupt the learning environment. Alternative education programs are structured and operated in a variety of ways and range from remedial reading and math programs for students with academic problems to in-school suspension for disruptive students (Hawkins and Wall, 1980: 2). Alternative schools are designed to create a more positive learning environment through lower teacher-to-student ratios, individualized self-paced instruction, and less structured and less competitive classrooms (Raywid, 1983). A self-paced curriculum and informal classroom structure enable teachers to provide more individualized instruction. A review of several empirical studies of alternative schools revealed that small school size, a supportive and noncompetitive environment, and a student-centered curriculum were the characteristics most associated with program success (Young, 1990). Students in alternative schools generally work under less pressure and competition from other students because their academic progress is measured by their own individual achievement, rather than in comparison with other students in the class (Gold and Mann, 1984). Denise Gottfredson (1987) noted that many alternative educational programs have been developed for disruptive and delinquent students because such programs purportedly help improve students' self-esteem, attitudes toward school, attendance, and academic performance and reduce their delinquent involvement. Stephen Cox, William Davidson, and Tim Bynum (1995) conducted a metaanalysis of fifty-seven evaluative studies of alternative education programs. The results of their study suggested that alternative education programs can have a small positive effect on school performance, school attitude, and self-esteem. Their analysis also indicated, however, that alternative schools have not been effective in reducing delinquent behavior. They suggested that even though alternative schools promote positive school attitudes, their effect on school performance and self-esteem is not large enough to influence delinquent behavior. Even though the students liked going to the alternative school and seemed to perform better academically, those improvements were not sufficient to overcome other influences (such as family problems and peer influences) that may have had a greater effect on delinquency (Cox et al., 1995: 229). It appears that alternative schools that are targeted at specific problem students have a greater impact than schools with a mix of students with different problems and needs. The school structure and curriculum can be more easily adapted for a more clearly defined student population. More research is needed to determine whether alternative schools can have a significant impact on delinquent students and to identify specific components of alternative education programs that may be most effective.

School-Based Violence Prevention Programs

The rate of serious violent crimes committed by high school-age youths armed with a weapon has increased dramatically. Several violence prevention programs have been developed in the past few years to teach anger management and conflict resolution skills to youths. In 1992 nearly half of all murder victims were related to (12 percent) or acquainted with (35 percent) their assailants, and 29 percent of all murders were the result of an argument. Most were committed impulsively, and about half of all perpetrators or victims had consumed alcohol before the homicide (DeJong, 1994: xi).

The nature of violent crime has led some to view the growing problem of violence from a public health perspective as well as from the criminal justice perspective (Rosenberg and Fenley, 1991). Criminal justice professionals concern themselves with investigation, arrest, prosecution, and conviction. Public health officials, on the other hand, approach health problems in terms of the interaction among persons, the agent, and the environment. The environmental factors that contribute to violence as a public health problem includes social, cultural, and institutional forces. Violence is often the product of the inability of families and communities to transmit positive values to young people and to teach nonviolent conflict resolution skills. The agents of violence are the weapons that are so readily available to young people, and the public health focus has increased efforts to restrict the sales of firearms and especially to limit their availability to young people. School-based violence prevention programs are based on the premise that violence is a learned behavior and that children must be taught nonviolent means of resolving conflict.

The *Resolving Conflict Creatively Program* (RCCP) is a school-based conflict resolution and mediation program sponsored by the New York City Public Schools and Educators for Social Responsibility—Metro (ESR), a nonprofit organization. The K–12 program was begun in 1985 and is now operating in 180 elementary, junior high, and high schools in New York City, with 3,000 teachers and 70,000 students participating (DeJong, 1994: 19). RCCP's year-long curriculum concentrates on active listening, assertiveness (as opposed to aggressiveness or passivity), expression of feelings, perspective taking, cooperation, and negotiation. Teachers are encouraged to include at least one "peace lesson" each week, to use "teachable moments" related to classroom situations or world events, and to infuse conflict resolution lessons into the regular academic program. By creating a "peaceable school," RCCP teachers strive to give their students a new image of what their world can be. In order to teach the RCCP curriculum most effectively, educators must learn a new set of skills for resolving conflict and adopt a new style of classroom management, sharing power with students so that they can learn how to deal with their own disputes. RCCP recently began a pilot program for parents, in which a few parents per school are trained to lead workshops for other parents on intergroup relations, family communication, and conflict resolution. By the end of 1994, nearly 300 parents had received training (DeJong, 1994: 29).

The *Violence Prevention Project* (VPP) is a community-based outreach and education project in Boston. The program is run by the Boston Department of Health and Hospitals as part of its Health Promotion Program for Urban Youth. The project was implemented in 1986 as a three-year pilot program in two neighborhoods, Roxbury and South Boston. It has now been expanded and has become an integral part of the mayor's citywide Safe Neighborhoods Plan. Providing the educational foundation for the Violence Prevention Project is the "Violence Prevention Curriculum for Adolescents," developed by Dr. Deborah Prothrow-Stith (1987; see also Prothrow-Stith, Spivak, and Hausman, 1987). The primary message of VPP is that violence is a learned behavior and is therefore preventable. The project directs attention to the acceptance of violence in American culture. There are elements of American culture that promote the use of violence to resolve conflict, not as a last resort, but as a first option. When parents teach their children to stand up to bullies by fighting, they promote violent behavior. When peers encourage each other to respond to any verbal insult, even mild ones, with verbal and physical threats and fighting, they promote violence. When the entertainment industry continues to produce films and television shows that depict violence as the hero's way to resolve conflict, they promote violence in a manner that has become very difficult to overcome. The goal of the Violence Prevention Project is to reduce students' acceptance of violence by helping them to discover that whatever gains fighting might bring are far outweighed by the risk of serious injury or death. The VPP teaches staff members from community-based youth agencies how to use lessons from the high school curriculum in their own violence prevention programs. The community education program of VPP was combined with a mass media campaign to raise public awareness of adolescent violence. The campaign featured a series of public service announcements on the role of peer pressure and the responsibility that friends have for helping to defuse conflict situations. The Advertising Club of Boston produced radio and television announcements with the theme "Friends for Life Don't Let Friends Fight." VPP's peer leadership program uses a small group of youth leaders who do conflict resolution and violence prevention work among their peers. VPP is also in the process of organizing a coalition of service providers, teachers, and school administrators, juvenile justice officials, parents, and other community residents. Organizers strongly believe that such coalitions are more likely to start their own violence prevention activities, which are a key objective of the Violence Prevention Project (DeJong, 1994: 36).

Beacons of Hope is a program of school-based community centers in New York City. Originally implemented in 1991 by a New York City Mayoral Commission, the program now has thirty-seven centers, one in each of the thirty-two school districts in the city; five districts have two centers. The goals of the program are to help residents, particularly youths, avoid crime and violence and to solve community problems. Included among the array of services are mentoring, tutoring, employment training and counseling, and cultural and recreational activities. Many of the services are aimed at addressing the risk factors associated with crime and violence by strengthening protective factors such as bonding with role models and developing healthy peer groups. Beacons of Hope centers include antiviolence programs and campaigns, conflict resolution training, public education about drugs, substance abuse treatment, community beautification projects, and Police Athletic League activities in which youth play basketball and interact informally with local police officers. Funding for the Beacons of Hope program comes from the New York City Department of Youth Services. Each center receives $450,000 per year for its operation, and the city Board of Education receives $50,000 per Beacon center for costs associated with the use of school space, such as the extra custodial services that are required (National Institute of Justice, 1996: 6).

Monitoring and evaluation of the Beacons of Hope program is being conducted by the New York City Youth Development Institute, which has been collecting information from the centers on a monthly basis. Each center submits weekly activity reports summarizing the specific programs, sponsoring groups, days and hours of operation, target populations, and the number of male and female youths served by each activity. Each of the Beacons typically enrolls approximately 1,000 community residents as ongoing participants (the highest enrollment was 1,848, and the lowest has been 628). Average daily attendance in the afterschool programs has been about 120 to 150 elementary and/or intermediate school students. A formal impact evaluation of the Beacons of Hope program has not yet been completed. Some of the outcome measures under consideration by the Department of Youth Services include improved school attendance, improved cognitive skills of program participants, improved relationships between youth and adults in the community, reduced drug activity, and fewer youth congregating on street corners in the Beacons' vicinities (National Institute of Justice, 1996: 9).

Mass media strategies can be very effective means for violence prevention when used in combination with school and community programs. The mass media, especially television, have an enormous influence on the ideas, values, and behavior of the American public (DeJong, 1994: 49). Educators, concerned parents, and community leaders have long been concerned about the negative impact of the media because of the abundance of violent shows and because of the portrayal of violence as an acceptable means of resolving conflict. As we noted above with the Violence Prevention Project, leaders in the antiviolence movement are now beginning to use the media as a strategy for violence prevention. William DeJong suggests that the best use of the mass media is to reinforce school and community programs in helping students learn new ways of resolving conflict. The mass media can be used in a number of ways: to educate the public about the nature and extent of the violence problem and to keep it at the top of the public agenda; to inform citizens about their community's attack on the problem and to inspire their full participation; to build support for changes in institutional arrangements, public policy, or laws that will reduce violence; and to reinforce the lessons of school and community programs by repeating key facts, demonstrating conflict resolution skills, and communicating a shift away from acceptance of violent confrontation (De-Jong, 1994: 49).

Mass media strategies include radio and television public service announcements as well as billboards prominently placed throughout a city. The Boston media campaign discussed earlier provided a support for that city's Violence Prevention Project. Other examples are the "Walk Away from Violence" media campaign sponsored by the Wayne County (Detroit), Michigan, Department of Public Health; the "Stop the Violence" campaign cosponsored by Jive Records and the National Urban League; and "Family Violence: Breaking the Chain," which was developed and aired by WBZ-TV in Boston (DeJong, 1994: 50).

Criminal justice professionals can also play an important role in violence prevention. We have noted the role played by police agencies in sponsoring the D.A.R.E. and the G.R.E.A.T. programs, which include components on resisting peer pressure and on the use of gang violence. The Police Athletic League (PAL) is active in many cities, providing programs for youth after school and during evenings and weekends. There are currently more than 500 PAL programs operating nationally, serving more than 3 million youth (DeJong, 1994: 61). Police and other criminal justice agencies can also take an active role in creating mass media campaigns against violence. The Minnesota Crime Prevention Officers Association (MCPOA) organized a "Turn Off the Violence" media campaign to raise parents' awareness of what their children watch and hear in the music, film, and television media.

Measuring and evaluating the impact that programs have on crime and delinquency is always a difficult and challenging task. Many programs have some kind of specific method for monitoring the outcome built into the program design, but some do not. At the minimum, it is important for all programs to specifically define the goals and objectives and the target population; to define some desired outcomes of the program; and to collect some information and data to assess the success of the program in meeting its objectives. A basic program evaluation should include the effort made in serving clients: number of staff members, hours and days of operation, number and types of activities and services provided, and the number of persons who participated in the program. It is more difficult to assess the effects of that effort on crime reduction. Programs are always affected to some extent by the presence of other variables, such as community policing and police patrol policies; changes in the economy of the area; employment opportunities; social factors; housing opportunities; the quality of city services; funding and resources for school building maintenance; and changes in school programs. These variables make it difficult to separate the specific reasons for changes in crime levels. Research can assess the level of criminal activity before and after implementation of a program and attempt to demonstrate a reduction in crime problems that may be attributable to the program. Program administrators must include some mechanisms for monitoring and assessing their programs if they want to improve their chances for receiving further support and funding from government agencies and foundations.

Preventing Bullying at School

Most Americans, including many school personnel, do not consider bullying a serious problem. This is surprising, considering that most bullying takes place in schools. Many persons think of bullying as a normal part of childhood and adolescence, just a passing stage experienced by "boys who will be boys." Although many are familiar with the bullying problem, only in the past couple of decades has bullying been the subject of systematic research. Initial research on bullying was confined mostly to Scandinavia with the work of Dan Olweus (1978), but bullying among schoolchildren has now been the subject of research in England, Japan, the Netherlands, Australia, Canada, and the United States (see Farrington, 1993). On the basis of surveys of more than 150,000 Norwegian students, Olweus estimates that 15 percent (1 in 7) of students in grades 1 through 9 are involved in bully/victim problems (about 9 percent as victims and 7 percent as bullies) (Olweus, 1994:1). According to Olweus, data from other countries indicate that the bullying problem exists outside Norway with similar or even higher prevalence rates.

Bullying occurs among both boys and girls, though many more boys than girls bully others. A high percentage of girls report that they are bullied mainly by boys, but a somewhat higher percentage of boys are victims of bullying. Bullying among boys is mostly physical. Girls typically use more subtle and indirect forms of harassment, such as slandering, spreading rumors, excluding victims from the group, and manipulating friendships (Olweus, 1994). All of these behaviors are encompassed by the definition of bullying as the repeated oppression, either physical or psychological, of a less powerful person by a more powerful one (Farrington, 1993: 381).

Three myths about bullying have been challenged by Olweus's research findings. First, many believe that bullying problems are more common in large schools or large classes. Empirical data indicate that the size of the class or school has little to do with the frequency or seriousness of bullying. Second, bullying behavior is often thought to be a reaction to school failure and frustration. Research data do not support a causal relationship between poor grades and school failure. Third, it is commonly believed that physical characteristics make some youth more vulnerable to bullying. Thus, for example, students who are fat, have red hair, wear glasses, or speak in an unusual manner are more likely to be victims of bullying. This belief also has not been supported by research (Olweus, 1994).

Victims of bullying tend to be more anxious and insecure than students in general. They are often cautious, sensitive, and quiet; have low self-esteem, are often lonely; and have few close friends at school. Bullies have a positive attitude toward violence and are characterized by impulsivity and a need to dominate others. They are usually physically stronger than most other boys, use violence and aggression more than most students, and express little empathy for victims. Contrary to the belief that bullying is a reaction to underlying insecurity, research indicates that bullies have little anxiety or insecurity and do not suffer from poor self-esteem (Olweus, 1994).

Bullying is not something that can be ignored or treated as simply normal adolescent behavior. Many children suffer greatly from bullying. Some respond by withdrawing and staying home from school. Others become more aggressive themselves. There are even documented cases of suicide among victims of bullying. A school program to prevent bullying should consider the following suggestions:

• Increase awareness of the bully/victim problem. Assess the extent of the problem in each school through an anonymous survey of students.

• Present an in-service training session for school personnel on the bullying problem; present results of the survey; compare with national and international data on bullying; and explain the characteristics of victims and bullies.

• Organize a parent-teacher meeting to inform parents about bullying and what the school is doing to prevent it. Provide parents with the information presented to teachers. Show a video on bullying (the National School Safety Center has produced one), and solicit parents' input on preventing bullying.

• Develop clear rules against bullying, including a definition of bullying and the various oppressive and harassing behaviors that are forbidden. Enforce the rules with appropriate sanctions that are agreed upon by school personnel, parents, and students.

• Ensure that school personnel provide adequate supervision on school grounds during recess and in school hallways, stairways, restrooms and areas where students are must vulnerable to bullying. Provide support and protection for the victims, and help them develop friendships.

• Have teachers discuss bullying with students in class, and use role-playing exercises and video presentations. Teachers should talk to identified bullies, their victims, and their parents (see Olweus, 1994: 4; and Farrington, 1993: 425–426)

The National School Safety Center

The National School Safety Center (NSSC)[1] was created by presidential directive in 1984 to meet the growing need for additional training and technical assistance to help prevent school crime and violence. The NSSC is funded jointly by the U.S. Departments of Education and Justice, in partnership with Pepperdine University in California. The purpose of the center is to promote safe schools and to help ensure quality education for all students. The NSSC attempts to focus national attention on cooperative solutions to school problems, with special emphases on efforts to rid schools of crime, violence, and drugs, and on programs to improve student discipline, attendance, achievement and school climate. NSSC provides technical assistance, legal and legislative aid, and publications and films as part of its work with local school districts, law enforcement agencies, legislators, and other key government policymakers. The center serves as a clearinghouse for current information on school safety issues and maintains a resource center with more than 50,000 articles, publications and films. Publications of the NSSC include *School Safety*, a newsjournal published three times each year, and *School Safety Update*, a newsletter published six times during the school year.

NSSC staff members have worked with governors, attorneys general, and school officials in all fifty states. The center sponsors conferences and workshops on specific school safety issues, assembling groups of experts and practitioners to develop new strategies and model policies to address school crime and violence problems. The participants' ideas are then incorporated into resources to assist others in developing safe schools. NSSC conducts about fifty training programs per year, involving 8,000 to 10,000 persons. Since 1984, the center has worked with more than 1,000 schools, and conducted more than 500 training programs involving more than 100,000 educators, administrators, and professionals concerned with school safety. Model school safety codes have been developed to help state officials and legislators respond to critical legal, constitutional, and educational issues. NSSC staff have provided expert testimony at the state and federal levels to support the enactment of school safety legislation. A list of the resources of the National School Safety Center is included in Appendix A.

Parents' Involvement in Schooling

School-based interventions cannot accomplish effective delinquency prevention without the support and assistance of parents. Educators generally complain that schools have been expected to take on many additional responsibilities that have traditionally been the responsibility of parents. Furthermore, teachers and principals complain that many of the teaching and discipline problems they face could be alleviated if they had more support from parents. Their complaints certainly have merit. Many discipline problems can be minimized if parents help to instill respect for teachers and support educators in disciplinary sanctions when their children have violated school regulations. Parents can help improve their children's school achievement when they inquire regularly about their required assignments and what they are studying week to week, encourage them to complete homework, and provide a place and a quiet time in the home to complete homework.

The idea of parental involvement in the schools has not always been welcomed by many educators, however. Many teachers and school administrators believe that parents have no right to exert influence on the schools. Gene Maeroff (1982) suggested that some school procedures seem intentionally to exclude parents and keep them uninformed. Parents have no role in the selection of teachers for their children or the assignment of principals to schools, for example, and most schools do not involve parents in decisions regarding curriculum development and selection of textbooks (1982: 208). Other examples of schools' failure to involve parents are in setting regulations for dress and behavior; issuing report cards that are complex and unintelligible or so simple that they report little about a child's progress; and scheduling meetings during the day, with little regard for parents' work schedules (Maeroff, 1982: 208). Many schools do encourage parental involvement and have implemented a number of programs and policies to maintain close communication with parents and to develop a cooperative team approach to enhance educational progress for children. In addition, parents may become involved through parent-teacher organizations, and through decisions and policies of school boards.

There is evidence that parental involvement in children's education makes a difference in school achievement. To determine why children of some low-income families were more successful in school, teams of teachers and principals visited the homes of these successful students. They found three common factors in the homes: (1) the parents knew what was happening in school and kept in touch with teachers to know what was expected of their children; (2) the parents viewed school as the key to their children's upward mobility and encouraged regular attendance; and (3) in addition to the parent, there was usually another adult, such as a grandparent, neighbor, or aunt, who provided additional emotional and psychological support (Maeroff, 1982: 227). The combination of these three factors resulted in a strong emphasis on regulated television viewing, completing assigned chores around the house, and doing homework. The organization and structure that began in these children's lives at home apparently carried over into the classroom.

School administrators and teachers have placed renewed emphasis on the need for more parental involvement in education. The Center for School Change at the University of Minnesota's Hubert H. Humphrey Institute surveyed about 1,800 teachers. Seventy-five percent of the teachers in the sample emphasized that attending parent/teacher conferences was the most important way for parents to get involved in their children's education; two-thirds of the teachers noted the importance of parental involvement in their children's homework (National School Safety Center, 1995: 5).

Recommendations for Educators, Justice Officials, and Policymakers

School disorder and delinquency are problems with causes that are as varied as the troubled students who engage in such behaviors. No one program or strategy will be sufficient to deal with school disruption and crime problems. As we study school problems and juvenile delinquency, we are struck by the complexity of the problem. We cannot study crime and delinquency in the schools apart from crime and delinquency in the community. Crime is a multifaceted problem with roots in the family. Young people who grow up without close parental ties and supervision are at risk of negative associations with antisocial peers and are more likely to experience problems in school and to engage in delinquent behavior. I have attempted in this book to outline the problem of juvenile delinquency and crime in schools and the role of schools in delinquency prevention. Juvenile delinquency evolves from problems in the family, the school, and the community. Schools are often criticized for educational failure, while at the same time they are expected to take on more of the responsibilities for the overall social development of young people. The general reluctance of the American public to approve tax increases for public education presents an additional challenge for educators to do more with less.

Schools are meeting the challenge. School retention and graduation rates are improving. Teachers, administrators, and students are successfully confronting and overcoming the problems of disruption, violence, and vandalism in schools throughout the United States and in other countries. Educators are implementing new school curricula and special programs to improve students' academic performance and reduce delinquent involvement in schools. Controlling school crime and providing a safe school environment for all students is a never-ending process. The National School Safety Center has outlined several steps that schools may take for developing safe schools. The Safe School Planning guide of NSSC is summarized in Table 10–1.

Developing a consistent policy and method for monitoring and recording school crime is essential. Educators are not required to report all violations of the law that occur in the schools. Loren Evenrud (1987) examined the crime-reporting policies of twenty-six Minnesota schools and found that most of the schools had no specific policy regarding the reporting of crimes committed in the schools. Most schools have a policy regarding the possession and use of tobacco, illegal drugs, and weapons, but few have a formal policy for reporting other criminal or delinquent conduct. School administrators prefer to maintain informal contact with law enforcement officials and use discretion in deciding whether to make a formal report of a criminal violation. Uniform and effective school crime reporting depends on the sophistication of the school management system. Evenrud found that crime incident classification systems varied greatly from school to school; 77 percent of the schools recorded crime incidents manually, while 23 percent used a computerized reporting system (1987: 220). An essential step in developing a safe school plan is developing a uniform system for monitoring crime incidents and keeping records.

Strong and effective leadership of school administrators is essential for maintaining a safe school environment. It is equally important for school administrators to develop cooperative interagency relations. Efforts to reduce school crime depend on the collaborative efforts of agencies such as law enforcement officials, the juvenile court, juvenile probation, and social service agencies. A major impediment against effective delinquency prevention in most cities is the absence of interagency relations between school districts and community agencies.

Many school districts have developed comprehensive and effective delinquency prevention programs. A great deal of effort is required, and it is essential to get the cooperative participation of students, parents, and community representatives. It is important to recognize that there are no easy and simple answers to providing a quality education for all young people in a safe school environment, free of crime and violence. In conclusion, I offer the following policy recommendations for school administrators, justice officials, community leaders, policymakers, and legislators. These recommendations encompass the school-based delinquency prevention programs that have been summarized, previous studies of school crime (see Gottfredson and Gottfredson, 1985: 179–180), and the Safe School Planning guide of the National School Safety Center (1993).

Table 10–1
Safe School Planning

A Safe Schools Plan is a continuing, broad-based, comprehensive, and systematic process to create and maintain a safe, secure, and welcoming school climate, free of drugs, violence, and fear—a climate which promotes the success and development of all children and those professionals who serve them.
Specific components include:

•Statistical Crime Tracking and Record Keeping
•Public Awareness Plan
•Education Plan
•Behavior Plan (Students and Staff)
•Supervision Plan
•Crisis Plan—Emergency Evacuation
•Attendance and Truancy Prevention
•Drug Prevention Plan
•Interagency Partnership Plan—Youth Service Network
•Cultural and Social Awareness Plan
•Student Leadership Component
•Parent Participation Plan
•Senior Citizens Plan
•Special Event Management Plan
•Crime Prevention Through Environmental Design
•Extra-curricular and Recreation Plan
•School/Law Enforcement Partnership Plan
•Screening and Selection Plan—Staff and Students
•Violence Prevention Pre-Service and In-Service Training Program
•School Security Plan
•Community Service/Outreach Plan
•Corporate Plan—Bring business to the educational marketplace
•Media and Public Relations Plan
•Health Service Plan
•Nuisance Abatement Plan
•Transportation Plan
•Legislative Plan

    Local, State and Federal Contacts including judges
•Evaluation and Monitoring Plan to constantly evaluate and assess the present structure
•Improvement/Strategic Plan

    Now that we have done the best we can, what else can we do?

Reprinted with permission. National School Safety Center © 1993

The recommended policies are these:

- School administrators and law enforcement officials should monitor and keep records on the nature and extent of school crime incidents.
- School boards and administrators should develop—with input from teachers, parents, and students—a clear statement of school policies and regulations and the sanctions that students and parents should expect for criminal behavior and violations of school rules.
- School districts should consider various options to reduce disruption and crime, including restructuring, reducing school size, and providing more resources and technical assistance for schools with the highest risks of problems.
- School administrators and teachers should take every opportunity to improve their skills in discipline, classroom management, and conflict mediation through available training sessions.
- Schools should implement promising ideas to reduce school disorder by developing model disciplinary procedures, increasing instructional resources, and offering a range of educational programs so that all students have the opportunity and the incentive to succeed in school.
- Schools should monitor the implementation and evaluate the outcomes of the programs. Administrators should closely study the conditions under which effective programs are achieved.
- Law enforcement and juvenile court officials should make every effort to assist schools in delinquency prevention, cooperate with their efforts, and communicate periodically regarding school policies and crime prevention programs.
- Business and community leaders should work closely with schools and justice agencies in crime prevention efforts, including participating in public information and media campaigns. Businesses can work with schools to offer employment-training opportunities. Employers should make job offers contingent upon students' records of school attendance and achievement and not allow students to work past 10 or 11 P.M. on school nights.
- Special emphasis should be focused on developing interagency relations among school administrators, law enforcement and justice officials, and community leaders; meeting regularly to discuss mutual concerns, monitor progress, and engage in joint program planning.
- State and federal legislators and policymakers must recognize the important role that education plays in reducing crime and delinquency and should increase funding for education at levels that are at least comparable to the funding increases for police, jails, and prisons.
- We must recognize that spectacular results cannot be expected immediately. We should expect some failures and be skeptical about any claims that there is any single solution to school crime. Program evaluations of good efforts do not always produce positive results. We must learn from each effort, design and implement new programs, and evaluate them.
- We should persist in our efforts. There is ample evidence that school-based delinquency prevention programs can succeed, especially when they have the support of criminal justice agencies, community leaders, parents, and students.

Summary

School crime and disruption is a serious problem with multiple causes. Law enforcement, the juvenile court, and juvenile corrections are not intended primarily for crime prevention. They can respond to crime only after it occurs. True delinquency prevention efforts must begin in the family, the community, and the schools. Several school-based delinquency prevention programs have been implemented, and many show promise in helping to improve young peoples' attendance and school performance and reducing their involvement in delinquent behavior. The task of providing safe schools that are free of crime, drugs, and weapons demands the consolidated efforts of the entire community. The goal of safe schools cannot be met without the aid of the federal and state governments and the coordinated efforts of school administrators, law enforcement officials, community leaders, parents, and students.

Note

1. The material for this section on the National School Safety Center was obtained from the Center and through correspondence and a telephone conversation with Ronald Stephens, executive director of the NSSC.

References

"A Model for Evaluating D.A.R.E. & Other Prevention Programs." 1995. *News & Views of the American Drug and Alcohol Survey* 22(Fall): 1–2.

Akers, Ronald L. 1985. *Deviant Behavior: A Social Learning Approach*, 3rd ed. Belmont, Calif.: Wadsworth.

Barker, Roger G., and Page V. Gump, eds. 1964. *Big School, Small School*. Stanford, Calif.: Stanford University Press.

Bayh, Birch. 1977. *Challenge for the Third Century: Education in a Safe Environment— Final Report on the Nature and Prevention of School Violence and Vandalism*. Report of the Subcommittee to Investigate Juvenile Delinquency. Washington, D.C.: U.S. Government Printing Office.

Berrueta-Clement, John R., Lawrence J. Schweinhart, William S. Barnett, and David P. Weikart. 1987. "The Effects of Early Educational Intervention on Crime and Delinquencyin Adolescence and Early Adulthood." In J. D. Burchard and S. N. Burchard, eds., *Prevention of Delinquent Behavior*. Newbury Park, Calif.: Sage.

Cloward, Richard A., and Lloyd E. Ohlin. 1960. *Delinquency and Opportunity*. Chicago: Free Press.

Cohen, Albert K. 1955. *Delinquent Boys*. New York: Free Press.

Cox, Stephen M., William S. Davidson, and Timothy S. Bynum. 1995. "A Meta-Analytic Assessment of Delinquency-Related Outcomes of Alternative Education Programs." *Crime and Delinquency* 41:219–234.

DeJong, William. 1994. *Preventing Interpersonal Violence Among Youth: An Introduction to School, Community, and Mass Media Strategies*. Washington, D.C.: National Institute of Justice.

Dryfoos, Joy. 1994. *Full-Service Schools*. San Francisco: Jossey-Bass.

Elliott, Delbert S., and Harwin Voss. 1974. *Delinquency and Dropout*. Lexington, Mass.: D.C. Heath.

Ennett, Susan T., Nancy S. Tobler, Christopher L. Ringwalt, and Robert L. Flewelling. 1994. "How Effective is Drug Abuse Resistance Education? A Meta-Analysis of Project D.A.R.E. Outcome Evaluations." *American Journal of Public Health* 84:1394–1401.

Esbensen, Finn-Aage. 1995. "The National Evaluation of the Gang Resistance and Education Training (G.R.E.A.T.) Program: An Overview." Paper presented at the Annual Meeting of the Academy of Criminal Justice Sciences, Boston, Mass.

Evenrud, Loren. 1987. "A Study of Crime Reporting in Minnesota Secondary Schools." Unpublished Ph.D. dissertation. Minneapolis: University of Minnesota.

Farrington, David P. 1993. "Understanding and Preventing Bullying." In M. Tonry, ed., *Crime and Justice: A Review of Research*, vol. 17. Chicago: University of Chicago Press.

Felson, Marcus. 1994. *Crime and Everyday Life*. Thousand Oaks, Calif.: Pine Forge Press.

Fox, James W., Kevin I. Minor, and William L. Pelkey. 1994. "The Relationship Between Law-Related Education Diversion and Juvenile Offenders' Social- and Self-Perceptions." *American Journal of Criminal Justice* 19:401–418.

Gold, Martin, and David W. Mann. 1984. *Expelled to a Friendlier Place: A Study of Alternative Schools*. Ann Arbor: University of Michigan Press.

Goldstein, Arnold P., Steven J. Apter, and Berj Harootunian. 1984. *School Violence*. Englewood Cliffs, N.J.: Prentice-Hall.

Gottfredson, Denise C. 1986. "An Empirical Test of School-Based Environmental and Individual Interventions to Reduce the Risk of Delinquent Behavior." *Criminology* 24:705–731.

Gottfredson, Denise C. 1987. "Examining the Potential for Delinquency Prevention Through Alternative Education." *Today's Delinquent* 6:87–100.

Gottfredson, Denise C., and Gary D. Gottfredson. 1986. *The School Action Effectiveness Study: Final Report*. Baltimore: Center for Social Organization of Schools, Johns Hopkins University.

Gottfredson, Gary D., and Denise C. Gottfredson. 1985. *Victimization in Schools*. New York: Plenum Press.

Harmon, Michele A. 1993. "Reducing the Risk of Drug Involvement Among Early Adolescents: An Evaluation of Drug Abuse Resistance Education (DARE)." *Evaluation Review* 17:221–239.

Hawkins, J. David, and Tony Lam, 1987, "Teacher Practices, Social Development, and Delinquency." Pp. 241–274 in J.D. Burchard and S.N. Burchard (eds.) Prevention of Delinquent Behavior. Newbury Park, CA:Sage Publications.

Hawkins, J. David and Denise Lishner. 1987a. "Etiology and Prevention of Antisocial Behavior in Children and Adolescents." In D. H. Crowell, I. M. Evans, and C. R. O'Donnell, eds., *Childhood Aggression and Violence: Sources of Influence, Prevention and Control*. New York: Plenum Press.

Hawkins, J. David, and Denise M. Lishner. 1987b. "Schooling and Delinquency." In E. H. Johnson, ed. *Handbook on Crime and Delinquency Prevention*. New York: Greenwood Press.

Hawkins, J. David, and John S. Wall. 1980. *Alternative Education: Exploring the Delinquency Prevention Potential*. Washington, D.C.: U.S. Department of Justice.

Hawkins, J. David, and Joseph G. Weis. 1985. "The Social Development Model: An Integrated Approach to Delinquency Prevention." *Journal of Primary Prevention* 6:73–97.

Hirschi, Travis. 1969. *Causes of Delinquency*. Berkeley, Calif.: University of California Press.

Howell, James C., ed. 1995. *Guide for Implementing the Comprehensive Strategy for Serious, Violent, and Chronic Juvenile Offenders*. Washington, D.C.: Office of Juvenile Justice and Delinquency Prevention, U.S. Department of Justice.

Jarjoura, G. Roger. 1993. "Does Dropping Out of School Enhance Delinqent Involvement? Results from a Large-Scale National Probability Sample." *Criminology* 31:149–171.

Lawrence, Richard. 1985. "School Performance, Containment Theory, and Delinquent Behavior." *Youth and Society* 17:69–95.

Maeroff, Gene I. 1982. *Don't Blame the Kids.* New York: McGraw-Hill.

McEvoy, Alan. 1990. "Combating Gang Activities in Schools." *Education Digest* 56:31–34.

Murray, C. A., B. B. Bourgue, R. S. Harnar, J. C. Hersey, S. R. Murray, D. D. Overbey, and E. S. Stotsky. 1980. *The National Evaluation of the Cities in Schools Program Report No. 3.* Washington, D.C.: National Institute of Education.

National Institute of Education. 1978. *Violent Schools—Safe Schools: The Safe School Study Report to the Congress,* vol. 1. Washington, D.C.: U.S. Department of Health, Education, and Welfare.

National Institute of Justice. 1996. *Beacons of Hope: New York City's School-Based Community Centers.* Washington, D.C.: U.S. Department of Justice.

National School Safety Center. 1993. *Safe School Planning.* Westlake Village, Calif.: National School Safety Center.

National School Safety Center. 1995. "Promising Strategies for Juvenile Crime Prevention." *School Safety Update* (February): 5.

Office of Juvenile Justice and Delinquency Prevention. 1990. "Education in the Law: Promoting Citizenship in the Schools." *OJJDP Update on Programs.* Washington, D.C.: U.S. Department of Justice.

Office of Juvenile Justice and Delinquency Prevention. 1995. *Delinquency Prevention Works: Program Summary.* Washington, D.C.: U.S. Department of Justice.

Olweus, Dan. 1978. *Aggression in the Schools.* Washington, D.C.: Hemisphere Publishing Corp.

Olweus, Dan. 1994. "Bullying: Too Little Love, Too Much Freedom." *School Safety Update* (May): 1–4.

President's Commission on Law Enforcement and Administration of Justice. 1967. *Task Force Report: Juvenile Delinquency and Youth Crime.* Washington, D.C.: U.S. Government Printing Office.

Prothrow-Stith, Deborah. 1987. *Violence Prevention Curriculum for Adolescents.* Newton, Mass.: Education Development Center.

Prothrow-Stith, D., H. Spivak, and A.J. Hausman. 1987. "The Violence Prevention Project: A Public Health Approach." *Science, Technology, and Human Values* 12:67–69.

Raywid, Mary A. 1983. "Alternative Schools as a Model for Public Education." *Theory into Practice* 22:190–97.

Rosenbaum, Dennis P., Robert L. Flewelling, Susan L. Bailey, Chris L. Ringwalt, and Deanna L. Wilkinson. 1994. "Cops in the Classroom: A Longitudinal Evaluation of Drug Abuse Resistance Education (DARE)." *Journal of Research in Crime and Delinquency* 31:3–31.

Rosenbaum, James E. 1989. "What If Good Jobs Depended on Good Grades?" *American Educator* 13(Winter): 10–15, 40,42–43.

Rosenberg, M. L., and M. A. Fenley, eds. *Violence in America: A Public Health Approach.* New York: Oxford University Press.

Rubel, Robert J., and Peter D. Blauvelt. 1994. "How Safe Are Your Schools?" *American School Board Journal* (January): 28–31.

Schafer, Walter E., and Kenneth Polk. 1967. "Delinquency and the Schools." In *Task Force Report: Juvenile Delinquency and Youth Crime.* Washington, DC: U.S. Government Printing Office.

Thornberry, Terence P., Melanie Moore, R. L. Christenson. 1985. "The Effect of Dropping Out of High School on Subsequent Criminal Behavior." *Criminology* 23:3–18.

Winfree, L. Thomas Jr., Finn-Aage Esbensen, and D. Wayne Osgood. 1995. "On Becoming a Youth Gang Member: Low Self-Control or Learned Behavior?" Paper presented at the Annual Meeting of the Academy of Criminal Justice Sciences, Boston, Mass.

Young, Timothy W. 1990. *Public Alternative Education: Options and Choice for Today's Schools*. New York: Columbia University Press.

Appendix

National School Safety Center Resources

The National School Safety Center serves as a national clearinghouse for school safety programs and activities related to campus security, school law, community relations, student discipline and attendance, and the prevention of drug abuse, gangs and bullying.

NSSC was created in 1984 by Presidential mandate through a partnership of the U.S. Department of Justice and U.S. Department of Education with Pepperdine University. The Center's primary objective is to focus national attention on the importance of providing safe and effective schools. The following resources have been produced to complement this effort. In addition to these resources, NSSC provides on-site training and technical assistance to school districts and law enforcement agencies nationwide in the areas of school crime prevention, gangs, weapons in school, crisis management and safe school planning. Please write to NSSC at 4165 Thousand Oaks Blvd., Suite 290, Westlake Village, CA 91362, for further information on training resources.

Publications

School Safety News Service includes three issues of *School Safety*, Newsjournal of the National School Safety Center, and six issues of NSSC's newsletter. These publications feature the insight of prominent professionals on issues related to school safety, including student discipline, security, attendance, dropouts, youth suicide, character education and substance abuse. NSSC's News Service reports on effective school safety programs, updates legal and legislative issues and reviews new literature on school safety issues. Contributors include accomplished local practitioners and nationally recognized experts and officials.

Developing Personal and Social Responsibility (1992). Human nature, all too often, seeks the lowest level of responsibility while seeking the highest expression of freedom and rights. When left unchecked, this often translates into disobedience, disruption, violence, truancy, early pregnancy, drug abuse and, in general, a lack of appropriate self-control and motivation in young people. Schools can play important leadership roles with students, parents and the community in teaching responsibility skills. The ideas, suggestions and model curricula set forth in **Developing Personal and Social Responsibility** are designed to serve as a framework on which to build successful programs aimed at training young people to be responsible citizens. 129 pages.

School Crime and Violence: Victims' Rights (1992) recently updated, is a comprehensive text on school safety law. The book offers a historical overview of victim's rights, describes how it has been dealt with in our laws and courts, and explains its effect on America's schools. Many educators are not familiar with the magnitude, import or specifics of the burgeoning phenomenon of liability and litigation in the United States. This lack of information and understanding can only breed more conflict and litigation. Schools must prepare themselves for the possibility of such liability. The authors cite legal case histories and cover current school liability laws. This useful tool provides advice to educators and school administrators in risk and liability prevention, and in implementing campus crime prevention programs. 134 pages.

School Discipline Notebook (1992) is a newly revised edition originally published in 1986. This book will help educators establish fair and effective discipline. It reviews student responsibilities and rights, including the right to safe schools. The correlation between orderly, disciplined schools and safe, productive schools is examined. Legal policies that regulate discipline methods used in schools are also explored. In addition, suggestions are offered for the many practical tasks required by educators, including preparing discipline codes, defining and tracking infractions, and disciplining special education students. A resource section suggests publications, films and policies providing further assistance with school discipline.

Child Safety Curriculum Standards (1991) helps prevent child victimization by assisting youth-serving professionals in teaching children how to protect themselves. Sample strategies that can be integrated for both elementary and secondary schools. The age-appropriate standards deal with the topics of substance abuse, teen parenting, suicide, gangs, weapons, bullying, runaways, rape, sexually transmitted diseases, child abuse, parental abductions, stranger abductions and latchkey children. Each of the 13 chapters include summaries, standard, strategies and additional resources for each grade level. 353 pages.

School Safety Check Book (1990) is NSSC's most comprehensive text on crime and violence prevention in schools. The volume is divided into sections on school climate and discipline, school attendance, personal safety and school security. Geared for the hands-on practitioner, each section includes a review of the problems and prevention strategies. Useful charts, surveys and tables as well as writeups on a wide variety of model programs are also included. 219 pages.

Set Straight on Bullies (1989) examines the myths and realities about schoolyard bullying. Changing attitudes about the seriousness of the problem is stressed. It studies the characteristics of bullies and bullying victims. And, most importantly, it provides strategies for educators, parents and students to better prevent and respond to schoolyard bullying. Sample student and adult surveys also are included.

The Need To Know: Juvenile Record Sharing (1989) deals with the confidentiality of juvenile records and why teachers, counselors, school administrators, police, probations officers, prosecutors, the courts and other professionals who work with juvenile offenders need to know and be able to share information contained in juvenile records. When information is shared appropriately, improved strategies for responding to serious juvenile offenders, and for improving public safety, can be developed. The second part of the book reviews the legal statutes of each state, outlining which agencies and individuals are permitted access to various juvenile records and how access may be obtained. A model juvenile records code and sample forms to be used by agencies in facilitating juvenile records sharing also are included. 88 pages.

Gangs in Schools: Breaking Up Is Hard to Do (1993) offers an introduction to youth gangs, providing the latest information on the various types of gangs—including ethnic gangs, stoner groups and satanic cults—as well as giving practical advice on preventing or reducing gang encroachment in schools. The book contains valuable suggestions from law enforcers, school principals, prosecutors and other experts on gangs. The concluding chapter describes more than 20 school- and community-based programs throughout the country that have been successful in combating gangs. 48 pages.

Educated Public Relations: School Safety 101 (1993) offers a quick course in public relations for school district public relations directors, administrators and others working to achieve safe, effective schools. The book explains the theory of public relations and successful methods for integrating people and ideas. It discusses how public relations programs can promote safe schools and quality education and gives 101 specific ideas and strategies to achieve this goal. The text includes a special chapter by Edward L. Bernays, considered by many as the father of contemporary public relations, which updates his classic work *The Engineering of Consent*. 72 pages.

School Safety Work Book (1995). Much of the writing about schools today takes the form of deficit models or problems. The *School Safety Work Book* reverses this trend by highlighting prevention models that show promise toward stemming the rising tide of school crime and violence. Researchers agree that effective programs must be tailored to each school, student population and community. The featured programs can be used as a starting point for developing a comprehensive violence prevention program for your school or community. *School Safety Work Book* showcases more than 100 school- and community-based programs. Contact information provides a resource for those who may seek more data to replicate these successful programs. The contents target conflict resolution, gang prevention, social responsibility, substance abuse prevention, truancy reduction, violence prevention and weapons prevention. Also included is a list of national violence prevention resources and organizations.

Student Searches and the Law (1995). With the alarming increase of drugs and weapons at American schools, school personnel have stepped up their efforts to search for contraband on campus in order to provide a safe environment for all students. Despite court-imposed safeguards on students' constitutional rights, school officials have greater leeway in conducting searches than do police officers. *Student Searches and the Law* takes a close look at the legality of conducting searches on school campuses. Included in the book is a discussion of the landmark U.S. Supreme Court case of *New Jersey v. T.L.O.*, which set the standard for conducting student searches. Since 1985 when the *T.L.O.* Court established the reasonable suspicions standard, court decisions have helped to further define what constitutes an appropriate search on school campuses. *Student Searches and the Law* examines recent court cases concerning student searches, including locker searches and strip searches. Other sections discuss searches conducted on school grounds by law enforcement and probation officers and school security personnel; the use of drug testing and surveillance equipment on campus; and searches using metal detectors or drug-sniffing dogs. *Student Searches and the Law* also covers practical matters such as sample school board policies and procedures for conducting legal searches at school. 80 pages.

NSSC Resource Papers provide a concise but comprehensive review of topical school safety issues. Papers include "Safe Schools Overview," "Increasing Student Attendance," "Drug Traffic and Abuse in Schools," "School Bullying and Victimization," "Student Searches and the Law," "Student and Staff Victimization," "Alternative Schools for Disruptive Youth," "Weapons in Schools," "Role Models, Sports and Youth," "Corporal Punishment in Schools," and "School Crisis Prevention and Response." "Safe Schools Overview" offers a review of the contemporary safety issues facing the country's schools and students, national statistics and court cases. Specific issue papers offer a general outline of the problem, national statistics, and prevention and intervention strategies. The papers conclude with reprints of relevant articles from newspapers and magazines and a list of related organizations and publications. New papers will continue to be published to address emerging school safety issues. 10–30 pages.

Films/Tapes

"School Crisis: Under Control" (1991) combines actual news footage of school crisis events with the insights and recommendations of school officials who have dealt firsthand with violent tragedies on their campuses. From having experienced deranged gunmen invading their campuses, hostage situations, bombings, and students killing teachers and each other, participants at the National School Safety Center's "School Crisis Prevention Practicum" offer other educators valuable advice about school crisis prevention, preparation, management and resolution. Acclaimed actor Edward James Olmos hosts this 25-minute, award-winning educational documentary that covers topics such as outlining staff roles and responsibilities, dealing with the media, providing adequate communications systems and signals, arranging transportation, and offering grief counseling. Available in VHS format.

"High Risk Youth/At the Crossroads" (1989) addresses drug abuse prevention by focusing attention on specific negative social, economic and behavioral problems that make youths more vulnerable to have drug abuse problems. Hosted by LeVar Burton, the program promotes a "risk-focused approach" to youth drug abuse prevention that goes beyond "just so no." The 22-minute documentary profiles several high-risk youth and examines their vulnerable characteristics through commentary from several nationally renowned authorities. Available in VHS format.

"Set Straight on Bullies" (1988). Whoever thought bullies were all talk and no action needs to view the film "Set Straight on Bullies." The National School Safety Center film was produced to help school administrators educate faculty, parents and students about the severity of the schoolyard bullying problem. The message is clear: bullying hurts everyone. The film tells the dramatic story of a bullying victim and how the problems adversely affects his life as well as the lives of the bully, other students, parents and educators. 18 minutes. Available in VHS or Beta tapes or 16mm.

"What's Wrong With This Picture?" (1986) is an award-winning film showing five scenarios that address the school safety issues of drug trafficking and abuse, intimidation and violence, teacher burnout and theft. The docudrama is narrated by the people who actually experienced the incidences portrayed. This "trigger" film is intended to generate emotional responses, discussions and action from its viewers. The film has received awards at the Houston, New York and Chicago film festivals, the U.S. Industrial Film Festival and the National Association of Government Communications. 18 minutes. Available in VHS and Beta tapes or 16mm.

Display Posters

"Join a team, not a gang!" (1989) Kevin Mitchell, home run leader with the San Francisco Giants, urges kids to enjoy a confrontation on the baseball diamond and not with a rival gang on a street corner. "It's an experience you'll live to remember," he concludes.

"The Fridge says 'bullying is uncool!' " (1989) is the caption on this 22- by 34-inch full-color poster of William "The Fridge" Perry, the 325-plus pound offensive lineman for the Chicago Bears. The Fridge urges youths to treat others as they would like to be treated.

"Facades . . ." (1987) is a set of two 22- by 17-inch full-color posters produced and distributed to complement a series of drug-free schools TV public service announcements sponsored by NSSC. The posters combine dramatic visual imagery with short introspective messages about self-respect from former youthful drug abusers.

To order these resources, or for information about multiple-copy purchases and discounts, write:

National School Safety Center
4165 Thousand Oaks Blvd., Suite 290
Westlake Village, CA 91362
805/373-9977

All resources are prepared under Grant No. 85-MU-CX-0003 and fully funded by the Office of Juvenile Justice and Delinquency Prevention, Office of Justice Programs, U.S. Department of Justice. Points of view or opinions in these documents are those of the authors and do not necessarily represent the official position or policies of the U.S. Department of Justice, U.S. Department of Education or Pepperdine University.
    Reprinted with permission.

Author Index

Subject Index